D1138686

025 502

RELIGION TODAY: A READER

This Reader is part of *Religion Today: Tradition, Modernity and Change* (AD317), an Open University third level course in Religious Studies for students of the Arts and Social Sciences. Details of this and other Open University courses can be obtained from the Call Centre, PO Box 724, The Open University, Milton Keynes, MK7 6ZS, United Kingdom; tel. +44 (0)1908 653231, email ces-gen@open.ac.uk. Alternatively, you may visit the Open University web site at http://www.open.ac.uk where you can learn more about the wide range of courses and packs offered at all levels by the Open University.

RELIGION TODAY: TRADITION, MODERNITY AND CHANGE – AN OPEN UNIVERSITY/ASHGATE SERIES

The five textbooks and Reader that make up this series are:

- *From Sacred Text to Internet* edited by Gwilym Beckerlegge
- *Religion and Social Transformations* edited by David Herbert
- *Perspectives on Civil Religion* by Gerald Parsons
- *Global Religious Movements in Regional Context* edited by John Wolffe
- *Belief Beyond Boundaries* edited by Joanne Pearson
- *Religion Today: A Reader* edited by Susan Mumm

Each textbook includes:

- an introduction to the issues and controversies relevant to the topic under discussion
- a series of detailed case studies, which allow readers to see the theories and debates at work today in the experience of religious practitioners from various parts of the world
- extracts from other publications, which address the same issue from different perspectives (except *Perspectives on Civil Religion*)
- extensive references to other published material on the same topics
- supporting colour and black-and-white illustrations

The series offers an in-depth introduction to contemporary themes and challenges in religious studies. The contents highlight the central issues and ideas that are shaping religion today – and will continue to do so tomorrow. The textbooks contain plentiful contemporary case studies spanning many countries and religions, and integrate methods of analysis and theoretical perspectives. They work to ensure that readers will understand the relevance of methodologies to lived experience and gain the ability to transfer analytic skills and explanatory devices to the study of religion in context. The textbooks focus on the following key issues in contemporary religious studies: representation and interpretation; modernity and social change; civil religion; the impact of globalization on religion; and the growth of alternative religion.

    The accompanying Reader presents primary and secondary source material structured around these core themes. It will serve as an invaluable resource book, whether used to accompany the textbooks in the series or not.

RELIGION TODAY: A READER

Edited by
SUSAN MUMM

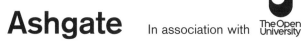

Ashgate In association with The Open University

This publication forms part of an Open University course AD317 *Religion Today: Tradition Modernity and Change*. Details of this and other Open University courses can be obtained from the Call Centre, PO Box 724, The Open University, Milton Keynes MK7 6ZS, United Kingdom: tel. +44 (0)1908 653231, e-mail ces-gen@open.ac.uk

Alternatively, you may visit the Open University web site at http://www.open.ac.uk where you can learn more about the wide range of courses and packs offered at all levels by the Open University.

To purchase this publication or other components of the Open University courses, contact Open University Worldwide Ltd, The Berrill Building, Walton Hall, Milton Keynes MK7 6AA, United Kingdom: tel. +44 (0)1908 858785; fax + 44 (0)1908 858787; e-mail ouwenq@open.ac.uk; website http://www.ouw.co.uk

British Library Cataloguing in Publication Data
Religion today: a reader. – (Religion today: tradition, modernity and change)
    1. Religions
    I. Mumm, Susan, 1961– II. Open University
    291

Library of Congress Cataloging-in-Publication Data
Religion today: a reader/edited by Susan Mumm.
    p. cm.
  Includes bibliographical references.
  ISBN 0-7546-0743-7--ISBN 0-7546-0821-2 (pbk.)
    1. Religion. 2. Religions. I. Mumm, Susan, 1961–

BL50 .R4267 2002
200--dc21   2001053710

Co-published by

The Open University	Ashgate Publishing Limited	Ashgate Publishing Company
Walton Hall	Gower House, Croft Road	Burlington, VT 05401-5600
Milton Keynes MK7 6AA	Aldershot Hants GU11 3HR	USA

Ashgate website: http://www.ashgate.com

First published 2002

Printed and bound by T J International Ltd, Padstow, Cornwall.

ISBN 0 7546 0743 7 (Hbk)
ISBN 0 7546 0821 2 (Pbk)

CONTENTS

PART III: PERSPECTIVES ON CIVIL RELIGION

PART IV: GLOBAL RELIGIOUS MOVEMENTS IN REGIONAL CONTEXT

PART V: BELIEF BEYOND BOUNDARIES

PREFACE

As the title of the Open University course that this Reader accompanies suggests – *Religion Today: Tradition, Modernity and Change* – the readings in this volume range over many countries and religions, but remain firmly fixed in the contemporary world. Religion has changed, and continues to change. The reciprocal interplay between religion and social and technological change continues, with each constantly modifying the other in endlessly fascinating ways. One of the goals of this Reader is to give examples of the tension between change and tradition in religion today: how religion copes with and participates in the modern world, how tradition gets interpreted, revived, reinvented or created in response to change.

There is a widespread perception in the West that we live in a secular age, which can lead to the assumption that religion is at best an optional extra, if not a false delusion completely out of place in the modern – or postmodern – world. The contention underlying this selection of readings is that informed understanding of the contemporary world requires an appreciation of the role of religion in shaping ideas, worldviews and actions that have an impact on politics, economics, social and cultural practices, as well as on the life of the individual. Religion still arouses passion and causes controversy; it can control and transform lives. It may not look like it used to, but it is still there, and its transformation should not be confused with decline.

It is our belief that there are five key areas of religious change today, and these five themes are explored in this volume. Briefly, these are:

RELIGION AND REPRESENTATION

The often contested and controversial representation of religion in picture, text, film, politics, and on the Internet is examined in the first section, and the readings selected range from Egypt to America to India. Issues of interpretation as well as of representation are highlighted in a wide-ranging introduction to the multiplicity of ways in which religion can be represented, and how its representation can in itself be transformative.

RELIGION AND SOCIAL TRANSFORMATIONS

The second section of this volume looks at the fluid and flexible reciprocal relationship between religion, modernity, and social change. Readings included engage with the role of religion in the fall of communism, the tension between religion and feminism, whether religion is compatible with modern ideas of human rights, and if ancient religions can accommodate new challenges such as environmentalism. This section includes documents derived from Europe, the USA, the Middle East and Asia.

RELIGION IN CIVIL SOCIETIES

The third section examines the shifting meaning of civil religion. Texts selected revolve around two key issues: the first involving the development of the idea of war grave pilgrimage, from its birth in the American civil war, through British adoption in the two world wars, and ending with the enormously controversial Vietnam Veterans Memorial in Washington. The second set of readings centre on a highly contrasted example of civil religion, the Palio festival in Siena. As extreme a contrast as this may seem, it illuminates key issues in the difficult concept of civil religion.

RELIGION GOES GLOBAL

The fourth section examines the issue of globalization, using the example of religious spread throughout the world, and examining the change and adaptation required of old religions in new places. The texts included here make the point that religious 'transplantation' is an inadequate and unsophisticated explanatory device in a global context, and religions that go global cannot remain unchanged by their importation into new cultures. The focus here is on the experience of Protestantism in the UK, the USA and Latin America, the world-wide spread of Islam, and the 'westernization' of Buddhism.

BELIEF BEYOND BOUNDARIES

The final section deals with one of the emerging phenomena of religion today: the exponential growth of what may be called alternative spiritualities, as people shift from communities of descent to communities of assent. With texts selected from the areas of paganism, Wicca, witchcraft, Celtic spirituality and North American indigenous religion, it offers a good introduction to the range of materials being produced in this area, and the controversies currently being debated. The final set of readings make important links between the ideas inherent in alternative spirituality to key concepts in the psychology of religion, focusing on the importance of Jung.

The texts selected for this volume include many of the major world religions, but it makes no attempt to provide equal coverage of all religions within all themes, which would have swelled this book to the size of an encyclopedia. The texts and the traditions from which they arise are selective rather than comprehensive, as this Reader is not intended to serve as an introduction to world religions or a comparative religion reader: there are plenty of these already available. Even within these limits, the range of viewpoints represented is dazzling. It does however offer a meaningful sample of the religious experience of humanity today, highlighting the issues and ideas that are shaping religion today – and will continue to do tomorrow.

Thanks to the following people for suggesting texts for inclusion: Gwilym Beckerlegge, Marion Bowman, Sophie Gilliat-Ray, David Herbert, Roderick Main, Gerald Parsons, Joanne Pearson, Helen Waterhouse and John Wolffe. The help of Adrian Roberts, Jonathan Hunt and Meridian was much appreciated. Special thanks are due to Denise Hall and Val Price, for taking charge of many crucial aspects of the Reader's production. Throughout the Reader, the spelling, grammar and punctuation of the original texts has been retained.

Part I:

From Sacred Text to Internet

All the readings in this section examine aspects of the representation of religion: representation in sacred texts, through images and pictures, across different cultures, and through new forms of media and communication. The first two readings deal with the relationship between scholarly reconstruction of the life of Jesus and the contemporary debate about the appropriate representation of this figure. Marsh and Moyise (1.1) describe the changing regard in which Mark's account of the life of Jesus has been held by Christians in the past and today; Borg (1.2) tackles the wider question of how Jesus himself has been understood. Moving from text to visual representation, the second set of readings (1.3–1.7) examine ideas about the sacred image in recent Hindu thinking and practice. The following readings (1.8–1.14) provide evidence for how a religion is variously represented while in the process of dissemination: charting the development of Buddhism from the Buddha's last instructions to the proliferation of Buddhist sects in the west, as well as reviewing the media through which the Buddha is represented in the west and the nature of different representations. 1.15 points up the issue of the interpretation and representation of Islam in a modernizing Egypt. The final reading in this section (1.16) moves to the electronic pulpit, and how the Internet is used by religions, and questions the future shape of religion as it increasingly relies upon electronic alternatives to the printed text and the real object.

1.1 'MARK'S GOSPEL'

Clive Marsh and Steve Moyise

From *Jesus and the Gospels*, Marsh, C. and Moyise, S., London, Cassell, 1999, pp. 14–25, 115–19.

Mark is the shortest of the four Gospels, beginning at Jesus' baptism (nothing about his birth) and ending at the empty tomb (no resurrection appearances). For much of church history, it was thought to be an abbreviation of Matthew and hence less important. Over 600 of its 661 verses find a parallel in Matthew, and although early tradition suggests that Mark drew on the memories of Peter, the fact remains that it was not written by an apostle. This probably explains why so few commentaries were written on Mark in the early church and the book fell into neglect (Lightfoot, 1950, p.2).

However, during the nineteenth century, scholars such as Lachmann (1835) and Holtzmann (1863) showed that the 'abbreviation' theory is untenable. For example, the story of the demoniac and the pigs (Matt 8:28–34) occupies seven verses in Matthew but Mark's account runs to twenty verses (Mark 5:1–20). The similarities between the Gospels, particularly their use of unusual Greek phrases, shows that the church was correct in seeing a relationship between them. But most scholars today believe that Matthew and Luke used Mark as one of their sources (Luke acknowledges that many have written before him). This would make Mark our earliest 'life of Jesus' and therefore of great importance.

. . .

Mark presents Jesus' ministry in two parts. The first ten chapters describe an itinerant ministry in and around Galilee. The last six chapters concern the last week of his life ('the passion') in and around Jerusalem. Unlike Matthew and Luke, Mark does not tell us anything about a miraculous birth or a child prodigy. Mark begins with Jesus' baptism and moves rapidly to his death. Over a third of Mark's Gospel is devoted to the final week of his life, earning it the description of 'a passion narrative with an extended introduction'.

Many scholars have also noted a thematic division in the Gospel. The first eight chapters present Jesus as a man 'mighty in word and deed'. But the incident at Caesarea Philippi (8:27–30) seems to be a turning point. Jesus asks his disciples, 'Who do people say I am?' They reply with a variety of answers: John the Baptist; Elijah; a prophet. He then asks, 'But who do you say that I am?', to which Peter replies, 'You are the Messiah'. Then

> *he began to teach them* that the Son of Man must undergo great suffering, and be rejected by the elders, the chief priests, and the scribes, and be killed, and after three days rise again. He said all this quite openly. And Peter took him aside and began to rebuke him. But turning and looking at his disciples, he rebuked Peter and said, 'Get behind me, Satan! For you are setting your mind not on divine things but on human things.' He

called the crowd with his disciples, and said to them, 'If any want to become my followers, let them deny themselves and take up their cross and follow me. For those who want to save their life will lose it, and those who lose their life for my sake, and for the sake of the gospel, will save it.' (8:31–35)

Though chapters 9–16 are not devoid of miracles (there are three), the emphasis is on Jesus' suffering. It is the focus of his teaching (9:30–2; 10:32–4; 12:1–12; 14:8; 14:18–25). And it is the climax of Mark's story (14:34; 14:65; 15:15–20; 15:34). As Gundry puts it: 'The basic problem of Marcan studies is how to fit together these apparently contradictory kinds of material in a way that makes sense of the book as a literary whole' (1993, p. 2).

· · ·

NO CHRISTIANITY WITHOUT THE CROSS

The majority view is that Mark intended to show that there can be no glory without the cross. As Paul discovered, God's glory is not revealed in strength but weakness. The burden of Mark's Gospel is to show that even with his mighty power and superior wisdom, Jesus could only accomplish his work through suffering. The same will be true for his followers. To an earlier generation of scholars (Taylor, 1953; Cranfield, 1959), this was seen as Jesus fusing together the glorious 'Son of Man' figure from Daniel 7 with the suffering servant of Isaiah 53. This is a rather neat solution, but it is probably too neat. There is little evidence that Jews of Jesus' day were expecting a messianic 'Son of Man' or a 'suffering servant'. And there are no actual quotations of Isaiah 53 in Mark's Gospel. The three quotations that do appear in connection with Jesus' death are Psalm 118:22–3 ('The stone that the builders rejected'), Zechariah 13:7 ('I will strike the shepherd, and the sheep will be scattered') and Psalm 22:1 ('My God, my God, why have you forsaken me?'). As Joel Marcus has shown, Mark seems to have drawn on a number of Old Testament figures in order to paint his picture of Jesus' passion (1992, pp. 153–98).

Many have suggested that Mark is writing at a time of extreme tension, either the Neronian persecution in Rome (c. 64 CE) or, more probably (in the light of 13:14), the Jewish war (c. 66–70 CE). It is often thought of as the 'suffering' Gospel. Thus Denis Nineham (1963, p. 33) thinks that the author of Mark's Gospel had three aims:

- to show how much Jesus suffered
- to show how he taught his followers that they would suffer
- to show how he promised great rewards to those who endure to the end.

· · ·

A NON-MESSIANIC JESUS

In 1901, William Wrede published his famous book on the 'messianic secret'. Prior to this, it was assumed that Jesus wanted people to know who he was and why he had come. Why else would God become incarnate if not to try and communicate with lost humanity? But Mark portrays Jesus as frequently *commanding* silence from those who are healed and *refusing* to work miracles to aid belief:

1:34 The demons are forbidden to say who Jesus is (see also 3:12).

1:44 The leprosy sufferer is told to tell no one about his cure.

5:43 Jairus is told to tell no one about the raising of his daughter.

7:36 The crowd must not tell of the healing of the deaf mute.

9:9   Peter, James and John are not to tell anyone about the transfiguration.

9:30 Jesus wants to keep his presence a secret.

Wrede believed that these are unrealistic and artificial. How could Jairus say nothing about the raising of his daughter when there is a crowd of mourners outside? And if Jesus is seeking to avoid attention, why does he insist on healing the man with the withered hand in the middle of a synagogue service? Why not wait until the next day? Why does he feed a crowd of 5000 if he wants to remain anonymous? Wrede concluded that this is really a literary device to cover up the fact that while the church proclaimed Jesus as Messiah, Jesus himself had no such pretensions. In order to get around this, the church introduced the 'messianic secret', the idea that Jesus knew himself to be the Messiah but wished to keep it quiet. But actually, Jesus was not conscious of being the Messiah and never made any such claims.

A NON-POLITICAL MESSIAH

Conservative scholars interpret this evidence differently. Jesus knew that he was the Messiah and Son of God (e.g. 13:32) but did not openly proclaim it, either for fear of creating sedition or of encouraging the wrong sort of faith (Cranfield, 1959, p.270). He knew that groups like the Zealots would pounce on such claims and try to lead a revolt against Rome (as in fact they did *c.* 66–70 CE). So he veiled his teaching in parables. He spoke about the kingdom rather than proclaiming himself as king. He preferred to use the obscure 'Son of Man' (the Aramaic simply means 'human') rather than openly declaring himself to be the 'Messiah' or 'Son of God'. But when asked at his trial, 'Are you the Messiah, the Son of the Blessed One?', he answered, 'I am' (14:61–2). At this stage, there was no longer any need to keep his true status quiet. Thus Wrede was correct in drawing attention to a key characteristic of Mark but had misinterpreted it. Peter is not rebuked for calling Jesus 'Messiah' but for his inability to see that the Messiah must suffer (8:32).

SON OF MAN AND SON OF GOD

Any interpretation of Mark must do justice both to the 'glory' passages and the 'suffering' passages. In terms of Mark's Christology, this has often been discussed with respect to his use of the titles 'Son of God' and 'Son of Man'. The distribution of these titles is curious, for 'Son of Man' appears to be Jesus' preferred title (fourteen times), while Mark clearly wishes his readers to think of Jesus as 'Son of God' (1:1, 11; 9:7; 12:6; 13:32; 15:39). This could be seen as a point in favour of Mark's reliability. Mark sees Jesus as Son of God but he does not make Jesus a mouthpiece for his own theology. Rather, he presents Jesus as preferring 'Son of Man', even though the early church (according to Acts) seems to have ignored it.

. . .

CONCLUSION

The early church believed that Mark was an abbreviation of Matthew and so the book fell into neglect. But most scholars today (Farmer is an exception) believe that Mark is the earliest Gospel and therefore of great importance. In particular, its candid portrayal of a suffering, forsaken Jesus (and the many failures of the disciples) has resonated powerfully with post-war readers (Moltmann, 1974). More recently, the paradoxical nature of the Gospel (on some readings) has appealed to what many have called our postmodern world. Far from providing answers, Aichele deduces from the Gospel's abrupt ending that Mark

> is not a story which ends happily or comfortably for readers who want the reinforcing of Christian faith. It does not end with a meeting between the disciples and the resurrected Jesus, nor with Jesus seated on the right hand of God. It does not end with an imperishable message of everlasting salvation spreading out from east to west, nor with the end of the reign of Satan, nor with a promise of heavenly glory; nor with Jesus transformed, nor with transformed disciples. (1996, p. 51)

For such things, we have to look to the other Gospels and the rest of the New Testament.

1.2 'DOES THE HISTORICAL JESUS MATTER?'

Marcus J. Borg

From *Jesus in Contemporary Scholarship*, Borg, M.J., Valley Forge, Pa, Trinity Press International, 1994, pp. 182–200.

The historical study of Jesus produces results very different from what Christians are accustomed to hearing and affirming about Jesus. Within Christian devotion, worship, and belief, Jesus is regularly spoken of as divine, indeed as the second person of the Trinity. The Nicene Creed, the great creed of the church formulated in the fourth century, speaks of him in the most exalted language:

> We believe in one Lord, Jesus Christ,
> the only Son of God,
> eternally begotten of the Father,
> God from God, Light from Light,
> true God from true God,
> begotten, not made,
> of one Being with the Father.
> Through him all things were made.
> For us and for our salvation
> he came down from heaven;
> by the power of the Holy Spirit
> he became incarnate from the Virgin Mary,
> and was made man.
> For our sake he was crucified under Pontius Pilate;
> he suffered death and was buried.
> On the third day he rose again
> in accordance with the Scriptures;
> he ascended into heaven
> and is seated at the right hand of the Father.
> He will come again to judge the living and the dead,
> and his kingdom will have no end.[1]

Yet historical scholarship about the pre-Easter Jesus affirms essentially none of this. We are quite certain that Jesus did not think of himself as divine or as "Son of God" in any unique sense, if at all. If one of the disciples had responded to the question reportedly asked by Jesus in Mark's gospel, "Who do people say that I am?," with words like those used in the Nicene

---

1. From *The Book of Common Prayer* (New York: Oxford University Press, 1979), 358, Rite II. The wording is identical in the *Lutheran Book of Worship* (Minneapolis: Augsburg, 1978), 84.

Creed, we can well imagine that Jesus would have said, "What???" Moreover, most Jesus scholars do not think Jesus was born of a virgin, or that he ascended into heaven in a visible way, or that there will be a literal second coming. Indeed, perhaps the only line from the Creed that would be seen as historical is the reference to his death: "he was crucified under Pontius Pilate, suffered death, and was buried."[2]

Thus the quest for the historical Jesus often seems to call into question some of the most common and cherished Christian beliefs. Indeed, its foundational claim — that Jesus of Nazareth was quite different from how he is portrayed in the gospels and creeds of the church — can seem threatening to and destructive of Christian faith. In this chapter, as one who is both a Christian and a Jesus scholar, I want to reflect on the relationship between Jesus scholarship and the Christian life. What is the significance of such scholarship for Christian theology, understanding, and life? Does the historical study of Jesus matter for Christians, and, if so, in what ways?

A HISTORICAL PERSPECTIVE

It is useful to see this issue as a sub-category of a larger question: what significance is to be given to the historical study of the Bible as it has emerged in the last few centuries of biblical scholarship? What happens to the claims of Christian theology, doctrine, dogma, and morals when the Bible is treated not as a divine product whose truth is guaranteed by its divine origin, but as a human product produced by two ancient cultures, namely, ancient Israel and the early Christian movement?

Until about three centuries ago, this was not an issue within the Christian world, any more than it was an issue for Muslims to wonder whether the Koran came directly from Allah through the prophet Mohammed. No effort was required to believe this, for it was part of the taken-for-granted world of shared conviction. The gospels and the Bible as a whole were understood in . . . the state of "natural literalism" or "pre-critical naiveté." They were seen as divine documents whose truth was guaranteed by God. Therefore, the history that they reported was taken for granted actually to have happened.

This is not to say that every passage was understood literally. Theologians and Scripture scholars could find the "spiritual" or "allegorical" meaning of a text to be more important than the literal meaning, and could deny the literal meaning of some texts.[3] Nevertheless, if the text

---

2. And even the claim that he was buried in a tomb has been questioned. Crossan argues that it was customary for the Romans to prohibit normal burial of victims of crucifixion as a final shaming and humiliation, and that Jesus' body may have been cast into a common grave or even devoured by dogs; Crossan, *Jesus: A Revolutionary Biography* (San Francisco: Harper, 1994), 123–58. To say, as I have suggested, that Jesus' death may be the only historical referent in the creed is not to deny the resurrection. It does, however, imply that the resurrection is not a historical event in the ordinary sense of the word; I do not think you could have "caught" the risen Christ on a videocam, though I assume that the crucifixion was the kind of event that could have been photographed.

3. Two examples, whose source I do not remember but which are recalled from usually reliable memory: About the part of the temptation narrative in which Satan takes Jesus to a high mountain from which he shows him all the kingdoms of the earth, Origen (early third century) commented: there is no such mountain; obviously, something else must be meant. About the passage in Genesis 3 in which we are told that Adam and Eve heard the sound of God walking in the garden of Eden in the cool of the day, Luther commented: God never walked in any garden; they must have heard something else, perhaps the sound of the wind; nature, which had previously seemed benevolent, had now become a source of fear.

looked like it described something that happened or was said, it was taken for granted that what it reported was historically true: Adam and Eve in the Garden of Eden, Noah and the flood, God speaking to Moses through a burning bush, the walls of Jericho falling down in the time of Joshua, the miraculous deliverance of Daniel from the lions' den, the virgin birth with shepherds and wisemen in attendance, the stories of Jesus walking on the water, and so forth.

Within this view of Scripture what Jesus was like could be known simply by combining together all that the Bible said about him.[4] No distinction had yet been made between Jesus as a historical figure and the Jesus who meets us on the surface of the gospels, between the pre-Easter Jesus and the post-Easter Jesus. The Jesus of history and the canonical Christ were seen as identical, and this identification was not even an article of faith. It required neither "belief" nor effort, but was as self-evident to our ancestors as the heliocentric solar system is to us.

It was this understanding of the Bible and the gospels that was initially undermined and ultimately overturned by modern biblical scholarship. Modern biblical scholarship was the child of two parents: the Protestant Reformation of the sixteenth century and the Enlightenment, which began about a century later. The Reformation emphasized the authority of the Bible (in contrast to church tradition), and thus gave to its study an importance that it had not had for over a thousand years. The Reformation also saw the Bible translated into popular languages, thereby making it widely accessible.

The Enlightenment, with its emphasis upon reason and scientific ways of knowing, engendered a revolution in knowledge. No longer could something be accepted as "true" simply on the basis of authority and tradition. Investigation and reason became the new basis for knowledge. Applied initially in the natural world of the sciences, the new way of knowing soon was applied in the human world of history and culture. Within the world-view of the Enlightenment, both sacred authority and supernatural causation were rejected, and instead the effort was made to understand everything within a natural system of cause and effect.

· · ·

EARLY PERIOD: THE HISTORICAL JESUS MATTERS

It was in this period that the quest for the historical Jesus began. Like the early forays in biblical criticism, it generated both controversy and conflict. Hermann Samuel Reimarus (1694–1768), a professor of Oriental languages in Hamburg, is usually credited with the honor of being its father.[5] The work for which he is famous — *The Aims of Jesus and His Disciples* (1778) — was published posthumously and anonymously by Gotthold Lessing, who

---

4. See the comment of Craig A. Evans, "Authenticity Criteria in Life of Jesus Research," *Christian Scholar's Review* 19 (1989): 6: "Prior to the critical period of biblical studies, canonicity was the only test for determining the authenticity of the sayings of Jesus. What was in the New Testament was authentic; what was not in the New Testament was suspect."

5. Ever since Albert Schweitzer's famous *The Quest for the Historical Jesus* (1906), it has been a scholarly convention to date the beginning of the quest to Reimarus's work. He did, however, have predecessors, as N. Thomas Wright ("Jesus, Quest for the Historical" in *Anchor Bible Dictionary* 3:796–802) and Colin Brown (*Jesus in European Protestant Thought* [Grand Rapids: Baker, 1985], 29–55) point out.

used a ruse to get it past state censorship, which forbad the publication of works injurious to religion. The identity of the author was not disclosed for several decades because of fear of bringing harm to his family. In 1835, a two-volume fourteen-hundred-page *Life of Jesus* by David Friedrich Strauss (remarkably, only twenty-seven years old) was published. Among other things, Strauss argued that the miracle stories were to be understood as myth, not history. He lost his academic position in Tübingen and was in effect banned for life from a university career. One reviewer referred to his book as "the Iscariotism of our day," and another called it the most pestilential volume ever vomited out of the bowels of hell.[6] To say the obvious, many people in this period thought that what one affirmed about the historical Jesus mattered a great deal. Civil authority still sometimes took a hand, and outrage among church officials was common.

Throughout the nineteenth century, there was widespread agreement that the historical Jesus had great significance for Christian faith. About this, hostile debunkers, orthodox defenders, and liberal revisionists agreed.

. . .

THE PENDULUM SWINGS

Around the end of the nineteenth century, the claim that the historical Jesus mattered changed. Indeed, it was turned on its head. Throughout much of the twentieth century, the dominant position has been that the historical Jesus (defined more precisely as *the historian's Jesus*, namely, as what the historian can affirm about Jesus) has little or no significance for Christian theology and faith.

The reversal was due largely to the work of two scholars, Martin Kähler (1835–1912) and Albert Schweitzer (1875–1965). In a book published in Germany in 1892 and translated into English as *The So-Called Historical Jesus and the Historic Biblical Christ*, Kähler, a professor of systematic theology, argued that the historical Jesus does not matter for Christian faith and theology; rather, only the biblical Christ does.[7] For Kähler, the historical Jesus was the historically reconstructed Jesus, the result of the historian's activity. The biblical Christ is the Christ of the gospels and the New Testament. The historical Jesus, he argued, cannot be decisively important for Christian faith, in part because the gospels do not provide adequate materials to write a life of Jesus, and in part because all historical reconstructions are relative and can at most be probable, not certain. Christian faith cannot be faith in constantly changing historical reconstructions accessible only through the work of scholars. If it were, it would, among other things, make Christian faith inaccessible to most Christians. Rather, Kähler argued, Christian faith is faith in "the biblical Christ," the Christ of early Christianity's proclamation as found in the New Testament as a whole. It is the Christ of the church's proclamation — the kerygmatic Christ — who matters for faith and theology. The historical Jesus does not.

In different terms, a similar position was articulated by Albert Schweitzer in the epilogue to his epochal *Quest for the Historical Jesus* (1906). In conclusion of a book in which he (at age

---

6. For the history of this period of Jesus scholarship, see the works by Schweitzer and Brown in the previous note.
7. The English translation by Carl E. Braaten (Philadelphia: Fortress, 1964) is from the 1896 German edition.

thirty) brilliantly systematized the history of the quest to his day and then argued for an eschatological understanding of Jesus that was to dominate scholarship throughout much of the twentieth century, he pronounced the whole enterprise theologically and religiously irrelevant. The Jesus discovered by historical research was, he wrote, "a stranger to our time." He was strange to a large extent because of the eschatological beliefs that, Schweitzer argued, animated his life: Jesus believed that the supernatural kingdom of God was at hand, and that he himself would be transformed into the apocalyptic "Son of man" who would rule that kingdom as God's vice-regent and Messiah. And, of course, he was wrong.[8] But that doesn't matter, Schweitzer continued, for it is *the spiritual Christ*, not the historical Jesus, who matters for us who live in the centuries since. The spiritual Christ is the one who is still known; the historical Jesus is a remote and strange figure from the distant past.

. . .

THE CURRENT SCENE

In broad strokes this was the situation at mid-century. In retrospect, one can see that Jesus scholarship from its beginning up to this period saw a pendulum swing between the poles of two related either/or's. The first either/or was *the historical Jesus or the Christ of faith* (who may also be spoken of as the biblical Christ or kerygmatic Christ). Who is normative for Christian faith and theology? Is it the historical Jesus or the Christ of faith? The second either/or was a common (though not necessary) corollary of the first: *either the historical Jesus is of normative importance, or he is of little or no significance at all.* To speak schematically, scholarship in the nineteenth century generally affirmed the Jesus of history (and thus the theological importance of the historical study of Jesus) and in much of the twentieth century affirmed the Christ of faith (and hence the theological unimportance of historical Jesus scholarship).

. . .

NORMAN PERRIN

In a work published in the late 1960s, Perrin (the most prominent Jesus scholar in North America at the time of his death in 1976) assigned considerable theological importance to the historical study of Jesus.[9] To see this, it is illuminating to begin with Perrin's useful notion of "faith-image" of Jesus. Every Christian has such a "faith-image," which is the product of

---

8. It should be noted that Schweitzer did not argue (as Kähler and others have done) that we cannot know much about the historical Jesus. That was not the point of Schweitzer's history of the quest; rather, Schweitzer used it as a springboard for creating his own sketch of the historical Jesus, which he himself (and others) found quite persuasive. His point is that the historical Jesus is irrelevant to our time because of his "strangeness," not because he is unknowable.

9. See the concluding chapter of Norman Perrin, *Rediscovering the Teaching of Jesus* (New York: Harper & Row, 1967), 207–48, still one of the best chapter-length treatments of the subject. Other works from the period that continue to be important include Van A. Harvey, *The Historian and the Believer*, and Leander Keck, *A Future for the Historical Jesus* (Nashville: Abingdon, 1971; reprint, Philadelphia: Fortress, 1981).

everything the Christian has assimilated about Jesus, whether from listening to sermons, hearing the gospels, reciting creeds, or singing hymns.[10] Faith-images are ultimately the product of Christian proclamation (in a comprehensive sense), not directly the result of historical research. Thus for Perrin (in continuity with Kähler and Bultmann, both of whom he explicitly cites), the proclaimed Christ is granted primacy.

What then is the relationship between the historical study of Jesus and the proclaimed Christ found in the faith-images of Christians? First, it can contribute to the formation and revision of the faith-image by providing content. Christian faith, Perrin writes, is: "…necessarily faith *in* something, a believer believes *in* something, and in so far as that 'something' is 'Jesus,' historical knowledge can help to provide the content, without thereby becoming the main source of that content."[11]

Second, Perrin affirms that historical knowledge about Jesus can be used as a basis for discriminating among the great variety of proclamations that claim to be Christian. In a situation in which everything from "radical right racism to revolutionary Christian humanism" is proclaimed as Christian kerygma, historical knowledge about Jesus can be "a means of testing the claims of the Christs presented in the competing kerygmata to be Jesus Christ." This leads to a striking statement: "The true kerygmatic Christ, the justifiable faith-image, is that consistent with the historical Jesus." It is a strong statement. The historical study of Jesus is assigned no less a role than the validation or invalidation of a given version of Christian proclamation as really *Christian*.[12]

If we were to emphasize only this part of Perrin, it would seem as if we had gone back to the nineteenth century: the historical Jesus is normative for discerning what is authentically Christian. What makes Perrin's position not simply a return to the nineteenth century is, of course, his strong affirmation of the primacy of the kerygmatic Christ, the Christ of faith. Rather than being a return to one pole of the "either/or" of earlier scholarship, Perrin (like the new quest) represents movement to a "both/and" position.

. . .

MY OWN POSITION

Thus the last few decades have seen affirmations that historical Jesus scholarship matters for Christian faith and life. In the last part of this chapter, I wish to describe how I presently see the issues myself. Two central claims seem important.

---

10. To quote Perrin, *Rediscovering*, 243–44: "[T]he Jesus of one's faith-image is a mixture of historical reminiscence, at a somewhat distant remove, and myth, legend and idealism." The validity of a faith-image is not directly dependent upon historical knowledge of Jesus, but upon "the fact that it grows out of religious experience and is capable of mediating religious experience."

11. Ibid., 244. The "main source," Perrin continues, "will always be the proclamation of the Church, a proclamation rising out of a Christian experience of the risen Lord."

12. In Perrin's own language: "To this limited extent our historical knowledge of Jesus validates the Christian kerygma; it does not validate it as *kerygma*, but it validates it as Christian." Though Perrin speaks of this as "limited," it is a broad claim. Why then call it "limited"? I construe his use of it to mean: although the central claims of the kerygma are beyond validation (for example, Jesus lives and is lord), claims about what Christianity means for life are testable by appeal to the historical study of Jesus. Quoted passages from Perrin, *Rediscovering*, 244.

First, . . . I agree that historical knowledge of Jesus is not essential to being a Christian. This seems self-evidently true; if it were not, then we would have to say that the vast majority of Christians throughout the centuries have not had authentic faith, for there was no possibility of historical knowledge of Jesus until the birth of the quest a couple of centuries ago.

Moreover, I do not think the truth of Christianity is at stake in the historical study of Jesus (or the Bible, for that matter). Its truth has a least a relative immunity to historical investigation. By this, I mean that Christianity seems obviously to be a viable religion. That may seem an odd way to talk about it. What I mean is that Christianity seems clearly to "work": it is a means or vehicle by which people experience "the sacred." And I cannot imagine any historical discovery or claim causing it immediately to cease to "work." I say this not simply because religious beliefs tend to persist even in the face of contradictory data, but also because religious traditions can mediate the sacred independently of their historical or literal truth.[13]

Finally, in affirming that historical knowledge of Jesus is not essential for Christian faith, it is important to be precise about what one means by "faith." I am using "faith" in a relatively narrow sense to refer to one's relationship to God, and Christian faith specifically is a trusting relationship to God as mediated by the Christian tradition. Faith in this sense — as one's relationship to God — is not dependent upon historical knowledge of Jesus.

If, however, one uses "faith" in a broad sense so that it refers not only to one's relationship to God but becomes virtually a synonym for the whole of Christianity (as in the phrase "the Christian faith"), then it seems obvious to me that historical knowledge of Jesus is relevant.

This leads to my second main claim: images of Jesus *in fact* very much affect images of the Christian life. Much of the scholarly debate about the significance of historical knowledge about Jesus for Christians has focused on the question of whether it *ought* to be significant. Reasons for and against are then marshaled: to say "yes" risks making authentic Christianity inaccessible to millions of Christians of the past and present; to say "no" risks docetism, gnosticism, and other illnesses. I prefer to begin in another place, namely, with the descriptive statement that images of Jesus do in fact have a strong effect on the lives of Christians. Because of his central place in the Christian tradition, how we as Christians think of Jesus shapes our understanding of the Christian life itself.

Let me illustrate this initially by speaking of the "popular image" of Jesus and how it affects one's image of the Christian life. By the popular image, I mean the widespread image of Jesus that most of us received as children, whether we grew up within the church or only on its fringes. It is an image of Jesus as the divine savior. Its answers to the classic questions of Jesus' identity, mission, and message are clear: Jesus was the divinely begotten Son of God, whose mission was to die for the sins of the world, and whose message was about himself, the saving purpose of his death, and the importance of believing in him. This image of Jesus leads to an understanding of the Christian life as consisting primarily of *believing*, whatever else it

---

13. Perhaps, over a long period of time, an absolutely outrageous discovery (what could it be?) would weaken Christianity enough so that it would cease to "work" for large numbers of people and cause it effectively to disappear. But my point is that the core validity of Christianity has to do with its ability to mediate the sacred, not with the historical accuracy of any particular claim.

may also lead to. It creates what we might call a *fideistic* image of the Christian life, one whose essential quality is believing that Jesus is one's savior. The point: the image of Jesus shapes the image of the Christian life.

A second image of Jesus is not as widespread as the first but still fairly common: not Jesus as savior, but Jesus as teacher. Generally a de-dogmatized image of Jesus, it is what most commonly results when persons are no longer certain about the doctrinal features of the popular image. What remains is Jesus as a teacher of ethics or morals, and it leads to a *moralistic* understanding of the Christian life, often expressed in quite banal terms. The Christian life consists of "being good" or of following "the golden rule."

. . .

The same relationship between how Christians think of Jesus and how Christians think of the Christian life is found if we move from global images of Jesus to more particular claims about him. To cite a few examples: if a Christian becomes persuaded that Jesus taught a subversive wisdom, it affects how that person sees the conventional wisdom of his or her own day; if a Christian becomes persuaded that Jesus countered the purity system of his day, it affects how she or he sees purity systems in our day; if a Christian becomes persuaded that Jesus indicted the ruling elites of his day, it affects how domination systems are seen in the present. Note that I am not saying that these perceptions *ought* to have an effect, but that they do. I have seen this happen again and again: a significant change in a Christian's perception of Jesus in fact affects that person's perception of the Christian life.[14]

My point is the correlation between images of Jesus and images of the Christian life. Given this correlation, the question is not so much *whether* images of Jesus *ought* to have theological significance. Rather, they *do* have theological significance at the very practical immediate level of Christian understanding, devotion, and piety. Our choice is to let that significance be largely unrecognized, unconscious, and unchallenged, or to be conscious and intentional about the relationship. In short, because historical scholarship about Jesus affects our image of Jesus and thus our image of the Christian life, it matters.

---

14. I am not claiming that the change in perception leads immediately to a change in how one lives one's life. For most people, the process is gradual and slow. But a change in one's perception of Jesus is most often accompanied by a change in one's vision of the Christian life and what it calls one to.

1.3 'SEEING THE SACRED'

Diana L. Eck

From 'Seeing the sacred: film images', in *Darśan: Seeing the Divine Image in India*, Eck, D.L., New York: Columbia UP, 1996, pp. 14–16.

The term *hermeneutics* has been used to describe the task of understanding and interpreting ideas and texts. In a similar way, we need to set for ourselves the task of developing a hermeneutic of the visible, addressing the problem of how we understand and interpret what we see, not only in the classical images and art forms created by the various religious traditions, but in the ordinary images of people's traditions, rites, and daily activities which are presented to us through the film-image.

Rudolf Arnheim, in his extensive work on visual perception, has shown that the dichotomy between seeing and thinking which runs through much of the Western tradition, is a very problematic one. In *Visual Thinking*, he contends that visual perception is integrally related to thought.[1] It is not the case, according to Arnheim, that the eyes present a kind of raw data to the mind which, in turn, processes it and refines it by thought. Rather, those visual images are the shapers and bearers of thought. Jan Gonda, in writing on the Vedic notion *dhi-*, sometimes translated as "thought," finds similarly that the semantic field of this word in Vedic literature does not correspond as much to our words for "thinking" as it does to our notions of "insight," "vision," and "seeing."[2] Susanne Langer has also written of the integral relation of thought to the images we see in the "mind's eye." The making of all those images is the fundamental "imaginative" human activity. One might add that it is the fundamental activity of the religious imagination as well. She writes, "Images are, therefore, our readiest instruments for abstracting concepts from the tumbling streams of actual impressions."[3]

Seeing is not a passive awareness of visual data, but an active focusing upon it, "touching" it. Arnheim writes, in language that echoes the Hindu notion of seeing and touching: "In looking at an object we reach out for it. With an invisible finger we move through the space around us, go out to the distant places where things are found, touch them, catch them, scan their surfaces, trace their borders, explore their texture. It is an eminently active occupation."[4]

According to Arnheim, the way in which we reach out for and grasp the "object we see, either in our immediate range of perception or through the medium of photography, is dependent upon who we are and what we recognize from past experience." The visual imprint of an image, an object, or a scene upon the eye is not at all "objective." In the image-making process of thinking, we see, sort, and recognize according to the visual phenomenology of our

---

1. Arnheim, Chapter 2, "The Intelligence of Visual Perception."
2. Gonda, *The Vision of the Vedic Poets*, Chapter I, "Introduction" and Chapter II, "*Dhih*" in the Rg Veda."
3. Susanne K. Langer, *Philosophy in a New Key*, 3rd edition (Cambridge: Harvard University Press, 1942), p. 145.
4. Arnheim, p. 19.

own experience.[5] What people notice in the "same" image — be it an image of the dancing Śiva or a film of a Hindu festival procession — depends to some extent on what they can recognize from the visual experience of the past. In the case of film, of course, it also depends on what the photographer has seen and chosen to show us. Arnheim writes that the eye and the mind, working together in the process of cognition, cannot simply note down images that are "already there." "We find instead that direct observation, far from being a mere ragpicker, is an exploration of the form-seeking, form-imposing mind, which needs to understand but cannot until it casts what it sees into manageable models."[6]

As students confronted with images of India through film and photography, we are challenged to begin to be self-conscious of who we are as "seers." Part of the difficulty of entering the world of another culture, especially one with as intricate and elaborate a visual articulation as India's, is that, for many of us, there are no "manageable models." There are no self-evident ways of recognizing the shapes and forms of art, iconography, ritual life and daily life that we see. Who is Śiva, dancing wildly in a ring of fire? What is happening when the priest pours honey and yogurt over the image of Viṣṇu? Why does the woman touch the feet of the ascetic beggar? For those who enter the visible world of India through the medium of film, the onslaught of strange images raises a multitude of questions. These very questions should be the starting point for our learning. Without such self-conscious questioning, we cannot begin to "think" with what we see and we simply dismiss it as strange. Or, worse, we are bound to misinterpret what we see by placing it solely within the context of what we already know from our own world of experience.

---

5. Arnheim, Chapter 5, "The Past in the Present" and Chapter 6, "The Images of Thought."
6. Arnheim, p. 278.

1.4 'IDOLATRY AND THE DEFENCE OF HINDU THEISM'

Rāmmohun Roy

From *A Source Book of Modern Hinduism*, Richard, G. (ed.), Richmond, Curzon Press, 1985, pp. 4–6.

The greater part of Brahmans, as well as of other sects of Hindoos, are quite incapable of justifying that idolatry which they continue to practise. When questioned on the subject, in place of adducing reasonable arguments in support of their conduct, they conceive it fully sufficient to quote their ancestors as positive authorities! And some of them are become very ill-disposed towards me, because I have forsaken idolatry for the worship of the true and eternal God! In order therefore, to vindicate my own faith and that of our early forefathers, I have been endeavouring, for some time past, to convince my countrymen of the true meaning of our sacred books; and to prove, that my aberration deserves not the opprobrium which some unreflecting persons have been so ready to throw upon me . . .

In pursuance of my vindication, I have to the best of my abilities translated this hitherto unknown work, as well as an abridgement thereof, into the Hindoostanee and Bengalee languages, and distributed them, free of cost, among my own countrymen, as widely as circumstances have possibly allowed. The present is an endeavour to render an abridgment of the same into English, by which I expect to prove to my European friends, that the superstitious practices which deform the Hindoo religion have nothing to do with the pure spirit of its dictates!

I have observed that, both in their writings and conversation, many Europeans feel a wish to palliate and soften the features of Hindoo idolatry; and are inclined to inculcate, that all objects of worship are considered by their votaries as emblematical representations of the Supreme Divinity! If this were indeed the case, I might perhaps be led into some examination of the subject: but the truth is, the Hindoos of the present day have no such views of the subject, but firmly believe in the real existence of innumerable gods and goddesses, who possess, in their own departments, full and independent power; and to propitiate them, and not the true God, are temples erected and ceremonies performed. There can be no doubt, however, and it is my whole design to prove, that every rite has its derivation from the allegorical adoration of the true Deity; but at the present day all this is forgotten, and among many it is even heresy to mention it! . . .

My constant reflections on the inconvenient, or rather injurious rites introduced by the peculiar practice of Hindoo idolatry which more than any other pagan worship, destroys the texture of society, together with compassion for my countrymen, have compelled me to use every possible effort to awaken them from their dream of error: and by making them acquainted with their scriptures, enable them to contemplate with true devotion the unity and omnipresence of Nature's God.[1]

---

1. *English Works of Raja Rammohun Roy*, edited by Dr Kalidas Nag and Debajyoti Burman, (Calcutta, 1945–51), Part II (1946), 59–61.

A DEFENCE OF HINDU THEISM IN REPLY TO ŚANKARA ŚASTRI, HEAD
ENGLISH MASTER AT THE MADRAS GOVERNMENT COLLEGE, ATTACKING
RĀMMOHUN ROY'S VIEWS AND ADVOCATING THE WORSHIP OF DIVINE
ATTRIBUTES AS DEITIES

The learned gentleman says that 'Their (the attributes and incarnations) worship under various
representations, by means of consecrated objects, is prescribed by the scripture to the
human race, by way of mental exercises,' etc. I cannot admit that the worship of these
attributes under various representations, by means of consecrated objects, has been prescribed
by the Veda to the HUMAN RACE; as this kind of worship of consecrated objects is enjoined
by the Sastra[2] to those only who are incapable of raising their minds to the notion of an
invisible Supreme Being. I have quoted several authorities for this assertion in my Preface to
the *Isopanishad*, and beg to repeat here one or two of them: 'The vulgar look for their
God in water; men of more extended knowledge in celestial bodies; the ignorant in wood,
bricks, and stones; but learned men in the Universal Soul.' 'Thus corresponding to the nature
of different powers or qualities, numerous figures have been invented for the benefit of those
who are not possessed of sufficient understanding.' Permit me in this instance to ask, whether
every Mussulman in Turkey and Arabia, from the highest to the lowest, every Protestant
Christian at least of Europe, and many followers of Kabir and Nanak, do worship God without
the assistance of consecrated objects? If so, how can we suppose that the human race is not
capable of adoring the Supreme Being without the puerile practice of having recourse to
visible objects?

. . . The learned gentleman is of opinion that the attributes of God exist distinctly from
God and he compares the relation between God and these attributes to that of a king to his
ministers as he says: 'If a person be desirous to visit an earthly prince, he ought to be
introduced in the first instance by his ministers', etc; and 'in like manner the grace of God
ought to be obtained by the grace through the worship of his attributes.' This opinion, I am
extremely sorry to find, is directly contrary to all the Vedanta doctrines interpreted to us by
the most revered Sankaracharya [a traditional authority], which are real adwaita or non-
duality; they affirm that God has no second that may be possessed of eternal existence, either
of the same nature with himself or of a different nature from him, nor any second of that
nature that might be called either his part or his quality . . .

The Veda very often calls the Supreme Existence by the epithets of Existence, Wise, and
Eternal and assigns as the reason for adopting such epithets, that the Veda in the first instance
speaks of God according to the human idea, which views quality separately from person, in
order to facilitate our comprehension of objects. In case these attributes should be supposed,
as the learned gentleman asserts, to be separate existences, it necessarily follows, that they must
be either eternal or non-eternal. The former case, viz, the existence of a plurality of beings
imbued like God himself with the property of eternal duration, strikes immediately at the root
of all the doctrines relative to the unity of the Supreme Being contained in the Vedanta. By
the latter sentiment, namely, that the power and attributes of God are not eternal, we are led
at once, into the belief that the nature of God is susceptible of change, and consequently that
He is not eternal, which makes no inconsiderable step towards atheism itself. These are the

---

2. Sacred texts.

obvious and dangerous consequences, resulting from the learned gentleman's doctrine, that the attributes of the Supreme Being are distinct existences.[3]

A SECOND DEFENCE OF HINDU THEISM AND THE MONOTHEISTIC SYSTEM OF THE VEDAS IN REPLY TO THE ATTACK OF AN ADVOCATE FOR IDOLATRY REPUTED TO BE THE WORK OF A LEARNED BRAHMIN FROM CALCUTTA.

As to the custom or practice to which the learned Braham so often refers in defence of idolatry, I have already, I presume, explained in the Preface of the *Isopanishad,* the accidental circumstances which have caused idol-worship to flourish throughout the greater part of India; but, as the learned Brahman has not condescended to notice any of my remarks on this subject, I beg leave to repeat here a part of them.

'Many learned Brahmans are perfectly aware of the absurdity of idolatry, and are well informed of the nature of the pure mode of divine worship; but as in the rites, ceremonies, and festivals of idolatry, they find the source of their comforts and fortune, they not only never fail to protect idol-worship from all attacks, but even advance and encourage it to the utmost of their power, by keeping the knowledge of their scriptures concealed from the rest of the people.' And again: 'It is, however, evident to every one possessed of common sense, that custom or fashion is quite different from divine faith; the latter proceeding from spiritual authorities and correct reasoning, and the former being merely the fruit of vulgar caprice. What can justify a man, who believes in the inspiration of his religious books, in neglecting the direct authorities of the same works, and subjecting himself entirely to custom and fashion, which are liable to perpetual changes, and depend upon popular whim? But it cannot be passed unnoticed, that those who practise idolatry, and defend it under the shield of custom, have been violating their customs almost every twenty years, for the sake of a little convenience, or to promote their worldly advantages.' . . .

The learned Brahman attempts to prove the impossibility of an adoration of the Deity, saying . . . 'That which cannot be considered, cannot be worshipped.' Should the learned Brahman consider a full conception of the nature, essence, or qualities of the Supreme Being, or a physical picture truly representing the Almighty power, with offerings of flowers, leaves, and viands, as essential to adoration, I agree with the learned Brahman with respect to the impossibility of the worship of God. But, should adoration imply only the elevation of the mind to the conviction of the existence of the Omnipresent Deity, as testified by His wise and wonderful works, and continual contemplation of His power as so displayed, together with a constant sense of the gratitude which we naturally owe Him, for our existence, sensation, and comfort — I never will hesitate to assert, that His adoration is not only possible, and practicable, but even incumbent upon every rational creature.[4]

REFERENCE

English Works of Raja Rammohun Roy, Part I–VI. Edited by Kalidas Nag and Debajyoti Burman, Calcutta: Sadharan Brahma Samaj, 1945–51.

3. Ibid., 89–90.
4. Ibid., 106–16.

1.5 'IDOL WORSHIP'

Dayānanda Sarasvati

From 'Idols', in *A Source Book of Modern Hinduism*, Richard, G. (ed.), Richmond, Curzon Press, 1985, pp. 52–3.

DURING THE SHIVARATRI VIGIL DAYĀNANDA WITNESSED A MOUSE CLIMBING ON THE IDOL OF SHIVA AND EATING THE AKSHATA (OFFERINGS)

I awoke my father and asked him to tell me whether the hideous emblem of Shiva in the temple was identical with the Mahadeva [Supreme God] of the scriptures? Why do you ask this? enquired my father. I feel it is impossible, I replied, to reconcile to the idea of an omnipotent, living god, with this idol which allows the mice to run over his body and thus suffers his image to be polluted without the slightest protest.

My father tried to explain to me that this stone representation of the Mahadeva of Kailash,[1] having been consecrated by the holy men, became in consequence the god himself, and is worshipped and regarded as such. As Shiva cannot be perceived, he further added, in this *Kaliyuga*,[2] we have the idol in which the Mahadeva of Kailash is imagined by his votaries. This kind of worship pleases the great deity as much as if instead of the emblem he were there himself. But the explanation fell short of satisfying me. I could not help suspecting misinterpretation and sophistry in all this.[3]

God being Formless and Omnipresent cannot have an image. If the sight of an idol puts God in one's mind why cannot this wonderful creation which comprehends the earth, water, fire, air, and vegetation and a hundred and one other things? . . .

Being All-pervading He cannot be imagined to exist in any particular object only.[4]

True happiness consists solely in giving up altogether the worship of idols and in serving another and other living gods. It is an awful shame that people should have given up the worship of the living gods that impart happiness and have taken to the worship of idols instead . . .

It is evil practices like idol worship that are responsible for the existence of millions of idle, lazy, indolent, and beggarly priests in India, who are mainly answerable for this widespread ignorance, fraud and mendacity in the country.[5]

O. — Idol-worship and pilgrimage to holy places have been in vogue since time immemorial. How can they be false?

A. — What do you call *time immemorial*? If you say that by the use of these words you

---

1. Mythical mountain abode of Shiva.
2. The current age of degeneration.
3. *Autobiography of Dayananda Sarasvati*, (New Delhi, 1978), 69.
4. *Satyarth Prakash*, 372–73.
5. Ibid., 383–84.

mean that these practices have *always* been in vogue it cannot be right, otherwise how would you account for the fact that there is no mention of these things in the *Vedas*, the *Brahmanas* and other ancient books of sages and seers. The practice of worshipping idols originated with the *Vama Margis* [followers of a tantric discipline] and the Jainees a little under 2,000 or 2,500 years back. It did not exist in India in ancient times, nor were there any *places held sacred* (*tirathas*) then.[6]

---

6. Ibid., 397.

1.6 'DEFENCE OF IMAGE WORSHIP'

Swami Vivekananda

From *The Complete Works of Swami Vivekananda*, volume III, Calcutta, Advaita Ashrama, 1990, pp. 218–19, 460–61.

This external worship of images has been described in all our Shastras [sacred texts] as the lowest of all the low forms of worship. But that does not mean that it is a wrong thing to do. Despite the many iniquities that have found entrance into the practices of image-worship as it is in vogue now, I do not condemn it. Ay, where would I have been if I had not been blessed with the dust of the holy feet of that orthodox, image-worshipping Brahmin!

Those reformers who preach against image-worship, or what they denounce as idolatry – to them I say, "Brothers, if you are fit to worship God-without-form discarding all external help, do so, but why do you condemn others who cannot do the same? A beautiful, large edifice, the glorious relic of a hoary antiquity has, out of neglect or disuse, fallen into a dilapidated condition; accumulations of dirt and dust may be lying everywhere within it, maybe, some portions are tumbling down to the ground. What will you do to it? Will you take in hand the necessary cleansing and repairs and thus restore the old, or will you pull the whole edifice down to the ground and seek to build another in its place, after a sordid modern plan whose permanence has yet to be established? We have to reform it, which truly means to make ready or perfect by necessary cleansing and repairs, not by demolishing the whole thing. There the function of reform ends.

. . .

It has become a trite saying that idolatry is wrong, and every man swallows it at the present time without questioning. I once thought so, and to pay the penalty of that I had to learn my lesson sitting at the feet of a man who realized everything through idols; I allude to Ramakrishna Paramahamsa. If such Ramakrishna Paramahamsas are produced by idol-worship, what will you have – the reformer's creed or any number of idols? I want an answer. Take a thousand idols more if you can produce Ramakrishna Paramahamsas through idol-worship, and may God speed you! Produce such noble natures by any means you can. Yet idolatry is condemned! Why? Nobody knows. Because some hundreds of years ago some man of Jewish blood happened to condemn it? That is, he happened to condemn everybody else's idols except his own. If God is represented in any beautiful form or any symbolic form, said the Jew, it is awfully bad; it is sin. But if He is represented in the form of a chest, with two angels sitting on each side, and a cloud hanging over it, it is the holy of holies. If God comes in the form of a dove, it is holy. But if He comes in the form of a cow, it is heathen superstition; condemn it! That is how the world goes. That is why the poet says, "What fools we mortals be!" How difficult it is to look through each other's eyes, and that is the bane of humanity.

1.7 'GLIMPSES OF RELIGION'

M.K. Gandhi

From *An Autobiography, or The Story of My Experiments with Truth*, Gandhi, M.K., Harmondsworth, Penguin Books, 1982, pp. 44–5. Translated by Mahadev Desai.

From my sixth or seventh year up to my sixteenth I was at school, being taught all sorts of things except religion. I may say that I failed to get from the teachers what they could have given me without any effort on their part. And yet I kept on picking up things here and there from my surroundings. The term 'religion' I am using in its broadest sense, meaning thereby self-realization or knowledge of self.

Being born in the Vaishnava faith, I had often to go to the *Haveli*.[1] But it never appealed to me. I did not like its glitter and pomp. Also I heard rumours of immorality being practised there, and lost all interest in it. Hence I could gain nothing from the *Haveli*.

---

1. The term used for 'temple' in the Vaishnava sect.

1.8 'IMAGES AS AN AID TO WORSHIP'

M.K. Gandhi

From *Selected Writings of Mahatma Gandhi*, Duncan R. (ed.), Fontana, 1971, pp. 177–8, 182.

In dealing with the problem of untouchability, I have asserted my claim to being a Sanatani[1] Hindu with greater emphasis than hitherto, and yet there are things which are commonly done in the name of Hinduism, which I disregard. I have no desire to be called a Sanatani Hindu or any other, if I am not such. And I have certainly no desire to steal in a reform, or an abuse under cover of a great faith.

It is therefore necessary for me once for all distinctly to give my meaning of Sanatana Hinduism. The work Sanatana is used in its natural sense.

I call myself a Sanatani Hindu, because,

(1) I believe in the Vedas, the Upanishads, the Puranas and all that goes by the name of Hindu scriptures, and therefore in avatars and rebirth.
(2) I believe in the Varnashrama dharma in a sense in my opinion strictly Vedic, but not in its present popular and crude sense.
(3) I believe in the protection of the cow in its much larger sense than the popular.
(4) I do not disbelieve in idol worship.

I am a reformer through and through. But my zeal never takes me to the rejection of any of the essential things of Hinduism. I have said I do not disbelieve in idol worship. An idol does not excite any feeling of veneration in me. But I think that idol worship is part of human nature. We hanker after symbolism. Why should one be more composed in a church than elsewhere? Images are an aid to worship. No Hindu considers an image to be God. I do not consider idol worship a sin.

---

1. An adherant of the 'external', or timeless essence, of Hinduism.

1.9 'THE PRINCIPLES OF THE FRIENDS OF THE WESTERN BUDDHIST ORDER'

FWBO, www.fwbo.org/principles

The institutions of the FWBO are run according to several mutually balancing principles.

OPERATING IN 'THE LOVE MODE'

The essence of Buddhist ethics is the attempt to act on the basis of awareness, respect and kindness. Borrowing a phrase from the psychologist, Erich Fromm, Sangharakshita calls this way of acting 'the love mode'. This is in contrast to 'the power mode', in which people are made to do things, possibly against their will. In Buddhist practice this principle is expressed in the first precept of the fundamental ethical code: not killing or causing harm to other living beings. The commitment implied in becoming a member of the Western Buddhist Order is to act ethically and according to the love mode. So FWBO Centres are founded on the principle of operating through co-operation and consensus.

SPIRITUAL COMMITMENT IS AT THE CORE

It is not enough to assert that the FWBO should be run through love and not power. This requires people who are committed to making this happen. So it is important that those who control FWBO activities have made an explicit and deep commitment to acting ethically, and in the light of Buddhist principles and practice. This is what is entailed in becoming a member of the Western Buddhist Order, so Order members hold the positions of responsibility for the FWBO. It is their responsibility to ensure that all FWBO activities are expressions of Buddhist ideals.

AUTONOMY

From a legal point of view the FWBO consists of many charities which are legally and financially autonomous. This means that the trustees of each FWBO charity are responsible for what happens in the centre or organization it governs. There is no central authority in the FWBO with the power to issue orders.

CONSENSUS

Decisions within FWBO Councils are always made by consensus, never by edict or by voting. This means that issues have to be talked through until there is mutual harmony and understanding, rather than dissenters being silenced through a vote.

SPIRITUAL HIERARCHY

As a spiritual community the WBO is based on communication and a desire that it should be based as fully as possible on wisdom, compassion, and maturity. Pragmatically, when a community enters into open communication it transpires that necessarily some members are inevitably more experienced, and more able to put Buddhist principles into effect in their lives than others. Consequently, some Order members are highly respected for their experience, maturity, and depth of practice and their voices are accorded their due weight. Most FWBO centres have a President, a senior Order member from outside the situation whose views are consulted on all major developments in the centre.

ACTING IN HARMONY WITH THE FWBO AS A WHOLE

There are many meetings between Order members, and people who hold similar positions in different FWBO situations – Centre Chairmen, people with responsibility for the mitra system, Presidents, and so on. The aim of these meetings is to provide peer support, ensure harmony, and prevent a centre from becoming isolated.

EXPERIMENT

Whilst FWBO centres follow generally the same teachings and practices, there is also a place for experiment. The FWBO is a creative endeavour, a collective attempt to explore how the Buddhist path can best be followed in the modern world. However, it is important that experimentation does not degenerate into change for change's sake. It needs to be conscious, and the results should be carefully assessed.

1.10 'THE FWBO AND THE BUDDHIST TRADITION'

FWBO, www.fwbo.org/tradition

Buddhism has now arrived in the West.

Over the last thirty years thousands of Buddhist Centres have opened across Europe, America, and other parts of the world. Most of these teach one of the many Buddhist traditions that have developed in Asia. Others have sought to understand Buddhism in the light of particular traditions of western thought such as psychotherapy, drawing on it as a source of techniques and instruction. The FWBO takes a third approach. It seeks to return to the basic principles of Buddhism and find ways of living them out in the context of the modern West. It seeks to be neither an importation of Buddhism to the West nor an adaptation of it; it seeks to be a re-expression of Buddhism in its new surroundings. In doing this the FWBO sees itself as following the example of Buddhist traditions throughout history that have been flexible and pragmatic in communicating Buddhist teachings in new environments, and yet have remained true to its core teachings and values.

The FWBO's approach is based on the perception that the varied and divided Buddhist tradition has an underlying unity. All schools teach a path to Enlightenment, and define this path through common principles. When Sangharakshita founded the FWBO in 1967 he wanted to strip the tradition back to this essence so that a new Western Buddhism could develop as experience showed how universal Buddhist principles could be expressed in the new context. The intention was to make Buddhism a viable spiritual path for the modern world and a force for good in society.

Thus the FWBO is committed to presenting Buddhism in a way that is relevant to the modern West. The modern environment of industry, technology and communications is far removed from the conditions under which traditional Buddhism evolved and thrived. This opens up new possibilities and new difficulties and the FWBO has recognized that some of the forms through which the central experiences of Buddhism have been expressed in Asia need to be adapted to our new circumstances.

We are heirs to the whole of Buddhism. This is why the FWBO does not define itself in relation to any one form of Eastern Buddhism but derives inspiration from the Buddhist tradition as a whole. The FWBO's attitude is not one of eclecticism, however. It has a coherent and well-worked out approach to Buddhist practice and it draws on particular techniques, texts and teachings in a systematic way that supports practice.

1.11 'LEARNING ABOUT BUDDHISM'

FWBO, www.fwbo.org/learning-about-buddhism

The Buddhist path needs to be reflected upon and understood if one is to practise it, so study of the Buddha's teachings, and reflection upon them are important at all levels of practice in the FWBO.

For the Dharma, or the Buddha's teachings, to take you to Enlightenment, Buddhist tradition says that you must do three things, listen, reflect, and meditate on it.

First it is important to know what Buddhism teaches. The Buddha had a radical and distinctive approach to life which underlies the meditation and other practices Buddhists engage in. These teachings are challenging and inspiring, and reveal a unique vision of human potential, but often they need interpretation and discussion if their relevance to our lives is to become clear. Talks, courses, and study groups, that are held at every FWBO centre, are opportunities to hear the Dharma in this way, and to make sense of it in terms of one's own life. Many centres also have bookshops with books from across the Buddhist traditions.

Reflecting on the Dharma can be done individually or with others. Study groups give a chance to clarify understanding, share experience, and learn new approaches along with others, so these are an important part of how teaching happens in the FWBO.

Some people in the FWBO have made very deep studies of aspects of Buddhism. Sangharakishita is a respected scholar whose works have been influential in both the East and the West. A number of Order members are academics, studying and teaching Buddhism in Europe and the US. The task for thinkers in the FWBO, academics or otherwise, is not simply to know how Buddhism has been articulated in the East, but also to make links between it and western culture, and to help show how the tradition applies in the modern world. Sangharakshita emphasizes the need for a critical and historical awareness of the Buddhist tradition that draws on a range of commentarial material in study, including the findings of modern scholarship, the Buddhist commentarial tradition, and even comparative literature.

Meditating on the Dharma is the third stage. Buddhism aims at an understanding of life which transforms one's entire being. Study often takes place in the context of retreats and seminars, and there is often an opportunity to reflect on Buddhist teachings in the context of meditation.

1.12 'KADAMPA BUDDHISM'

www.kadampa.net

NKT – HELPING KADAMPA BUDDHISM FLOURISH THROUGHOUT THE WORLD

Kadampa Buddhism was first introduced into the west in 1977 by the renowned Buddhist Master Geshe Kelsang Gyatso.

Since then Geshe Kelsang has worked tirelessly to spread Kadampa Buddhism throughout the world by giving extensive teachings, writing many profound books on Kadampa Buddhism, and establishing over 300 meditation centres.

Each centre offers study programmes, meditation instruction, and retreats for all levels of practitioner. The emphasis is on integrating Buddha's teachings into daily life to solve our problems and to spread lasting peace and happiness throughout the world.

The New Kadampa tradition (NKT) is an association of Buddhist centres and practitioners that derive their inspiration and guidance from the example of the ancient Kadampa Buddhist Masters and their teachings, as presented by Geshe Kelsang Gyatso.

The Kadampa Buddhism of the NKT is an entirely independent Buddhist tradition and has no political affiliations.

1.13 'TRAINING AS A QUALIFIED DHARMA TEACHER'

Geshe Kelsang Gyatso

'Training as a qualified Dharma teacher', Gyatso, G.K., *Full Moon*, Summer 1992.

People who are taking part in the Foundation Programme and Teacher Training Programme study subjects in great depth during the classes. At the end of a particular subject, when an examination is due, they try strongly to improve their understanding and to memorize the essential meaning of the book. On the day of the examination it seems as if they have the entire meaning of the book in their mind. For example, if the subject is *Universal Compassion*, on the day of the examination some people have the entire meaning of that book in their mind. At that time they have very special qualifications. Whatever question they are asked, they are ready to give an answer so beautiful, such a good qualification.

When the examination has finished, however, say after one week, our understanding has already become a little bit unclear. After another week it has become more unclear, and after a few months almost nothing remains. Eventually we have forgotten everything. Then, if someone asks us a question for example, yesterday I asked you what is the eighth commitment of training the mind we have to think for a long time and probably have to look it up in the book before we can answer. This indicates that we have forgotten what we previously learned. I think that this is not good. If we do this we waste our study and prevent ourself from gaining any real results from our study. We become like a leaky pot that cannot retain anything that is put into it. During our classes, and especially during our revision for examinations, we put so many things into our mind, but after the examination is over we lose everything.

I beg you not to become like this, but to try to retain whatever understanding and Dharma knowledge you have gained. During your examination you have everything very clearly here in your heart, but you should keep it there. You should try to retain what you have learned by recalling it again and again, by discussing it with your fellow students, and by trying to teach it. Never waste your study. At least you should memorize the essential meaning such as the root text or the condensed meaning of the text. Then, if someone asks you a question you are ready to give the answer clearly. Also when you teach you can immediately remember the root text and can quote from it. Then you will find it very easy to give a commentary. Otherwise, even though you may have passed the examination, if after a few months you have forgotten everything you have learned and it is no longer manifest in your mind, how can you put it into practice? You cannot, because you cannot remember it. Therefore please always keep all the Dharma you have studied and understood in your mind.

Perhaps there are some old people who have difficulty in retaining things, but there are many who can remember very clearly what they have learned, and certainly young people can because they have stronger powers of memorization. Unfortunately, we do not use these powers. Perhaps we think 'Now my examination is over I have finished with this subject, later I will receive my certificate.' Thinking like this is very wrong.

We need qualified Teachers. The New Kadampa Tradition cannot buy qualified Teachers, nor can we invite them from outside. We need Teachers who can teach the twelve texts that we have chosen as our objects of study in the Teacher Training Programme and the Foundation Programme. Other Teachers cannot teach these books because they have not studied them and they do not have the transmissions. Therefore, qualified Teachers within the New Kadampa Tradition can come only from our own students.

Qualified Teachers are very important for us. If you are like a leaky pot you will not become a very qualified Teacher. This is because although you may have studied many things and passed examinations the knowledge does not remain in your mind. If you cannot remember it you will have no confidence in giving teachings. Therefore I think you will be able to give a few lectures, but it will be difficult for you to teach continually, for a long time, and when you do teach there will be a great danger of your making mistakes. Without remembering the meaning of Dharma how can we put it into practice? Without putting Dharma into practice how can we gain experience? Without gaining experience of Dharma how can we help others? Therefore, it is very important that we keep our Dharma knowledge in our mind. We should not be satisfied with mere intellectual understanding, thinking 'I can read the book later', or 'I can read my notes.' We should not think like this. After we have completed an examination we should try to keep the knowledge we have gained in our heart. We should think 'I need to recall the subject again and again, re-read the book, discuss with my friends, and try to teach it to others.' In this way, gradually we try to bring the Dharma books into our heart. Otherwise if Dharma books always remain separate from us we will find it difficult to become a qualified Teacher.

My understanding is this. For example, if I have one thousand students of whom one hundred attain enlightenment and become Buddhas through studying and practising my teachings, but one student becomes a qualified Teacher, then for me that single person is more important than all the others. This is not just for me, but for all the people in this country and throughout the entire world – that one person who becomes a qualified Spiritual Guide is more important than the hundred who become Buddhas. Why is this? It is because those Buddhas are too high for us. We cannot communicate with them. Their body, speech, and mind are completely pure but our mind is impure, so we cannot communicate with them and they cannot give us teachings directly. We can only visualize them; but it is very difficult for us to make progress just through visualization. For the Buddhas to teach us directly we need to see them, to talk to them and communicate with them. Therefore, even though they are Buddhas, for us they are almost useless. The humble qualified Spiritual Teacher, on the other hand, is very useful for us. He or she is like a real wishfulfilling jewel. Perhaps that person is an emanation of Buddha, but conventionally he or she looks just like an ordinary person, and as a Teacher is working directly to help us. Although his or her aspect is like that of an ordinary person, externally the same as us, he or she is performing the deeds of a Buddha by giving clear instructions, leading us into the spiritual path, and setting a good example for us to follow. Therefore, this single person is more important than those hundred Buddhas. There are already a thousand Buddhas in this Fortunate Aeon, and in general there are countless

Buddhas, but for the moment they are useless for us. What we need is a qualified Teacher. Therefore we prostrate to this single person, to the one who is very qualified.

Why do we need qualified Teachers? If we look around us we can see that all living beings have minds filled with ignorance. They have no knowledge, and so from a spiritual point of view they are very poor. Although they may be skilled at worldly activities, from a spiritual point of view, which is what really matters, they are ignorant. Their minds are completely filled with ignorance and wrong views. Even though they have access to Dharma books, simply reading such books does not help them much. Because of their ignorance and wrong views it is difficult for them to appreciate these books and to believe what they say. What they need, therefore, are qualified Dharma Teachers who can dispel their ignorance, overcome their wrong views, and lead them into correct spiritual paths. From this we can see how important it is to have qualified Teachers. Therefore, please understand that our main purpose in organizing the Teacher Training Programme and the Foundation Programme is to provide qualified Teachers. I would like to request you to train to become fully qualified Spiritual Teachers. If you do this, the benefits will be experienced by countless people throughout the world.

We can consider the example of Atisha. From a conventional point of view he was ordained, but in reality he was already an enlightened being. According to his life story, Atisha thought 'Maybe I will become an enlightened being quickly by practising Highest Yoga Tantra in the aspect of a Yogi and relying upon an action mudra.' However, Tara appeared to him and said 'You should not think like this; you should become a Spiritual Guide. You have been a Spiritual Guide many times in your previous lives, and if you also become a Spiritual Guide in this life you will bring great benefit to many people.'

When I was young, I used to wonder why Tara told Atisha to become a Spiritual Guide when he was already an enlightened being, because a Buddha is the highest Spiritual Guide. At first I found this difficult to understand, but now I understand it clearly. If we become an enlightened being like Buddha, we will be of little use to ordinary beings because it is difficult for them to communicate with a Buddha. However, if we remain as a humble practitioner and become a qualified Teacher we will be able to benefit many people. By remaining with ordinary people we can become their Spiritual Guide and help them greatly. Therefore, what Tara said was correct. Atisha followed her advice and became a very qualified Spiritual Teacher who benefited countless people in India and Tibet. From this we can understand why our Spiritual Teacher is more important for us than the Buddhas. We can communicate directly with our humble Spiritual Guide, and he or she can act in exactly the same way as Buddha acts. Therefore, in reality, the Spiritual Guide is an emanation of Buddha.

In conclusion, it is very important to train qualified Spiritual Guides. The New Kadampa Tradition can buy houses, open new Dharma Centres, and do many other things to facilitate the study and practice of Dharma, but we cannot easily find qualified Teachers. As I already said, we cannot buy them, we cannot borrow them, and we cannot invite them from elsewhere. They have to come from within our tradition, from our students. Therefore it is very important that every month, every year, you try to improve your qualifications as Spiritual Teachers. While you are doing this, you are laying the foundations for benefiting others. In the future you will be able to dispel the ignorance of many others and give them wisdom and Dharma knowledge. In this way you are becoming great benefactors of all living beings. Even now, while you are improving your qualifications, you are working for all living beings. For example, if you use your money to support yourself while you are training as a Teacher, you are using this money to benefit all living beings.

This is my message. I am not saying this only to the students of Manjushri Mahayana Buddhist Centre, I am saying it to all the students in all the Centres. Please give them my message. I am waiting for qualified Teachers.

Whether or not qualified Teachers appear depends upon how skilful you are right now. Generally, if you become a qualified disciple you can become a qualified Teacher. This is also important to understand. In particular you should make sure that your studies such as those of the Teacher Training Programme and Foundation Programme are never wasted. After your examinations are finished try to keep all your previous knowledge in your mind. Do not forget it but try to keep it in your heart by recalling it again and again, by re-reading the books, by discussing with others, and by trying to teach.

If we remember the meaning of what we have learned we will be able to put it into practice, but if we cannot remember it we will find it difficult to practise Dharma, and our daily practice will be very weak. We need to use our Dharma practice to help our daily life, but to do this we need to remember Dharma. Therefore please do not waste your studies, please do not waste your knowledge. We all like to study new things, but this is of little value. What matters is to remember the Dharma we have already studied. If we can keep all the knowledge we have gathered our mind will become like a great ocean of knowledge. Then we will have great confidence. Because our wisdom will be strong, we will be able to solve all our own problems and we will be able to help many other people by giving them teachings. This is the real meaning of becoming a qualified Teacher.

1.14 'BHIKKU SANGHA: THE ORDER OF MONKS'

Stephen Batchelor

From *The Awakening of the West: The Encounter of Buddhism and Western Culture*, Batchelor, S., Aquarian, 1994, pp. 36–48.

It was to Wat Pah Bong that a newly ordained American monk, Ven. Sumedho, was taken to meet Ajahn Chah in 1967. In his former existence as Robert Jackman, Sumedho had served as a medical officer in the Korean war, completed a degree in South Asian Studies at Berkeley and taught English with the Peace Corps in Borneo. His first year as a novice in Thailand had been spent mainly in solitary retreat, where he had experienced an overwhelming sense of spiritual well-being but found himself incapable of coping with other people. As a foreigner he was used to being pampered by the Thais. When he arrived in Wat Pah Bong people said: 'He's American; he can't eat our kind of food!' Ajahn Chah responded with a mischievous grin: 'He'll have to learn.' Sumedho spent the next ten years under the guidance of his kind, humorous but uncompromising teacher, learning the principles that underlay Ajahn Chah's approach: living harmoniously in a community, practising mindfulness under all conditions, and ceaselessly letting go of clinging and conceit.

By 1974 the number of Westerners arriving to ordain and practise with Ajahn Chah led to the founding of Wat Pah Nanachat, a monastery dedicated to the training of Western monks. Sumedho was appointed abbot, the first Westerner to hold such a post in Thailand. But in 1977 this idyll in the Thai jungle was interrupted. Ajahn Chah received an invitation from the English Sangha Trust, a lay organization that since 1955 had been trying, as yet unsuccessfully, to establish an order of Western Buddhist monks in Britain. . . .

With him Ajahn Chah brought Sumedho – now Ajahn Sumedho – and left his disciple in charge of three other Western *bhikkhus* in the Vihara, a cramped house at 131 Haverstock Hill, in the less salubrious end of Hampstead, that rattled with the groan of passing traffic. . . .

One morning the following spring, while out on the daily ritual with their begging bowls in search of non-existent alms, the *bhikkhus* attracted the attention of a jogger on Hampstead Heath who offered them a forest. This was Hammer Wood in West Sussex, that the jogger had bought with the intention to restore it to its original state. Recently he had realized that his plan was too ambitious to accomplish unassisted. Although not a Buddhist himself, he felt that these monks would be ideal wardens. By-laws, however, forbade any permanent structures to be built in the wood. The forest monks had a forest but nowhere to live. So the following year the English Sangha Trust sold the Hampstead property and purchased a dilapidated Victorian house about a mile from the woodland in the village of Chithurst. At this point Ajahn Chah returned from Thailand to see how his disciples were getting on.

Over the years the previous owners had let Chithurst House fall into ruin, retreating from the leaking roofs and decaying floors until only four of the twenty or so rooms were habitable. The electricity had long since failed, only one cold water tap worked, dry rot infested the woodwork, the cesspit had not been emptied for twenty-five years, more than thirty abandoned cars littered the gardens, and the house was packed with hoarded pre-war bric-à-brac. It took a week just to burn all the newspapers and magazines. Ajahn Chah gave his approval to the place and the monks and their lay supporters set to work on the task of restoring the building and the grounds.

For two years they put aside their monastic routines and turned into builders, carpenters, metal-workers and plumbers, pausing for contemplation only during the Rains Retreat or when funds ran out.

In 1981 three events signalled, if not completion of their task, at least that its end was in sight. In February the radiant half-ton golden Buddha arrived as a gift from a devout lay-supporter in Thailand and was manoeuvred into the newly prepared shrine room. On 3 June, Ven. Anandametteya, an elder from Sri Lanka, established a *sima* (monastic boundary) in the garden and conferred on Ajahn Sumedho the authority to perform ordinations. And on 16 July the first Theravada Buddhist ordination in Europe to be carried out by a Westerner took place as Ajahn Sumedho ordained three Western postulants as *bhikkhus*.

This flourishing of Buddhism in Sussex coincided with the collapse of Ajahn Chah's health in Thailand. Earlier that summer the diabetes which had affected him for years became suddenly worse and he was rushed to Bangkok for an operation. This was of little help. By the autumn he had lost his speech and shortly afterwards the use of his limbs. By the end of the year he was paralysed and bed-ridden.

By 1992, Chithurst House had been immaculately restored in every detail from the spiralling brick chimneys to the well-tended lawns, from the scrupulously polished floors, up the caringly recrafted banisters, to the sparkling bathrooms. In this sanctuary from the turmoil of modern life, where radio, television and newspapers are forgotten rather than banished, where the days are regulated by bells and lunar cycles instead of clocks and calendars, a vital stillness absorbs anxiety and precipitates 'wise reflection on the Dharma', silent meditation, bowing and chanting, in short: a life of awareness.

Chithurst is no longer an eccentric outpost of Thai Buddhism in a corner of England, but the nucleus of a growing monastic community throughout Europe. It has become a Buddhist 'seminary', where newly ordained monks are trained before being sent to serve in Amaravati, the main public centre north of London, or in the two smaller centres in Britain – in Harnham, Northumberland, and Honiton, Devon – or even to the newly opened *viharas* in Switzerland and Italy. At the time of writing, there are around fifty *bhikkhus*, nine ten-precept nuns and about thirty male and female postulants living in the different European centres.

The success of Chithurst has surprised not only sceptical outsiders, but even members of the English Sangha Trust. One of the stumbling blocks to Ananda Metteyya's mission in 1908 had been the sheer incongruity of the traditional lifestyle of a Buddhist monk in the context of British society. Perceptions had not changed greatly in the seventy years since. The very notion of shaven-headed *bhikkhus* in thin cotton robes and sandals going on a daily alms-round through English towns and villages, where not only Buddhism but monasticism and mendicancy in general are alien, seemed ludicrous. Surely the sensible thing to do would be to modify certain aspects of the monastic rule so that the contrast between the monks and the rest of society would be lessened. But Ajahn Chah and Ajahn Sumedho – as well as the ethnic Thai community in Britain – would hear nothing of it. If change comes, it will come in its own time, they said. Our sole task is to place unconditional trust in the rule and the Dharma. If the conditions are ripe in Europe, it will work; if not, then we'll go back to Thailand.

Throughout its history Buddhism has regarded the establishment of a monastic *sangha* – of at least five *bhikkhus* – as the indispensable condition for a country to qualify as a place where the Dharma has taken root. Symbolically, such a community represents the living presence of the Buddha's dispensation; in real terms, it shows a society sufficiently conscious of the value of the Dharma to support a community of men and women dedicated to its practice. Chithurst Forest Monastery may not be the first place in Europe to house a settled community of Buddhist monastics (ethnic Tibetan, Vietnamese, Sri Lankan and Thai monasteries have existed for some years), but it is the first such community to be run entirely by Western monks and nuns, with the wholehearted backing of an orthodox tradition.

How has Chithurst succeeded in establishing such a community in Europe? It was not a deliberately plotted campaign to implant Buddhism; the British supporters saw it as a gamble, the monks as merely a response to circumstances. The Thai community in Britain (as well as supporters in Thailand) may have seen it as a mission of sorts and were proud to witness an aspect of their culture received with enthusiasm in the West. But while they provided, and still provide, a great deal of funding, money alone cannot account for the coherence, vitality and growth of a religious community.

At the root of Chithurst Monastery lies the encounter between Ajahn Chah and the straggling procession of disaffected Westerners who drifted into Thailand during the 1960s and 70s. Ajahn Chah, himself a rebel against the lax clerical Buddhist establishment of the towns, appealed to these veterans of the hippy trail and the Vietnam War as someone who offered not only a radically simple and sane philosophy of life but an embodiment of it in his daily existence. The austere lifestyle he followed was infused not with the dour, world-denying outlook one might expect but with a sparkling, roguish and above all contented personality. Years of hedonistic excess, together with a loss of faith in Christianity, had led these young Europeans and Americans not to unfettered freedom but to spiritual despair. And this pot-bellied little monk, who looked more like a bullfrog than a saint, turned their world-view on its head.

The long hair and beards were shaved off, the embroidered Afghan shirts and baggy Indian trousers were exchanged for hand-dyed ochre robes, and total unrestraint was replaced by 227 rules of conduct. 'I know that you have had a background of material comfort and outward freedom', Ajahn Chah would tell them:

> By comparison you now live an austere existence. Food and climate are different from your home . . . This is the suffering that leads to the end of suffering. This is how you learn . . . I know some of you are well educated and very knowledgeable. People with little education and worldly knowledge can practise easily. But it is as if you Westerners

have a very large house to clean. When you have cleaned the house, you will have a big living space. But you must be patient.

The explicit emphasis on a simple and harmonious community life and the implicit need to train with a teacher wiser than oneself are at the basis of Ajahn Chah's understanding. An inscription carved in a stone embedded in the lawn in front of the monastery's *sima* reads *Vinayo Sasanassa Ayu*: 'The rule is the life of the teaching.' No matter how uncomfortable or irrational the monastic rule may seem at times, unconditional confidence that it is vital to Buddhist practice is the act of faith upon which the community is founded. The danger of it becoming constricting and legalistic is avoided by emphasizing moment to moment examination of the mind and letting go of fixations. This combination of literal adherence to the rule with open-minded, warm-hearted awareness not only endeared Ajahn Chah to his Western disciples but also endears the monks and nuns at Chithurst to the lay community that supports them. Thus a relationship of mutual, freely offered provision is established: the community gives spiritual nourishment to the laity and the laity provide physical nourishment for the monks and nuns.

'If you want to really see for yourself what the Buddha was talking about,' Ajahn Chah would say, 'you don't need to bother with books. Watch your own mind.' This non-scholastic, experience-based approach to Buddhism is central to the community at Chithurst. It does not mean that books are forbidden – there is an extensive library of Buddhist scriptures in the monastery – but it teaches one to treat intellectual knowledge with caution.

1.15 'ZAYNAB AL GHAZALI: ISLAMIST FEMINIST?'

Denis J. Sullivan and Sana Abed-Kotob

Reprinted from *Islam in Contemporary Egypt: Civil Society vs. the State*, Sullivan, Denis J. and Abed-Kotob, Sana, London, L. Rienner, 1999, pp. 104–109.

One of the most interesting actors in the struggle for greater freedom in both spheres of the sacred (the Islamic *umma*, or community of faith) and the profane (the social-political-economic structure known as Egypt) is Zaynab al-Ghazali al-Jubayli. Al-Ghazali began her feminist career working for Huda Sha'rawi at the Egyptian Feminist Union in 1935, at the age of 17. She left the following year and founded her own organization the Muslim Women's Association.[1] Al-Ghazali felt that . . . it was "a grave error" to speak of the liberation of women in an Islamic society. Islam provided women with "everything – freedom, economic rights, political rights, social rights, public and private rights,"[2] even if these rights were not present in contemporary Islamic societies and politics. Al-Ghazali's association "helped women study Islam and carried out welfare activities, maintaining an orphanage, assisting poor families, and helping unemployed men and women to find useful employment."[3]

Zaynab al-Ghazali developed a strong relationship with the Muslim Brotherhood, beginning in 1937 when she delivered a lecture to the Muslim Sisters Association at the Brotherhood headquarters. Following the lecture, al-Banna, who founded the Muslim Sisters as a division of the Muslim Brotherhood, asked al-Ghazali to merge her organization with his.[4] Al-Ghazali consulted the board of her organization, and it declined the merger, preferring to maintain the independence of the Muslim Women's Association.[5] (After al-Banna's death in 1949 'Abd al-Qadir 'Auda delivered a message to al-Ghazali on behalf of the Brothers: "It would please us if Zaynab al-Ghazali al-Jubayli were to become one of the Muslim Brotherhood," an invitation that she immediately accepted – as an individual, while maintaining a separate status for her organization.)[6] Al-Ghazali's ability to refuse the request of the leader of the Islamist movement speaks volumes about her independence, integrity, and commitment to her cause. "From the beginning [al-Ghazali] conceived of the Association as

---

1. Both "association" and "society" are used in English as translations of the Arabic word *jam'iyya*. Either is acceptable to speak of NGOs generally; but use of "society" often connotes political motivations. For example, the Society of Muslim Brothers, founded by al-Banna, or the Society of Muslims, founded by Shukri Mustafa.

2. Valerie J. Hoffman, "An Islamic Activist: Zeinab al-Ghazali," in Elizabeth Warnock Fernea, ed., *Women and the Family in the Middle East* (Austin: University of Texas Press, 1985); cited in Leila Ahmed, *Women and Gender in Islam* (Yale University Press, 1992), p. 198.

3. Ibid., Ahmed, p. 197.

4. The establishment of the Muslim Sisters Association is discussed by Layla Salim in "Al-Mar'a fi Da'wat wa Fikr Hasan al-Banna: Bayn al-Madi wa al-Hadir [Woman in the Call and Thought of Hasan al-Banna: Between the Past and present]," *Liwa' al-Islam*, January 1990, p. 52.

5. Al-Ghazali's relationship with Hasan al-Banna is discussed in her prison memoirs: Zaynab al-Ghazali, *Ayam min Hayati* [*Days of My Life*] (Cairo: Dar al-Shuruq, n.d.).

6. Al-Ghazali, *Ayam min Hayati*, p. 25.

being equal to and equivalent with, yet deliberately separate from, the Muslim Brothers . . .
She must have known that had she accepted alliance any notion of equivalence and equality
would certainly have degenerated into complementarity at best, subordination at worst."[7]
While declining to merge her organization into (and under the control of) al-Banna's, al-
Ghazali pledged her organization's and members' full cooperation with the leading Islamist
organization and its leader. What is more, she took an oath pledging her personal efforts to
the cause advanced by al-Banna. And she paid for this loyalty.

The government ordered the Muslim Women's Association disbanded in the late 1940s,
in keeping with its campaign against Islamist groups, seen in the crackdown on the Muslim
Brothers and the assassination of Hasan al-Banna in 1949. While she fought the government
and won her case in court, persecution persisted. After al-Ghazali resisted repeated attempts
by the government to co-opt her allegiance to the Brotherhood, President Nasser dissolved the
association on 15 September 1964 and shut down their headquarters. In response, the Muslim
Women's Association sent a letter of complaint to government agencies and to Nasser himself.
According to al-Ghazali, the letter stated:

> The Muslim Women's Association was established in 1936 to spread the *da'wa* of God
> and to work towards the goal of a Muslim *umma*. . . . The message [of the association]
> is a call to Islam, and the recruitment of men and women, young and old, . . . to establish
> a state ruled by what God has revealed. . . . And we, the Muslim Women's Association,
> reject the decision. The President of the Republic . . . has no authority over us . . . Nor
> does the Ministry of Social Affairs. . . . The government can confiscate assets but it
> cannot confiscate our creed.[8]

After the shutdown of the association's headquarters, members of the organization began
to hold meetings in their homes, including al-Ghazali's. The government reacted by issuing
warnings to the women, which resulted in fewer meetings and reduced their *da'wa* activities
to the individual level.

Nasser then had al-Ghazali imprisoned and tortured for nearly seven years (1965–1972).
She recounts in her memoirs the numerous attempts by her torturers to break her bond to the
Brotherhood, Nasser's primary domestic opposition.

Before her imprisonment, throughout the development of building an independent
nation in the 1940s and 1950s, al-Ghazali was a critical figure. She served as intermediary
between her friends in the Islamist movement (the Brotherhood) and her friends in
government, in particular Mustafa al-Nahas, leader of the Wafd Party that controlled the
government during this time.[9]

To one of many who have interviewed her, al-Ghazali recounted her life and her cause
for women's rights within Islam. Women are, she said,

> a fundamental part of the Islamic call. . . . They are the ones who build the kind of men
> that we need to fill the ranks of the Islamic call. So women must be well educated,

---

7. Miriam Cooke, "Zaynab al-Ghazali: Saint or Subversive?" *Die Welt des Islams* 34 (1994), p. 2.

8. Al-Ghazali, *Ayam min Hayati*, pp. 14–15.

9. Hoffman, "An Islamic Activist", pp. 197–8.

cultured, knowing of the precepts of the Koran and sunna, informed about world politics, why we are backward, why we don't have technology. The Muslim woman must study all these things, and then raise her son in the conviction that he must possess the scientific tools of the age, and at the same time he must understand Islam, politics, geography, and current events. *He* must rebuild the Islamic nation.

Islam does not forbid women to actively participate in public life. It does not prevent her from working, entering into politics, and expressing her opinion, or from being anything, as long as that does not interfere with her first duty as a mother, the one who first trains her children in the Islamic call. So her first, holy, and most important mission is to be a mother and wife. She cannot ignore this priority. If she then finds she has free time, she may participate in public activities. Islam does not forbid her.[10]

Al-Ghazali has been selective in practising what she preaches. She has been prominent in Egypt's political and social arenas. Although her public statements emphasize that a woman's primary "mission" is to be a "wife and mother,"[11] her personal life demonstrates that, in practice, she has emphasized a public role in which women are encouraged to take part in actively spreading the Islamic *da'wa*. When al-Ghazali's first husband could not support her active role in the Islamic cause, the two were divorced. "She had stipulated before marrying him that her mission came first and that they would separate if there was any major disagreement between them."[12] Her stipulations before marriage were the same with her second husband, Muhammad Salim Salim.

> There is something in my life that you must know because you are going to be my husband. . . . I must tell you about it so that afterwards you will not ask me about it. I will not compromise on my demands with regard to this matter. I am the director of the Muslim Women's Association. . . . I believe in the message of the Muslim Brotherhood. . . . If [one day] your personal well-being and your economic work conflict with my Islamic work, and if I find that my marital life will get in the way of the *da'wa* and establishing an Islamic state, we will part roads. . . . It is my right to demand that you not prevent me from undertaking my *jihad* for God. And when responsibility places me in the ranks of the *mujahidin* [holy warriors], do not ask me what I am doing. . . . If the needs of marriage conflict with the *da'wa* for God, the marriage will end and the *da'wa* will remain.[13]

When her *da'wa* activities raised Muhammad Salim's concern for her safety, al-Ghazali reminded him that he had agreed to these conditions before their marriage. She said: "Today I ask you to stand by your promise. Do not ask me whom I meet."[14]

Thus, although Zaynab al-Ghazali preaches that family responsibilities are important in a woman's life, her life's work does not suggest that a woman cannot simultaneously be a

---

10. Ibid., pp. 236–37; see also Ahmed, p. 199. Emphasis added.
11. See al-Ghazali's regular column in *Liwa' al-Islam* for the advice she gives to Muslim women.
12. Ahmed, "Women," p. 200.
13. Al-Ghazali, *Ayam min Hayati*, pp. 34–35.
14. Ibid., p. 35.

public figure and have a family. She explains that her public work did not lead to neglect of her "familial obligations" toward her husband.[15] Al-Ghazali asserted her independence before and after her marriage, and she placed her religious work above the marital obligations of which she often speaks. Her actions serve as a prominent example that women do not have to be relegated to a second class, subservient role in their marriages: the woman who is aware of her rights may stipulate conditions that her husband is then legally bound to uphold.

Al-Ghazali's second husband did support her ambitions, although he did not play an active role besides agreeing to serve as her "assistant." He facilitated her regular meetings at her home with other activists and allowed her to play a leading role in preparing new generations for the activism demanded by Hasan al-Banna. Her husband did not interfere in these activities, recognizing her right to work for the realization of an Islamic state. At no time did he suggest that her meetings with other men were improper. In the middle of the night, al-Ghazali writes, her husband would answer a knock at the door, admit one of her visitors, and then go back to bed, while al-Ghazali would join the visitor for a discussion. For this woman activist, there is no talk of female seclusion or segregation. Her role is similar to that of the veiled Islamist women described by Nilüfer Göle: "The prevailing image of a fatalist, passive, docile, and obedient traditional woman was replaced by that of an active, demanding, and, even, militant Muslim woman who is no longer confined to her home."[16]

Although al-Ghazali's work is not overtly feminist, the example she sets is that of a strong, independent woman who could not be held back either by her husband (who expressed concern for her safety) or by the state that tried to torture her into submission. She does not openly call for equality between men and women, but al-Ghazali's experiences demonstrate that the Islamist woman is not necessarily seeking to relegate women to the private sphere; on the contrary, in her activism against the secular state al-Ghazali shows strength, fortitude, and commitment to public change.

> By her own example, she emphasizes that women should be active in seeking to apply duties to God and the Islamic state above rights of individuals. This hierarchy allows her to use the Islamic legal system to empower herself…. She continues to use patriarchal discourse because like all women advocating radical reform in power relations she must hone her language so as to be heard…. Zaynab al-Ghazali may claim in interviews and write in Islamic journals that women should restrict themselves to the home, but in her life, and significantly, in writing her life, she marginalizes domesticity.[17]

In fact, in "writing her life" in her memoirs, al-Ghazali virtually avoids mention of a woman's responsibilities to her family. She does not seem to differentiate between her public role as a woman and that of a man. In her opinion both are equally responsible for upholding God's word. What is also noteworthy in al-Ghazali's memoirs is that she does not discuss women's rights, nor is she an advocate for women's causes. Rather, her advocacy is for an Islamic society that encompasses men and women alike. She calls not only on men to

---

15. Ibid., p. 33.
16. Nilüfer Göle, *The Forbidden Modern: Civilization and Veiling* (Ann Arbor: University of Michigan Press, 1996), p. 84.
17. Cooke, "Zaynab al-Ghazali," p. 20.

eliminate the *jahili* society but addresses both men and women, for the latter are also responsible for advancing the *da'wa* and building an Islamic society.

Islamist women's rights advocates (from various perspectives) abound in Egypt, including Safinaz Qasim, Ni'mat Fu'ad[18] and Kariman Hamza[19] though Zaynab al-Ghazali remains the best known and leading force in the women's Islamist movement through most of the 1990s.[20]

---

18. For discussion of Fu'ad and Qasim, as well as detailed analysis of the views and life work of Zaynab al-Ghazali, see Sherifa Zuhur, *Revealing Reveiling: Islamist Gender Ideology in Contemporary Egypt* (Albany: SUNY Press, 1992).

19. On Hamza, see Fedwa Malti-Douglas, *A Woman and Her Sufis*, the Kareema Khoury Annual Distinguished Lecture in Arab Studies. Published by Georgetown University's Center for Contemporary Arab Studies, 1995. Malti-Douglas examines Hamza's autobiographical *My Journey from Unveiling to Veiling*, which "recounts the dramatic story of a born-again young woman who travels from a secular to a religious lifestyle" (p. 3).

20. See Elizabeth Warnock Fernea, *In Search of Islamic Feminism: One Woman's Global Journey* (New York: Doubleday, 1997), for a discussion of Islamic women's movements in comparative perspective, including the Egyptian case.

1.16 'THE PEARLY GATES OF CYBERSPACE'

Margaret Wertheim

From *The Pearly Gates of Cyberspace: A History of Space from Dante to the Internet,* Wertheim, M., Virago Press, London, 1999, pp. 291–8.

It is well to remember that until very recently the digital "agora" was in fact an extremely exclusive place. Up until 1993 (when "browser" software for the World Wide Web first became available), few people outside universities and research settings had access to the Net. Even now there are many people who still cannot afford an appropriate computer and a monthly Internet access fee. And that is true even in rich countries like America. If cyberspace is to become a truly equitable place then we are going to have to face the question of how to ensure that *everyone* has equal access. Not just people who are well-off, but also those who aren't. Moreover, if we are serious about creating some kind of cyber-utopia then the rich developed world is going to have to take seriously the task of making the Internet available to developing countries as well.

One aspect of early coffeehouse culture that was *never* egalitarian was its gender mix. Whatever else may have been in flux, male authority was maintained there, and few women participated in this scene. Cyberspace *is* accessible to women, but how much, really, is the "second sex" welcome? Although the wired world does offer genuine opportunities for women, all is not rosy in this supposed paradise of gender dissolution. Behind the utopian rhetoric, the bits can still pack a hefty sexist bite. . . . Online nastiness toward women is not unusual; It is a common reason women give for not wanting to participate in many cyberspace forums. In the face of online harassment women are often told to "just fight back," but that may be easier said than done. . . .

For many women it is so much easier to just log off.

And that is the primary reason for concern about rampant cyber-misogyny. Under the guise of the First Amendment the cyber-elite has mounted a mantra-like defense of freedom of speech, this supposedly core feature of cyber-utopia. But one has to ask: *Freedom of speech for whom?* . . .

When women who make postings to *alt.feminism* are called "bitches" by angry young men, is *that* freedom of speech? When, on *X-Files* newsgroups, women are told that their lusty postings in praise of David Duchovny are obscene, is *that* freedom of speech? When, on *Star Trek* newsgroups, women are flamed for expressing dissatisfaction with the female roles in the series, is *that* freedom of speech? . . .

Thus we must ask, *who* is this cyber-utopia really going to be for?

Women aren't the only ones encountering obstacles in the digital domain. Similar barriers also confront homosexuals, non-whites, and non-Anglos. The heavenly vision of a place where "men of all nations will walk in harmony" is one of the prime fantasies under which cyberspace is being promoted, yet despite many cyberspace enthusiasts' public paeans to pluralism, all cultures are *not* equally welcome in cyberspace. On the contrary, commentator Ziauddin Sardar suggests that what we are seeing is not so much a space for vibrant pluralism but a new form of Western imperialism.

Sardar notes that much of the rhetoric used by cyberspace champions is drawn from the language of colonization. Cyberspace is routinely referred to as a "new continent" or a "new frontier" and its conquest and settlement often compared to the conquest and settlement of the "New World." A typical example comes from Ivan Pope, editor of the British cyberspace magazine 3W, who described it as "one of those mythical places, like the American West or the African Interior, that excites the passions of explorers and carpetbaggers alike." The headline for a cover story from the San Francisco-based cyberpunk journal *Mondo 2000* declared simply, THE RUSH IS ON! COLONIZING CYBERSPACE.

The theme of colonization is also reflected in a widely quoted document titled "Cyberspace and the American Dream: A Magna Carta for the Knowledge Age," which was put together by right-wing think tank the Progress and Freedom Foundation, and based on the ideas of a group that included Esther Dyson and Alvin Toffler. This cyber Magna Carta states bluntly, "what is happening in cyberspace...[calls to mind] the spirit of invention and discovery that led...generations of pioneers to tame the American continent".[1] In a similar vein, the Electronic Frontier Foundation's John Perry Barlow has written that "Columbus was probably the last person to behold so much usable and unclaimed real estate (or unreal estate) as these cybernauts have discovered."[2]

But of course the "real estate" of the Americas *was* claimed. The "taming" of the American West that the writers of the cyber Magna Carta would emulate also entailed the "taming" (and often erasure) of dozens of other cultures. According to Sardar, that is also the hidden danger of cyberspace. Rather than embracing other cultures and their traditions, he suggests that "cyberspace is particularly geared towards the erasure of all non-Western histories." As he explains: "If Columbus, Drake and other swashbuckling heroes of Western civilization were no worse than pioneers of cyberspace, then they [too, by association] must have been a good thing."[3] The implications, Sardar notes, is that the colonized people "should be thankful" for all the "wonderful" technologies the Westerners brought. It is certainly worth asking, as Sardar does, why is it that at a time when colonial frontier metaphors are being so critiqued elsewhere they should be embraced by champions of cyberspace.

Whatever this cyberspatial frontier rhetoric implies about our past, perhaps more insidiously it hints at an *ongoing* cultural imperialism. A frontier, by definition, is a place where things are being formed anew. And newness is exactly what many cyber-enthusiasts prize above all else. For too many of them, history is of little interest, because what *really* matters is the future, a glorious unprecedented future that will supposedly emerge Athena-like from their heads. In such an atmosphere of future-worship, Sardar says, there can be no genuine respect for the traditions of any culture. With the world constantly being formed anew at the digital frontier, traditional ways of thinking and being are all too easily reduced to quaint curiosities: "Other people and their cultures become so many 'models', so many

---

1. Bhabha, *The Location of Culture* (London and New York: Routledge, 1994), p. 67.
2. Abelove et al. (eds), *Lesbian and Gay Studies Reader* (London: Routledge, 1993), p. xv.
3. Butler, 'Identity and Gender Subordination', p. 21 in Fuss (ed.), *Inside/Outside: Lesbian Theories, Gay Theories* (London and New York: Routledge, 1992), pp. 13–31.

zeros and ones in cyberspace."[4] It is a process that Sardar decries as "the museumization of the world."

On a global scale, moreover, cyberspace provides unprecedented opportunities for "corporations [to] trade gigabytes of information about money and death." Let us never forget the role of the military in the initial development of cyberspace, and their continuing presence at the forefront of this technology. It is not insignificant that the first-ever application of multiuser online virtual reality was for an intercontinental battle simulation.[5] Beyond the military one of the greatest users of cyberspace is the financial industry, and it is already known that billions of crime dollars slosh undetected through the world's computer networks, dissolved into apparent legitimacy by the purifying power of silicon. If, as Sardar and others suggest, "cybercrime is going to be *the* crime of the future," then rather than bringing to mind the New Jerusalem, one might wonder if cyberspace will be more like a new Gomorrah.[6] . . .

Now cyberspace too is an inner space of humanity's own making, a space where the vilest sides of human behavior can all too easily effloresce. In the past few years neo-Nazi and skinhead sites have proliferated on the web, while USENET groups make it all the easier for racists and bigots to spread their messages of hatred. Surfing such sites, with their openly violent, antisocial, and antigovernment diatribes, is truly to descend into a new circle of Hell. To say nothing of pornography, for which the Web has undoubtedly been the greatest boon since the invention of photography. As Sardar notes, the underbelly of cyberspace is indeed "a grotesque soup."

---

4. McCutcheon, *Manufacturing Religion: The Discourse on Sui Generis Religion and the Politics of Nostalgia* (Oxford University Press, 1997), p. 22.
5. Noddings, *Caring: A Feminist Approach to Ethics and Moral Education* (Los Angeles: University of California Press, 1984).
6. See Ashcroft, *The Empire Writes Back: Theory and Practice in Post-colonial Literature* (Oxford and Cambridge, MA: Blackwell, 1989); Gates (ed.), 'Race', *Writing and Difference* (Chicago University Press, 1985); Moore-Gilbert, *Postcolonial Theory: Contexts, Practices, Politics* (London and New York: Verso, 1997), pp. 5–11.

Part II:

Religion and Social Transformations

The readings in this section centre around Buddhism, Christianity and Islam, the world's three major missionary faiths, intentionally universal in scope. They all engage with the question of how these three traditions are responding to some of the ethical challenges associated with globalization and the social transformations that have resulted. They focus on the relationship between politics and religion, the increasing emphasis on human rights (HR) norms, the changing role of women, and our human responsibility for the environment. Reading 2.1 deals with the dilemma faced by the Christian churches in the post-communist period, especially in the transition to political pluralism. Reading 2.2 provides insight into the issue of human rights faced by Muslims at an individual level; readings 2.3 and 2.4 allow readers to consider whether human rights are a product of cultural modernity, and to compare and contrast the HR perspectives of the United Nations and the Organization of the Islamic Conference (OIC), which represents the governments of Muslim societies. The readings that follow (2.5–2.9) illustrate the tension between the role of women as understood by traditional Christianity and feminist thought, especially as applied to the interpretation of scripture. The final set of readings (2.10–2.13) illustrate the stance of Buddhists on the ethical issues surrounding the environment.

2.1 'CHRISTIANITY IN THE POST-COMMUNIST VACUUM'

Jósef Tischner

From *Religion, State and Society*, Vol. 20, nos 3 and 4, 1992, pp. 331–7.

The confrontation of Christianity with communism in Poland made a most interesting spectacle. Two opposing theories, brought down to earth from the world of ideas, were now to have their true worth put to the test in the process of being put into practice. As long as both remained in the heavenly realm of abstract ideas both managed to radiate a certain attractiveness and develop an appeal. However, as soon as both descended into this vale of tears and became the driving force for human actions they were seen very differently. Ideas which claimed that they would judge reality at the bar of justice, in order then accordingly to transform reality, were themselves summoned to the court of reality and condemned.

However, it would be a simplification to work from the premise that in recent decades it was only these two ideas – Christianity and communism – which confronted one another on the stage of time. From the beginning there was a third player in this confrontation: the idea of freedom. Admittedly freedom at first stood on the sidelines in this arena. For a while it looked as if it was the communists who should be regarded as the true champions of freedom, and this brought a lot of kind-hearted liberals under their spell. Then the church stepped forward as the mainstay of freedom, and this brought the liberals over to the church's camp. But now doubts are spreading in the church's camp as well. Before our eyes there is a turning away from the church – both Christianity and religion in general have to accept a sharp drop in the number of followers. Might it be that liberalism will prove to be the only idea that is victorious?

The penetration of the social fabric with ideas is described by the not altogether felicitous term 'acculturation'. We have in mind a mutual enrichment of cultures as a result of their contact and interpenetration. We can conceive of an idyllic development which begins with the encounter of cultures – two cultures penetrate each other, enrich each other and as a result bring forth undreamed-of fruit on either side: highly prized works of art and literature. This beautiful, idyllic dream was dispelled, however, by the reality of the confrontation which we experienced at first hand during the era of communism. The struggle between ideas soon turned into a full-blooded struggle between people, which brought forth quite different fruit: prisons, labour camps, new atrocities and new forms of martyrdom. The ultimate criterion of truth should have been the obvious validity of the idea, but as ever what counted was the steadfastness of the martyr. The whole tragedy of the conflict was laid bare in the martyr's death: the idea could put its viability to the test only by finding people who were prepared to lay down their lives for it.

Let us turn to some basic questions. What did communism mean for man? What change did Christianity undergo in the confrontation with communism? What were the most important consequences of this conflict?

The rivalry of communism and Christianity has had a decisive impact on our age. This period is now coming to an end. On this giant battlefield, as far as the eye can see, there are no more heroes, only the starving still wandering around. We are all surrounded by a feeling of emptiness. One looks back nostalgically to the time when there were motivations other than rapaciousness.

IN THE COMMUNIST ELEMENT

What did communism mean for Christians? Depending on the situation different elements were emphasised. The deeper Christians were immersed in the communist element, the stronger was their impression that communism is not a negation of Christianity, but rather a parody of it. It is true that communism fought vehemently with Christianity, but at the same time it wanted to imitate it in everything, and thus ended up as a parody of it. Communism bore within itself a great envy of religion. What was it actually that communism wanted? It wanted to take possession of man, it wanted to have man absolutely, undivided and exclusively for itself – in the way that, in the communist perception, God has man. Communism is a power that is greedy for man.

As early as 1959 Leszek Kołakowski wrote about the way that communism parodies Christianity in his article 'The priest and the court jester' on the theme of 'the theological legacy in modern thought' (*Twórczość* no. 10). For part of this legacy was also to be found in the Marxist stream of thought. The fundamental questions of Marxism were in origin and content questions of Christian theology. Belief in the ultimate meaning of history, the question of the relationship between freedom and necessity, the principle of the unique significance of the working class, dialectical thinking and many other elements were of theological provenance. Communist power – and here it is like religious power – wants to keep a tight reign on everybody with the 'bridle of the catechism'. Ultimately the most important Marxist guidelines for the process of decision-making were in the theological mould. Kołakowski mocked: 'At the burial of one god who has outlived his time [new] gods are raining down from heaven. The godless have found their own saints and the blasphemers are building themselves new chapels.' Kołakowski thereby provoked a wave of indignation among the Marxists. Catholic intellectuals felt so flattered by this daring criticism of Marxism, all the more since it came from the pen of an until recently important Marxist, that they were blind to the corollary of this criticism: namely to the conclusion that follows from it that, seen in this way, communist absolutism can ultimately be nothing else than a continuation of religious absolutism.

So we found ourselves confronted with a parody. Between the parody and its subject there is a point of contact, for without contact no spark would cross over. This point of contact between communism and Christianity was the community. Both communism and Christianity made men the offer of entering into a community with other men; but their starting points were opposing ideas of what community is. '*Religio*' means 'union/communality', '*Kommune*' also means 'community', but they denote opposite poles. The difference is not only that '*religio*' means a community with God and '*Kommune*' one with other men, but the understanding of interpersonal relations is also fundamentally different.

What kind of relationship is meant by '*Kommune*'? Our starting point must be that communism from its origin was more than just an approach to solving the economic and political problems of the early capitalist era. Alongside the economic and political content there was also a 'new ethic'. This ethic was like a light which illuminated the path of the revolution and which justified its bearers, i.e. absolved them of guilt. Communism was striving for a 'transvaluation of values, a revolution in the realm of values', as a consequence of which the meaning of good and evil would be newly defined. From then on it became clear that the exploitation of man and the root of all evil was to be seen in private *property*, and especially in the private ownership of the means of production. Communism launched a frontal attack on private ownership and praised to the skies 'socialised', 'state' and 'collective' property.

At this point the taking up of Christian ideals was unmistakable. After all, we read also in the Acts of the Apostles that the early Christians shared everything with one another. Were not Ananias and his wife Sapphira punished by death for keeping back for themselves part of the proceeds from the sale of a piece of land, although they pretended to have placed everything at Peter's feet? The abolition of private ownership of the means of production seemed to be a way of realising Christian ideals, namely justice, equality and brotherhood. It was to be hoped that under the influence of communism Christian societies would become more Christian.

The criticism of private property had varying consequences at different periods and in different countries. The boundaries between what was allowed and what was forbidden were not always drawn in the same place. But the principle stood, and was summed up in the following question: is man as man also 'collective property' or can he be regarded as 'the private property of himself'? Thus man as such was at stake. Communism insisted that man in his totality was a 'product of society' and as such 'collective property'. Man is at his own disposal only to the extent that the '*Kommune*' permits it.

Here too there were parallels with Christianity. Unlimited surrender to God – the love of God 'before all else' – was replaced by unlimited surrender to the community. The community thus took on the role of the absolute. There is nothing higher than the community. Just as the Christian was to subordinate his will completely to the will of God, so too the communist was to subordinate his will completely to the '*Kommune*'. And therein freedom was supposed to lie. To be free meant grasping the inner logic of history and getting in tune with it. For the Christian does not freedom also mean unity with the grace of God and following God's directions?

From a certain point the differences become clear. Communism was accompanied by atheism, materialism and the idea of revolution. One could certainly find intellectuals who would object that the above-named elements became part of communist teaching purely by chance, or that they are also among the less important contents of Christianity; for one could conceive of communism without the atheist and materialist components, just as Christianity would be feasible without renunciation of the theory of revolution. Those intellectuals would furthermore assert that negative theology in fact contains some elements of atheism and that the universal understanding of creation as the 'raw material' for human work is to be found to some extent already in the book of Genesis. These and similar ideas became the theoretical basis for the movement of 'progressive Catholics', who were prepared without great reservations to support the social policy of the communists and to enter into an alliance with the communist party. In return they were allowed to practise their religion in very narrow parameters – and in fact as a 'private matter'.

Finally, what was communism? It was an ideal, a never-realised idea of community which, however, had an effect strong enough to destroy existing social relationships. According to this ideal the whole came before the part and only the whole gave meaning to the part. At the same time everything was based on power and force. Power – understood as the capacity to perform work – was the most important bond in the construction of society. Power was also to be seen in action: he who acts, is. But one might act only within the limits set by the 'Kommune' and only in its interests. Within the communist state structure totalitarian might reigned. It had two important distinguishing features: firstly, it believed that the compulsion it exercised was an expression of the Power that governs the whole of reality; secondly, it worked on the premise that it could control the whole of man, because there is nothing in man which he did not first receive from might. In this way the communist desire 'for the whole man' could be satisfied.

The communist ideal could never be fully put into practice because society (social matter) and man as an individual resisted it. There was no lack of attempts to put it into practice, and each one was inaugurated by force and each one claimed new victims. This developed into the tragedy of whole peoples and states. In parallel the experience of evil grew – in breadth, height and depth. And this evil returned again and again, spreading horror mixed with fascination. Was it possible for one person to plan such a fate for another? If after the Enlightenment people asked how it was still at all possible to believe in God, after these immense crimes of communism – after Kolyma – one wonders whether and how it will ever be possible again to rely on man. Doubt in man was a significant factor in the destruction of social bonds and finally undermined communism itself. And today this doubt is the greatest hindrance in the search for a way to democracy. The communist disease in the post-communist era is based on calling man totally into question – doubt is all-embracing.

FAITH AT THE CROSSROADS

Confrontation with the parody makes man feel the need to go back to his roots. The first question was: what is Christianity? In this question there was a note of great longing for authenticity. Where can one find an answer to all these problems? In the gospel, of course. And so in Polish Catholicism there was a growing tendency to return to Christianity. People made a pilgrimage back to the gospel. At first only academic circles were affected; but after the Second Vatican Council other circles were drawn into the movement. This return was no simple process. But the obstacles were overcome and the goal was reached: on several levels in varying degrees the identity of Christianity was affirmed.

However, if one wishes to identify the main motive for this search one must bear in mind the context in which the search took place. And this was the direct, living and constantly recurring experience of evil – the picture of fallen man. Man proved to be extremely unreliable, a being capable of treachery at any time. This tendency was not a fully developed Manichaeism with its belief in the ultimate triumph of evil over good, but rather a Manichaean fear of evil, which is constantly and everywhere lying in wait and which after even the longest absence will inevitably return, so that one must for ever tirelessly search for new hiding places, for good is like a flower in premature bloom which will be killed by the frost. Manichaeism also cast its shadow over thinking about freedom. On the one hand man's right to freedom would soon turn into brute tyranny. This thought gave rise to a certain conception of power. Power is ambivalent: it is evil when it offers the force it has available in the service of evil; but it can also be good when it devotes itself to good. Manichaeism mostly accompanies the cult of absolutism.

What is the first fruit of this return to the roots of Christianity? Within the framework of Catholicism there was a polarisation – there were two currents, one 'evangelical' in character, the more strongly orientated towards 'catechism'. It was not a matter of dogmatic differences, it was merely that the path to the roots seemed to have a varying length. Take the example of human value. In the catechism-oriented current it was based on the dogma of creation: man is the image of God. In the evangelical current of the other hand it was derived from the fact of redemption. 'What value must man have had in the eyes of the creator to deserve so mighty a Redeemer, for God to give his Only Begotten Son, in order that man might not be lost' (*Redemptor hominis*, 10). This varying perspective is also clearly seen in the attitude to the crucifixion: in the catechism-oriented view it was a further proof of how wretched man is that he did not shrink from nailing his God to the cross; the gospel-oriented view discovered man's greatness in it. The first viewpoint is a breeding-ground for Manichaeism, the second places grace in the foreground. As a consequence catechism saw a point in religious education: if you believe then behave according to God's law; the gospel directed attention to participation: if you have a part in the mystery of Christ then you will know yourself what you have to do. Some are of the opinion that one can derive faith from good works – put it into practice and you will find your faith; others nurture their faith in order to be able to do good as a result. If the former are intent on making a show of their convictions, the latter are constantly striving to deepen them. The perspective of the gospel brings us new perceptions which can become the foundation of a religious renewal. The following are the most important ones.

First and foremost is the discovery of the heroic dimension of the gospel – there is quite simply no faith without heroism. Christianity is strong through the blood of its martyrs, for the testimony of blood is far more important than any instruction. We do not mean martyrs for abstract ideas, but martyrs for love of one's neighbour: my neighbour is an absolute value for me. Thereby my attitude to human rights is pre-determined: the rights of man are thus first and foremost not *my* rights, but my *neighbour*'s rights. My right is in the form of an obligation to my neighbour – I should make a sacrifice, any sacrifice, for his freedom, his dignity and his wellbeing and constantly overcome anew my own egoism. In heroic love there may be the 'danger' of loving one's neighbour more than oneself, but not in the liberal countries of Western Europe, where for the present the rights of man are perceived as '*my*' rights, which furthermore are often used against the church. We are in an age in which one set of Christians is engaged in a determined struggle for the loosening of church discipline, while the others accept persecution and years of imprisonment for faithfulness to the church and her discipline. With the same dogmatic position and the same textbooks on ethics the gospel is lived in quite different ways.

Evangelical heroism, however, contains within itself a certain ambiguity which has only recently come to light. The question is whether this heroism is ethical or religious in character. What is the meaning of the Sermon on the Mount? What is the parable of the Good Samaritan all about? The return to the gospel brings out the ethical dimension of the gospel. The strictly religious element remains in the background. Does the gospel thereby lose something? The gospel does not lose out, because as an ethical text it achieves a far wider effect, and consequently appeals not only to those consciences that have found faith in 'Christ as God'. Each one of them is and can be a Samaritan. This realisation is of enormous significance.

Certain consequences flow from it. From the point of view of ethics communism must take particularly hard criticism. One cannot emphasise forcibly enough that communism appeared 'amoral' to Catholics – despite all the features in common with Christianity that were highlighted by the 'movement of progressive Catholics'. Communist morality approved things and forms of behaviour which were unacceptable for Christians and Catholics – for example, abortion, divorce, the use of force. And yet for a while it looked as though the communists would be able to lay claim to universal ethical justification. In the last analysis in this world you have got to help justice to break through. Killing the enemy on the way to a just order is after all right and proper if we are all property of the community. Communist terror, ever increasing and with no end in sight, and coupled with absolute economic inefficiency, showed clearly enough how absurd such a view is. The communists wondered how many more millions of people would have to be sacrificed before the survivors understood that they did not belong to themselves. Under the influence of Kolyma the realisation gradually dawned that the origin of all evil is a fatal contempt for man, and not any form of private property. First comes the commandment 'Thou shalt not kill' and only then 'Thou shalt not steal'. These facts brought about a rejection of the transvaluation of values. The Christian principle of love for one's neighbour came back into favour. The communist ethic gradually dwindled to a painful and bloody myth.

Christianity found a common language with those dissident groupings which broke away from communism. The throng of good Samaritans grew and the church felt duty bound to take them all under her wing. In a world shaped by Kolya, the Samaritan, for whatever reason, was ready to accept the Christian *ethos*, but not yet the Christian *logos*.

This circumstance was bound to provoke controversies which seemed to be a distant echo of Pelagianism.[1] It had to be decided who the *true* Christian is. Was this question a consequence of returning to the roots? Let us proceed from the assumption that everybody who knows who his neighbour is should be regarded as a Christian. The dissidents saw their neighbour above all in every victim of totalitarian oppression. The dissidents took up a struggle against the system in power. Many were imprisoned; it cost some their lives. This

---

1. The word derives from Pelagius, a 4th/5th century British monk who opposed the doctrine of original sin, in particular arguing that infants are not born depraved but become so through their own choice, or through contact with society. In this context it refers to the idea that one can be a Christian by behaving according to Christian ethos, but without an explicit declaration of belief.

heroism was treated with wonder and respect. Against this background those Catholics – like the 'progressive' group – who were able to make an accommodation with the regime looked really pathetic. Of course, they were only a handful, by no means all Catholics. To generalise from them would be totally out of place. After the fall of communism, however, the question of one's neighbour returned, for example in the discussion on abortion: 'So who is my neighbour?' And it happened that many a hanger-on of yesterday pushed the dissident into a corner because the latter had quite a blurred conception of the matter. Isolated exceptions apart, do we not recognise here a struggle of ideas that have not been properly thought through?

In the midst of the argument about the meaning and the scope of the gospel *ethos* one constantly meets the problem of the community. What is a community? Putting this question at all is an expression of protest against the recent past. In any case the experience of communism teaches what a community is not. But in positive terms what is it? The answer to this question requires a still more important decision on whose property man is. In this we touch on the problem of the 'greed (of power) for man', to which two opposite attitudes are possible.

One attitude has the premise that man belongs exclusively to himself and no community or neighbour can lay any claim to him. The community always has a tendency to suppress. Other people are my hell. Man's freedom presupposes freedom from the community. From this arose post-communist individualism, which has thrived on very different soils and has developed very diverse forms. If it rejected the national community, then it was out of fear of nationalism; if it opposed a religious community, then it was because it was afraid of the inquisition. It accepted the state only as a guarantee of individual freedom. This individualism does not oppose religion, but keeps its distance from the church. Religion is acceptable to it only as a relationship with God; one's neighbour – especially in church – gets in the way and is perceived as an obstacle on the path to redemption. A characteristic of the flight from community is a sense of pain, which is significant for any kind of romantic religiosity: man bears suffering for millions, but holds it against those millions that he has to do it. Rejection of community is a distant echo of Manichaeism which has thrown its shadow over community.

On the other hand, the second position was determined to make man part of a community again. In this instance it was the Manichaean attack on individualism which brought about the turn towards community. The dominant idea here was solidarity. The experience of Solidarity as a movement constituted the context. This integration in the community is no easy process because first of all the irksome legacy of communism with the monster of 'pseudo-community' has to be overcome. So, what should a national community be like if it does not want to foster nationalism and zenophobia? How should a state be designed so that it cannot degenerate into a totalitarian structure? The same concerns accompany any reflection on the model of an authentic political party, a trade union or a form of local government. How can all these institutions be established by people who are highly allergic to words like 'community', 'cooperative', 'team' and 'collective'?

The role of the church in this process requires especially great sensitivity. Hegel once said something which must also be worthy of note for a non-Hegelian: 'Religion is the place where a people defines for itself what it holds to be the truth.' Later he writes: 'but torn apart in this way from innerness, from the last shrine of conscience, from the quiet place where religion has its seat, the constitutional principles and institutions no more come to a real focus than they remain in abstraction and vagueness' (*Vorlesungen über die Philosophie der Geschichte* (Suhrkamp Verlag), vol. 12, pp. 70 and 72). What the communists were about was building a state of the 'dictatorship of the proletariat' without or even against the 'principle of conscience'. Should anybody who wants to rebuild the state even consider this way again? Is it sensible to ignore historical wisdom and the experience of the church with community? The role of the church should not be confused with the 'leading role of the party'. What has already been a parody cannot become the subject for another parody.

A key position must be accorded to the consciousness of power. In the time of persecution it was obvious that the church achieved a position of power only when it was robbed of all power. In the soul of every man there is a deep-rooted religious restlessness and a need for God. And this is where we find the origin of the power that the church has over man; but this power has nothing to do with force. Just as illness gives a doctor a certain power over the patient, so the human longing for God opens the way into man's heart for the church. This longing is original, everything else is secondary. Do then the representatives of the church need any other power over man than the one that they have as a result of this natural original longing? Should the church succumb to the temptation of the 'other power', then doing so will deprive the church of the power which it has. The church has power only when it has none. The 'other', wordly, power of the church could all too quickly completely undermine its real position of power.

2.2 'HOW CAN A MUSLIM LIVE IN THIS ERA?'

Shaik Hamid Al Nayfar

Interviewed by Francois Burgat, in *Political Islam: Essays from Middle East Report*, Beinin, J. and Stork, J. (eds), London, I.B. Tauris, 1997, pp. 370–75.

WHAT IS THE MEANING OF THE NAME OF YOUR MAGAZINE, 15/21?

The basis of our project is to ask how one can be simultaneously a Muslim and live in this era – how to be a Muslim today. Fifteen stands for the fifteenth century of the *hijra*, the beginning of the Islamic community. Twenty-one signifies the fact that we are living now on the edge of the twenty-first century, with all the problems that poses for the world community.

CAN YOU RECALL THE ROUTE WHICH LED YOU INTO RELIGIOUS THOUGHT AND THEN POLITICAL ACTION?

The end of the 1960s in Tunisia saw some fundamental changes. The departure of the Ben Salah government in 1970 marked the end of the socialist period, particularly the experience of the [agricultural] cooperatives. The change was very abrupt. Ben Salah was put on trial. Young people saw that the very same government could strike a leftist pose and then switch to right-wing economic policies. Many were completely disoriented. We realized that this was proof that there was no fundamental policy orientation.

WHO JOINED THE ISLAMIST MOVEMENT?

They were neither leftists nor rightists. They were uprooted. There was no longer any ideology that they could connect with. A search for identity became characteristic of this period.

To this Tunisian problem, you have to add what was occurring in France. I was living in Paris in May 1968. The question there was: "Where is the West going?" I discovered that we shared the same type of intellectual angst. It wasn't only a Tunisian or Arab problem.

The third thing that helps explain the emergence of the Islamist movement in Tunisia is the defeat in the 1967 Six-Day War. This represented a failure of the nationalist-Arab factor.

HOW DID THINGS FALL INTO PLACE IN THE ISLAMIST MOVEMENT?

A number of intellectuals, including Rashid al-Ghannoushi, began meeting together. Al-Ghannoushi was in Paris at the same time I was. Before that we had been together in Damascus. Immediately the question of religion was posed. None of those programs, which for so long had seemed to offer certain solutions, could provide the answer – neither Arab nationalism nor Tunisian nationalism nor the West.

HAD RELIGION ALWAYS PLAYED A SIGNIFICANT ROLE?

I'm from a very conservative family that was active in the University of Zaytuna. Religion and religious studies have always had an important place in my family.

SO YOU NEVER DISTANCED YOURSELF FROM RELIGION?

Well, I was like everybody else. I didn't practice at all. Religion was part of the past, it was no longer current.

WHY DID YOU DECIDE TO ORGANIZE YOURSELVES INTO SOMETHING BESIDES INFORMAL MEETINGS?

At that time there was the Qur'anic Preservation Society (QPS), set up by the ministry of religion. We began to congregate there. There was also Jama'at al-Da'wa (the Preaching Association), a group that used to visit us every year from Pakistan. Soon Tunisians also joined their group. Jama'at al-Da'wa people travel around the world preaching a return to Islam, to religious practice. We were influenced by their simplicity, a way of life that seemed old-fashioned in Tunisia.

Jama'at-Da'wa was apolitical; it spread the "good news" and beseeched people to return to the straight path. There was a more intellectual tendency in the cadre of the QPS. They wanted to organize conferences and meetings.

We functioned like that until 1973. Those years now seem to me ones of groping. But we were certain of one thing – that the religious aspect had become essential. By contrast, the political aspect was still very vague. No one agreed with the government, of course, but neither did anyone have a well-thought-out plan of political action.

HOW WAS THIS VACILLATION RESOLVED?

First, we came in contact with a Mr. Benslama, who was educated at Zaytuna. He had ideas that were a bit old-fashioned, of course, but he was very nice. Everyone readily agreed to relaunch the magazine, *Al-Ma'rifa*, which had published one issue in 1962.

The second new element was al-Sadat's release of the Muslim Brothers in Egypt. The Brothers resumed their literary production. Even before this, publications from Egypt had been very important. The sheikhs of Zaytuna were disappearing one by one, until we didn't have any more. Zaytuna University was completely closed. So the Egyptians encouraged us to engage more directly in political action, as well as in underground planning.

WHAT KIND OF IDEOLOGICAL FORMATION DID YOU AND RASHID AL-GHANNOUSHI BRING BACK FROM SYRIA?

I believe it was in Syria that al-Ghannoushi had his first contact with the Brothers. At the end of the 1960s the Islamist tendency was very weak, so upon returning from Damascus our political formation was still rather sketchy.

SO IT WAS FROM THE RESERVOIR OF MUSLIM BROTHERS' THOUGHT THAT THE FUTURE ISLAMIC TENDENCY MOVEMENT (ITM) TOOK ITS PRINCIPAL IDEOLOGICAL REFERENCES, STRATEGIES, AND TACTICS?

Yes. We read about how the Brothers in Egypt established their first cells. We lived in a country that was quite different from Egypt. The Tunisian government didn't concern itself much with the mosques. We could therefore meet very easily, outside the usual Friday sermon. We also organized in the high schools. We held meetings during recess and lectured the students.

THE GOVERNMENT IGNORED YOU, BUT YOU CONSIDERED YOURSELVES ESSENTIALLY AS POLITICAL OPPONENTS?

We were tacitly against the government, but our ideology and plan of action weren't clear. We were against all Western forms of society, but we did not know what alternative society we should propose.

Things became clearer when our first high school students entered the university. There they came into contact with people from the left and the extreme right. This confrontation between traditional Islamic thought and the thought and modes of action of leftist groups radicalized our group. I believe it was at that moment that the political profile of the ITM was formed. The Islamist students couldn't escape the university methods: political protest, meetings, graffiti, political "analyses."

Imperialism – before no one ever spoke of imperialism. Only when we came in contact with leftist elements did we discover that there was a history of foreign intervention in the lives of underdeveloped countries.

DID THE MOVEMENT THEN BECOME MORE STRUCTURED?

Not really. A bureau wasn't established until 1981. But by that time I had already left the movement. In 1977 there was what we called a "central nexus" which, under the direction of al-Ghannoushi, planned activities, decided what was to be done in this or that mosque.

WHY DID YOUR ATTITUDE TOWARD THE ORGANIZATION CHANGE?

Well, after 1975 I traveled to Egypt, where I met a number of religious personalities, especially among the Muslim Brothers, many well-known personalities who wrote in the newspapers and journals. In the end it turned out to be a deception.

YOU MEAN THAT THEIR DOCTRINE SEEMED INSUFFICIENT TO YOU?

Precisely. Let's take the example of Muhammad Qutb, whom I met in 1974 in Saudi Arabia. I explained to him that I was editor-in-chief of a magazine called *Al-Ma'rifa*. He shouted at me, "You are the agents of Bourguiba!" I realized that this man knew nothing about what was happening in Tunisia. He undoubtedly wrote very well. I read everything he published. But regarding the reality of the Arab countries, or at least Tunisia, he knew nothing whatsoever.

The second disillusion I had was with 'Abd al-'Alim 'Uways, who was reputed to be the political theoretician of the Muslim Brothers and a specialist in the political history of the Muslim world. I asked him what the Brothers sanctioned in matters of curriculum and scholarly reform. He referred me to a text by Hasan al-Banna, who had died in 1949. We were then in 1974! The problems had changed.

I came to realize that the Brothers of Egypt corresponded more to legend than anything else. What they called their methodology slowly appeared to me to be totally obsolete and could only lead to disaster. They spoke of three million members and sympathizers. I asked myself how a movement of such importance could have been broken up in a couple of months by 'Abd al-Nasir – broken up not only physically, but ideologically! This organization hadn't been capable of creating an ideological movement that could survive repression. A brotherhood of four thousand members depending on three million sympathizers – and in a few months they were imprisoned as if one was herding a flock of sheep. Obviously something had gone wrong. Besides, what they wrote was too general. This disillusionment gave me another way of seeing.

failure of the M. Bro.

YOU SOMEHOW RECLAIMED YOUR INDEPENDENCE OF THOUGHT?

Yes, but the problem was that our magazine, *Al-Ma'rifa*, was essentially that type of literature. I began to distance myself from the people there. Still, the movement spread and the audience for that type of literature grew.

With the radicalization going on inside the university and with what was happening at the trade union headquarters, you couldn't take time to reorient yourself. We perceived the danger from the left to be imminent. If I put myself in al-Ghannoushi's shoes, I understand that it was quite difficult to make any changes during that period. But I couldn't continue. I felt we needed to create something Tunisian. I began to apply a notion that was completely taboo during that period: "Tunisian Islam."

We also fought against what I called "the new sufism," which ignored the uniqueness of each Arab country and only addressed Islam as a whole. For me, to emphasize solely the spiritual side of Islam is a form of sufism. Our project cannot have a real impact on our societies as long as we do not understand the workings of those societies, their recent history, their problems.

AND ON THIS BASIS YOU BROKE WITH WHAT BECAME THE ITM?

At the end of some articles that I wrote for *Al-Ma'rifa* I pointedly attacked Hasan al-Banna. I wrote that this man was certainly a brave man, a militant, but he had not understood the ropes and he was dead. D-e-a-d. To die physically is not important, but when one leads a movement that is dismantled with surprising ease after one is gone, that proves that the ideology was not in step with the real problems of society. We should not reemploy that strategy. We should study him, understand why all al-Banna's work went up in smoke. That's what I wrote.

Since I was editor-in-chief of the magazine, I brought the text to the printer. Later, when I had the issue in hand, I noticed that the entire paragraph where I discussed Hasan al-Banna had been deleted. The director of the magazine had cut it out without even consulting me.

I requested that a statement be published in the next issue and it did appear. Then I withdrew. I remained alone for almost a year. "He's someone whose faith is weak," they insinuated. "He no longer believes in certain things." But at that time, I have to say that they were hardly concerned with those problems. Not as long as the meetings and sermons were successful. And the Iranian revolution was about to occur and give the movement greater significance.

THAT'S ANOTHER IMPORTANT DATE IN THE HISTORY OF THIS MOVEMENT, RIGHT?

Absolutely. But I remember that at first the leadership of the ITM kept their distance. Rashid al-Ghannoushi thought that it was above all a Shi'i revolution. After seeing the magnitude of the revolution, the participation of the entire Iranian population, it was no longer possible to remain neutral. So they threw themselves onto the side of the Iranian revolution, especially in the magazines *Al-Ma'rifa* and *Al-Mujtama'*. In its last issue, *Al-Mujtama'* published a huge picture of Khomeini on the cover. It was from that moment on that the authorities started to become alarmed. They arrested al-Ghannoushi for a few days and seized internal documents of the movement. I had met with Rashid al-Ghannoushi months before his arrest. I said that now that they were involved in this political business they could never turn back. He told me he didn't think he was risking more than six months in prison – if the government had the guts to put them on trial. They truly believed they were too strong for the government to dare to try. But all those people who followed them in the mosques did not constitute a real base.

A movement can only be important if it fulfills two conditions – first, if it has structures and associations involved with various social classes and represents a definite social phenomenon, not marginal, frustrated people. Otherwise it's some kind of crowd. The second condition is that the movement provide a plan that society can identify with. A plan must have a well-developed social profile, and that is something that the ITM has never had.

FOR YOU, THE ITM STEPPED INTO POLITICAL ACTION MUCH TOO SOON, WITHOUT THE NECESSARY THEORETICAL REFLECTION ON WHICH TO BASE ITS ACTIVITIES?

It's true. Theoretical reflection and reflection on reality. But they couldn't engage in this reflection as long as they believed that everything that took place between 1881 and 1956, and even between 1956 and the emergence of the Islamist movement – the Bourguiba project of modernization and all that – amounted to nothing, just a historical parentheses.

Translated from the French by Linda G. Jones

2.3 'HUMAN RIGHTS DECLARATION, 1948'

From *Encyclopedia of the United Nations*, Osmanozyek, E.J. (ed.), London, Taylor and Francis, 1985, pp. 361–2.

HUMAN RIGHTS. UNIVERSAL DECLARATION OF 1948. The name of the UN document adopted Dec 10 1948 by the UN General Assembly by 48 votes in favor and eight members abstaining: Saudi Arabia, Czechoslovakia, Yugoslavia, Poland, the Republic of South Africa, Ukrainian SSR and the USSR. The socialist States abstained because the majority deleted amendments proposed by those states which postulated: equality not only of all people, but of all nations; (2) abolition of capital punishment in peacetime; (3) a ban on fascist propaganda, as well as militarist and racist propaganda as anti-human. The Republic of South Africa and Saudi Arabia abstained because they considered the Declaration too progressive. The text of the Declaration reads:

"Whereas recognition of the inherent dignity and of the equal and inalienable rights of all members of the human family is the foundation of freedom, justice and peace in the world, whereas disregard and contempt for human rights have resulted in barbarous acts which have outraged the conscience of mankind, and the advent of a world in which human beings shall enjoy freedom of speech and belief and freedom from fear and want has been proclaimed as the highest aspiration of the common people,

whereas it is essential, if man is not to be compelled to have recourse, as a last resort, to rebellion against tyranny and oppression, that human rights should be protected by the rule of law,

whereas it is essential to promote the development of friendly relations between nations,

whereas the peoples of the United Nations have in the Charter reaffirmed their faith in fundamental human rights, in the dignity and worth of the human person and in the equal rights of men and women and have determined to promote social progress and better standards of life in larger freedom,

whereas Member-States have pledged themselves to achieve in cooperation with the United Nations, the promotion of universal respect for and observance of human rights and fundamental freedoms,

whereas a common understanding of these rights and freedoms is of the greatest importance for the full realization of this pledge. Now, therefore, the General Assembly proclaims this Universal Declaration of Human Rights as a common standard of achievement for all peoples and all nations, to the end that every individual and every organ of society, keeping this Declaration constantly in mind, shall strive by teaching and education to promote respect for these rights and freedoms and by progressive measures, national and international, to secure their universal and effective recognition and observance, both among the peoples of Member-States themselves and among the peoples of territories under their jurisdiction.

Art. 1. All human beings are born free and equal in dignity and rights. They are endowed with reason and conscience and should act towards one another in a spirit of brotherhood.

Art. 2. Everyone is entitled to all the rights and freedoms set forth in this Declaration, without distinction of any kind, such as race, color, sex, language, religion, political or other opinion, national or social origin, property, birth or other status.

Furthermore, no distinction shall be made on the basis of the political, jurisdictional or international status of the country or territory to which a person belongs, whether it be independent, trust, non-self-governing or under any other limitation of sovereignty.

Art. 3. Everyone has the right to life, liberty and security of person.

Art. 4. No one shall be held in slavery or servitude; slavery and the slave trade shall be prohibited in all their forms.

Art. 5. No one shall be subjected to torture or to cruel, inhuman or degrading treatment or punishment.

Art. 6. Everyone has the right to recognition everywhere as a person before the law.

Art. 7. All are equal before the law and are entitled without any discrimination to equal protection of the law. All are entitled to equal protection against any discrimination in violation of the Declaration and against any incitement to such discrimination.

Art. 8. Everyone has the right to an effective remedy by the competent national tribunals for acts violating the fundamental rights granted him by the constitution or by law.

Art. 9. No one shall be subjected to arbitrary arrest, detention or exile.

Art. 10. Everyone is entitled in full equality to a fair and public hearing by an independent and impartial tribunal, in the determination of his rights and obligations and of any criminal charge against him.

Art. 11.(I) Everyone charged with a penal offence has the right to be presumed innocent until proved guilty according to law in a public trial at which he has had all the guarantees necessary for his defence. (II) No one shall be held guilty of any penal offence on account of any act of omission which did not constitute a penal offence, under national or international law, at the time it was committed. Nor shall a heavier penalty be imposed than the one that was applicable at the time the penal offence was committed.

Art. 12. No one shall be subjected to arbitrary interference with his privacy, family, home or correspondence, nor to attacks upon his honor and reputation. Everyone has the right to the protection of the law against such interference or attacks.

Art. 13.(I) Everyone has the right to freedom of movement and residence within the borders of each state. (II) Everyone has the right to leave any country, including his own, and to return to his country.

Art. 14.(I) Everyone has the right to seek and to enjoy in other countries asylum from persecution. (II) This right may not be invoked in the case of prosecutions genuinely arising from non-political crimes or from acts contrary to the purposes and principles of the United Nations.

Art. 15.(I) Everyone has the right to a nationality. (II) No one shall be arbitrarily deprived of his nationality nor denied the right to change his nationality.

Art. 16.(I) Men and women of full age, without any limitation due to race, nationality or religion, have the right to marry and to found a family. They are entitled to equal rights as to marriages, during marriage and at its dissolution. (II) Marriage shall be entered into only with the free and full consent of the intending spouses. (III) The family is the natural and fundamental group unit of society and is entitled to protection by society and the state.

Art. 17.(I) Everyone has the right to own property as well as in association with others. (II) No one shall be arbitrarily deprived of his property.

Art. 18. Everyone has the right to freedom of thought, conscience and religion: the right includes freedom to change his religion or belief, and freedom, either alone or in community with others and in public or private, to manifest his religion or belief in teaching, practice, worship and observance.

Art. 19. Everyone has the right to freedom of opinion and expression: this right includes the right to freedom to hold opinions without interference and to seek, receive and impart information and ideas through any media and regardless of frontiers.

Art. 20.(I) Everyone has the right to freedom of peaceful assembly and association. (II) No one may be compelled to an association.

Art. 21.(I) Everyone has the right to take part in the government of his country, directly or through freely chosen representatives. (II) Everyone has the right of equal access to public service in his country. (III) The will of the people shall be the basis of the authority of the government; this will shall be expressed in periodic and genuine elections which shall be by universal and equal suffrage and shall be held by secret vote or by equivalent free voting procedures.

Art. 22. Everyone, as a member of society, has the right to social security and is entitled to realization, through national effort and international cooperation and in accordance with the organization and resources of each State, of the economic, social and cultural rights indispensable for his dignity and the free development of his personality.

Art. 23.(I) Everyone has the right to work, to free choice of employment, to just and favorable conditions of work and to protection against unemployment. (II) Everyone, without any discrimination, has the right to equal pay for equal work. (III) Everyone who works has the right to just and favorable remuneration ensuring for himself and his family an existence worthy of human dignity, and supplemented if necessary, by other means of social protection. (IV) Everyone has the right to form and to join trade unions for the protection of his interests.

Art. 24. Everyone has the right to rest and leisure, including reasonable limitation of working hours and periodic holidays with pay.

Art. 25.(I) Everyone has the right to a standard of living adequate for the health and well-being of himself and of his family, including food, clothing, housing and medical care and necessary social services, and the right to security in the event of unemployment, sickness, disability, widowhood, old age or other lack of livelihood in circumstances beyond his control. (II) Motherhood and childhood are entitled to special care and assistance. All children, whether born in or out of wedlock, shall enjoy the same social protection.

Art. 26.(I) Everyone has the right to education. Education shall be free, at least in the elementary and fundamental stages. Elementary education shall be compulsory. Technical and profession education shall be made generally available and higher education shall be equally accessible to all on the basis of merit. (II) Education shall be directed to the full development of the human personality and to the strengthening of respect for human rights and friendship among all nations, racial or religious groups and shall further the activities of the United

Nations for the maintenance of peace. (III) Parents have a prior right to choose the kind of education that shall be given to their children.

Art. 27.(I) Everyone has the right freely to participate in the cultural life of the community, to enjoy the arts and to share in scientific advancement and its benefits. (II) Everyone has the right to the protection of the moral and material interest resulting from any scientific, literary or artistic production of which he is the author.

Art. 28. Everyone is entitled to a social and international order in which the rights and freedoms set forth in this Declaration can be fully realized.

Art. 29.(I) Everyone has duties to the community in which alone the free and full development of his personality is possible. (II) In the exercise of his rights and freedoms, everyone shall be subject only to such limitations as are determined by law solely for the purposes of securing due recognition and respect for the rights and freedoms of others and of meeting the just requirements of mortality, public order and the general welfare in a democratic society. (III) These rights and freedoms may in no case be exercised contrary to the purposes and principles of the United Nations.

Art. 30. Nothing in this Declaration may be interpreted as implying for any State, group or person any right to engage in any activity or to perform any act aimed at the destruction of any of the rights and freedoms set forth herein."

UN Yearbook, 1948, UN Bulletin, 1948 and 1949: R. CASSIN, *La Déclaration Universelle de Droit de l'Homme et sa mise en oeuvre,* Paris, 1956; *The UN and the Human Rights,* New York, 1968.

2.4 'CAIRO DECLARATION ON HUMAN RIGHTS IN ISLAM'

United Nations General Assembly, 1993, 'The Organization of the Islamic Conference: Cairo declaration on human rights in Islam', *World Conference on Human Rights*, 4th Session, Agenda Item No. 5, UN Doc.A/CONF.157/PC/62/Add.18(1993) [selection].*

The Member States of the Organisation of the Islamic Conference.

Reaffirming the civilizing and historical role of the Islamic Ummah which God made the best nation that has given mankind a universal and well-balanced civilization in which harmony is established between this life and the hereafter and knowledge is combined with faith; and the role that this Ummah should play to guide a humanity confused by competing trends and ideologies and to provide solutions to the chronic problems of this materialistic civilization.

Wishing to contribute to the efforts of mankind to assert human rights, to protect man from exploitation and persecution, and to affirm his freedom and right to a dignified life in accordance with the Islamic Shari'ah.

Convinced that mankind which has reached an advanced stage in materialistic science is still, and shall remain, in dire need of faith to support its civilization and of a self motivating force to guard its rights;

Believing that fundamental rights and universal freedoms in Islam are an integral part of the Islamic religion and that no one as a matter of principle has the right to suspend them in whole or in part or violate or ignore them in as much as they are binding divine commandments, which are contained in the Revealed Books of God and were sent through the last of His Prophets to complete the preceding divine messages thereby making their observance an act of worship and their neglect or violation an abominable sin, and accordingly every person is individually responsible – and the Ummah collectively responsible – for their safeguard.

Proceeding from the above-mentioned principles,

Declare the following:

ARTICLE I:

(a)   All human beings form one family whose members are united by submission to God and descent from Adam. All men are equal in terms of basic human dignity and basic obligations and responsibilities, without any discrimination on the grounds of race, colour, language, sex, religious belief, political affiliation, social status or other considerations. True faith is the guarantee for enhancing such dignity along the path to human perfection.

---

* The United Nations is the author of the original material.

(b)   All human beings are God's subjects, and the most loved by Him are those who are most useful to the rest of His subjects, and no one has superiority over another except on the basis of piety and good deeds.

ARTICLE 2:

(a)   Life is a God-given gift and the right to life is guaranteed to every human being. It is the duty of individuals, societies and states to protect this right from any violation, and it is prohibited to take away life except for a Shari'ah prescribed reason.
(b)   It is forbidden to resort to such means as may result in the genocidal annihilation of mankind.
(c)   The preservation of human life throughout the term of time willed by God is a duty prescribed by Shari'ah.
(d)   Safety from bodily harm is a guaranteed right. It is the duty of the state to safeguard it, and it is prohibited to breach it without a Sharia-prescribed reason.

ARTICLE 3:

(a)   In the event of the use of force and in case of armed conflict, it is not permissible to kill non-belligerents such as old men, women and children. The wounded and the sick shall have the right to medical treatment; and prisoners of war shall have the right to be fed, sheltered and clothed. It is prohibited to mutilate dead bodies. It is a duty to exchange prisoners of war and to arrange visits or reunions of the families separated by the circumstances of war.
(b)   It is prohibited to fell trees, to damage crops or livestock, and to destroy the enemy's civilian buildings and installations by shelling, blasting or any other means.

ARTICLE 4:

Every human being is entitled to inviolability and the protection of his good name and honour during his life and after his death. The state and society shall protect his remains and burial place.

ARTICLE 5:

(a)   The family is the foundation of society, and marriage is the basis of its formation. Men and women have the right to marriage, and no restrictions stemming from race, colour or nationality shall prevent them from enjoying this right.
(b)   Society and the State shall remove all obstacles to marriage and shall facilitate marital procedure. They shall ensure family protection and welfare.

ARTICLE 6:

(a)   Woman is equal to man in human dignity, and has rights to enjoy as well as duties to perform; she has her own civil entity and financial independence, and the right to retain her name and lineage.

(b)   The husband is responsible for the support and welfare of the family.

ARTICLE 7:

(a)   As of the moment of birth, every child has rights due from the parents, society and the state to be accorded proper nursing, education and material, hygienic and moral care. Both the fetus and the mother must be protected and accorded special care.

(b)   Parents and those in such like capacity have the right to choose the type of education they desire for their children, provided they take into consideration the interest and future of the children in accordance with ethical values and the principles of the Shari'ah.

(c)   Both parents are entitled to certain rights from their children, and relatives are entitled to rights from their kin, in accordance with the tenets of the Shari'ah.

ARTICLE 8:

Every human being has the right to enjoy his legal capacity in terms of both obligation and commitment; should this capacity be lost or impaired, he shall be represented by his guardian.

ARTICLE 9:

(a)   The question for knowledge is an obligation and the provision of education is a duty for society and the State. The State shall ensure the availability of ways and means to acquire education and shall guarantee educational diversity in the interest of society so as to enable man to be acquainted with the religion of Islam and the facts of the Universe for the benefit of mankind.

(b)   Every human being has the right to receive both religious and worldly education from the various institutions of education and guidance, including the family, the school, the university, the media, etc., and in such an integrated and balanced manner as to develop his personality, strengthen his faith in God and promote his respect for and defence of both rights and obligations.

ARTICLE 10:

Islam is the religion of unspoiled nature. It is prohibited to exercise any form of compulsion on man or to exploit his poverty or ignorance in order to convert him to another religion or to atheism.

ARTICLE 11:

(a)   Human beings are born free, and no one has the right to enslave, humiliate, oppress or exploit them, and there can be no subjugation but to God the Most-High.

(b)   Colonialism of all types being one of the most evil forms of enslavement is totally prohibited. Peoples suffering from colonialism have the full right to freedom and self-determination. It is the duty of all States and peoples to support the struggle of colonized peoples for the liquidation of all forms of colonialism and occupation, and all States and peoples have the right to preserve their independent identity and exercise control over their wealth and natural resources.

ARTICLE 12:

Every man shall have the right, within the framework of Shari'ah, to free movement and to select his place of residence whether inside or outside his country and if persecuted, is entitled to seek asylum in another country. The country of refuge shall ensure his protection until he reaches safety, unless asylum is motivated by an act which Shari'ah regards as a crime.

ARTICLE 13:

Work is a right guaranteed by the State and Society for each person able to work. Everyone shall be free to choose the work that suits him best and which serves his interests and those of society. The employee shall have the right to safety and security as well as to all other social guarantees. He may neither be assigned work beyond his capacity nor be subjected to compulsion or exploited or harmed in any way. He shall be entitled – without any discrimination between males and females – to fair wages for his work without delay, as well as to the holidays, allowances and promotions which he deserves. For his part, he shall be required to be dedicated and meticulous in his work. Should workers and employers disagree on any matter, the State shall intervene to settle the dispute and have the grievances redressed, the rights confirmed and justice enforced without bias.

ARTICLE 14:

Everyone shall have the right to legitimate gains without monopolization, deceit or harm to oneself or to others. Usury (riba) is absolutely prohibited.

ARTICLE 15:

(a)   Everyone shall have the right to own property acquired in a legitimate way, and shall be entitled to the rights of ownership, without prejudice to oneself, others or to society in general. Expropriation is not permissible except for the requirements of public interest and upon payment of immediate and fair compensation.

(b)   Confiscation and seizure of property is prohibited except for a necessity dictated by law.

ARTICLE 16:

Everyone shall have the right to enjoy the fruits of his scientific, literary, artistic or technical production and the right to protect the moral and material interests stemming therefrom, provided that such production is not contrary to the principles of Shari'ah.

ARTICLE 17:

(a)   Everyone shall have the right to live in a clean environment, away from vice and moral corruption, an environment that would foster his self-development and it is incumbent upon the State and society in general to afford that right.

(b)   Everyone shall have the right to medical and social care, and to all public amenities provided by society and the State within the limits of their available resources.

(c)   The State shall ensure the right of the individual to a decent living which will enable him to meet all his requirements and those of his dependents, including food, clothing, housing, education, medical care and all other basic needs.

ARTICLE 18:

(a)   Everyone shall have the right to live in security for himself, his religion, his dependents, his honour and his property.

(b)   Everyone shall have the right to privacy in the conduct of his private affairs, in his home, among his family, with regard to his property and his relationships. It is not permitted to spy on him, to place him under surveillance or to besmirch his good name. The State shall protect him from arbitrary interference.

(c)   A private residence is inviolable in all cases. It will not be entered without permission from its inhabitants or in any unlawful manner, nor shall it be demolished or confiscated and its dwellers evicted.

ARTICLE 19:

(a)   All individuals are equal before the law, without distinction between the ruler and the ruled.

(b)   The right to resort to justice is guaranteed to everyone.

(c)   Liability is in essence personal.

(d)   There shall be no crime or punishment except as provided for in the Shari'ah.

(e)   A defendant is innocent until his guilt is proven in a fair trial in which he shall be given all the guarantees of defence.

ARTICLE 20:

It is not permitted without legitimate reason to arrest an individual, or restrict his freedom, to exile or to punish him. It is not permitted to subject him to physical or psychological torture or to any form of humiliation, cruelty or indignity. Nor is it permitted to subject an individual to medical or scientific experimentation without his consent or at the risk of his health or of his life. Nor is it permitted to promulgate emergency laws that would provide executive authority for such actions.

ARTICLE 21:

Taking hostages under any form or for any purpose is expressly forbidden.

ARTICLE 22:

(a)   Everyone shall have the right to express his opinion freely in such manner as would not be contrary to the principles of the Shari'ah.
(b)   Everyone shall have the right to advocate what is right, and propagate what is good, and warn against what is wrong and evil according to the norms of Islamic Shari'ah.
(c)   Information is a vital necessity to society. It may not be exploited or misused in such a way as may violate sanctities and the dignity of Prophets, undermine moral and ethical values or disintegrate, corrupt or harm society or weaken its faith.
(d)   It is not permitted to arouse nationalistic or doctrinal hatred or to do anything that may be an incitement to any form of racial discrimination.

ARTICLE 23:

(a)   Authority is a trust; and abuse or malicious exploitation therefore is absolutely prohibited, so that fundamental human rights may be guaranteed.
(b)   Everyone shall have the right to participate, directly or indirectly in the administration of his country's public affairs. He shall also have the right to assume public office in accordance with the provisions of Shari'ah.

ARTICLE 24:

All the rights and freedoms stipulated in this Declaration are subject to the Islamic Shari'ah.

ARTICLE 25:

The Islamic Shari'ah is the only source of reference for the explanation or clarification of any of the articles of this Declaration.

Cairo, 14 Muharram 1411H

5 August 1990

2.5 'WHO IS MARY FOR TODAY'S ASIAN WOMEN?'

Kyung Hyun Chung

From *Struggle to Be the Sun Again: Introducing Asian Women's Theology*, Chung, K.H., London, Orbis Books, 1990, pp. 77–9, 81, 83, 95.

MARY AS VIRGIN: SELF-DEFINING WOMAN

Asian women are beginning to view the virginity of Mary, not as a *biological* reality, but as a *relational* reality. Indonesian theologian Marianne Katoppo articulates this point. For her, Mary's virginity means she is a "liberated human being, who – not being subject to any other human being – is free to serve God."[1] Virginity lies in her true connectedness to her own self and to God. It is "an inner attitude, not a psychological or external fact."[2] When a woman defines herself according to her own understanding of who she really is and what she is meant for in this universe (and not according to the rules and norms of patriarchy), she is a virgin. Therefore, her virginity persists "in spite of sexual experience, child bearing and increasing age."[3] Actually her virginity, her ability to be a self-defining woman, grows because of her full range of life experience.

Virgin is "the symbol for the autonomy of women."[4] Virgin primarily means not "a woman who abstains from sexual intercourse" but a woman who does not lead a derived life, as "daughter/wife/mother" of men.[5] She is a "woman who matures to wholeness within herself as a complete person, and who is open for others."[6]

Han Kuk Yum, a Korean woman theologian, pushes the meaning of virginity one step further. Quoting another Korean woman theologian, Park Soon Kyung, she argues that Mary's virgin birth of Jesus means that "the human-male is excluded" from this important event of the birth of new humanity.

> The fact that in Jesus' birth, human-male is excluded connotes that a new human image, a new saving world could no longer be sustained through a patriarchal order. The human-saving Messiah who saves humanity has nothing to do with the patriarchal view of value or patriarchal order, but is totally the birth of new human image.[7]

---

1. Katoppo, *Compassionate and Free*, p. 21.
2. Ibid., p. 20.
3. Ibid.
4. Ibid.
5. Ibid.
6. Ibid.
7. Han Kuk Yum, "Mariology as a Base for Feminist Liberation Theology," Consultation on Asian Women's Theology – 1987, p. 3.

The virgin birth, then, means the overture of the end of the patriarchal order. It is the symbol of God's judgment against men's sinning against women. Through the event of the virgin birth, God shows men that they cannot control and oppress women. This event also shows women that salvation is sufficient without men. The church's emphasis, therefore, of the virgin birth as a miraculous, clean birth that is not "corrupted" by human sexuality only shows its sickness as "a marked sexual neurosis."[8] Korean theologian Han thinks that if the miraculous virgin birth is important for the patriarchal church, it would be more convincing for them to insist that Jesus was born from an egg rather than a woman's body.[9] For many Asian women Mary's virginity is an active symbol of resistance against patriarchal order. Mary as a virgin is a complete human being within herself. She defines her life. By defining herself by her experience and her faith in God (and not by patriarchal norms), she becomes a model of full womanhood and liberated humanity for many Asian women.

MARY AS MOTHER: GIVER OF LIFE TO GOD AND NEW HUMANITY

Since Mary is a virgin who is not domesticated by the patriarchal order, she can give birth to God and new humanity. The new order of God, the new redeemed humanity, cannot be brought to the world through the old order of patriarchy, which is based on the principle of domination. By defying the patriarchal order in her decision to have a child out of wedlock, and by her believing in God and herself, Mary enables God to be born through her own body. Mary matures to wholeness by believing in God and herself and through her openness to an unknown future. "Through this maturing process, she is *fertile*, she *gives life* for God."[10]

Mary's giving birth to both the Messiah and to a new humanity starts with her saying yes to God's plan for salvation for a broken humanity. This affirmation of God's plan through her motherhood of Jesus and the new humanity is not mere obedience and submission to a male God but a conscious choice on her part. Mary's choice is based on her historical consciousness "as a young Jewish girl thoroughly steeped in the traditions of Israel and the historical struggle of her people."[11] With fear and trembling she takes the risk of participating in God's plan out of her vision of redeemed humanity. Mary takes this risk not as a heroic superwoman, but as an ordinary woman who is receptive to God's calling, which draws her from her own private safety. She is fully aware of the consequences of her choice: social ostracism or even the possibility of being stoned to death according to Jewish custom. But Mary still chooses to give birth to the Messiah and thereby makes possible the liberation of her people. This courageous action, her risk for life-giving reality, is the beginning of her journey to become a "mature committed woman, growing in her faith in God and the Son."[12]

Indian theologian Astrid Lobo emphasizes Mary's feelings at the annunciation as an Asian woman who wants to make her own choices in her life:

---

8. "Summary Statement on Mariology," Consultation on Asian Women's Theology – 1987, p. 1.

9. Han Kuk Yum, p. 3.

10. Katoppo, *Compassionate and Free*, p. 21.

11. Who Is Mary?" in *Proceedings: Asian Women's Consultation* (Manila: EATWOT, 1985), p. 156.

12. Lobo, "Mary and the Woman of Today," p. 7.

I can feel her fear. Her world is suddenly being turned upside down. God asks her to bear the Son…and Mary says "yes." It is a "yes" that reverberates throughout her life, as time and time again she is put to the test…When Mary makes her choice, human odds are against her. She must have realized that she would probably lose Joseph; that once her pregnancy began to show she would face the possibility of being stoned to death. In her place we would have let common sense prevail, and said, "I'm sorry. Please find someone else." We would forget the one thing that Mary never forgets: the one who asks is God. And so she is willing to pay the price. But the world cannot understand. Not even Joseph. Mary has to be ready to walk alone.[13]

Jesus was born through the body of this woman, "a liberated, mature woman, who had a mind and will of her own, capable of self determination and perseverance in her decisions."[14]

Jesus also did not grow up in a vacuum. Jesus was nurtured and taught by a mother who embodied his people's aspiration for liberation. Asian women theologians claim that Mary announced "what kind of messiah her son will be" through her Magnificat.[15] . . .

When Mary overcomes her fear by being affirmed by her sister in the same struggle, she regains the power to tell the truth. Mary sings a song of revolution, the Magnificat. She expresses her yearning for the liberation of the oppressed people in the words of Hannah – another strong woman of Israel. Mary claims her power and history as a woman whose consciousness is deeply rooted in the heritage and wisdom of the strong women of Israel. Mary makes the forgotten power of her foremother, Hannah, alive by taking action, by accepting the work of the spirit through her pregnancy and by prophesying the "complete change in the present patriarchal order using the words of Hannah."[16] Mary makes connections vertically and horizontally by discovering her foremother and by announcing justice for the oppressed in her own time. Mary's Magnificat is addressed "to an older woman, Elizabeth, who like Hannah, has become pregnant after years of infertility."[17] Elizabeth becomes the first audience for Mary's Magnificat. This shows an important truth: Women need women's presence and affirmation to dare to dream the revolution and to celebrate their power for life.

MARY AS A CO-REDEEMER FOR HUMAN SALVATION

Some Asian women think Mary's role in the salvation of humanity must be recognized as redeemer with Jesus Christ in the Christian tradition. There are two major positions for this claim. One is envisioning Mary as a co-redemptrix by her role as a model for the liberation and salvation of humanity. The other is depicting Mary as a helper and mediator for the redemption of humanity.

---

13. Ibid., pp. 7–8.
14. Nalaan, Navaratnarajah, "Mariology", Consultation on Asian Women's Theology—1987, p. 1.
15. "Summary Statement on Mariology," p. 1.
16. "Summary Statement on Mariology", p. 2.
17. Ibid., p. 2.

2.6 'ASIAN WOMEN WRITING THEOLOGY'

Kyung Hyun Chung

From *Struggle to Be the Sun Again: Introducing Asian Women's Theology*, Chung, K.H., London, Orbis Books, 1990, p. 102.

Only a few Asian women have articulated their theology through writing. This written theology among Asian women was begun only during the last decade. Most Asian women who write and publish theologies in Asia today have had some kind of traditional theological training, are of middle-class background (by origin or educational status), and have been exposed to Western feminist theologies. Many Asian women theologians write their theology in English. These middle-class, educated, and English-speaking women talk about Asian women's pain – poverty, physical and psychological battering, prostitution, and so on. They talk about poor women's suffering in Asia. But what right do they have to talk about poor Asian women's struggles? How can they speak of the poor Asian women's faith with authenticity using the language of their colonizers, which the poor women in their respective countries cannot even understand? What is the relationship between the educated middle-class women theologians who *write* theology and the illiterate, poor women theologians who *live* theology in their everyday lives?

This is a great problem for Asian women theologians. It is discussed often as they seek to overcome their separation from their poor sisters. It is not an alienation easy to overcome; it is perhaps a lifetime struggle. What is important for our study is that Asian, Western-educated women have identified this problem and are fighting to bridge the gulf between them and their sisters. Asian middle-class women have identified *solidarity* with poor women as the goal of their struggle.

Many educated women theologians in Asia know that they are not doing theology *for* the poor women. They articulate theology in order to enhance the liberation process in their broken communities, seeking the common future of the communities. These women do theology as a form of repentance and self-criticism. They also do theology in order to become more critically aware of their privilege and their responsibility in relation to the poor women in their communities. These middle-class, educated Asian women theologians are learning how to work with poor women and how to be transformed by the wisdom of the poor through the process of doing theology. Asian women theologians know that this process of *metanoia* to poor women is the only way to regain their wholeness.

2.7 'MARY IN THE CHRISTIAN COMMUNITY: MODEL FOR LIBERATION'

Ana Maria Bidegai

From *Through Her Eyes: Women's Theology from Latin America*, Tamez, E. (ed.), New York, Orbis Books, 1989, pp. 33–6.

MARY IN THE CHRISTIAN COMMUNITY: MODEL OF LIBERATION

Mary has been held out to Christians as a model of the feminine. But like the image of Jesus, so also that of Mary has frequently been utilized to justify a patriarchal mentality that marginalizes women. Mary has been simplified. She has become the model of self-denial, passivity, and submission as the essential (or worse still, the only) attributes of woman.

We are altogether accustomed to this predominantly patriarchal discourse. Despite efforts like those of Paul VI in *Marialis Cultus*, or of Peubla, Mary's genuine quality does not "come through" sufficiently to rescue the whole prophetic, liberative dimension that her mystery can offer the Latin American woman and man of today.

Jesus not only reminds us insistently that the female human being is God's daughter as much as the male is God's son. He not only incorporates this daughter of his into his church. He not only values her pedagogy highly enough to summon the people of God to hear her word and experience her prophetic role of proclamation. He actually takes a woman and makes her his mother, to fulfill God's plan by taking flesh within her.

From our Latin American viewpoint, the figure of the mother of Jesus helps us rediscover the role of woman and man, and calls us to be converted and sanctified by accepting her liberative dimension.

Luke 1:26–33 teaches us that the humility of Mary consists in the daring to accept the monumental undertaking proposed to her by God. At first Mary is in wonder. She is unsettled and disturbed, as a woman, at what God proposes to her. But the angel promises that the shadow of the Spirit will cover her. Then Mary says: "I am the servant of the Lord. Let it be done to me as you say" (Luke 1:38).

Mary's yes is a free, responsible yes by which she accepts being the vessel of the new creation to be embodied by her son Jesus. It is not the yes of self-denial, almost of irresponsibility, as it has been traditionally presented to us. Mary knows to whom she is committing herself. . . .

We understand Mary's submission as a free act of surrender and self-bestowal for the purpose of co-creating, together with us, a new kind of humanistic and humanizing culture – one that will permit us to deliver ourselves from the rationalistic, inhumane, dehumanizing, hence discriminatory and utilitarian, culture of domination around us. . . .

Mary is blessed because she bears and communicates life even though she knows the suffering her son will undergo in pursuit of the liberation of his people. What a blessing for our faith that she believed! Mary, a woman, is the model disciple for Latin American men and women performing the joint task of giving birth to a new society.

In a society like ours in Latin America, which has denied us the right to motherhood by sterilizing us psychologically (through the radical birth control campaigns) and economically (on a continent drowning in foreign debt) – where, politically, we are denied the right to life because dissent is silenced with prison, torture, and the threat of being put on a death list – where those who do their duty are murdered – where the use and abuse of drugs in the United States and the drug traffic in Latin America is killing our children, husbands, brothers, and friends – Mary, the prophet of the Magnificat, gives us the strength to fight, in solidarity and in community, for the right to life. . . .

Mary the lowly servant of God – woman Mary – is God's decree of liberation, and the model of our action today. Woman – Latin American mother, eternal Eve, everlasting communicator of life – is also, like Mary, ever the first to communicate the good news, and thus to engender in her offspring a sense and feeling for their own life. The figure of Mother Mary helps us re-create woman's role, her identity and sense of belonging in the world. Man alone cannot create that world.

2.8 'BLACK FEMINISM AND THEOLOGY'

Jacquelyn Grant

From *White Women's Christ, Black Women's Jesus: Feminist Christology and Womanist Response*, Grant, J., The American Academy of Religion, 1989, pp. 195–6, 201–202, 210.

FEMINIST THEOLOGY AS WHITE THEOLOGY

Feminist theologians are white in terms of their race and in terms of the *nature of the sources* they use for the development of their theological perspectives. Although there are sharp differences among feminist theologians, as we have seen, they are *all* of the *same* race and the influence of their race has led them to similar sources for the definition of their perspectives on the faith. Of course, chief among the sources is women's experience. However, what is often unmentioned is that feminist theologians' sources for women's experience refer almost exclusively to White women's experience. White women's experience and Black women's experience are not the same. Indeed all experiences are unique to some degree. But in this case the difference is so radical that it may be said that White women and Black women are in completely different realms. Slavery and segregation have created such a gulf between these women, that White feminists' common assumption that all women are in the same situation with respect to sexism is difficult to understand when history so clearly tells us a different story.

. . .

FEMINIST THEOLOGY AS RACIST

It would be inaccurate to assert that because feminist theology is White, it is also racist. To be White does not necessarily mean to be racist, though the behavior of Whites makes the distinction difficult. Nevertheless, my claim that feminist theology is racist is best supported by a definition of racism.

Racism, according to Joel Kovel "…is the tendency of a society to degrade and do violence to people on the basis of race, and by whatever mediations may exist for this purpose."[1] These mediations are manifested in different forms, and are carried on through various media: the psychology, sociology, history, economics and symbolism of the dominant (White) group. Racism is the domination of a people which is justified by the dominant group on the basis of racial distinctions. It is not only individual acts but a collective, institutionalized activity.

. . .

---

1. Joel Kovel, *White Racism: A Psychohistory* (New York: Columbia University Press, 1984), p. x.

To say that many Black women are suspicious of the feminist movement, then, is to speak mildly about their responses to it. Put succinctly, women of the dominant culture are perceived as the enemy. Like their social, sexual and political White male partners, they have as their primary goal the suppression, if not oppression, of the Black race and the advancement of the dominant culture. Because of this perception, many believe that Black feminism is a contradiction in terms.

TOWARDS A NEW BLACK WOMEN'S CONSCIOUSNESS

In spite of the negative responses of Black women to the White women's liberation movement described, there has been a growing feminist consciousness among them, coupled with the increased willingness to do an independent analysis of sexism. This is creating an emerging Black perspective on feminism. Black feminism grows out of Black women's tri-dimensional reality of race/sex/class. It holds that full human liberation cannot be achieved simply by the elimination of any one form of oppression. Consequently, real liberation must be "broad in the concrete;"[2] it must be based upon a multi-dimensional analysis. Recent writings by secular Black feminists have challenged White feminist analysis and Black race analysis, particularly by introducing data from Black women's experience that has been historically ignored by White feminists and Black male liberationists.

---

2. This phrase is used by Anna Cooper in *A Voice From the South By a Black Woman of the South* (Xenia, Ohio, 1892), quoted in hooks *Ain't I A Woman*, pp. 193–94. I use it here to characterize Black women's tri-dimensional experience. To be concerned about Black Woman's issues is to be *concrete*. Yet because of their interconnectedness with Black men (racism), White women (sexism) and the poor (classism), it is also to be, at the same time, concerned with broad issues.

2.9 'SELF-UNDERSTANDING OF BIBLICAL SCHOLARSHIP'

Elisabeth Schüssler Fiorenza

From *Bread Not Stone: The Challenge of Feminist Biblical Interpretation*, Schüssler Fiorenza, E., Edinburgh, T&T Clark, 1984, pp. 137–9, 141.

Liberation theologies challenge biblical scholars, preachers, and the entire Christian community to articulate their theological commitment and engagement in the liberation struggle of those who suffer from patriarchal oppressions: from racial, sexual, colonial, economic, and technological exploitation. The basic methodological starting point of liberation theologies is the insight that all theology knowingly or not is by definition always engaged for or against the oppressed.[1] Intellectual neutrality is not possible in a historical world of exploitation and oppression. If this is the case, then theology cannot talk about human existence in general, or about biblical theology in particular, without identifying whose existence and whose God is meant. This "advocacy stance" of all liberation theologies is the major point of disagreement between liberation and academic theology.[2]

Academic biblical scholarship with a positivist posture rejects liberation-theological interpretations of the Bible as "ideological" and "unscientific" because they are influenced by present-day concerns. A feminist or liberationist interpretation in turn cannot acknowledge the claims and assumptions made by positivistic scholarship if it does not want to relinquish its own interests in women's biblical past and heritage. While a value-neutral, detached, scientific biblical scholarship, for example, can collect the biblical passages on *woman*, it cannot conceive of women as equally involved in shaping early Christian origins and articulating its religious vision. It cannot do so because it accepts androcentric biblical sources as "data" and "evidence" and its own androcentric linguistic interpretive models and narrative as totally divorced from contemporary concerns.[3] Scholarship claiming to be "objective" and "neutral" is not more value-free and less ideological because it hides its subjectivity and contemporary interests from itself.[4]

In contrast with interpreters who claim to be free of institutional interests, liberation theologians maintain that theology as well as biblical interpretation are never done in an institutional and personal vacuum but consciously or not are always "interpretation for." In order to sustain the "advocacy stance" the scholar of the Bible must first understand her own experience, adopt a clear political-social-theological analysis and then act upon her commitment to the oppressed and the marginalized. . . .

1. See especially Lee Cormie, "The Hermeneutical Privilege of the Oppressed: Liberation Theologies, Biblical Faith, and Marxist Sociology of Knowledge," *Proceedings of the Catholic Theological Society of America* 32 (1977): 155–81.
2. See for example Schubert M. Ogden, *Faith and Freedom: Toward a Theology of Liberation* (Nashville: Abingdon, 1979).
3. See my *In Memory of Her: A Feminist Theological Reconstruction of Christian Origins* (New York: Crossroad, 1983), pp. 41–96.
4. Cf. F. Herzog, "Liberation Hermeneutics as Ideology Critique," *Interpretation* 27 (1974): 387–403; D. Lockhead, "Hermeneutics and Ideology," *Ecumenist* 15 (1977): 81–84.

Liberation theologians maintain further that their pre-understanding – the option for the poor – is not *eisegesis* but exegesis, since this message is already found in the text: The God of the Bible is the God of the poor and oppressed.[5] At this point it becomes apparent that the critical hermeneutical task of feminist theology is more complicated, since it cannot state without qualification that the "God of the Bible is the God of women,"[6] because there is considerable evidence that the Bible not only was used against women's liberation but also had no clear "option" for women's liberation. . . .[7]

Feminist theology therefore insists that we have to bring to bear a critical evaluation and "hermeneutics of suspicion" both upon the content and the process of biblical interpretation as well as upon the biblical texts themselves. . . .

Whenever one cannot accept the religious, political, and personal ethos and ethics of a biblical text, one cannot accept its authority as revealed and as Holy Scripture, that is, if one does not want to turn the biblical God into a God of oppression. Such a critical evaluation of biblical texts cannot locate inspiration in the text, not even in its "surplus" or polyvalence of meaning. Instead it must place it in biblical people and their contexts. As J. Barr has proposed, inspiration must be understood "as the inspiration of the people from whom the books came."[8] Inspiration cannot be located in texts or books, but its process is found in the believing community and in its history as the people of God. The feminist liberation theologian would qualify this statement by insisting that the process of inspiration must be seen as the inspiration of those people, especially of poor women, struggling for human dignity and liberation from oppressive powers, because they believe in the biblical God of creation and salvation despite all experiences to the contrary.

Therefore, feminist biblical hermeneutics . . . cannot respect the "rights" of the androcentric *text* and seek for a "fusion" with the patriarchal-biblical horizon. Its goal is not "identification with" or "consent to" the androcentric text or process of biblical reception but faithful remembrance of and critical solidarity with women in biblical history. In other words, it does not focus on *text* as revelatory word but on the story of women as the people of God. Its "canonical" hermeneutics insists that the people of God are not restricted to Israel and the Christian church but include all of humanity, because the Bible begins with creation and ends with the vision of a new creation.[9]

---

5. Cf. for example, E. Tamez, *Bible of the Oppressed* (Maryknoll, N.Y.: Orbis Books, 1982), who has very little to say about women.

6. This was underlined by both B. Birch's and T. Ogletree's response to my "Discipleship and Patriarchy," pp. 173–89.

7. For a different position emphasizing the prophetic traditions in the Bible as such a liberating tradition and principle see Rosemary Radford Ruether, "The Feminist Critique in Religious Studies," *Soundings* 64 (1981): 388–402, and "Feminism and Patriarchal Religion: Principles of Ideological Critique of the Bible," *JSOT* 22 (1982): 54–66.

8 James Barr, "The Bible as a Document of Believing Communities," in Hans Dieter Betz (ed.), *The Bible as a Document of the University* (Chico, Calif.: Scholars Press, 1981), p. 38.

9 This seems to me the most of what one can say about the "overall theological coherence" of the canon. See the review by B.W. Anderson of B.S. Childs, *Introduction to the Old Testament as Scripture* in *Theology Today* 37 (1980): 100–108; for a contrasting evaluation of B.S. Childs and J. Sanders see E.E. Lemicio, The Gospels and Canonical Criticism," *BTB* 11 (1981): 114–22, and J. Sanders' response, pp. 122–24. For an integration of "canonical" criticism into liberation theology see L.J. White, "Biblical Theologians and Theologies of Liberation: Part I, Canon-Supporting Framework," *BTB* 22 (1981): 35–40, and "Part II, Midrash Applies Text to Context," ibid.: 98–103.

2.10 'GOD AS MOTHER'

Sallie McFague

From *Models of God: Theology for an Ecological Nuclear Age*, McFague, S., London, SCM Press, 1987, pp. 97–100.

"Father-Mother God, loving me, guard me while I sleep, guide my little feet up to thee." This prayer, which theologian Herbert Richardson reports reciting as a child, impressed upon his young mind that if God is both father and mother, then God is not like anything else he knew.[1] The point is worth emphasizing, for as we begin our experiment with the model of God as mother, we recall that metaphors of God, far from reducing God to what we understand, underscore by their multiplicity and lack of fit the unknowability of God. This crucial characteristic of metaphorical language for God is lost, however, when only one important personal relationship, that of father and child, is allowed to serve as a grid for speaking of the God-human relationship. In fact, by excluding other relationships as metaphors, the model of father becomes idolatrous, for it comes to be viewed as a description of God.[2] Hence, one reason for including maternal language in a tradition where paternal language has prevailed is to underscore what the negative theological tradition has always insisted: God is unlike as well as like our metaphors.[3]

But there are additional reasons for using female as well as male metaphors of God. The most obvious is that since human beings are male and female, if we seek to imagine God "in the image of God" – that is, ourselves – both male and female metaphors should be employed. Because the point is self-evident, one wonders what all the fuss is about when the suggestion is made that God be imaged in female terms or addressed as "she." But fuss there is, and it is best to address it head on. For whatever reasons, Western thought – certainly Western theology – has been deeply infected by both a fear of and a fascination with female sexuality.[4] The most basic reason, it appears, for uneasiness with female metaphors for God is that unlike

---

1. Elizabeth Clark and Herbert Richardson, eds., *Women and Religion* (New York: Harper & Row, 1977), 164–65.

2. For a fuller treatment of this point, see my book *Metaphorical Theology: Models of God in Religious Language* (Philadelphia: Fortress Press, 1982; 2d printing with new preface, 1985), chap. 5.

3. Virginia Mollenkott makes this point eloquently, when after quoting Schubert Ogden's statement that God is "the most truly absolute Thou any mind can conceive," continues, "This *Thou*, this Absolute Relatedness, may be referred to as He, She, or It because this *Thou* relates to everyone and everything. . . . This Thou is a jealous God . . . jealous . . .that He/She/It be recognized everywhere in everyone and everything . . ." (*The Divine Feminine: The Biblical Imagery of God as Female* [New York: Crossroad, 1983], 113–14).

4. For different but complementary views on this point, see Carolyn Merchant, *The Death of Nature: Women, Ecology, and the Scientific Revolution* (New York: Harper & Row, 1980); Brian Easlea, *Fathering the Unthinkable: Masculinity, Scientists, and the Nuclear Arms Race* (London: Pluto, 1983); Rosemary Radford Ruether, *Sexism and God-Talk: Toward a Feminist Theology* (Boston: Beacon Press, 1983), chap. 2; Mary Daly, *Gyn/Ecology: The Metaphysics of Radical Feminism* (Boston: Beacon Press, 1978); and Rita M. Gross, "Hindu Female Deities as a Resource for the Contemporary Rediscovery of the Goddess," in *The Book of the Goddess Past and Present: An Introduction to Her Religion*, ed. Carl Olson (New York: Crossroad, 1983).

the male metaphors, whose sexual character is cloaked, the female metaphors seem blatantly sexual and involve the sexuality most feared: female sexuality.

There are at least three points being made here that need to be addressed briefly. First, to speak of God as father has obvious sexual connotations (as is evident in the Trinitarian language of the "generation" of the Son from the Father), but given the Hebraic tradition's interest in distinguishing itself from Goddess religions and fertility cults, as well as the early and deep ascetic strain in Christianity, the sexual implications of paternal imagery were masked. This leads into the second point: the blatant sexuality of female metaphors. It is by introducing female metaphors for God that the sexuality of both male and female metaphors becomes evident, though it appears, because we are familiar with the male metaphors, that only the female ones are sexual. In other words, the shock of unconventional language for God – female imagery – jolts us into awareness that there is no gender-neutral language if we take ourselves as the model for talk about God, because we are sexual beings. Hence, traditional language for God is not nonsexual; on the contrary, it is male. The third point, the fear and fascination associated with female sexuality, is related to the first two points: female sexuality would not, I suspect, be so feared or found so fascinating if sexuality, both female and male, had been accepted in a more open and healthy manner both as a human good and as an important way to model the activity of God in relation to the world.[5] It is treated in this fashion in many religions, and Western thought, including Christianity, with its warped view of female sexuality as well as its reluctance to imagine God in female terms, has much to learn from these sources.

The first thing to insist upon, then, is that in spite of Western and Christian uneasiness over female imagery for God, since the *imago dei* is twofold, female as well as male, both kinds of metaphors ought to be used.[6] The question then arises how God should be imaged as both female and male (as well as, of course, beyond both). I would make two points here: first, God should be imagined in female, not feminine, terms, and second, the female metaphors should be inclusive of but not limited to maternal ones. On the first point: the distinction between "female" and "feminine" is important, for the first refers to gender while the second refers to qualities conventionally associated with women.[7] The problem with introducing a feminine

---

5. One example of the danger inherent in twisted thinking concerning sexuality surfaces in the birth metaphors used by scientists involved in creating the atomic bomb. Brian Easlea in his book *Fathering the Unthinkable* has collected these materials, and I quote a few. Kenneth Bainbridge, the physicist in charge of the Trinity test: "The bomb was [Robert Oppenheimer's] baby" (p. 95). General Farrell: "Atomic fission was almost full grown at birth" (p. 96). Henry Stimson received the following telegram after the Trinity test: "Doctor has just returned most enthusiastic and confident that the little boy is as husky as his big brother" (p. 96), which meant that the plutonium bomb was as good as the uranium. William Laurence, a reporter at the Trinity test: "The big boom came about a hundred seconds after the great flash – the first cry of a new-born world" (p. 96). Easlea traces the history of science as the conquest of female nature – the taming of Mother Nature – back to Francis Bacon and his call to men to unite and, "turning with united forces against the Nature of things, to storm and occupy her castles and strongholds" (quoted pp. 20–21).

6. Janet Morley, a British theologian, in commenting on the fact that many natural images are used as metaphors of God in the church's hymns (light, sun, sea, rocks, castles, etc.), whereas God is seldom if every spoken of as mother, wife, sister, midwife, etc., concludes, "Non-human objects may symbolize God's glory, but, by their almost universal absence in this respect, must we conclude that human women cannot?" ("In God's Image?" *Cross Currents* 32 [1982]: 315).

7. Many feminists are concerned to make this distinction. See, e.g., Ruether's rejection of "masculine" and "feminine" characteristics: there is, she says, no evidence that women are caring and nurturing whereas men are not. "We need to affirm…that all humans possess a full and equivalent human nature and personhood, *as male and female*" (*Sexism and God Talk*, 111).

dimension of God is that it invariably ends with identifying as female those qualities that society has called feminine. Thus, the feminine side of God is taken to comprise the tender, nurturing, passive, healing aspects of divine activity, whereas those activities in which God creates, redeems, establishes peace, administers justice, and so on, are called masculine. Such a division, in extending to the godhead the stereotypes we create in human society, further crystallizes and sanctifies them.[8]

But to image God in female personal terms, as she as well as he, is a very different matter. It is not, at the outset, to identify God with any particular set of characteristics, unless one is slipping in feminine stereotypes under the cover of simple gender appellation. All that has been done is to use a personal pronoun for deity and this, we have insisted, is not only our tradition, the tradition of addressing God as Thou, but desirable and necessary in our time. Since all agents are either male or female, either pronoun and both pronouns can and should be used. If we use only the male pronoun, we fall into idolatry, forgetting that God is beyond male and female – a fact that the use of both pronouns brings home to us as the opening prayer to "Father-Mother God" illustrated. If we refuse to use any pronouns for God, we court the possibility of concealing androcentric assumptions behind abstractions.[9] If we are, then, to be concrete, personal, and nonidolatrous in our talk about God, we have no alternative but to speak of God in female as well as male terms, to use "she" as well as "he," and to realize that in so doing we are not attributing passive and nurturing qualities to God any more than we are attributing active and powerful qualities. Or to say it differently, we are attributing human qualities: we are imaging God on analogy with human beings, and so far that is all that we are doing: God is she and he and neither.

We come now, however, to the second point: female metaphors for God should be inclusive of but not limited to maternal ones. One of the important insights emerging from

---

8. There are two ways that the feminine dimension of God can be imagined, as Elizabeth A. Johnson suggests in her excellent article "The Incomprehensibility of God and the Image of God Male and Female," *Theological Studies* 45 (1984): 441–65. Feminine *qualities* can be given to God so that God the father displays motherly qualities and, hence, God becomes a more holistic "person," having integrated the feminine side into a basically male character. But as Johnson points out, "The female can never appear as an icon of God in all divine fullness equivalent to the male" (p. 456). Or a feminine *aspect* can be attributed to God, and this is usually the Holy Spirit. Here, not only do masculine and feminine stereotypes emerge, but as Johnson notes, given the historically indefinite character of the Holy Spirit, we end "with two males and an amorphous third" (p. 458). I would add that even the attempt by process theologians to introduce the feminine dimension of God as God's consequent nature falls into stereotyping, since the qualities associated with God's consequent nature are receptivity, empathy, suffering, and preservation. Two unfortunate examples will illustrate Johnson's main points. Jürgen Moltmann claims that God "is the *motherly Father* of his *only-born Son*, and at the same time *the fatherly Father* of his *only-begotten Son*.... The Son was...made...from the womb of the Father" ("The Motherly Father: Is Trinitarian Patripassionism Replacing Theological Patriarchalism?" in *God As Father?* Ed. Johannes-Baptist Metz and Edward Schillebeeckx [New York: Seabury Press, 1981], 53). Nonetheless, Moltmann sees this use of feminine terminology only as a way to limit the use of masculine terminology; anything more, he says, would be in danger of "changing over to matriarchal conceptions" (ibid.). Donald L. Gelpi in his book *The Divine Mother: A Trinitarian Theology of the Holy Spirit* (Washington, D.C.: Univ. Press of America, 1984) elevates all positive feminine qualities to the Divine Mother as Jungian transformational categories (with none of the negative qualities), thus providing an excellent example of the "eternal feminine" sanctified by the Deity – with the dark side repressed.

9. Rosemary Radford Ruether makes this point tellingly with the comment that those unwilling to give up the male monopoly on God-language often reply to objectors, "God is not male. He is Spirit" (*Sexism and God-Talk*, 67). For the most part, I have avoided using personal pronouns for God in this essay – except for the male pronoun in relationship to the monarchical and patriarchal models – until the issue could be clarified. Henceforth, I shall use both male and female pronouns.

current research into Goddess religions is that in these traditions all divine activities are imaged by both male and female deities: both Ishtar and Horus, for instance, engage in creating, governing, nurturing, and redeeming.[10] In other words, neither masculine nor feminine characteristics are attributed to deities; rather, divine activities are attributed equivalently to male and female agents. Both male and female deities operate in both the private and the public arena; both engage in activities of power as well as care.[11] The Hebraic-Christian tradition does not, of course, worship multiple deities, but this fact in no way lessens the point being made – that if we accept the reasoning behind addressing God as "she" as well as "he," we should do so in a fashion that does not stereotype divine activities. This is not a new or radical notion in Christianity, despite the fact that the only female "component" in the tradition has been the quasi-divine figure of Mary, whose characteristics have certainly been stereotypically feminine.[12] But an earlier hypostasis of God – Sophia, or Wisdom, in Hebrew religion – was identified not only with the earth and sexuality but also with order and justice.[13] Moreover, medieval piety freely attributed a wide range of activities to God, some in female form, some in male, some in both.[14]

What, then, about the model of God as mother? Is that not stereotyping by suggesting as a major model for God *one* activity of females and the one most closely identified as stereotypically feminine, namely, giving birth to and raising children? My answer is twofold. First, although this particular essay will focus on God as mother in order to balance and provide a new context for interpreting God as father, other divine activities will also be imaged in female form, especially those concerned with creation and justice. Second, although mothering is a female activity, it is not feminine; that is, to give birth to and to feed the young is simply what females do – some may do it in a so-called feminine fashion, and others may not. What is more important for our purposes is that the symbolic material from the birthing and feeding process is very rich and for the most part has been neglected in establishment Christianity. It is also, . . . powerful imagery for expressing the interrelatedness of all life, which is a central component in both a holistic sensibility and an understanding of Christian faith as an inclusive vision of fulfillment.

---

10. For a sampling of this literature, see Judith Ochshorn, *The Female Experience and the Nature of the Divine* (Bloomington: Indiana Univ. Press, 1981); Carol Christ, "Symbols of Goddess and God in Feminist Theology," in *The Book of the Goddess*, ed. Olson; Gross, "Hindu Female Deities"; and Ruether, *Sexism and God-Talk*, chap. 2.

11. This point is made by many feminist theologians and is succinctly summarized by Johnson: "...the goddess is not the expression of the feminine dimension of the divine, but the expression of the fullness of divine power and care shown in a female image" (The Incomprehensibility of God," 461).

12. See, e.g., Rosemary Radford Ruether, *Mary – The Feminine Face of the Church* (Philadelphia: Westminster Press, 1977), and E. Ann Matter, "The Virgin Mary: A Goddess?" in *The Book of the Goddess*, ed. Olson.

13. In Elisabeth Schüssler Fiorenza's study of Sophia in Israelite religion, Sophia is in a symbiotic relationship to God with a variety of appellations (sister, wife, mother, beloved, teacher) and tasks (leading, preaching, teaching, creating, and so on). See *In Memory of Her: A Feminist Theological Reconstruction of Christian Origins* (New York: Crossroad, 1983), 130ff.

14. See Eleanor McLaughlin, "'Christ My Mother': Feminine Naming and Metaphor in Medieval Spirituality," *St. Luke's Journal of Theology* 18 (1975): 356–86; and Caroline Walker Bynum, *Jesus as Mother: Studies in the Spirituality of the High Middle Ages* (Berkeley and Los Angeles: Univ. of California Press, 1982).

2.11 'A BUDDHIST LIFE IS A GREEN LIFE'

Chris Pauling

From *Golden Drum*, February–April 1990, Windhorse Publications, pp. 4–7.

Buddhism has something fundamental to say on the environmental issue, because it addresses the basic human attitudes that lie at the heart of our planet's problems.

The root cause of our problems – personal *and* planetary – is our view of ourselves as separate, isolated individuals, walled off from the universe around us. This view leads us to see selfishness as necessary. It leads us to put narrow limits on what we see as our responsibility. And it leads us to live a life that is out of harmony with the universe, so that *we* suffer, and the world suffers with us.

But the Dharma tells us that this view of ourselves is mistaken. Our idea of separate selfhood is a delusion, and a profoundly damaging delusion. We are all part of each other and the world we inhabit, and whenever we harm another being or injure our environment, what we are hurting is ourselves.

Buddhism exists to help us break out of the prison of isolated selfhood and wake up to the true nature of reality – to help us become Enlightened. The Enlightened person is fully aware that everything in the universe is interconnected, not just as an intellectual concept, but in every fibre of their being. Such a person will inevitably live in harmony with the world around them. They will no more willingly hurt another being or desecrate the environment – no matter how far away the damage takes place – than they will willingly hurt themselves. In a world of Enlightened beings there could be no environmental problem.

This is not to suggest that the answer to the world's problems is for everyone to become Enlightened – at least not immediately. Our problems are urgent, and something more practical is needed in the short term.

But Buddhism is above all a practical tradition. It recognizes that for most of us the state of 'Final, Unsurpassed Enlightenment' is still a long way off. And it offers us ways in which we can invite some degree of Enlightenment to take root in the midst of our delusion, gradually altering the way we think and feel, and – more important from a purely practical point of view – immediately changing the way we act, so that the effect we have on the world around us becomes more like that of an Enlightened being.

In the short term Buddhism helps us live a more harmonious life in two main ways. Firstly, it offers us a vision of what it means to be a human being that is very different from the one our society trains us to accept – a vision in which life is a spiritual quest rather than a fight for survival or material goods. Simply changing our image of ourselves in this way does not add up to Enlightenment, but it helps. We may not be able to transcend our egotism in one bound, but we can quite quickly refine our image of ourselves so that we judge our richness by what we *are* rather than by what we own or consume.

And this change is vital. The only real answer to our planet's problems is for all of us – all those who enjoy the affluent life-style of mainstream culture in the West – to own and consume much, much less. Our most important environmental problems are the result of the sheer level of economic activity in our societies. The greenhouse effect, for example, is mainly due to CO_2 from the burning of coal, oil, and gas – the fuels that power our economic machine. We have no large-scale alternatives to these fuels except nuclear power, which is not an option many people will relish. The prosperity that we largely take for granted is based on making major changes to the composition of our planet's atmosphere, and hoping that future generations will find some way of dealing with the problems we cause.

But as long as we see ourselves as essentially material beings, judging the richness of our lives by our material 'standard of living', we will never willingly give up even a little of this prosperity. Before we can persuade people to let go of the myth of economic growth as the way to human happiness we need to put something in its place – something spiritual rather than physical.

As well as giving us a vision of what it means to be a human being that makes a return to a sustainable life-style possible, Buddhism also offers a set of practical guide-lines to help us live in concord with our surroundings. As a way of moving towards Enlightenment the Dharma encourages us to behave *as though we were already* Enlightened – as though we were already fully aware of the interconnectedness of all things in the universe, down to the very depths of our being. To help us to do this provides a set of norms which describe the way an Enlightened being would behave, which Buddhists undertake to observe as training principles. We may not become fully Enlightened tomorrow, next week, or next year. But if we make the decision to work towards Enlightenment by living according to the Buddhist precepts, our behaviour will immediately become more like that of an Enlightened person, and our life will become more in harmony with our environment.

The first – and most important – of these training principles is to refrain from harming other living beings, and instead to engage in acts of loving-kindness. This precept is basic to the Buddhist approach to life, and it is also basic to any solution to the world's environmental problems. It encourages us to soften our usual antagonism towards what is foreign to ourselves, and instead develop an attitude of caring, nurturing concern for the world around us.

Traditionally the Dharma encourages us to cultivate this attitude mainly towards other sentient beings – human and animal – starting with those near to us, then extending our goodwill to the global and even cosmic plane. But loving-kindness does not confine itself even to what we normally recognize as sentient beings. It is a basic attitude of heart which expresses itself in our relationship with *everything* that lies outside the boundaries of the self. We express it by caring for and nurturing our friends, our colleagues, our garden, our local countryside, its wildlife – and our planet. It is an attitude that springs from a deep reverence for the entire universe, from realizing that the world we live in is an astonishing miracle, and from seeing every part of it as holy.

2.12 'A ZONE OF PEACE'

The 14th Dalai Lama Tensin Gyatso

Nobel Peace Prize lecture, The 14th Dalai Lama Tensin Gyatso, Oslo 1989 in *Buddhism and Ecology*, Batchelor, M. and Brown, K. (eds), Cassell, 1992, pp. 110–14. Reproduced by permission of The Continuum International Publishing Group Limited.

Thinking over what I might say today, I decided to share with you some of my thoughts concerning the common problems all of us face as members of the human family. Because we all share this small planet earth, we have to learn to live in harmony and peace with each other and with nature. That is not just a dream, but a necessity. We are dependent on each other in so many ways that we can no longer live in isolated communities and ignore what is happening outside those communities. We need to help each other when we have difficulties, and we must share the good fortune that we enjoy. I speak to you as just another human being, as a simple monk. If you find what I say useful, then I hope you will try to practise it.

The realization that we are all basically the same human beings, who seek happiness and try to avoid suffering, is very helpful in developing a sense of brotherhood and sisterhood – a warm feeling of love and compassion for others. This, in turn, is essential if we are to survive in this ever-shrinking world we live in. For if we each selfishly pursue only what we believe to be in our own interest, without caring about the needs of others, we not only may end up harming others but also ourselves. This fact has become very clear during the course of this century. We know that to wage a nuclear war today, for example, would be a form of suicide; that to pollute the air or the oceans, in order to achieve some short-term benefit, would be to destroy the very basis for our survival. As individuals and nations are becoming increasingly interdependent we have no other choice than to develop what I call a sense of universal responsibility.

Today, we are truly a global family. What happens in one part of the world may affect us all. This, of course, is not only true of the negative things that happen, but is equally valid for the positive developments. We not only know what happens elsewhere, thanks to the extraordinary modern communications technology, we are also directly affected by events that occur far away. We feel a sense of sadness when children are starving in Eastern Africa. Similarly, we feel a sense of joy when a family is reunited after decades of separation by the Berlin Wall. Our crops and livestock are contaminated and our health and livelihood threatened when a nuclear accident happens miles away in another country. Our own security is enhanced when peace breaks out between warring parties in other continents.

But war or peace; the destruction or the protection of nature; the violation or promotion of human rights and democratic freedoms; poverty or material well-being; the lack of moral and spiritual values or their existence and development; and the breakdown or development of human understanding, are not isolated phenomena that can be analysed and tackled independently of one another. In fact, they are very much interrelated at all levels and need to be approached with that understanding.

Peace, in the sense of the absence of war, is of little value to someone who is dying of hunger or cold. It will not remove the pain of torture inflicted on a prisoner of conscience. It does not comfort those who have lost their loved ones in floods caused by senseless deforestation in a neighbouring country. Peace can only last where human rights are respected, where the people are fed, and where individuals and nations are free. True peace with ourselves and with the world around us can only be achieved through the development of mental peace. The other phenomena mentioned above are similarly interrelated. Thus, for example, we see that a clean environment is not sufficient to ensure human happiness.

Material progress is of course important for human advancement. In Tibet, we paid much too little attention to technological and economic development, and today we realize that this was a mistake. At the same time, material development without spiritual development can also cause serious problems. In some countries too much attention is paid to external things and very little importance is given to inner development. I believe both are important and must be developed side by side so as to achieve a good balance between them. Tibetans are always described by foreign visitors as being a happy, jovial people. This is part of our national character, formed by cultural and religious values that stress the importance of mental peace through the generation of love and kindness to all other living sentient beings, both human and animal. Inner peace is the key: if you have inner peace, the external problems do not affect your deep sense of peace and tranquillity. In that state of mind you can deal with situations with calmness and reason, while keeping your inner happiness. That is very important. Without this inner peace, no matter how comfortable your life is materially, you may still be worried, disturbed or unhappy because of circumstances.

Clearly, it is of great importance, therefore, to understand the interrelationship among these and other phenomena, and to approach and attempt to solve problems in a balanced way that takes these different aspects into consideration. Of course it is not easy. But it is of little benefit to try to solve one problem if doing so creates an equally serious new one. So really we have no alternative: we must develop a sense of universal responsibility not only in the geographic sense, but also in respect to the different issues that confront our planet.

Responsibility does not only lie with the leaders of our countries or with those who have been appointed or elected to do a particular job. It lies with each of us individually. Peace, for example, starts within each one of us. When we have inner peace, we can be at peace with those around us. When our community is in a state of peace, it can share that peace with neighbouring communities, and so on. When we feel love and kindness towards others, it not only makes others feel loved and cared for, but it helps us also to develop inner happiness and peace. And there are ways in which we can consciously work to develop feelings of love and kindness. For some of us, the most effective way to do so is through religious practice. For others it may be non-religious practices. What is important is that we each make a sincere effort to take seriously our responsibility for each other and for the natural environment.

It is my dream that the entire Tibetan plateau should become a free refuge where humanity and nature can live in peace and in harmonious balance. It would be a place where people from all over the world could come to see the true meaning of peace within themselves, away from the tensions and pressures of much of the rest of the world. Tibet could indeed become a creative centre for the promotion and development of peace.

The following are key elements of the proposed Zone of Ahimsa (Non-Violence):

- the entire Tibetan plateau would be demilitarized;
- the manufacture, testing and stockpiling of nuclear weapons and other armaments on the Tibetan plateau would be prohibited;
- the Tibetan plateau would be transformed into the world's largest natural park or biosphere. Strict laws would be enforced to protect wildlife and plant life; the exploitation of natural resources would be carefully regulated so as not to damage relevant ecosystems; and a policy of sustainable development would be adopted in populated areas;
- the manufacture and use of nuclear power and other technologies which produce hazardous waste would be prohibited;
- national resources and policy would be directed towards the active promotion of peace and environmental protection. Organizations dedicated to the furtherance of peace and to the protection of all forms of life would find a hospitable home in Tibet;
- the establishment of international and regional organizations for the promotion and protection of human rights would be encouraged in Tibet.

Tibet's height and size (the size of the European Community), as well as its unique history and profound spiritual heritage make it ideally suited to fulfil the role of a sanctuary of peace in the strategic heart of Asia. It would also be in keeping with Tibet's historical role as a peaceful Buddhist nation and buffer region separating the Asian continent's great and often rival powers.

Tibet would also not be the first area to be turned into a natural preserve or biosphere. Many parks have been created throughout the world. Some very strategic areas have been turned into natural 'peace parks'. Two examples are the La Amistad park, on the Costa Rica-Panama border and the Si A Paz project on the Costa Rica-Nicaragua border.

When I visited Costa Rica earlier this year, I saw how a country can develop successfully without an army, to become a stable democracy committed to peace and the protection of the natural environment. This confirmed my belief that my vision of Tibet in the future is a realistic plan, not merely a dream.

In conclusion, let me share with you a short prayer which gives me great inspiration and determination.

> For as long as space endures
> And for as long as living beings remain
> Until then may I, too, abide
> To dispel the misery of the world.

2.13 'SAVING FORESTS SO THERE CAN BE FOREST MONKS'

Ajahan Pasanno and Nick Scott

From *Forest Sangha Newsletter*, 2001, http://www.abm.ndirect.co.uk/fsn/35/forests

Nick: Ajahn, you have been a forest monk in Thailand for over twenty years now. In that time what have you seen happening to the forests?

Ajahn Pasanno: Basically, I've told Thai people that there just isn't going to be any more forest in Thailand if they don't act soon, the devastation is so complete. About fifty years ago around 70% of the country used to be covered in forest and now the government estimate it to be 20%; in reality it's more like 5% or 8%.

The big logging companies are partially responsible, but that's actually a small part of it. Logging is banned nowadays. And even when they used to come in, they only wanted the big trees and then they were out. What happened was that they opened up areas of forest, and after they left, people came in. Round where we are they cut the smaller timber for furniture – you can get that out without being seen – and a lot goes as charcoal. The government allows people to sell two sacks of charcoal, so everyone has two sacks at the front of their house for sale.

N: What about National Parks?

AP: The area of the country that has been made into National Park is a much higher percentage than, say, America. But the trouble is they're not protected. One of our monasteries is in a new National Park. The director of the park has got a budget for just one civil servant to act as his assistant – and one gun for his protection. Luckily, where this branch monastery is, the director is a young guy, really honest and dedicated. But many of the others are crooked.

Like the park at one of our other branch monasteries – the monastery protects not only its own area but the whole forest around it. But in order for the director of the park to sign the piece of paper which would allow that project to be submitted to the forestry department, it cost the monastery five hundred pounds – which goes to him personally! You'd think he'd be keen to help. So if he's expecting bribes from the monastery to protect his forest, you can think what else he must be doing, you can imagine the scams.

N: Ajahn, in that case you have got a small monastery with a large amount of forest being protected. How does that work?

AP: The dynamic, particularly in the N.E. of Thailand, but generally throughout the country, is that people respect monks – especially the disciples of Ajahn Chah. And if you respect people, you respect the place where they are at. So if the monks ask people not to encroach on an area, they respect that – generally.

There are several hundred monasteries in Ajahn Chah's tradition and they're all in forest – for some it's only a small area, but whatever, the forest is respected by the people and left alone. At Wat Pah Nanachat, before we finally got a wall around the monastery this last year, the villagers used to keep an eye out for fires during the dry season. Sometimes they would notice fires coming near the monastery. Many trees had been planted, so if a fire swept through there, three, four, five years of work would be wiped out. An alarm would be sent out, the villagers would come and put it out, and I would only find out about it later. They were really watching out for the monastery.

But you have to be careful in some places. When we first started one monastery I told the monks not to bother the people who were coming to poach logs from the forest; it was too dangerous to obstruct them. It was being done by the local village headman, the representative of the government. He was supposed to be looking after such things, but he was cutting down the forest right round the spring which was our water source. So I suggested to him that that area should be left undisturbed for future generations. He was very polite, there was nothing aggressive about him, "I can't do that", he said, "I've already paid the police, I've already paid the forestry. I'll lose a lot of money".

N: Am I right in thinking that other abbots have got into real problems with conservation projects?
AP: Oh sure. You have to be careful. There was a large area of good forest along the Cambodian border and the military and local merchants were trying to get it all. It was a big scam. They called it a 'reforestation project' – but what they were doing was cutting the native trees to plant Eucalyptus, so they were making money both ways! However, the abbot there was getting in the way, so he had grenades thrown at his monastery, the roof of his hut was splattered with M16 shots. He was harassed a lot. He ended up being taken to court – that's a big thing taking a monk to court in Thailand – and he finally ending up disrobing.

We started Nature Care when we set up a retreat place in Poo Jom Gom – that's the monastery in the National Park. I specifically chose that area because it is very rocky and the forest isn't very nice – we didn't want the hassle.

N: You deliberately chose it because there wasn't good forest left?
AP: Yes, it can be pretty distracting when you're practising, and then there's the struggle with the system to try to save it. But then when you see how things are – you feel that with a little bit of input, it's not that difficult to protect what's left.

If the people in the area have a different way to make a living, then they won't have to destroy the forest. They need to learn about the forest. In order to have a sustainable livelihood they have to live harmoniously with the environment. They also have to feel in control of the situation, and not just pawns in someone else's game.

One of the things we focus on most is getting people involved from different backgrounds. Previously there was no communication there. We're also providing a bridge between the administration, which means well, and the villagers. There can be so much corruption. For example, there was this project making toilets. It was a good project. In the local village there were 120 families and only 16 toilets.

N: How many televisions?
AP: About 40! So it was a great project, and the government had the budget for it. It started

off with a roof and bricks to build the cubicle, a tank to hold waste and a toilet. But by the time it got to the village, you've got the toilet bowl, eight bricks and a bag of cement! So the villagers don't take the government very seriously.

N: So what kind of practical things have you been doing?

AP: Nature Care has been focusing on providing alternative means of livelihood. You look at what they have already and consider how to use it more effectively. For example, they grow a lot of bananas. They take them to the market and they get beat every time by the merchants. They don't have the confidence to bargain. And, of course, if they can't sell them, they can't take them home again because they would go bad. So we help them to change what they're doing. Rather than taking the fresh bananas to the market, they make different products out of them; dried bananas, sweets, roasted bananas. Things that they can keep and sell for more. They can store them and wait till they get a good price. So they get more from their crop.

Also they grow cotton, but it's always been sold raw. So we have given training in weaving and dyeing using natural dyes. And there's a good market for that.

N: Are you doing anything more direct for the forest?

AP: One of the ways of protecting forest is to be involved in education, so that people can see the benefits of the forest. This involves stimulating interest, getting people keen to help. It's quite obvious to the people that there is a big difference in their lives and the quality of life around them, compared to 20, 30 years ago. In that area, you could walk around and be walking in shade. But now a lot of it has been cut for tapioca plantations. Most of it was just cut and burnt – it wasn't logged at all – just to plant cash crops. But then the soils degraded very quickly, the cash crops don't grow and they find that their livelihoods are threatened. They used to rely on the forest. Before cash crops they didn't actually use cash that much, because everything they needed they got from the forest. They were very self-sufficient.

N: Yes, but how do you go about improving things?

AP: Things like taking them out to see other projects – both places where there are natural forests well preserved and they can see the benefits for the people living nearby; and also seeing places that have been destroyed and where they are starting to work replanting and protecting, so that they can see what other people are doing. That's very successful. It stimulates many ideas and it gets them thinking. It inspires them to realize, "We can do that".

Also working with children, getting children involved is important. The children are at the heart of the family structure in Thailand, very well loved. If you get the children involved you tend to pull the parents in as well. So we've been putting on plays and skits in schools, taking children out into the forest, having fun, getting the children to love the forest.

In Thailand, the words that they use for forest are usually words that imply dangerous, messy, tangled – language which has a negative connotation. Also, somebody who goes out, clears the forest, makes fields and builds houses for themselves is someone who used to be praised. So that conditioning is there. The language and the way we talk about something is very ingrained, so now you're having to work against those values. It's going to take a while.

You have to see what's meaningful to them rather than have all these plans. Their needs have to be understood. Also, as a monk, you have contact with all levels of society, so that if

liaison

the villagers have a need or desire or hope, you have the opportunity to bring it to the attention of other people from different strands of society who could give them a hand. That does happen a lot – the monks creating a bridge between people.

In Thailand, monks are regarded as leaders in society. What we're doing isn't new. It is a function that monks have played traditionally and will continue to do so. You notice at Ajahn Chah's funeral, when the King and Queen came they bowed to the remains of Ajahn Chah – just the same as ordinary people who came to pay their respects. You have got to be able to preserve the purity of the life to deserve that – but when you manage it, it's very powerful.

Monks are able to draw in different people and provide a harmonious focal point for them to work together; they act as a catalyst. Say, like myself for instance, it's not that I'm all that directly involved, I'm more in the background providing advice, support and encouraging them.

N: Is anyone employed by Nature Care?

AP: Yes. They started with volunteers, people who were interested. At first it was manageable for the volunteers, because in the beginning they weren't doing all that much. But as they got involved in more projects, got more interest from the villagers and made more contacts, it needed more continuity, so that we have asked four of the volunteers to work full time.

N: So how is it funded?

AP: Well, we've got very good at scrounging and everything is done very cheaply – we've one motorcycle between everybody. So far we've got by on donations from a few individuals and some small grants from the Canadian and Belgian embassies. The salaries for the workers are being paid at present with some money offered for my travel to come to do this retreat in England.

N: Would you say, Ajahn, that by looking after the forest that you are looking out for the Sangha and future monks?

AP: Yes, definitely. Because if we don't have forests we're not forest monks! We're definitely protecting areas where monks can practise within a forest setting, because you need to have a stable and quiet environment for practice. If monasteries are set up in areas which are being encroached upon by settlements, or in degraded areas where there is no longer water or shelter, these are not conducive places to practise in. So definitely, I'm looking out for myself.

Our tradition has always been connected to the forest. I can remember walking with Ajahn Chah around the monasteries when he would point out different trees and plants, telling us their uses for medicine or food or their special characteristics. It was always interesting being with him. The old forest monks really relied on the forest for everything.

N: Through my work in conservation, I've come to realize that it is this kind of small scale effort that you are making which is important, rather than trying to 'save the world'.

AP: Yes, an example needs to be set. The project demonstrates what can be done with a small number of people, a small amount of effort. But if it's done in the right way it can be effective. I try to keep it very practical, keep it centred on a couple of issues, which actually starts to expand into others, but it provides something for others to consider. So we're planting seeds that will get more people involved. If you push people into a corner, they'll defend themselves. You have to give people the space to back out. One of the problems oftentimes is the kind of confrontation you get into between the people who are destroying the forests, the vested interest, the civil service, people who want to preserve it. If you're not including everybody in the process, the forest just isn't worth it to protect. Everyone has to be included, seeing that this is something which belongs to all of us, that we also have a part to play in it. In the Theravada tradition there's always been a very close relationship between the society you live in and the monastic community. In Thailand, as a monk, I don't have the amount of free time or space that you'd expect. You're actually so much a part of the community that the monastery is an open space. That's why I had to come to England to do this one year retreat.

[handwritten annotations:]

it belongs to no one
it belongs to everybody

Links to Church in Poland & E Germany
(its only one for people to meet + plan)

this is helping local community to
freedom also — to live in harmony
self sustaining manner.

Part III:

Perspectives on Civil Religion

The extracts in this section provide sources relevant to the study of aspects of the phenomenon of 'civil religion', a concept central to much contemporary debate within religious studies. The extracts here are divided broadly, into three groups. First come two lengthy extracts and one shorter extract that discuss the concept of civil religion in the context of modern America. Of these, 3.1 is taken from an influential article on civil religion in America, which has subsequently proved key to the discussion of the concept of civil religion in general, while 3.2 discusses the concept of civil religion in relation to the Southern experience of defeat in the American civil war. Reading 3.3 is a critique of the concept of American civil religion from a Native American perspective. A brief reading about war memorials, 3.4, provides a transition to a larger group of shorter extracts, all of which examine or describe the experience of visiting war memorials and the various emotions and actions to which this activity is apt to give rise (3.5–3.11). The final group of extracts provides four sources that are relevant to the application of the concept of civil religion to the history, culture and experience of modern Siena. Readings 3.12 and 3.13 translate key texts relating to the rededication of the city of Siena to the Virgin Mary – its traditional patron and protectess – in 1944, at a time when Siena was threatened with destruction during the Second World War. The last two readings (3.14–3.15) are taken from influential studies of the traditional Sienese festival of the Palio.

3.1 'CIVIL RELIGION IN AMERICA'

Robert Bellah

First published* in *Daedalus*, American Academy of Arts and Sciences, Winter 1967, pp. 21, 28–33, 30–42. Reprinted in *American Civil Religion*, Richey, Russell E. and Jones, Donald G. (eds), New York, Harper and Row, 1974.

While some have argued that Christianity is the national faith, and others that church and synagogue celebrate only the generalized religion of "the American Way of Life," few have realized that there actually exists alongside of and rather clearly differentiated from the churches an elaborate and well-institutionalized civil religion in America. This article argues not only that there is such a thing, but also that this religion – or perhaps better, this religious dimension – has its own seriousness and integrity and requires the same care in understanding that any other religion does.[1] . . .

The words and acts of the founding fathers, especially the first few presidents, shaped the form and tone of the civil religion as it has been maintained ever since. Though much is selectively derived from Christianity, this religion is clearly not itself Christianity. For one thing, neither Washington nor Adams, nor Jefferson mentions Christ in his inaugural address; nor do any of the subsequent presidents, although not one of them fails to mention God.[2] The God of the civil religion is not only rather "Unitarian," he is also on the austere side, much more related to order, law, and right than to salvation and love. Even though he is

---

* Reprinted, with permission, from "Religion in America," the Winter 1967 issue of *Daedalus*, Journal of the American Academy of Arts and Sciences, Boston, Massachusetts.

1. Why something so obvious should have escaped serious analytical attention is in itself an interesting problem. Part of the reason is probably the controversial nature of the subject. From the earliest years of the nineteenth century, conservative religious and political groups have argued that Christianity is, in fact, the national religion. Some of them have from time to time and as recently as the 1950s proposed constitutional amendments that would explicitly recognize the sovereignty of Christ. In defending the doctrine of separation of church and state, opponents of such groups have denied that the national polity has, intrinsically, anything to do with religion at all. The moderates on this issue have insisted that the American state has taken a permissive and indeed supportive attitude toward religious groups (tax exemption, et cetera), thus favoring religion but still missing the positive institutionalization with which I am concerned. But part of the reason this issue has been left in obscurity is certainly due to the peculiarly Western concept of "religion" as denoting a single type of collectivity of which an individual can be a member of one and only one at a time. The Durkheimian notion that every group has a religious dimension, which would be seen as obvious in southern or eastern Asia, is foreign to us. This obscures the recognition of such dimensions in our society.

2. God is mentioned or referred to in all inaugural addresses but Washington's second, which is a very brief (two paragraphs) and perfunctory acknowledgement. It is not without interest that the actual word *God* does not appear until Monroe's second inaugural, 5 March 1821. In his first inaugural, Washington refers to God as "that Almighty Being who rules the universe," "Great Author of every public and private good," "Invisible Hand," and "benign Parent of the Human Race." John Adams refers to God as "Providence," "Being who is supreme over all," "Patron of Order," "Fountain of Justice," and "Protector in all ages of the world of virtuous liberty." Jefferson speaks of "that Infinite Power which rules the destinies of the universe," and "that Being whose power regulates the destiny of nations," and "Heaven," Monroe uses "Providence" and "the Almighty" in his first inaugural and finally "Almighty God" in his second. See, *Inaugural Addresses of the Presidents of the United States from George Washington 1789 to Harry S. Truman 1949*, 82d Congress, 2d Session, House Document No. 540, 1952.

somewhat deist in cast, he is by no means simply a watchmaker God. He is actively interested and involved in history, with a special concern for America. Here the analogy has much less to do with natural law than with ancient Israel; the equation of America with Israel in the idea of the "American Israel" is not infrequent.[3] What was implicit in the words of Washington already quoted becomes explicit in Jefferson's second inaugural when he said: "I shall need, too, the favor of that Being in whose hands we are, who led our fathers, as Israel of old, from their native land and planted them in a country flowing with all the necessaries and comforts of life." Europe is Egypt, America, the promised land. God has led his people to establish a new sort of social order that shall be a light unto all the nations.[4]

This theme, too, has been a continuous one in the civil religion. We find it again in President Johnson's inaugural address:

> They came here – the exile and the stranger, brave but frightened – to find a place where a man could be his own man. They made a covenant with this land. Conceived in justice, written in liberty, bound in union, it was meant one day to inspire the hopes of all mankind; and it binds us still. If we keep its terms, we shall flourish.

What we have, then, from the earliest years of the republic is a collection of beliefs, symbols, and rituals with respect to sacred things and institutionalized in a collectivity. This religion – there seems no other word for it – while not antithetical to, and indeed sharing much in common with, Christianity, was neither sectarian nor in any specific sense Christian. At a time when the society was overwhelmingly Christian, it seems unlikely that this lack of Christian reference was meant to spare the feelings of the tiny non-Christian minority. Rather, the civil religion expressed what those who set the precedents felt was appropriate under the circumstances. It reflected their private as well as public views. Nor was the civil religion simply "religion in general." While generality was undoubtedly seen as a virtue by some, as in the quotation from Franklin above, the civil religion was specific enough when it came to the topic of America. Precisely because of this specificity, the civil religion was saved from empty formalism and served as a genuine vehicle of national religious self-understanding.

But the civil religion was not, in the minds of Franklin, Washington, Jefferson, or other leaders, with the exception of a few radicals like Tom Paine, ever felt to be a substitute for Christianity. There was an implicit but quite clear division of function between the civil religion and Christianity. Under the doctrine of religious liberty, an exceptionally wide sphere

---

3. For example, Abiel Abbot, pastor of the First Church in Haverhill, Massachusetts, delivered a Thanksgiving sermon in 1799. *Traits of Resemblance in the People of the United States of America to Ancient Israel*, in which he said, "It has been often remarked that the people of the United States come nearer to parallel with Ancient Israel, than any other nation upon the globe. Hence OUR AMERICAN ISRAEL is a term frequently used; and common consent allows it apt and proper." Cited in Hans Kohn, *The Idea of Nationalism* (New York, 1961), p. 665.
4. That the Mosaic analogy was present in the minds of leaders at the very moment of the birth of the republic is indicated in the designs proposed by Franklin and Jefferson for a seal of the United States of America. Together with Adams, they formed a committee of three delegated by the Continental Congress on July 4, 1776, to draw up the new device. "Franklin proposed as the device Moses lifting up his wand and dividing the Red Sea while Pharaoh was overwhelmed by its waters, with the motto 'Rebellion to tyrants is obedience to God.' Jefferson proposed the children of Israel in the wilderness 'led by a cloud by day and a pillar of fire by night.'" Anson Phelps Stokes, *Church and State in the United States*, Vol. 1 (New York, 1950), pp. 467–68.

of personal piety and voluntary social action was left to the churches. But the churches were neither to control the state nor to be controlled by it. The national magistrate, whatever his private religious views, operates under the rubrics of the civil religion as long as he is in his official capacity. This accommodation was undoubtedly the product of a particular historical moment and of a cultural background dominated by Protestantism of several varieties and by the Enlightenment, but it has survived despite subsequent changes in the cultural and religious climate.

CIVIL WAR AND CIVIL RELIGION

Until the Civil War, the American civil religion focused above all on the event of the Revolution, which was seen as the final act of the Exodus from the old lands across the waters. The Declaration of Independence and the Constitution were the sacred scriptures and Washington the divinely appointed Moses who led his people out of the hands of tyranny. The Civil War, which Sidney Mead calls "the center of American history,"[5] was the second great event that involved the national self-understanding so deeply as to require expression in the civil religion. . . .

With the Civil War, a new theme of death, sacrifice, and rebirth enters the civil religion. It is symbolized in the life and death of Lincoln. Nowhere is it stated more vividly than in the Gettysburg Address, itself part of the Lincolnian "New Testament" among the civil scriptures. Robert Lowell has recently pointed out the "insistent use of birth images" in this speech explicitly devoted to "these honored dead": "brought forth," "conceived," "created," "a new birth of freedom." He goes on to say:

> The Gettysburg Address is a symbolic and sacramental act. Its verbal quality is resonance combined with a logical, matter of fact, prosaic brevity . . . In his words, Lincoln symbolically died, just as the Union soldiers really died – and as he himself was soon really to die. By his words, he gave the field of battle a symbolic significance that it had lacked. For us and our country, he left Jefferson's ideals of freedom and equality joined to the Christian sacrificial act of death and rebirth. I believe this has a meaning that goes beyond sect or religion and beyond peace and war, and is now part of our lives as a challenge, obstacle and hope.[6]

Lowell is certainly right in pointing out the Christian quality of the symbolism here, but he is also right in quickly disavowing any sectarian implication. The earlier symbolism of the civil religion had been Hebraic without being in any specific sense Jewish. The Gettysburg symbolism ("...those who here gave their lives, that that nation might live") is Christian without having anything to do with the Christian church.

The symbolic equation of Lincoln with Jesus was made relatively early. Herndon, who had been Lincoln's law partner, wrote:

---

5. Sidney Mead, *The Lively Experiment* (New York, 1963), p. 12.
6. Allan Nevins, *Lincoln and the Gettysburg Address* (Urbana, 1969), pp. 88–9.

For fifty years God rolled Abraham Lincoln through his fiery furnace. He did it to try Abraham and to purify him for his purposes. This made Mr Lincoln humble, tender, forbearing, sympathetic to suffering, kind, sensitive, tolerant: broadening, deepening and widening his whole nature: making him the noblest and loveliest character since Jesus Christ. . . . I believe that Lincoln was God's chosen one.[7]

With the Christian archetype in the background, Lincoln, "our martyred president," was linked to the war dead, those who "gave the last full measure of devotion." The theme of sacrifice was indelibly written into the civil religion. . . .

Without an awareness that our nation stands under higher judgment, the tradition of the civil religion would be dangerous indeed. Fortunately, the prophetic voices have never been lacking. Our present situation brings to mind the Mexican-American war that Lincoln, among so many others, opposed. The spirit of civil disobedience that is alive today in the civil rights movement and the opposition to the Viet-Nam war was already clearly outlined by Henry David Thoreau when he wrote, "If the law is of such a nature that it requires you to be an agent of injustice to another, then I say, break the law." Thoreau's words, "I would remind my countrymen that they are men first, and Americans at a late and convenient hour,"[8] provide an essential standard for any adequate thought and action in our third time of trial. As Americans we have been well favored in the world, but it is as men that we will be judged.

Out of the first and second times of trial have come, as we have seen, the major symbols of the American civil religion. There seems little doubt that a successful negotiation of this third time of trial – the attainment of some kind of viable and coherent world order – would precipitate a major new set of symbolic forms. So far the flickering flame of the United Nations burns too low to be the focus of a cult, but the emergence of a genuine trans-national sovereignty would certainly change this. It would necessitate the incorporation of vital international symbolism into our civil religion, or, perhaps a better way of putting it, it would result in American civil religion becoming simply one part of a new civil religion of the world. It is useless to speculate on the form such a civil religion might take, though it obviously would draw on religious traditions beyond the sphere of Biblical religion alone. Fortunately, since the American civil religion is not the worship of the American nation but an understanding of the American experience in the light of ultimate and universal reality, the reorganization entailed by such a new situation need not disrupt the American civil religion's continuity. A world civil religion could be accepted as a fulfillment and not a denial of American civil religion. Indeed, such an outcome has been the eschatological hope of American civil religion from the beginning. To deny such an outcome would be to deny the meaning of America itself.

Behind the civil religion at every point lie Biblical archetypes: Exodus, Chosen People, Promised Land, New Jerusalem, Sacrificial Death and Rebirth. But it is also genuinely American and genuinely new. It has its own prophets and its own martyrs, its own sacred events and sacred places, its own solemn rituals and symbols. It is concerned that America be

---

7. Quoted in Sherwood Eddy, *The Kingdom of God and the American Dream* (New York, 1941), p. 162.
8. Quoted in Yehoshua Arieli, *Individualism and Nationalism in American Ideology* (Cambridge, Mass., 1964,), p. 274.

a society as perfectly in accord with the will of God as men can make it, and a light to all the nations.

It has often been used and is being used today as a cloak for petty interests and ugly passions. It is in need – as is any living faith – of continual reformation, of being measured by universal standards. But it is not evident that it is incapable of growth and new insight.

It does not make any decision for us. It does not remove us from moral ambiguity, from being, in Lincoln's fine phrase, an "almost chosen people." But it is a heritage of moral and religious experience from which we still have much to learn as we formulate the decisions that lie ahead.

3.2 'BAPTIZED IN BLOOD'

Charles Regan Wilson

From 'Origin and Overview', in *Baptized in Blood: The Religion of the Lost Cause 1865–1920*, Wilson, C.R., Athens, The University of Georgia Press, 1980, pp. 3–5, 10–17.

ORIGIN AND OVERVIEW

This is a study of the afterlife of a Redeemer Nation that died. The nation was never resurrected, but it survived as a sacred presence, a holy ghost haunting the spirits and actions of post – Civil War Southerners. Embodying the dream of Southerners for a separate political identity, the Confederacy was defeated by Father Abraham and an apparently more blessed, as well as more self-righteous, Redeemer Nation. But the dream of a separate Southern identity did not die in 1865. A Southern political nation was not to be, and the people of Dixie came to accept that; but the dream of a cohesive Southern people with a separate cultural identity replaced the original longing. The cultural dream replaced the political dream: the South's kingdom was to be of culture, not of politics. Religion was at the heart of this dream, and the history of the attitude known as the Lost Cause was the story of the use of the past as the basis for a Southern religious-moral identity, an identity as a chosen people. The Lost Cause was therefore the story of the linking of two profound human forces, religion and history. This study examines the product of this connection in the South from the end of the Civil War until the end of World War I. It was a Southern civil religion, which tied together Christian churches and Southern culture. . . .

Southern religion also contributed to the defense of Southern society against the growing criticisms of it by militant abolitionists in the North. In the 1840s and 1850s Southerners advanced a pro-slavery argument that defended their society as a high achievement of civilization and attacked the Northern industrial, free society as an inhumane one. Southerners by this time were united in the defense of slavery on the grounds of protection of property and public safety, and these intellectuals who articulated the pro-slavery argument suggested the positive benefits derived from a slave civilization. South Carolina was the leader in this defense, with Southern clergymen playing a prominent role. The pro-slavery argument leaned more heavily on the sanction of the Bible than on anything else. Ministers cited biblical examples of the coexistence of Christianity and slavery, quoted Old Testament approvals of slavery, and interpreted a passage from Genesis to mean that blacks were descendants of the sinner Ham and destined to be forever bondsmen.

By 1861 Southern churches, like other regional institutions, had thus laid the basis for secession. For a generation they had preached of slavery's divine nature and the need to protect it. Unionist sentiment did exist among ministers, and those in the border states urged a policy of moderation after Lincoln's election. But in the crisis of secession and the attack on Fort Sumter in the spring of 1861, Southern clergymen and their institutions made clear their commitment to what they believed was God's cause. Like their counterparts in the North,

Southern clerics preached that their cause was a holy one; they interpreted battle victories as God's blessings, and defeats as God's punishments for their failings. A recurring phrase in the Confederate religious lexicon was "baptism of blood." In his sermon "Our National Sins," preached on November 21, 1860, before Lincoln's inauguration, the distinguished Presbyterian theologian James H. Thornwell called for secession, even though "our path to victory may be through a baptism of blood." In 1862 the Episcopal Bishop Stephen Elliott observed, "All nations which come into existence at this late period of the world must be born amid the storm of revolution and must win their way to a place in history through the baptism of blood." "A grand responsibility rests upon our young republic," said the Episcopal rector B.T. Lacy in 1863, "and a mighty work lies before it. Baptized in its infancy in blood, may it receive the baptism of the Holy Ghost, and be consecrated to its high and holy mission among the nations of the earth." This evocative, powerful terminology suggested the role of war in bringing a redemption from past sins, an atonement, and a sanctification for the future. . . .

Judged by historical and anthropological criteria, the civil religion that emerged in the postbellum South was an authentic religious expression. As Clifford Geertz has said, the anthropological study of religion (in this case, the Lost Cause religion) is a twofold undertaking: first, one must analyze the symbols and the myth of the Southern faith for the meanings they embody; second, one must explore the relationship of these meanings to "social-structural and psychological processes." The South faced problems after the Civil War which were cultural but also religious – the problems of providing meaning to life and society amid the baffling failure of fundamental beliefs, of extending comfort to those suffering poverty and disillusionment, and of encouraging a sense of belonging in the shattered Southern community. The anthropologist Anthony F.C. Wallace argues that religion originates "in situations of social and cultural stress," and for postbellum Southerners such traditional religious issues as the nature of suffering, evil, and the seeming irrationality of life had a disturbing relevancy. Scholars stress that religion is defined by the existence of a sacred symbol system and its embodiment in ritual. As Geertz has said, the religious response to the threat of disorder in existence is the creation of symbols "of such a genuine order of the world which will account for, and even celebrate, the perceived ambiguities, puzzles, and paradoxes in human experience." These symbols create "long-lasting moods and motivations" which lead men to act on their religious feelings.[1] At the heart of the religion of the Lost Cause were the Confederate heroes, who came to embody transcendent truths about the redemptive power of Southern society. In fact, the Lost Cause had symbols, myth, ritual, theology, and organization, all directed toward meeting the profound concerns of postwar Southerners.

In addition to fulfilling the role of religion as, in Geertz's words, interpreter of "social and psychological processes in cosmic terms," the Lost Cause religion also fulfilled another function of religion by shaping these processes. Southerners used the Confederate past for

---

1. Anthony F.C. Wallace, *Religion: An Anthropological View* (New York, 1966), pp. 30, 102; Clifford Geertz, "Religion as a Cultural System," in Michael Banton, ed., *Anthropological Approaches to the Study of Religion* (New York, 1966), pp. 4, 8–12, 14, 23, 28. See also Andrew M. Greeley, *The Denominational Society: A Sociological Approach to Religion in America* (Glenview, Ill., 1972), p. 28; Mircea Eliade, *Myth and Reality* (New York, 1963), pp. 8, 17–18.

their own purposes in the late nineteenth century. Businessmen and politicians employed the glorious legacy for their own needs; Southern ministers did the same. As the guardians of the region's spiritual and moral heritage, they used the Lost Cause to buttress this heritage. This study stresses that Christian clergymen were the prime celebrants of the religion of the Lost Cause. They were honored figures at the center of the Southern community, and most of them had in some way been touched by the Confederate experience. Not All Southern preachers were celebrants of the religion of the Lost Cause, but those who were true believers were frequently prominent church leaders; the phrase "minister of the Lost Cause" identifies those who were most clearly committed to it. These ministers saw little difference between their religious and cultural values, and they promoted the link by constructing Lost Cause ritualistic forms that celebrated their regional mythological and theological beliefs. They used the Lost Cause to warn Southerners of their decline from past virtue, to promote moral reform, to encourage conversion to Christianity, and to educate the young in Southern traditions; in the fullness of time, they related it to American values. Anthony F.C. Wallace has speculated that all religions originate as cultural revitalization movements, and it is clear that Southern ministers and their churches achieved this revitalization by shaping their culture. While some revitalization movements have been utopian, looking to the future, the Lost Cause religion was a revivalistic movement, aiming, as Wallace has said, "to restore a golden age believed to have existed in the society's past."[2]

Race, of course, was of fundamental importance to Southern culture. Indeed, Samuel Hill argues that Southern "racial traditions and practices have served as the cement for the South's cultural cohesion," and that white supremacy was the "primary component" of Southern culture.[3] This study explores another component providing cultural cohesion: the link between Southern history and religion. Race was intimately related to the story of the Lost Cause but was not the basis of it, was not at the center of it. In recent years the needed concentration on the racial dimensions of religion's relationship to culture in the South has left the impression that the secular culture entirely modified and distorted religion. It should now be (and is) historical orthodoxy to assert that the Southern churches were culturally captive. By focusing on this related but still separate issue of the role of religion and history in Southern culture, one can see that the churches exploited the secular culture, as well as vice versa. The culture was a captive of the churches.

The Southern civil religion assumes added meaning when compared to the American civil religion. Sociologist Robert N. Bellah's 1967 article on that topic and his subsequent work have focused scholarly discussion on the common religion of the American people. Bellah has argued that "an elaborate and well-institutionalized civil religion" existed, which was "clearly differentiated" from the Christian denominations. He has defined "civil religion" as the religious dimension of a people "through which it interprets its historical experience in the light of transcendent reality." Like Sidney E. Mead, Bellah saw civil religion as essentially prophetic, judging the behavior of the nation against transcendent values. Will Herberg has proposed that the civil religion has been a folk religion, a common religion emerging out of the life of the folk. He has argued that it grew out of a long social and historical experience that established a heterogeneous society. The civil religion came to be the American Way of

---

2. Wallace, *Religion*, pp. 30–165.
3. Hill, Samuel S. "South's Two Cultures," in *Religion and the Solid South*, S. Hill, (ed.), (Nashville, 1972), p. 24.

Life, a set of beliefs that were accepted and revered by Protestants, Catholics, and Jews. "Democracy" has been the fundamental concept of this civil religion. Scholars have identified the sources of the American public faith in the Enlightenment tradition and in the secularized Puritan and Revivalist traditions. Clearly born during the American Revolution, it was reborn, with the new theme of sacrifice and renewal, in the Civil War.[4]

In the post-Civil War and twentieth-century South, a set of values existed which could be designated a Southern Way of Life. Those values constituted the basis for a Southern civil religion which differed from the American civil religion. Dixie's value system varied from the one Herberg discussed – Southerners undoubtedly were less optimistic, less liberal, less democratic, less tolerant, and more homogeneously Protestant. In their religion Southerners stressed "democracy" less than the conservative concept of "virtue". The Enlightenment tradition played no role in shaping the religion of the Lost Cause, while the emotionally intense, dynamic Revivalist tradition was at its center. The secularized legacy of idealistic, moralistic, Puritanism also helped form its character. While the whole course of Southern history provided the background, the Southern civil religion actually emerged from Dixie's Civil War experience. Just as the Revolution of 1776 caused Americans to see their history in transcendent terms, so the Confederate experience led Southerners to a profound self-examination. They understood that the results of the Civil War had clearly given them a history distinct from that of the North. The story of the civil religion included the founding of Virginia in the colonial period, the Southern role in the American Revolution and World War I, and the myths of the Old South and Reconstruction. These aspects were adjuncts to the religion of the Lost Cause, which contained ritualistic, mythological, theological, institutional, educational, and intellectual elements that were simply not present in the other aspects of the civil religion. Without the Lost Cause, no civil religion would have existed. The two were virtually the same.

A civil religion, by definition, centers on the religious implications of a nation. The Southern public faith involved a nation – a dead one, which was perhaps the unique quality of this phenomenon. One of the central issues of the American faith has been the relationship between church and state, but since the Confederate quest for political nationhood failed, the Southern faith has been less concerned with such political issues than with the cultural question of identity. Because it emerged from a heterogeneous immigrant society, the American civil religion was especially significant in providing uprooted immigrants with a sense of belonging. Because of its origins in Confederate defeat, the Southern civil religion offered confused and suffering Southerners a sense of meaning, an identity in a precarious but distinct culture.

The institutional aspect is perhaps the most controversial part of the civil religion debate. The civil religion possesses a basic conceptual ambiguity: Has it been a separate religious tradition? Or simply an aspect of other societal institutions? Recent historical studies have cast

---

4. Robert N. Bellah, "Civil Religion in America," Sidney E. Mead, "The 'Nation with the Soul of a Church,'" Will Herberg, "America's Civil Religion: What It Is and Whence It Comes," all in Russell E. Richey and Donald G. Jones, eds., *American Civil Religion* (New York, 1974), pp. 21–44, 45–75, 76–88; Bellah, *The Broken Covenant: American Civil Religion in Time of Trial* (New York, 1975); Will Herberg, *Protestant, Catholic, Jew: An Essay in American Religious Sociology* (Garden City, N.Y., 1960); Catherine L. Albanese, *Sons of the Fathers: The Civil Religion and the American Revolution* (Philadelphia, 1976); James H. Moorhead, *American Apocalypse: Yankee Protestants and the Civil War, 1860–1869* (New Haven, 1978).

doubt on Bellah's assumption of the continuing existence of the American public faith in permanent organizations. Scholars increasingly believe the term "civil religion" should be used to denote episodes of religious nationalism, heavily influenced in the nineteenth century by evangelical Protestantism. This study of the religion of the Lost Cause extends the conceptual debate on this controversial issue of the civil religion. Bellah's original insight seems to have qualified validity for the South; the Southern public religion was not a formal religion, but it was a functioning one. It possessed well-defined elements – mythology, symbolism, theology, values, and institutions – which combined to make a religion. Its elements were not unrelated parts, but interactive aspects of a well-organized, multidimensional spiritual movement. Even more than in the North, a strong connection existed between the Southern civil religion and the Protestant churches. Although support of the Lost Cause was indeed a prominent theme of Southern Protestantism, certainly not all religious leaders supported it. This is a study of the Southern civil religion and should not be seen as a study of Southern Protestantism. Its conclusions do not apply to all Southern clergymen; in addition, many important concerns of Southern Protestantism did not touch on the Lost Cause.

The religion of the Lost Cause, moreover, had its own distinctive structure of institutions. John Wilson has shown that voluntary associations have been perhaps the key organizational embodiment of the American public faith, and similar groups (the Confederate veterans' groups and the Ku Klux Klan, as well as the churches and denominational schools) expressed the religion of the Lost Cause. Because of this complex structure of well-defined, interactive institutions, the Southern civil religion, again, should not be seen simply as the equivalent of Southern Protestantism. Southern ministers who believed in the Lost Cause were the indispensable individuals who mediated between their own denominations and the other institutions of the Lost Cause. They were frequently members of these voluntary associations and directed their organizational and ritualistic activities. While they shaped the religion of the Lost Cause in the image of Southern Protestantism, organizationally the two were not precisely the same.[5]

The persistent Bible Belt image suggests that the South has been long regarded as a sacred society. To be sure, secular values have been potent, especially in the twentieth century; nevertheless, the South's historical development resulted in longer dominance of an "old-time religion." The pioneering sociologist Emile Durkheim argued that all societies have a sacred quality, a spiritual dimension, and that members may even regard their society itself as holy. But postbellum Southerners saw their culture, rather than their society, as enduring. The reality of Southern culture's alleged sacredness was less important than the Southerner's conviction that his regional values and cultural symbols were holy. Another of Durkheim's insights helps to clarify further the question of the South's sacred or secular quality. He pointed out that religion divides existence into two realms, the sacred and the profane, based upon the perception of holiness, rather than upon the inherent qualities of the sacred items. Sacredness depends not on the item itself, but on the perception of its holiness by a religious person or group. The South was sacred to its citizens because they saw a sacred quality in it. The religious culture in Dixie, including the Confederate memory, promoted the self-image

---

5. In his *Public Religion in American Culture* (Philadelphia, 1979), esp. chs. 6 and 7, John F. Wilson skillfully clarifies the conceptual problems of the civil religion.

of virtue and holiness and thus helped maintain the cohesiveness of Southern society in a critical postwar period.[6]

As historians and novelists have shown, the Southern historical experience that was the basis of the civil religion has been an existential one. Defeat, poverty, guilt, disillusionment, isolation, dread of the future – all have characterized the Southern past. Samuel Hill has recently urged Southerners to look to this past for an authentic religious revelation to set beside their literalistic reading of the biblical revelation. "Surely living this way," he says of the Southern experience, "provokes acknowledgement of the transparency of earthy events to the depths, to ultimate meaning."[7] In fact, Southerners have tapped this existential religious resource in their Lost Cause religion. Taking a profound historical experience based in suffering and linking it with the deeply felt Christian forms resulted in institutionalizing a distinctly existential outlook among Lost Cause devotees.

However, the mythmaking or religious frame of mind represents an effort to overcome existential chaos, substituting a simplified, more comprehensible view of life for the ambiguities and contradictions that give rise to existentialism. Existentialism is a philosophy, attempting to interpret human activities in cosmic terms – but most people are not philosophers. Human beings seem to need some way to control events, if only symbolically; this is what religion does, which distinguishes it from philosophy. Southerners have indeed been existentialists, but (like other human beings) they could not bear their experience without the support of religion – the Lost Cause religion. They have remembered their suffering and have cultivated the memory, in order to affirm that it was not meaningless.

Samuel Hill compassionately hopes that the recovery of the existential dimension of the Southern experience by today's Christian churches in the South will make them somehow wiser and more humane in race relations. One might hope that would be true; however, in the Lost Cause religion the perception of transcendence in the Southern experience did not make the participants in the spiritual mysteries ethically wiser, mainly because Southern ministers tied the Lost Cause religion to the religion of the Southern churches – evangelical Christianity. On the racial question, indeed, the Southern historical experience as embodied in the Lost Cause provided the model for segregation that the Southern churches accepted. In short, the Lost Cause religion did not have the prophetic, ethical dimension that Hill calls for. Its prophetic aspects were not focused on racial issues. As the Southern churches did not judge regional racial ethics from the standpoint of the Christian love ethic, so the Lost Cause religion failed to judge the society's racial patterns. The Southern civil religion also failed after 1900 to perform a prophetic function in regard to the American civil religion. Rather than questioning the nation's purposes in terms of transcendent values, Southerners showed an eagerness to identify with the sometimes self-righteous dreams of glory and virtue of the American nation. Robert Penn Warren has observed that the Confederates offer the lesson that human dignity and grandeur are possible, even amid human weakness and vice. The lesson of the ministers who constructed a religion of the Confederate past is perhaps that they

---

6. Emile Durkheim, *The Elementary Forms of the Religious Life* (New York, 1965), 52, 56, 59, 261; Wilson, *Public Religion*, 153–59; Lloyd A. Hunter, "The Sacred South: Postwar Confederates and the Sacralization of Southern Culture" (Ph.D. dissertation, St. Louis University, 1978), 12–15. The latter study deals with many of the same phenomena that the present volume does, but is an attempt at, in the author's words, "a theological interpretation of the Lost Cause myth." Unaccountably, he overlooks the role of ministers in this and does not use church records.

7. Hill, "Toward a Charter for a Southern Theology," in *Religion*, pp. 182–84.

should have paid more attention to human weakness and vice, to the moral ambiguities and uncertainties of life, to the possibility that their society, indeed, any society, might not be virtue incarnate.[8] Southerners, then, made one attempt to utilize the spiritual resources of their historical experience, but, as in all things human, they fell short of perfection.

8. Robert Penn Warren, *The Legacy of the Civil War: Meditations on the Centennial* (New York, 1961), pp. 108–109.

3.3 'COMPLETING THE THEOLOGICAL CIRCLE: CIVIL RELIGION IN AMERICA'

Vine Deloria Jr.

From *For this Land: Writings on Religion in America*, Deloria, V., Jr., edited by Treat, J., London, Routledge, 1999, pp. 166–8, 174.

In his response to his commentators in *The Religious Situation*, Robert Bellah writes that "what I mean by civil religion is a set of religious beliefs, symbols, and rituals growing out of the American historical experience interpreted in the dimension of transcendence." It is, perhaps, as close and precise a definition as we can expect but when it is placed in tandem with C. Eric Lincoln's remark in his essay, "Civil Religion and the American Presidency," published in the preconvention issue of *Religious Education*, that "[p]residential politics is clearly the arena in which the implicit religion of the people is made explicit," we have the necessary context in which to ask the ultimate question which people seem unwilling or unable to ask. Is not the United States government and its informal political processes the latest denominational expression of the Christian religion? Does not the American understanding of social and world reality really derive from and depend upon the Christian theological and metaphysical understanding of the world to such a degree that America would not make sense aside from this context?

The assumption which Bellah, as far as I can tell, and his critics and admirers, fail to examine is whether when they discuss "civil religion" as a phenomenon they have not avoided an examination of the metaphysics of American existence. That is to say, the civil religion and its doctrines did not really spring out of "the American historical experience interpreted in the dimension of transcendence" at all. Rather the Christian interpretation of the meaning of the universe and its peculiar emphasis on the reality of history over and against geography structured the understanding of the Western European immigrants to North America so that they understood their experiences in the context of the Christian religion.

The various slogans and doctrines which Bellah and others find in the present phenomenon of civil religion were not ideas that randomly occurred to people over the course of four centuries but were an integral part of their outlook as they arrived on these shores. To the degree that these beliefs vary from traditional theological doctrines of the Christian faith, we can determine the impact of the North American continent and the values and beliefs of its original inhabitants on the conglomerate of beliefs and values that made up the Christian intellectual universe prior to its encounter with the New World.

Thus believing that the New England coast was a New Israel, a promised land, that the American people had a "Manifest Destiny" to control and settle, exploit and eventually destroy the interior of the continent, and that God was always on the side of the American people are all objective manifestations of the fundamental Christian belief that the world was intended for a certain group of people who followed the commands of Genesis to populate and subdue. The continuing myth perpetrated by American thinkers that the Europeans landed on an empty continent is merely a subconscious wish to put aside the immorality of reality in favor of a subjective doctrine that justifies the continued existence of American social and political existence.

American history can be neatly divided into two phases, pre-Revolution and post-Revolution. In the pre-Revolutionary period we find the articulation of a variety of Old Testament doctrines which serve to provide a secular context within which a growing concern for unity is manifested. How else were the scattered little colonies of immigrants to find a common basis for existence and mutual support except by believing that they shared part of a greater and transcendent purpose? The great variety of religious communities and their conflicting views of specific theological doctrines of the church, baptism, the role of the ministry, and the identification of true believers had to reach a common expression at some point and what Bellah and others find as the evolution of "civil religion" is the coming together of a new Christian metaphysic which is not dependent upon creeds nearly as much as it is dependent upon the acting out of a common purpose.

This common purpose is spelled out in the American State Papers and in the classic state documents such as the Declaration of Independence and the Constitution, which are really credal statements of the new overarching Christian denomination known as the United States of America. The true measure for understanding this phenomenon is not to distinguish from among the variety of the existing Christian denominations a new "civil religion," for all of these institutions exist and relate to each other and justify their existence within the framework of the Christian understanding of the universe. Rather the proper method of checking out the civil religion thesis is from the standpoint of a group which has never shared that understanding of the universe and which has always rejected it emotionally and intellectually. That group is the American Indian communities.

. . .

As the institutions of the federal government have eroded in recent years, religious freedom has increased for Indians and to the degree that secular humanism has dominated the ideology of the federal government, in that degree Indians have been able to practice their tribal religions. But what do we do when in a recent Wounded Knee trial involving the Sioux holy man Leonard Crow Dog, who wished to swear his oath upon the Sacred Pipe, a prospective juror blurts out, "My God, he doesn't believe in our Lord Jesus Christ!" And Leonard is convicted of criminal charges for his presence at Wounded Knee although all Indian testimony indicates that he was asked to come to Wounded Knee to perform religious ceremonies for the people who were there?

The bumper stickers telling us to "Kill a Commie for Christ" are not to be taken lightly. Nor is the perennial slogan of the right-wing Christian denominations, "Christianity or Communism" to be dismissed as simply overblown patriotism. In the minds of a substantial number of Americans, when a crisis of major proportions rises on their horizons, there is no real difference between the Christian religion and the United States of America and its political institutions. To distinguish this worldview from the institutional churches and discover a "civil religion" that is parallel to denominations but not one of them seems to me to be a false distinction which is possible only because the people who want to make this distinction exist and derive their tools of analysis from within the Christian religion and culture. It is like an Indian making a careful distinction between the various bands and warrior societies of his tribe. From the outside there is really no difference in a practical sense and it is the world of practicality, not the world of ideas, in which we live.

3.4 'WAR MEMORIALS'

Tony Walter

From 'Memorials', in *Funerals and How to Improve Them*, Walter, T., London, Hodder and Stoughton, 1990, pp. 211–13.

The Cenotaph, London's permanent memorial to the unknown warrior, was not planned by some high-up committee, but forced on the authorities by spontaneous public sentiment. Originally, the architect Sir Edwin Lutyens was asked to design a temporary wood and plaster shrine. When unveiled in July 1919, pictures of the saluting generals appeared in newspapers throughout the land, and in the days that followed wreath after wreath appeared at the base of the plaster shrine. No such response had been anticipated. Only eleven days later the Cabinet agreed to replace it with an identical and permanent structure.

I grew up in a London suburb created around the Metropolitan railway station and having no natural focus like a village green or old parish church. With the suburb only a couple of decades old, the memorial to those who died in the First World War became the focal point. Likewise in town after town in Australia, where often more than a quarter of those who went to fight the mother country's war did not return, it is the war memorial that has become the town's focal point. In this federal nation where loyalty to the local state or city is intense, the one building that symbolizes the entire nation of Australia is the War Memorial in Canberra.

But war memorials need not be grand. I recall driving west out of one old Australian gold-mining town; for mile after mile the road was an avenue of trees, all the same height, all planted at the same time. I did not understand why the avenue was so long until we stopped the car, and I could see that each tree had a name attached. There must have been several thousand in all. For the remaining few minutes as we completed the tree-lined section, a vacation to the bush turned into a pilgrimage.

I also recall walking across the Mall, that lovely two miles of grass down the middle of Washington DC, when a middle-aged man asked me the way to the Vietnam memorial. He was in town on business, but twenty years ago in South East Asia he had lost a buddy.

Later I arrived at the memorial myself, designed by Yale student Maya Ying Lin and dedicated in 1982. Unlike so many war memorials that rise in triumph high above the ground, the Vietnam memorial is sunk into the ground. As you walk down below the grass of the mall, you pass the names of the 57,692 Americans who died, each carved into a low 492-foot long wall of black marble, while in the polished stone you see the pale reflections of mourners. At places at the foot of the wall, in varying states of health, are potted plants. One or two people lean over the top, pressing crayon on paper to get a tracing of the name they have been looking for.

Unlike the Canberra memorial, where each name is listed in alphabetical order and by battalion, at Washington the names are simply in chronological order of death. There is no regimental pride here, just 57,692 sets of individual pain. Seekers after a name are told which section theirs is in, and then they have to seek among the dead to find their man. My path again crossed that of the middle-aged businessman. I too, a foreign tourist, had come to feel the universal sorrow of war.

Tourists by the million become pilgrims in such places. It happens in the concentration camp at Dachau; in Amsterdam's Anne Frank house; at Jerusalem's Yad Vashem memorial to the Holocaust. In such places, the chattering children and the clicking cameras fall silent.

3.5 'SAY GOODBYE TO GRANDAD'

Timothy Pain

Weekend Guardian, 3–4 November 1990.

I have never believed that the dead can speak to the living, and I'm not quite sure what the visit achieved, but something deep within me is convinced that my grandfather is pleased.

Sometime on September 3, 1917, somewhere near Ypres in Belgium, a German shell exploded on a British Lewis gun; and Sergeant Alfred Thomas Richard Jones was blown to bits.

Alfred was only one among many millions killed in the 1914–1918 war. And his story was far from unique; just 23, he had been married for under two years to my grandmother, and had a baby daughter whom he had never seen or held. It wasn't any harder for my mother and grandmother than for the other bereaved millions, but Alfred's death was the only one which directly affected me.

I was born nearly 40 years after he died, but Remembrance Sunday remains my most powerful memory of childhood. Each November through the late Fifties and early Sixties I stood on my parent's hearth watching Nan's red eyes, waiting to hear the guns in Hyde Park end the ordeal, wondering why the years had not healed her hurts.

My own discomfort began when I became a teenager. My grandmother started telling me how much I reminded her of Alfred. I tried comparing what I saw in the mirror with the fading sepia photographs on the wall, but fashionably long hair clashed with a military short-back-and-sides. Then other relatives of Nan's generation commented on an astonishing likeness. I found this embarrassing, but slowly a sense of responsibility developed – yet a responsibility for something unknown.

As I reached my early 20s I wore my hair shorter, and the likeness became obvious even to me. Once I grew a moustache; it lasted only a few weeks, but while it existed I visited Nan and noticed that last photo taken of Alfred before he died. He too had a moustache; somehow I had never noticed it before, then I realized that I was the age which he had been when he died. I was gripped by his eyes, and something happened which I can neither understand nor rationalize. I knew that there was something for me to do.

As Nan grew older, so we grew closer. She never recovered from Alfred's death, never remarried, never found satisfying work, never travelled far from her council flat. Her early bitterness of grief was partially assuaged by growing Christian faith. But that only brought back memories of a wedding night when she had refused to pray with Alfred, and had mocked his belief in God. She lived wanting to die, but even death seemed to be denied her. Twice she tried to commit suicide and failed. Eventually she died alone in hospital aged 94. I arrived at her bedside 10 minutes too late. I'd thought it might have helped her to see my face.

When my mother and I went through her things we found at the back of her wardrobe a stick which no one had ever seen. The wood was pale, flexible and scratched; the head was made of silver, and was engraved, dented and dirty. When this had been cleaned we read that the stick was a wedding present to Alfred from the other sergeants of the London Regiment. It was his sergeant's drill cane, and it bore the marks of war. Clearly it had been sent home from Belgium as all that remained of Sergeant A.T.R. Jones, 450881, and Nan had kept it hidden for 70 years.

They now seem such obvious questions, and I don't know why I had never thought of them before. I suppose the seventieth anniversary celebrations in 1988 of the end of the war must have sparked them off.

Visiting mother one day I glanced at the photos of Alfred, and suddenly asked her: "Do you know where your father is buried?" "Did Nan ever visit his grave or the place of his death?" Mum replied that Nan had always told her there had been no body to bury and that there was no grave to visit, "'blown to bits by a German shell' was what she always cried."

Instantly I knew what I had to do. I knew what I had seen in the eyes of my grandfather. I knew what the burden of my resemblance meant. "Would you like to go to Belgium?" I asked my mother. "I'll take you."

I'm not sure why it took two years to arrange. Distance, work, children, time and money, all got in the way. But another glance at his eyes last Christmas was enough. I rang the Commonwealth War Graves Commission and asked what information they needed to search for a grave or memorial. I pumped mother for the necessary details, and rang back the Commission with his rank, regiment, battalion, service number, and date of death.

The lady at the other end pressed a few buttons and announced that there was no recorded grave, and that the only memorial was on the Ypres Menin Gate – "Panel 54," she added.

I thought we could just make it there and back in one day. I booked a crossing on the Dover-Calais ferry, and Mum came to stay for a few days. We left home at 5.15 am, driving through the darkness to Dover. We landed in Calais at 10am, and drove to Dunkirk where I dropped my wife and four children for the day. Mum and I hurried on across flat, hedgeless, desolate countryside, to the killing fields of Belgium.

We didn't know whether the memorial was in Ypres, Menin, or somewhere between the two. We reached Ypres at 11.45 am, found nothing, and drove on to Menin, passing dozens of immaculately kept small military cemeteries. We didn't talk.

At Menin we learnt that the Gate was back in Ypres, so turned round and arrived there at 1.00 pm. I don't know how we had missed it, for the Menin Gate is huge. A magnificent stone arch straddling the main road where it crosses a canal. It is the only memorial to the 56,000 men of the British Army who died in Ypres salient with no known grave.

The panels were so tall that I dreaded finding Alf's name in some dark corner or high out of my mother's failing range of vision.

But the panel 54 (there are 56, each with 1,000 names) was bathed in bright sunlight; and there in the centre, about 12ft off the ground was his name. It stood out, for the names were grouped in ranks and he was the only sergeant.

A.T.R. Jones. Those letters had been carved over 60 years ago and never once in all those years had anybody gazed at them with such love and sadness. Somehow those stone letters transferred Alfred from a fading photographic image, from a phantom unreal figure, into a flesh and blood man who had lived, fought and died in a far off foreign country.

I placed his sergeant's stick against the panel and took a few photos. Mother wept. Tourists stared. And I prayed that Alfred would know we had come.

We had no time to wander around Ypres or visit the endless graves of the unknown dead. But we didn't need to. We had seen his name. That was enough.

Of course I realize that the visit was really about meeting emotional needs in my mother and myself, and of course I know that Alf is probably unaware of our visit. But an irrational, incomprehensible part of my inner being needs to believe that he knows and is pleased by our overdue visit.

I won't be going back to the Menin Gate. I don't need to; for now I can look into those eyes without any sense of discomfort. I have done my duty. Someone has at last said "Goodbye."

3.6 'HOW DID UNCLE EDMUND DIE?'

Paul Barker

The Observer Review, 7 November 1999.

We didn't mean to go to Ypres. But my wife's mother had just died, aged 93, and she used to talk about a favourite uncle who had been killed in the First World War. Among the old photographs we brought away from her cold Yorkshire cottage after the funeral was a picture of Edmund Ashworth in uniform. There was also a picture of Edmund's brother Will, my wife's grandfather, in the uniform of an ambulance volunteer in the Boer War. Will Ashworth sent reports on the Boer War to the local paper, the *Hebden Bridge Times*, which the Ashworth family owned, and where he succeeded his father as editor.

I knew that Edmund Ashworth was in his late twenties when he was killed in France. Young as he was, he had had more of a life than many of the dead. Until he enrolled for the war, he had been a teacher. In the late Thirties, when my brother-in-law was a pupil at the same junior school, his great-uncle Edmund's photograph was on the wall of the assembly hall, as a local hero.

Sally, like all her immediate family, also became a teacher. It was half-term. We decided to take Le Shuttle, partly to see the Goya exhibition at Lille, and partly to drift around all those places we usually drove past on our way to some sun in the south. I wanted to visit Lutyens's great memorial at Thiepval in northern France. I had never been to a war cemetery before. I wasn't a great fan of the new upsurge in First World War novels, not quite understanding why this nostalgia for unbearable pain should hit us 80 years on.

But if Thiepval, why not also a cemetery where we had some connection, however slender? But where was Edmund Ashworth buried? All I knew was that his parents went out to visit the grave, once, after the war. No one else had ever been.

A few days before we set off, I look in the phone book and find the Commonwealth War Graves Commission's number. An efficient staff member soon finds Edmund's file and reads me its contents: 'Lance-Corporal Edmund Lord Ashworth, son of Handley and Alice Ashworth of 4 Sandy Gate, Hebden Bridge. [A house I used to go to when I was walking out with Sally.] Died 13 December 1915, aged 29. He was in the lst/4th Battalion of the Duke of Wellington's West Riding Regiment. He is buried at the Talana Farm cemetery, near Ypres: plot three, row D, grave one. We can send you instructions on how to get there.'

We cross under the Channel, eat lunch in St Omer, walk around the deathly cold cathedral, and drive north. The fields are glazed over with snow as we try to find the back roads towards Ypres. The villages we pass are small and crushingly dull. Nothing looks as closed-down as French provincial life.

Before long, we are in Belgium and I can see the spire of Ypres cathedral. The view is as pretty as a calendar. I am beginning to feel anxious, even slightly ill – like before a funeral. The road is built up into a causeway, like driving through the Fens. It is even flatter than East Anglia. We go slowly. Then, 200 yards away, across a field, I see a plain white wall with a little classical entrance. This must be Talana Farm cemetery, although there is no sign to say so. We get out and see a clear green walk between fields. The fields are full of twisted black stalks about a foot high. They look like charred crucifixes.

We walk up to the cemetery and in through the brick porch. There are 529 graves in the usual neat rows. The identical shapes and sizes create a surreal effect. At the far corner from where we came in is a tall white cross. The cemetery is on a slight slope. Plot three is just above us. We walk up among the gravestones. Most of them have a little shrub at the foot. Plots three and four have many graves of the Duke of Wellington's Regiment. I find row D first. We go along through the snow, towards a neat boundary hedge. Here is grave number one. It is under a small tree which is leafless now, but has made Edmund Ashworth's stone greener, and harder to read, than the others. Anyone who has visited Haworth church will know what I mean. The stone gives only the regimental details and below (barely visible through the green) are the words: 'At Rest'.

Both Sally and I find it strange to be here. After all, Edmund Ashworth is someone we have never met, only heard about and seen in a photograph. We know almost nothing about his life or his death. I feel an odd mixture of abstraction and overwhelming sadness. I don't think it relates directly to Edmund Ashworth. It is the emotion produced by the cemetery on this cold, clear, inappropriately beautiful day.

We take snapshots, feeling like out-of-place tourists (we get edgy about which shots to take and how many). We make sure that the snapshots show only his grave and the cemetery. We don't want pictures of ourselves. It would be wrong. This isn't a seaside outing.

I had thought that we would want to stay and look. But it is too much. I notice, as we go back down the slope, that some graves are set closer together, in pairs or threes. These soldiers musts have been killed together and no one knows which limb is which. A niche behind the porch has a list of the dead and a visitors' book. We sign our names and leave. We walk back down through the blackened stumps, saying nothing.

Back home I decide to find out more about Edmund. The family story was that he had been made up to lance-corporal because he had been a good bowler on the local cricket team and this meant that he was good at throwing grenades. It was also said that he died because another soldier was ill and Edmund offered to take his place in the front line. My eldest son says I should try to find the regimental war history. I dig it out in the London Library: *The History of the 1st/4th Battalion Duke of Wellington's (West Riding) Regiment 1914–19* by Captain P.G. Bales MC, formerly adjutant to the battalion and keeper of its war diary.

The 1st/4th Battalion were part of the Territorial Army, founded in 1908, as anxieties about Germany mounted. When war broke out, they were billeted at Hull where they did odd jobs: digging trenches, guarding the docks, trying to round up supposed German spies – or just Germans. They were cross at not being sent out to the front. In April 1915, they finally left the north. By the summer, they were in the Ypres Salient, the only corner of Belgium not conquered by the Germans. To abandon Ypres would have straightened out the front line and cut down the cross-fire in the Ypres Salient. It became a point of principle for the British that Ypres should not be taken. And it never was, although in the Third Battle of Ypres, better known as Passchendaele, about 200,000 British soldiers died late in 1917, trying to break the German line. The Germans lost almost as many. Sometimes Hitler was in the German trenches.

A map in Captain Bales's book shows the lines the battalion occupied. The soldiers gave them names from home: Barnsley Road, Colne Valley, Skipton Road, Huddersfield Road. Captain Bales's dry military prose begins to show the reality behind these comforting place names. The battalion arrived, he said, keen to 'bag a Bosch'. But they only had two old Maxim machine guns, so they mostly relied on rifles. Hand grenades were 'just coming to the fore'. (And with them Edmund Ashworth's old skills as a bowler.) The Germans had mortars and the battalion 'had nothing effective to retaliate with'.

'The Ypres Salient,' Captain Bales writes, 'bore an evil reputation – not without cause.' Water lay close to the surface. Even in the mild rains of July 1915, the ground became sodden. No orders had been given to put in drainage. 'It was obvious that, as soon as the autumn rains began, the trenches must become waterlogged. Yet nothing was done.'

Working at night, the battalion built up earthwork defences with sandbags and wooden props. In the daytime, they wrote shoals of letters home. So far as I know, none of Edmund Ashworth's has survived. At the end of October, the rains began. The trenches were barely above the level of the canal. Water poured into them from higher ground. Even as the soldiers moved in, after only two days' steady rain, much of the front line was two feet deep in semi-liquid mud. As the rain want on, earthworks caved in.

'In a few days, hundreds of yards of trenches had become nothing but cavities filled with mud and water. Men who were wounded had to lie in the mud until they could be picked up after dark, assuming they were still alive. The earthworks often collapsed on top of the soldiers.'

No one had planned for such conditions. Men often got stuck in the mud and had to be pulled free, leaving their boots behind. They then had to fight in their socks. Soldiers were supposed to put protective grease on their feet. But there was nowhere dry to do this. All there was plenty of was rum.

In such conditions, the Duke of Wellington's held the line in November and December 1915. And somewhere in all this Lance-Corporal Ashworth was killed.

I go to the newspaper racks of the British Library in north London to try to glean more from the 1914 and 1915 editions of the *Hebden Bridge Times*. From one item, I gather that Edmund Ashworth and six other local teachers enroll in September 1914. Soon afterwards, the first of a series of weekly newsletters appears in the *Hebden Bridge Times* 'from a local Territorial' – who must be Edmund – reporting cheerfully on life near Grimsby, where he is sleeping in a chapel and having 'quite a jolly time of it'.

The first report appears of a local soldier's death. Private J.W. Greenwood 'fell asleep' during 'the Kaiser's vicious attack'. Slowly the deaths begin to rise. The back page carries more and more photographs of the dead – 'the fallen heroes' – usually in the Sunday best they wore to the studio before they departed.

In early 1915, as the news gets worse, the cheery newsletters from Territorial Army camps cease to appear. At the back, the deaths fill column after column. In the issue of 25 December 1915, on the back page, is Edmund Ashworth, in a reproduction of the photograph we brought back from Hebden Bridge after Sally's mother died.

'He met his death with the calm indifference he always showed,' a fellow soldier ('WHM') writes. 'At 6.30 am on the morning of 13 December, he had just finished giving the rations out to his section and was stretching his weary and wet limbs when the bullet of a

German sniper pierced his heart. He said, "I am hit; fetch the stretcher-bearers" and then he peacefully passed to rest.' On 14 December, a party of soldiers took his body to 'our ever-increasing cemetery'.

My niece has just sent me the latest edition of the *Hebden Bridge Times*. The newspaper is running a series of reproductions of old prints, taken by a local portrait photographer. This week's picture shows, blurrily, local dignitaries gathered at the new memorial gardens in 1938. Rather late in the day, Hebden Bridge was unveiling its tribute to those who had died in the First World War. Will Ashworth is there taking notes for his report. You can tell him by his shock of white hair. It turned white during his experiences as a young man in the Boer War.

Four years after the photograph was taken, the Art Deco, wrought-iron memorial gates were taken down for scrap metal for the Second World War.

3.7 'WAR GRAVE PILGRIMAGE'

Tony Walter

From *Pilgrimage in Popular Culture*, Walter, T., and Reader, I. (eds), Basingstoke, Macmillan Press, 1993, pp. 69–77, 83–8.

Among certain sections of the British population there has been a dramatic shift since the mid 1960s in approaches to death and bereavement: the dignified dying or bereaved person is no longer the one who stoically declines to mention the subject, but the one who expresses their feelings (Walter 1991). In some families members in their forties or younger may well feel that it would be good if grandpa or grandma were able to visit the grave; and middle aged people who never knew a father who died in World War Two may begin to feel that rather than sweeping their loss under the carpet as was done in the 1950s and 1960s, it is time that they too went to see the grave.

Coinciding with the generational factor are the demands of television. Producers love anniversaries – they can research and film well in advance, get footage both of visually dramatic ceremonies and of personal reminiscences, and present it on the day as topical news – something very useful for the news team to have 'in the bag'. TV coverage of the 40th and 70th anniversaries of battles have brought the subject into the living room at just the time when family members have become prepared to talk about it.

One might expect the current nostalgia boom (Hewison 1987) to be a major factor in the popularity of battlefield tourism. There may well be an element of this for some ex-soldiers and for some tourists, but there is much about pilgrimages to war graves in a foreign land that militates against nostalgic glorification of war. They are usually small scale affairs, without pomp and circumstance. An elderly widow, alone with her thoughts in a rainy Belgian cemetery, while the taxi driver waits for her to compose herself for the return trip to the main tour, is hardly a celebration of glamour and glory. If nostalgia is characterized by a falsification of history, then there is little nostalgia here: the woman is grieving an all-too-real human being. Grief for a young husband, or for a twenty year old brother, is not grief for a mythological version of what was, but grief for what might have been; grief not for a lost past, but for a lost future. . . .

PILGRIMS, TOURISTS AND ENTHUSIASTS

Whatever subsidiary reasons they have for travelling, pilgrims have one purpose: to visit a particular grave or memorial. Many are widows and other close family members of the one killed. I have come across several mother (in her seventies) and daughter (in her forties) combinations, with the same story – he died in World War Two, with daughter an infant or still in the womb. Reaching middle age and therefore more aware of human mortality, the daughter becomes overtly interested in the unknown father, and travels to the grave both for her own sake and to take mother before she becomes too infirm to travel. Other pilgrims are survivors, veterans who, often with son or grandson, make a pilgrimage to pay respect to their mates who died. They too seek a name, or names.

Others still are representative pilgrims, coming on behalf of someone else. An early example is described by Basil Farrer, one of the few Old Contemptibles still surviving in 1991: 'The first time I visited the battlefields was in the early 1920s, when I went in search of the grave of the son of a Nottingham couple on whom I had been billeted in 1917. My search was before the wooden crosses on the graves had been replaced by the present head-stones; I located the grave of my friends' son, took a photograph and sent it to them.' It is not uncommon today for a woman to be the keeper of the family's letters and to maintain an interest in relatives killed in war, but it may be her husband or son who actually goes overseas to visit the grave. . . .

Then there are family historians who come in search of a particular grave or name on a memorial, but are not closely related to the one who died – they may have developed a personal interest in a parent's brother, or a grandfather or great-grandfather, killed in the First World War. As the years go by more, not less, people find themselves with an ancestor who died in World War One. The deaths of these men are intrinsically interesting, often well documented in letters that may still be in the family, forming a link with a lost Victorian world. Anyone who grew up before 1914 somehow seems to belong to a different world, and if they died – tragically or heroically – in the trenches, they can take on for today's family a unique aura. Family members may find the visit to the grave unexpectedly moving, as one woman said of the trip she and her husband made to her great Uncle Cecil's grave on the Somme: 'We spent ages there, it was so sad never to have known him. I felt awful leaving him, what with nobody having visited before.' But family historians do not go so far as to say – as do widows – that now their life is complete and they can die in peace.

Many people, however, travel simply as tourists – out of curiosity, because they want to try something different, to keep a spouse company, or because they chance across a war cemetery en route to elsewhere. Some of these become unintentional pilgrims, finding that for a few moments they have ceased to be tourists and have connected with something very deep. Elsewhere (Walter 1990: 212–13), I have written of several occasions when this has happened to me, which at the time I described as 'the tourist becoming a pilgrim'.

The feelings of many, both tourists and pilgrims, were expressed by King George V during his 1922 pilgrimage (quoted in Longworth 1985: 79–80): 'I have many times asked myself whether there can be more potent advocates of peace upon earth through the years to come, than this massed multitude of silent witnesses to the desolation of war.' The outbreak of world war again within a generation, however, proved that memory of one great war would not prevent another and shattered the role of the cemeteries as icons of the peace movement. Peace protesters are rarely to be found on battlefield tours and pilgrimages today, but that does not reduce for many a visitor the cemeteries' power as a vivid statement of the desolation of war.

For those with no one grave to visit, the hundreds or thousands of graves in a war cemetery can be too much to grasp. I recall myself in a Royal Air Force cemetery meditating at just one stone, whose fallen 20 year old pilot somehow came to stand for all the others. A 16-year-old on a battlefield tour with his parents was particularly struck by a grave to a father and his twin teenage sons, and to the graves of soldiers younger than himself. On a school trip, a brash 17-year-old keen to join the army broke down on chancing across the grave of a lad his own age and in the regiment he planned to join; he still wants to become a soldier, but is more realistic now as to what it is all about.

Focusing on one representative grave is a strategy of some tour operators. At Hyde Park Corner near Ypres, in the front row of the cemetery is the grave to a 16-year-old, to which five years ago a relative attached a photo; at least one tour operator brings his tourists to this stone so they can stop and ponder on this one lad among the many.

A history teacher in a public school uses the same technique of following up not the scores of ex-pupils killed in the First World War, but the fourteen who died on the Somme. Having researched the fourteen, his pupils visit just one representative grave – of a lad who had been just two years older than them and had been in the very rugby team to which some of them are destined. The pupils identify with this lad more than they might a remote relative of their own. At the grave, the teacher says a few words about the lad and his death, lays a wreath, and leaves the boys to their own thoughts for a few minutes. . . .

Almost all tour operators have a space on the booking form where customers can indicate if there is a particular grave they wish to visit. Hence, many tours include a handful of pilgrims. Tours are usually arranged so that any pilgrims can absent themselves from the group for a couple of hours in order to take off in a taxi to a nearby cemetery. On British Legion pilgrimages, by contrast, the whole trip is geared to visits to individual graves.

On tours, far from the seventy year old veteran or widow having nothing in common with the nineteen-year-old button collector, they typically get on famously. The widows and pilgrims often become stars of the show, giving first hand accounts of the site being visited and making it come graphically alive for the younger tourists, while the interest of the younger tourists gives the older pilgrim an appreciation not usually accorded the elderly in our society. For the group, their pilgrim becomes a hero. One guide told me of a D-Day veteran who had never talked about the war to his children, but who on arrival at Omaha Beach proceeded to give a gripping account of the landings to the entire group. Guides as well as tourists are continually learning from their pilgrim veterans.

Another commercial operator told me,

We've had some such moving moments, with widows and relations. We were doing a World War One battlefield tour, and we had a booking from a little old lady who was well into her eighties, and she requested a special cemetery visit. When we got there – we often ask 'Can you tell us why you asked to come to this particular cemetery? I know the rest of the group would be interested.' So she said, 'Well it's very private, but I'll tell you my dears, this is my fiancé's grave.' She'd never been back, and didn't know how to get back, and then she heard about us. I think he was 21. And of course, for her, he's always 21. She asked me to take her to the grave, so I took her there and just left her. You know, she had kept faithful to that man all these years. So that pilgrimage was something that all her life she'd been dreaming about.

The tourists on that trip will not forget her either.

THE MEANING FOR THE PILGRIM: FROM CHAOS TO ORDER

One history teacher who arranges school trips to Flanders and Northern France suggested to me that battlefield visits are about creating order out of chaos. Out of the chaos of mud and meaningless death, out of the personal disintegration that is bereavement, out of the child's suppressed fears of non-existence, the visit to the battlefield and to the grave offer opportunities to create some meaning in that which most threatens human civilization: war and death. In this section, I will describe how individual pilgrims attempt to create order from their personal chaos.

More than anything else, pilgrims say they go to pay their respects to the ones who have died, to affirm that their death was not in vain, that they are not forgotten. Relatives may feel that at least one person from the family should visit the grave or the memorial on which the name is inscribed. Haunted by the photograph of the young man on his mother's wall, Timothy Pain (1990) tells of his desire to pay his respects to his grandfather, even though he was killed at Ypres four decades before Pain was born. He took his mother, concluding his account of the visit: 'A part of my inner being needs to believe that he knows and is pleased by our overdue visit… Now I can look into those eyes without any sense of discomfort. I have done my duty. Someone has at last said "Goodbye".'

Ex-soldiers feel a debt of honour to their comrades who died; often they feel guilty that they survived, knowing it could so easily have been they who were killed had they been less lucky or more brave. As one senior officer put it, 'You were damned lucky, and you've got a debt to pay.'. . .

For the bereaved, however, paying respect has a particular meaning. Again and again, they talk of it completing their life. As pilgrims on the 1928 pilgrimage put it (British Legion 1928: 45, 134): 'I have had the dearest wish of my life.' 'We have had a great yearning fulfilled in having seen the last resting place of our beloved sons.' 'I came all the way from home for this; now I can die content.' In 1991, the leader of a British Legion pilgrimage used similar language:

> We had a woman who went to her husband's grave on the Somme in, I think 1988. She last saw her husband at a station in Northumberland, she last waved goodbye pressing a little handkerchief and a Bible into his hand, in 1915. She went to her husband's grave for the very first time, ever, in 1988 or 1989. She was aged 93. We wrote to her last year…never had a reply. Then this year, we had a reply from the executors, saying that she'd passed away six months after her pilgrimage and that she had talked of nothing else.

Many speak of how the physical presence of the grave or the carved name on the memorial changes their life. One women wrote, in the mid 1980s: 'My father was killed and buried in Italy during the War when I was a baby. Two years ago, when I was 40, we went for the first time to visit his grave. It was an amazing experience – after all those years I felt complete having seen his gravestone. It is difficult to describe how much it meant then and since to me and the rest of the family. Without a gravestone, his identity would be lost.'

Timothy Pain (1990) expands, writing of his visit to the Menin Gate in search of his grandfather's name: 'A.T.R. Jones. Those letters had been carved over 60 years ago and never once in all those years had anybody gazed at them with such love and sadness. Somehow those stone letters transferred Alfred from a fading photographic image, from a phantom unreal figure, into a flesh and blood man who had lived, fought and died in a far off foreign country.'. . .

Arrival at the grave or memorial typically triggers an emotional response. Couriers attempt to give the pilgrim a balance of support and privacy. The pilgrim lays a poppy wreath or spray of flowers at the grave, and someone takes a photograph. British Legion pilgrimage leaders offer to take a photograph, and try to persuade the widow to be included in the picture so she can show the family back home that *she* was there.

As at the funeral that the pilgrimage replaces, words cannot say what is felt. Feelings have to be expressed in ritual, largely through flowers. Beyond the formal laying of the wreath, these rituals are typically initiated by the individual mourner. 'I picked a poppy near where they told me my boy was last seen' (St Barnabas 1927: 36). One middle aged journalist who travelled to Singapore to see the grave of the father she had never known told me that tending the flowers on the grave felt like caring for him – something she had never been able to do in real life. Finding it difficult to leave, as though she were leaving him, she understood for the first time why people tend graves.

A woman visiting the grave of her first husband in North Africa said to the local paper, 'I was overwhelmed by the beauty of the cemetery, there were flowers everywhere.' The article continues, 'Marigolds were growing on the grave. On asking later if it was possible to obtain some seed to grow at home, the man in charge of the cemeteries promised to post seeds from the same marigolds to her.'

If each individual pilgrim has their own personal goal whose attainment marks the culmination of their pilgrimage, British Legion pilgrimages also have a group climax in the form of a service of remembrance, usually at a memorial to the missing. Several commercial and educational tours also include a service of remembrance, including pilgrims and tourists alike. The personal vigil at the graveside, and the communal service of remembrance, involve both the participation of pilgrims and the spontaneous creation of personal rituals within an overall historic ritual framework – both notably absent from the typical British funeral which these ceremonies to some degree belatedly have to stand in for (Walter 1990: ch. 13). . . .

CONCLUSION: PILGRIMAGE AND TOURISM

I have made comparisons between the dynamics of modern battlefield pilgrimages and medieval religious pilgrimages. But how far do the comparisons go? Are battlefield pilgrimages really so very like traditional religious pilgrimages? Or are they better described as a form of tourism?

Battlefield pilgrimages have six characteristics that place them closer to traditional religious pilgrimage than to modern tourism. Firstly, operators clearly distinguish between the commercial tour and the British Legion pilgrimage; and in interview they used the word *pilgrim* for those travellers with a specific personal goal, and could distinguish them from their other travellers – whom I term *tourists*.

Secondly, the battlefield pilgrim has only one goal – the grave or memorial – and this is a key characteristic of the pilgrim over against the tourist who literally tours around (Urry 1990: 9). This is expressed in different schedules for British Legion pilgrimages and commercial tours.

Thirdly, the pilgrim's goal is, in Turner's (1974) evocative phrase, 'the centre out there'. Cohen (1979) has used Turner's concept of 'the centre' to identify five different forms of tourist, ranging from those socially adjusted individuals whose centre is in the home society and who travel for pleasure and refreshment, to those alienated individuals who seek on holiday to experience another culture or another way of living. These latter have their centre 'out there', but what they discover 'out there' is poorly related to their home culture – so they will either have to accept simply playing at being different for a couple of weeks a year, or they will have to leave their own society and join the kibbutz or ashram or whatever nirvana they have discovered.

Traditional religious pilgrimage and modern battlefield pilgrimage are different from all Cohen's tourist experiences in that the pilgrim's centre out there is well connected to core values of his home society, a point Cohen himself (1979: 188, 190–91) makes about pilgrimage. Although pilgrims in medieval Christendom had to leave their society in order to go on pilgrimage, their goal was nevertheless legitimate in terms of the values of that society. The same is true of most battlefield pilgrims: although a piece of their heart is with their comrades or their fiancé in Flanders fields, this psychological 'centre' is legitimated by a society that honours its military dead and that values romantic love. They are pilgrims, not tourists. Pilgrims talk of their journey as *completing* their life, of being able now to die in peace; tourists do not. Pilgrims can talk of completion only because there is a coherent link between their centre out there and their life back home. (This analysis, of course, does not fit those pilgrims who are disillusioned with how society's values have changed since the war, who are alienated from current society, and who go on pilgrimage in order to connect themselves with the centre *back* there.)

Fourthly, like medieval pilgrimages, battlefield visits are usually folk events, initiated from low in the social hierarchy. It was not till widows themselves put pressure on the UK government that, 40 years after the end of World War Two, it offered help to those who had not already visited their husbands' graves. Even the commercial tour operators are responding to a latent demand; they are not creating it out of nothing, even if by offering tours and pilgrimages they stimulate it.

Fifthly, and crucially, the battlefield and the grave are sacred because those we love and admire have died there. Like the medieval pilgrim, we come to pay homage to the relics of the saints – though we call them not saints but heroes. This is what makes battlefield pilgrimage different from tourism. And it is why tourists, on chancing by a Flanders cemetery or a Dachau, may find their cameras falling silent and themselves turning momentarily into pilgrims.

Sixth, the pilgrim is healed and becomes whole, complete, in the presence of the bones of the saints, or at the hero's grave. Medieval shrines often developed because of stories of physical healing; with the modern war grave, the talk is more of emotional healing.

The comparison with traditional religious pilgrimage, however, should not be taken too far. The healing power of the shrine is believed to be psychological rather than spiritual – it is seen within a modern psychological understanding of the grief process, even if tour and pilgrimage leaders do not articulate this in detail. If, as Durkheim suggested, traditional religion tends to bind people together, modern psychology tends to see them as isolated individuals, and it is therefore difficult to see how pilgrimages in which experience of the sacred is essentially psychological rather than religious can develop anything like the institutional solidity of the major medieval pilgrimage centres. . . .

The six ways I have listed in which modern war grave pilgrimage differs from modern tourism show that, despite the obvious structural similarities between tourism and pilgrimage, the two are *not* the same. On the twentieth century battlefield, we find both tourism *and* pilgrimage, and operators and travellers alike know the difference. When heroes die, when their relics heal, that is when you find pilgrimage. And at a shrine containing such relics, the orientation and behaviour of the pilgrim is easily distinguishable from that of the tourist.

BIBLIOGRAPHY

British Legion, *A Souvenir of the Battlefields Pilgrimage*, 1928.

E. Cohen, 'A Phenomenology of Tourist Experiences', *Sociology*, 1, 1979, pp. 179–210.

R. Hewison, *The Heritage Industry: Britain in a climate of decline*, London, 1987.

P. Longworth, *The Unending Vigil: a history of the Commonwealth War Graves Commission*, London, 1985.

T. Pain, 'Say Goodbye to Grandad', *Guardian*, 3–4 November 1990.

Society of St. Barnabas, *The Menin Gate Pilgrimage*, 1927.

V. Turner, *Dramas, Fields and Metaphors*, Ithaca and London, 1974.

J. Urry, *The Tourist Gaze*, London, 1990.

T. Walter, *Funerals*, London, 1990.

T. Walter, 'Modern Death: taboo or not taboo', *Sociology*, 25, 1991, pp. 293–310.

3.8 'COMMUNION AT THE WALL'

Cara Sutherland

From the Preface to *Hunger of the Heart: Communion at the Wall*, Powell, L., Dubuque, Islewest Publishing, 1995, pp. x–xi.

The Vietnam Veterans Memorial is almost austere in its simplicity. Two polished walls stretch toward the Washington Monument on the east and the Lincoln Memorial on the west, linking America's past with the present. Unlike the other memorials, you can't see the Wall from the car. You have to approach it. Enter its domain. At its outer edges, the Wall is less than a foot high, hardly appropriate for a national monument. Yet at the apex where the two walls meet, the memorial rises toward the sky, engulfing us with its height. At its center the Wall begins to make sense. The names, which began on a single line, have multiplied to the point where they surround us. All of a sudden the implication is clear: the Wall represents what might have been.

Looking at the Wall, we see the world reflected: sun, moon, clouds, the trees in the distance, the people standing next to us. Finally, we see ourselves on its surface. These reflections remind us that the Wall is as much about the present as the past. We see our world mirrored in the names we find there and realize that the slightest movement changes the view. No image is permanent on the Wall. Only the names are eternal.

Most of us touch the Wall. Our touch is tentative at first, but grows more assured as we discover its warmth. The black granite captures the sun, giving it back to our fingertips as they trace the names carved on its face. The list is chronological, beginning in July 1959 and ending in May 1975. Everyone is equal on the Wall; there is no rank, only the order of casualty. Each name has a diamond or a plus next to it. Diamonds confirm death, a plus means unanswered questions for families who still wait.

The Wall is a quiet place. There might be two people or twenty thousand present, but the sounds are still the same: hushed whispers, reverential comments, or just silence. Being at the Wall is a holy experience. It is Mecca for the Vietnam generation—America's Wailing Wall. It is the place where we come to mourn, to grieve, to reflect as a nation on the true cost of war. Personal opinion about the legitimacy of the war is irrelevant at the Wall. The only thing that matters is the recognition of life interrupted, the loss of potential, the families and friends who go on alone, comforted only by memory. It doesn't matter that we didn't know any of them personally. The act of coming to the Wall unites us with the people who did and from them we glimpse meaning.

I spent hours at the Wall during that week in 1993. I'd go in the morning right after dawn to watch the sun rise through the autumn mist. I'd stay until late at night after the tourists had gone home. I was at the Wall at mid-day, when bus loads would arrive on their choreographed tours of the city, when office workers strolled by on their lunch hours, when joggers cut through on their way to the reflecting pool. I saw the Wall in light and in darkness.

With crowds and with solitary veterans. It is where I now go during every visit to Washington. The Wall is no longer a foreign place.

For many the Wall is a place where they come to say good-bye and lay the past to rest. For others, the Wall is a beginning, the start of a journey as they seek to understand. For the Vietnam veterans, their families and friends, it is a place where finally they are "welcomed home." It is a place of reconciliation and healing.

Upon completion of the Wall, many people thought the job was done. But it was really only the beginning. The memorial not only honors the dead and missing, but offers the hope of healing to those left behind.

3.9 'THE THINGS THEY LEAVE BEHIND'

Charles Harbutt

The New York Times, 12 November 1995, p. 38.

In the 13 years since its dedication, the Vietnam Veterans Memorial has become the most visited monument in the capital; more than two million pilgrims are expected this year. Many who visit will leave behind something of their own: a medal, a note, combat boots with a packet of Kool-Aid inside. Preserved by the National Park Service, these items are accumulating into a social history collection as emotionally charged as the war itself was.

'There have always been mementos left at war memorials, but not of the intensity and volume that we are receiving,' says Duery Felton, curator of the collection. 'It's unique in that the items were not selected by a museum curator. History is being written from the bottom up, instead of from the top down.'

The items are left by every kind of visitor – friends, family, battle comrades, Girl Scouts – and for every reason – sorrow, longing, outrage at a Government they feel betrayed them. 'During the day we get tourists,' Felton says. 'At night, that's when the real ones come: the jungle grunts and those guys who saw too much combat. Some do it for a catharsis, a cleansing act. Some do it as an offering or to satisfy a pledge or a promise made.' The visiting season will hit full stride this weekend. 'Veterans Day now runs from October, November, through the first of the year. The park rangers may bring in 2,000 objects.'

The tradition allegedly began during the wall's construction, when the brother of a dead Navy flier tossed a Purple Heart into the wet concrete of the foundation. Months later, while cleaning up after the dedication, Tony Migliaccio, a maintenance foreman for the National Park Service, found objects that stood out from the usual park litter: a framed photograph of a 1955 Chevy, spontaneous poetry scrawled on Park Service pamphlets. 'I was touched by it,' he says. 'Obviously there was something going on here that was bigger than any of us thought it would be.'

For two years his workers saved the objects, stashing them in a toolshed. Then the Park Service decided the objects must be preserved more professionally. Now everything is saved except plants and flags – even the rocks and pebbles that visitors leave as tributes. The collection contains some 48,000 items, 'although that's a very conservative estimate,' Felton says. He describes a recent acquisition: a leather jacket festooned with medals, its pockets stuffed with motel receipts and restaurant checks that the owner evidently accumulated on his cross-country journey to the wall.

His staff goes to great lengths to unravel the significance of such items, calling the editor of a military newsletter to identify an unusual insignia, encouraging donors to explain what they've left and why. 'Each item, even the mass-produced objects, stubbornly insists on telling you that they are from an individual tragedy,' says Kim Robinson, a former assistant curator for the Park Service. 'They represent not one grief, but a whole cluster of griefs.'

That range is apparent in the letters left behind. A veteran wishes 'Merry Christmas' to a former high-school rival. Felton has even begun seeing notes expressing regret for not having gone to Vietnam.

'I read everything,' Felton says. 'Letters from medical corpsmen apologizing that they didn't do enough. Letters from another group saying, "You saved my life." I often wonder if these medical corpsmen will ever meet the people saying "Thanks."

Felton has observed subtle changes in the collection. Early donations were often spontaneous, like notes written on paper bags from the nearby Lincoln Memorial bookstore. As word spread that items were being preserved in perpetuity, visitors began leaving larger and premanufactured objects; longer letters, written at home, were placed in Ziploc bags. New generations are drawn to the Memorial as well: the collection contains letters from children of the deceased, and even from grandchildren 4 and 5 years old.

Asked to account for the tradition's endurance, Felton retrieves another letter, one that accompanied a dollar bill left last year on Veterans Day: 'On Nov. 12, 1994, my dad and I walked down the brick path past the increasing rows of names on the black wall of the Vietnam Memorial. He stopped at a panel and pointed to a spot between two names, "That is where my name would be." I didn't know what to say, I just stood there silently, selfishly realizing that if he had died that day I would not have been born. . . .

'He pointed to a white lettered name on the polished black surface, and said: "He had just cut my hair. Larry charged $2 for a haircut and I only had $1 on me. I told him I would pay him later. He was killed that evening. I try and come down at least once a year and pay for my haircut." We stood there silently, my dad remembering. On that day I saw only one of the infinite memories that live within the Vietnam wall. . . . Each name is a reminder, each tribute left at the wall has a story, whether it's this dollar for a haircut or a single wildflower, they all say, "I will not forget." Dad, I will not forget.'

3.10 'NIGHT ROUNDS: A VISIT TO THE VIETNAM MEMORIAL'

Marilyn Knapp Litt

From *Night Rounds – A Visit to the Vietnam Memorial*, Litt, M.K., 1998, www.illyria.com.

It was Sunday, Veteran's Day weekend 1996, and earlier that day I saw the Vietnam Memorial for the first time. Several people had attempted to explain to me how the names on the Wall were arranged chronologically. I looked at the dates and the names on the panels, but couldn't grasp it. I tried to listen, but the part of me that could process that information was busy with other business. The Wall was higher than I had imagined, and longer, and infinitely more terrible.

It was well into evening now as I walked along the Wall again, this time with a friend. As you make the long pass from one end to the other, you reach a slight bend in the middle. We didn't walk as far as the bend, but only walked along a short section of the Wall before turning to retrace our steps.

There weren't as many people at the Wall as there had been during the day, and everyone spoke softly if at all. Veterans tell you not to see the Wall by yourself and to go in the evening. After dark, the visitors are mostly veterans and all are people with a purpose, unlike some tourists who march past during the day.

We walked slowly and didn't talk. I was cold and tired and overwhelmed. My friend was a veteran who served as a nurse in Vietnam and had been to the Wall many times. She carried a penlight and, her head down, followed the small circle of light that slipped along the ground a few feet in front of us. As we passed certain panels, she somehow knew where she was, and would stop and flash the light briefly up to the Wall, illuminating a small section to read a name. Then, almost as if reassured the name was still in place, she would drop the light down again and stroll slowly on, not even looking up, before stopping again to swing a soft arc of light over more names.

We didn't walk the length of the Wall, or even very far along the Wall, before turning back to view again the same set of panels. A few times she broke the slow rhythm of our pacing by abruptly retracing a few feet to check on a name or by pausing to give a name extra scrutiny.

As we made the short circuit for perhaps the third time, she started to quietly explain about the chronology. The Wall is linear, but the dates make a circle. The dates on either end of the memorial are not from the beginning or the end of the Vietnam war. To follow the names in chronological order, you start in the middle of the Wall at the bend and walk to your right all the way to the end, then loop back to the left end of the Wall and follow it until you are back at the centre. As you do this you complete the circle and gradually come to the understanding that the Wall, like the war, does not have an end.

3.11 'TO HEAL A NATION'

Jan C. Scruggs and Joel L. Swerdlow

From 'Intro' and 'November 1982', *To Heal a Nation: The Vietnam Veterans Memorial*, Scruggs, J.C. and Swerdlow, J.L., New York: Harper and Row, 1985, pp. 3–4, 141–3, 146–8.

It is a place for people. You can feel alone or linked as never before with the people you love. You can feel uncomfortable or exhilarated. The Memorial dictates nothing.

This seeming simplicity is deceptive. The names keep you from remaining indifferent. You become part of them, and they become part of you. They search for something within you, and they stimulate you to search for something with greater meaning than yourself.

Many people come to see a special name. Every day someone leaves a flag, a flower, a snapshot, a memento, a poem, or a personal note.

Most visitors have no particular vet in mind. They come because they know that the Memorial has something important to offer.

These visitors include both the generation that got America involved in Vietnam and the Vietnam generation: 9 million men and women who served in the military and 30 million women and 20 million men who never served.

Always, there are countless young people – members of the post-Vietnam generation upon whom America depends to fight its wars.

Most of these young people know little about Vietnam. A child of draft age in 1986 was not born until three years after U.S. Marines first landed at Da Nang. For a six-year-old in 1985, Vietnam seems as far back as George Washington or Abraham Lincoln.

So they ask questions. Why is this here? Who are these names? What did they do? Why did they die? Did you know them? What does it mean to me? . . .

VIGIL

The vigil was scheduled from 10:00 a.m Wednesday, November 10, to midnight of Friday, November 12.

At either end of the chapel was a large slow-burning candle. There were twelve rows of seats, red roses, and the soft echoes that followed each breath and each footstep.

It was a simple ceremony: Volunteers worked in half-hour shifts reading the names, throughout the day and night. Every fifteen minutes there was a pause for prayer.

For weeks, volunteers had been practicing their allotted names. The hardest part was preparing not to cry, so that each name could be read loudly and clearly. Pronunciation was also a problem; and a Polish priest, a Spanish teacher, and a rabbi supplied expert advice.

"Rhythmic Spanish names. Tongue-twisting Polish names, guttural German, exotic African, homely Anglo-Saxon names," wrote *Newsweek* editor-in-chief William Broyles, who served in Vietnam as a Marine infantry lieutenant. "Chinese, Polynesian, Indian, and Russian names. They are names which run deep into the heart of America, each testimony to a family's decision, sometime in the past, to wrench itself from home and culture to test our country's promise of new opportunities and a better life. They are names drawn from the farthest corners of the world and then, in this generation, sent to another distant corner in a war America has done its best to forget. But to hear the names being read . . . is to remember. The war was about names, each name a special human being who never came home."

When you lost a son in Vietnam, you did everything you could to never forget anything about him. You made yourself remember conversations and scenes over and over again. You studied family photographs and realized there were far too few. You climbed to the attic and opened the cedar chest in which he'd stored his things. You touched the American flag that had come home with him, and you reread letters of condolence from the President.

So much had been taken from you, so you clung to the one thing they could never take away, something that had been with you since the joy of his birth: his name.

As they were read in the chapel, each name was like a bell tolling. Each ripped through the heart, into old wounds that could heal only after they were reopened.

They were read in alphabetical order, from Gerald L. Aadland of Sisseton, South Dakota, to David L. Zywicke of Manitowoc, Wisonsin.

Time slots when names would be read were announced, so their sound could reach across America to people who loved them. In Oklahoma, for example, at the exact moment her son's name was being said out loud, a woman stopped feeding her chickens and whispered a prayer.

Families and friends crowded into the Cathedral, where they waited, with cold hands and thumping hearts, for the precious moment. The father of an infantryman who had died in 1968 at age 19 explained to the volunteer reader: "It is important to have other people hear his name."

Another reader asked a mother if she would like to say her son's name when the time came. "You won't cry, will you?" the reader said.

The woman sat and waited, noting how every name was read slowly and clearly and with feeling—as if to say, We know your pain. We know this was a very special person who did not want to die.

She became tense as her time approached. Thoughts and emotions had to be forced aside. The reader nodded, and she stood, and in a loud, clear voice said her son's name in the crowded chapel, and added, "Our son."

Shortly afterwards, another woman rushed in late, so her son's name was read again. As she sat alone, a vet took her hand. Tears ran down his cheeks. They hugged and never said a word.

A journalist asked one vet who had just read names what it all meant to him. "I hope," he said, "that the Vietnam Veterans Memorial constantly reminds those who make foreign policy decisions of the costs of those decisions, and that it reminds the American people that they are ultimately responsible for what their government does."

A Medal of Honor winner who had volunteered to read names lasted five minutes before he broke down. He read the rest of the names on his knees. . . .

THE WALL

All week the American people discovered the wall.

At night they used matches and cigarette lighters and burned torches of rolled newspapers to find names. Volunteers stayed until dawn passing out flashlights. One father struck match after match, and then said to his wife in a hushed voice, "There's Billy."

They always touched the names. Fingertips traced out each letter. Lips said a name over and over, and then stretched up to kiss it.

Sunlight made it warm to the touch. Young men put into the earth, rising out of the earth. You could feel their blood flowing again.

Perhaps by touching, people regained a sense of life; or perhaps they finally came to peace with death.

We're with you, they said. We never forgot.

The panels of names were like mirrors. The more you looked, the deeper inside you saw. The names floated all around you, along with the clouds.

"As you saw your living reflection mixed with the names, a strong bond, a sharing, came forth."

"As I looked at and touched the names, a jolt went through me that rendered me stationary for a couple of seconds. It was as though time had stopped."

"I wouldn't have been born if Daddy had died in Vietnam."

"The names reach out and grab you and they scream, 'I don't want to be here!'"

"All the little children looking for their fathers' names. God!"

"It's depressing, but the war was depressing."

"What a waste. All those boys died, and for what? For fighting a war they had no way of winning."

"How did it happen? Why? Why does it hurt so much? Why my son?"

"The waste. The waste."

"I hate the reason he died."

"I never expected it to be passionless," Maya Lin explained to reporters. "The piece was built as a very psychological memorial. It's not meant to be cheerful or happy, but to bring out in people the realization of loss and a cathartic healing process. A lot of people were really afraid of that emotion; it was something we had glossed over."

A small group of protesters arrived shouting slogans denouncing the Vietnam War. Hundreds of Vietnam vets surrounded them. Violence seemed likely. Then the vets started to sing "God Bless America." The protesters looked embarrassed and left.

The vets had their own rituals of remembrance.

A vet carried a paper bag and a pack of cigarettes as he approached the wall. He found a name and took a beer out of the bag. He snapped open the beer, poured some on the ground, and drank the rest without pausing to breathe. He lit a cigarette, and smoked it slowly. Then he moved on to another name until the six-pack was gone.

A vet took out a bottle of whiskey and a dozen shot glasses. He stood in front of a name, saluted, filled all the glasses, drank them rapidly, saluted again, and left.

A vet struggled to keep ten candles lit. The wind kept blowing them out. Other vets stood around to block the wind. No one asked questions.

A small group of vets scattered the ashes of a comrade who had committed suicide. Another group arrived with a large American flag, and planted it in front of the wall.

"I want my daughter to see it," one man said. "I want her to stand up and be proud that her father fought."

Vets read the wall like an epic poem about the war in Vietnam: "There are the names of the guys who took bullets for me." "There's my whole platoon together!" "That's the day my helicopter went down." "Shit, here's half my platoon." "Ten guys died on the day I got hit."

One volunteer guide had her arm around a vet as she led him along the wall and showed him three names. The vet was shaking and crying. At a fourth name, he ran his fingers along the letters and cried out, "I loved him, and I love this wall."

A former medic searched for the name of a GI he had worked to save. Images of this man suffering had haunted the medic for years. "He lived! He lived!" the medic screamed. "I can't find the name."

Other vets found names of people they thought had made it home.

"Why am I here now, no longer young, with even less answers than I had then?" one vet wrote. "My name could have been on that wall. Six inches lower and I wouldn't have a leg. One man to the left and Sergeant Masso would be here and I'd be up there. I had no more right to life than they. What would they feel now if we had traded places? Would they have used their 14 years more wisely than I?"

Many vets went to the wall alone. They were afraid they would hate it, and afraid of the memories it would bring back. The smells. The filth. The horror. The loneliness. The sadness.

After seeing the wall, however, they needed each other, so they gathered in little groups. Men who had been strangers cried together. Many hugged. You have to touch the wall, they said to each other. They had never before been more strong or more fragile.

Promises to friends that they would never be forgotten had now been kept.

3.12 'NOTICE ANNOUNCING THE PROPOSED REDEDICATION OF SIENA TO THE VIRGIN, JUNE 18 1944'

P. Ciabattini

From *Quando I Senesi Salvarono Siena*, Rome, Edizioni Settimo Sigillo, 1997, p. 159. Translated by Gerald Parsons.

Sienese!

While war now overshadows our city, this Civil Authority, representing common feelings, intends to fulfil a solemn act of faith which will sustain the strength that will be necessary to overcome the extremely difficult days through which we have to pass. Following the example of our ancient forefathers, animated by the same zeal and inspired by the same devotion as them, we wish to repeat their promise of devotion to the most Holy Virgin, again offering our city to her, in purity of feeling and actions. The donation of the city will be renewed to the Venerable Image of the Madonna del Voto, Queen of Siena.

Be willing, Heavenly Patron, to hear the prayer that is raised from our hearts in this tormenting hour and give your help and your protection to our people in your Siena [that has been] faithful [to you] across the centuries.

From the Palazzo Comunale
17th June 1944

The Mayor Luigi Socini Guelfi

3.13 'ACT OF DONATION OF THE CITY OF SIENA TO THE MOST HOLY VIRGIN MARY'

(On display in Siena cathedral.)

Translated by Gerald Parsons

ACT OF DONATION OF THE CITY OF SIENA TO THE MOST HOLY VIRGIN MARY

The year nineteen hundred and forty four and the eighteenth of June, at 8.30 pm in the Cathedral Church of Siena:

> To execute the decision already made on the sixteenth of the same month, which interpreted the feelings of the entire population and decided to make a new donation of the city to the most glorious Virgin Mary, invoking her protection and help in the dangers of the present war, the illustrious Doctor Luigi Socini Guelfi, Mayor of Siena, with the deputy mayor, Doctor Gino Mazzeschi, with members of the Council and the Secretary of the Comune, preceded by the City Banner, escorted by pages and trumpeters, together with Count Guido Chigi Saracini, Rector of the Magistrato delle Contrade and the seventeen Priors of the Contrade themselves, with their pages carrying their respective banners as is customary, followed by numerous Sienese of every class, [processed] from the Palazzo Pubblico to the Cathedral where, near the chapel dedicated to the Most Holy Mary of Thanks, also called the Madonna del Voto, they were received by the most Reverend Mons. Mario Toccabelli, Archbishop of Siena, to whom they made homage.

The authorities and representatives took the places that had already been prepared for them, while in the cathedral a huge crowd was gathered, that also extended onto the steps [of the cathedral]. Litanies of the Madonna were sung, after which the Mayor went into an especially erected pulpit and read the following appeal:

> Most Holy Virgin, since you kindly deigned to accept the City of Siena that our fathers offered as a gift to you for the first time almost seven centuries ago, the people [of Siena] have always been faithful to your most high patronage and, counting the favours granted, have always had recourse to you in every hour of danger and anguish. With the profound devotion of our Fathers and, like them, proud of a deep faith that has not dimmed with time, and that all the gravity of the hour does not undermine, we return today to renew and confirm the gift of Siena to you.

We return, O Queen of Siena, because we intend to honour you and hold you in our hearts: the voice of our conscience, the light of our spirit, and the inexhaustible source of love for our neighbours that alone can save our country.

Therefore we call upon your help, in the name of all the people present in their glorious contrade, in the presence of the pastor of this city and archdiocese; we consecrate Siena once again to you, in the solemn promise to be worthy, therefore, of your name, of your protection, of your grace.

In faithfulness to this high promise we make ourselves ready, together with the honoured Priors of the Contrade – the true and genuine expression of the popular spirit of the Sienese – to sign below this act that will remain perpetually on your altar and is engraved in the history of Siena as a testimony to the faith that illuminates our hearts [even] in all the darkness of the times.

And we salute you with the words that the immortal genius of our people wrote, in your honour, indelibly on the arch of one of the gates of the city, where in the glory of art your power is exalted:

> "O Worthy Queen, Crowned by the High Father
> Perpetual Virgin, Protect Your Siena."

The donation, offered in such a form, was received and accepted by the archbishop, Mons. Mario Toccabelli, with expressions of great satisfaction and exhortations to know how to deserve the grace requested.

The mayor then placed the banner of the city near to the altar of the Madonna del Voto, ordering that it should be left there while the sacred image remained exposed to the veneration of the faithful, and likewise arranged that, as a permanent record of the new donation, the present deed would remain forever on the aforesaid altar.

The ceremony was closed, after a recitation of the Salve Regina and the singing of the hymn 'Maria, Mater Gratiae', by a blessing from the archbishop.

[Below this appear the signatures the Mayor, the Deputy Mayor, the Rector of the Magistrato dell Contrade, and the Priors of the seventeen Contrade of Siena.]

3.14 'THE DAY OF THE PALIO'

Alan Dundes and Alessandro Falassi

From *La Terra in Piazza: An Interpretation of the Palio of Siena*, Dundes, A. and Falassi, A., Siena, Nuova Immagine Editrice, pp. 96–8.

There is a certain sense in which the act of bringing a horse inside a church is a profanation of the church. Normally animals are not permitted to enter a church. However, the palio like so many festivals provides a special time of license, an opportunity for reversing reality. It is a day when a horse is not only allowed to enter the church, but it is required to do so. (A report from the end of the nineteenth century indicated that if the horse were a mare, it was customary for her to wear a white cap, for women were not allowed to enter a church with an uncovered head.)[1] The degree of profanation is further revealed by the belief that if the horse defecates while inside the church it is a sign of good luck in the forthcoming race.[2] If the nervous horse does defecate, one can see the immediate response of the contradaioli assembled – they break out in broad smiles. It is regarded as an omen that optimism and great hopes will not be in vain. The capitano may express his delight by carefully stepping in the auspicious sign. Should the horse relieve himself outside the church, either before or after the blessing, it would be regarded only as a normal bodily function. The horse must defecate in the church in order for the act to be regarded as a sign of good fortune.[3]

It is tempting to see a parallel between the profanation of the church and the sanctifying of the stable of the horse. During the days that the contrada stable is occupied by the horse, the stable becomes somehow sacred. No one is allowed to enter the stable without permission, and the horse itself becomes more and more a symbol of the destiny of the contrada. As the

---

1. "The Siena Races," *Temple Bar*, 117 (1899), p. 220.

2. There is absolutely no doubt that considering the horse's defecation in the church as a good omen is of considerable antiquity. However, relatively few accounts of the palio have bothered to mention it. There are several reports, e.g., André Bellessort, "La Joie de Sienne," *Revue des Deux Mondes*, 53 (1919), p. 400; Gerardo Righi-Parenti, *L'Anima del Palio di Siena*, 2nd ed. (Siena, 1926), p. 80; Toor, *Festivals and Folkways of Italy*, p. 294; Herbert Kubly, *American in Italy* (New York, 1955), pp. 190–92. Paolo Cesarini, *Il Palio* (Firenze, 1960), p. 48; and Laura Archera Huxley, *This Timeless Moment* (New York, 1968), p. 5; but it is strangely absent in the standard works by Brogi, Cecchini and Neri, Heywood, Marchetti, and Pepi.

3. Several informants volunteered explanations of the sign. One suggested that defecating made the horse lighter in weight and hence faster in the race. Another hypothesized that any horse which dared to defecate in a church is bound to be a horse with great courage and spirit. Accordingly, it was a horse likely to win the palio. We suspect that a possible explanation might be related to the equation of feces and money. This equation, which is found in many cultures, is evidently known in Italy. There is a proverb "I soldi sono lo sterco del diavolo" ("Money is the feces of the devil") which makes the association explicit. From this perspective, if the horse acting as a representative of the contrada defecates, he may be prefiguring the spending of money by the contrada. Spending money is something only the winner does. Hence the horse defecating is a sign of victory in the palio. Another possible aspect of the symbolism may be related to the infantile notion that the act of defecation calls for one's mother's attention and normally succeeds in bringing her into close physical contact. Thus by analogy, defecating in church ensures the presence or intervention of a supernatural "parent" figure. For further discussion of this train of thought, see Alan Dundes, "The Folklore of Wishing Wells," *American Imago*, 19 (1962), 27–34.

day of the palio approaches, the horse takes on some of the aura of a sacred animal. One indication that the stable becomes a church and the horse becomes sacred is an older tradition in which the winning horse is given bread and wine back in his stable following the victory. These elements, constituting a kind of communion, were in addition to the horse's regular food.[4] As the secular stable becomes sacred so the sacred church becomes partially secularized by the entrance of the horse. The transformation of church into stable is perhaps complete with the act of defecation.

After the blessing of the horse and jockey, the contradaioli assembled in the church mark the end of the ceremony by yelling the contrada cheer, e.g., "gi, gi, raffa!" Again, the mass yelling in what is normally a conspicuously silent church constitutes further proof of the temporary profanation of a sacred space.[5]

---

4. Valery, *Curiosités et Anecdotes Italiennes* (Paris, 1842), p. 190.
5. The curious mixture of sacred and profane was also evident right before Montaperti. During the ceremony dedicating the city of Siena to the Virgin, one could hear in between the prayers the cries of curses against the hated Florentines. See L. Zdekauer, *La Vita Pubblica dei Senesi nel Dugento* (Siena, 1897), p. 99.

3.15 'PALIO'

Alessandro Falassi and Giuliano Catoni

From 'Conclusion', in *Palio*, Evans, C.H. and Mann Borgese, E. (trans), Monte dei Paschi di Siena, 1983, p. 77.

The Palio is a festival that has been many festivals. Born as a secondary event in a great civic celebration, it has become its central point and essential moment; begun as a pastime for nobles and dignitaries, it has ended up the popular festival of an entire city; intended as a simple horse race it has turned into a game complicated and enmeshed by a thousand twists and turns.

As elsewhere in the Europe of the Middle Ages,[1] there was at Siena a city, a community with a habitat of its own, huddled within its walls and united by an unavoidably common destiny in those centuries of real insecurity. The civic festivals, with their system of symbols, their aesthetic, theatrical and ritual scenery, celebrated the unity, glory and felicity of the mother city. Just as country festivals celebrated the fertility of nature, the urban ones vaunted, more indirectly, the prosperity of the city state.[2] The opportunity they gave for pomp and ostentation spoke of its wealth; grandiose religious rituals celebrated the divine blessing, for which the rite of offerings both gave thanks and made supplication; the parading of former enemies reduced to subjection and alliance displayed the military prowess and political successes of the city.

When the great nation states made their appearance in Europe, the City States gradually and irrevocably lost their financial, political and military power. The ancient sentiments on which the festivals were founded abandoned the microcosm of the city to be invested in more abstract and distant entities. Everywhere civic festivals lost their original meaning and disappeared or, at most, survived.

Not in Siena though.[3] After the tragic end of the Republic, the Palio assumed on the contrary ever greater importance, until it reached its present form. Why Siena of all places, and why only in Siena?[4] Because the city held on to economic and demographic stability; because republican habits were more deeply engrained than elsewhere; because her culture, or at least what the Sienese took as its symbol, did not have time to change by degrees and refused

---

1. See the illuminating chapter "The Civic Ideal," in W. Bowsky, *A Medieval Italian Commune*, pp. 260–98.
2. On mediaeval and Renaissance festivals and their function see Yves-Marie Bercé, *Fête et révolte*, Paris, Hachette, 1976; Marianne Mesnill, *Trois essays sur la fête*, Brussels. Editions de l'Université, 1974. On the function and meaning of festivals in general see also A. Falassi, *Time out of Time, Essays on the festival* (in printing) and Victor Turner, *Celebration. Studies in Festivity and Ritual*, Washington, Smithsonian Institution Press, 1982.
3. On the end of the Republic see for example Langton Douglas, *A History of Siena...*, pp. 231–64; R. Cantagalli, *La Guerra di Siena (155–59)*, Siena, Accademia Senese degli Intronati, 1962; M. Filippone, *L'assedio di Siena. Dal III Libro dei Commentari di Blaise de Montluc*, Siena, Cantagalli, 1976; B. Aquarone, *Gli ultimi anni della Repubblica di Siena (1551–1555)*, Siena, tip. Sordomuti, 1869.
4. Notes on this recurrent question in A. Falassi, *Per forza e per amore*, p. 6; D. Balestracci-R Barzanti-G. Piccinni, *Il Palio. Una Festa*, p. 29.

to do so by force; because the memory of Montaperti[5] could never fade among her people. And then the city entrusted her most sacred and jealous memories to the festival, and turned it into evocation of history, mythologized return to the golden age, symbolic celebration of the greatest victory of her past to compensate for the defeats of the present; an image that set out to make imperishable a greatness that had once been real and that history had forever denied her.

The Palio is much more than a pageant and a horse race. There are those who have taken it for a splendid exercise in aesthetics, produced by a culture that had been through a period in which it created great art. "The Palio is just a show," wrote Aldous Huxley, "having no particular meaning."[6] Others on the contrary have seen it as the complex metaphor of a world view, specific to Siena, to her history and to her culture, whose elements can all be found, one by one, in the symbolism of the Festa.[7] Others have considered it an interplay of concord and discord, in which civic solidarity periodically breaks down into its opposite, factionalism, only to be reaffirmed, as new, at the end of each festival.[8] For some the Palio is the Middle Ages brought back to life;[9] for others a supreme expression of nationalism. Marinetti said that the Palio was "a mailed fist to be shaken at any enemy of Italy."[10] E.R.P. Vincent described it as a melting-pot into which all the innumerable elements of Italian national life are poured: "the Christianity and the paganism, the art, the history, the social virtues and the social failings – the very essence of the Italian character – blended harmoniously in one remarkable fusion."[11]

In the Palio the Sienese resort to the most subtle machinations of rationality and strategy, but they want it to be a game of chance at the same time; they set about it with fairness and prevarication, by force and for love. Preparing, living, awaiting and winning it require all the resources of reason and of chance.[12]

---

5. On Montaperti see W. Heywood, *Our Lady of August...*, pp. 11–44; L. Zdekauer, *La Vita Pubblica...*, p. 99; L. Douglas, *A History of Siena...*, pp. 91–104. The resentment of the Sienese against Florence crops up continually in many forms typical of Italian municipalism, but it is unusual in the fact that it almost invariably makes Montaperti (seven centuries after the battle took place) stand as an eloquent metaphor and antonomasia for anti-Florentine feeling. See A. Dundes-A. Falassi, *La Terra in Piazza*, p. 9. Explosions of this sort of feeling have been recorded after recent defeats by sports teams from Florence. A car sticker produced in a limited edition in Siena at the beginning of the eighties declares eloquently "Montaperti – I was there too." An extreme case of this is suggested by the anecdote about the contradaiolo who went to the football match between Celtic and Fiorentina held in Glasgow in 1970 to show his support for Celtic.

6. A. Huxley, *The Palio...*

7. A. Dundes-A. Falassi, *La Terra in Piazza*, pp. 185–240. The chapter is devoted to the Palio as a metaphor of the Sienese world view, as revealed by the different symbolic codes of the Festa.

8. See also A. Pomponio Logan, *The Palio of Siena...* and Don Handleman, *The Madonna and the Mare: Symbolic Organization in the Palio of Siena*. I am grateful to the author, from the University of Jerusalem, for a manuscript of this as yet unpublished article.

9. For this attitude, much in vogue in Savoyard and English *fin de siècle* and retained in oleography of the Palio, see for example A.H. Brewster, *Siena's Medieval Festival...*; M.L. Handley, *Siena's Palio, An Italian Inheritance from the Middle Ages...*; W. Hough, *The Palio of Siena: A curious Mediaeval Horse Race*; M.A. Taylor, *A Race at Siena: Medium Aevum Redivivum*.

10. Quoted in V. Grassi, *Le Contrade...*, vol. II, p. 65. For comments on the Palio see A. Tailetti, *Aneddoti...*, pp. 33–49; Aldo Cairola, "Poesia e Poeti del Palio," in A. Pecchioli, *Il Palio di Siena*, pp. 53–64.

11. See E.R.P. Vincent in *The Tradition of the Palio...* Siena as utopia is discussed in Nicholas Hildyard, *An Ideal City...*

12. On the Festa of Siena as *coincidentia oppositorum* see A. Falassi, *Saggio di mitologia senese*, in *Per forza e per amore*, pp. 9–29. For fortune in mediaeval tradition see Howard R. Patch, *The Goddess Fortuna in Mediaeval Literature*, Cambridge, Harvard Univ. Press. 1927.

Winning the Palio means the regeneration and continuation of an entire community (the newly-won banner is called in slang *il cittino*, the newborn son) but just as intensely private joy and the meaning of life for each of its members.[13]

"It was like when my first child was born." "You can't explain." "The finest moment of your life." "A joy no words can express." "The greatest joy I have ever experienced." These are the words of those who have had the opportunity and the fortune to experience this world as protagonists, to take part in this festival of festivals; they are echoed even by its most ambivalent heroes, the jockeys. Beppe Gentili spoke for all when he said: "There is nothing like winning the Palio, you just can't put it into words."[14]

The myth, the ineffable, is more real than the history that created it.

13. For the winning of the Palio as rebirth and regeneration of the contrada-family see A. Dundes-A. Falassi, *La Terra in Piazza*, pp. 187–88, 232, 234. Contrada songs on this theme in A. Falassi, *Per forza e per amore*, pp. 193–94, 217. The phrases quoted in the text were said to me by winning captains. See also M. Barni, "Ha vinto la mia Contrada," in *La Nazione*, XCVI (1954), no. 156, p. 4 (Sienese edition); *K'8*, special publication of the Tartuca, Siena, Meini, 1933, p. 8.
14. Quoted by R. Barzanti in the introduction to D. Magrini, *I Guerrieri...*, p. 12.

Part IV:

Global Religious Movements in Regional Context

The readings in this section examine the phenomenon of how religions adapt as they spread around the world. While the majority of readings deal with Christianity, Buddhism and Islam are also represented. Reading 4.1 was written by Oliver Barclay, a leading figure in the generation that promoted the post-war revival in British Evangelicalism. His position is a conservative one, and displays relative caution towards Charismatics and more recent cultural shifts in Evangelicalism. The report of the General Synod working group in the Church of England (4.2) is a balanced appraisal at the point at which Charismatics received a degree of official acceptance in the Church of England. Reading 4.3 is representative of both 1990s shifts in Evangelicalism. Tomlinson was a leading figure in the 'house'/new church movement, but then in the late 1980s began to experiment with an unconventional church, meeting in a south London pub on Tuesday evenings. His approach is one kind of Evangelical response to postmodernism, not necessarily representative, but interesting and provocative. Reading 4.4 offers an American counterpart to Barclay in offering critical insider appraisal, although his formative experience of Evangelicalism was in the 1950s–1960s, rather than the 1930s–1940s. Reading 4.6 gives insight both into Wimber's spirituality and that of the Vineyard in general. Latin American Evangelicalism is represented by 4.7–4.9.

Readings 4.10 and 4.11 point up key elements of the tensions and challenges thrown up by the world-wide spread of another missionary faith, Islam. The experience of Soka Gakkai as it goes global is presented in the readings which follow (4.12–4.18).

4.1 'LOOKING BACK, REACHING FORWARD'

Oliver Barclay

From *Evangelicalism in Britain 1935–1995*, Leicester, Inter Varsity Press, 1997, pp. 133–42.

It seems clear that the evangelicals (particularly the CEs [Conservative Evangelicals]) of the 1930s were generally too anti-intellectual and too anti-theological. As a result, they were often superficial and their apologetics quite inadequate. They could be negative about secular 'high' culture because they did not know how to relate to the 'modern mind' of their day. They had, of course, a rich popular culture of their own, but they had become defensive and sometimes sharply contentious, though that was difficult to avoid when they were constantly under fire. To the exclusion of all else, they concentrated on the basics – sometimes called 'the simple gospel' – teaching the Bible and getting on with straightforward evangelism and missionary work, at which they were very good. That gave them plenty of scope, but they failed to recapture the theological training that they had left to others, and few of them who studied theology were uninfluenced by the prevailing liberalism. They had a splendid, if not very deeply doctrinal, knowledge of the Bible, and that gave great toughness to ordinary church members; but they lost many of their ablest young people and ministers in training to other traditions. For lack of a well-thought-out position they tended towards negative pietism and a legalistic stance in ethics – a short-cut solution to complex questions. In reaction to liberal 'social gospel' advocates they defended a negative attitude to social action, apart from immediate local philanthropy.

MISTAKEN REACTIONS

In an attempt to break out of this too tight and too negative position, two different strategies started to be developed in the 1920s, and became important in the 1930s and 1940s. One, represented by the Oxford Group/Moral Rearmament, sought direct words from God ('guidance') apart from the Bible, and this gradually replaced the Bible in authority, both in personal 'quiet times' and in corporate strategy. It also led to a gradual loss of biblical and doctrinal content in the stress on experience and superficial 'life-changing' evangelism.

The other strategy, represented by the Anglican Evangelical Group Movement and the Fellowship of the Kingdom, was to borrow from the current culture, and that meant borrowing from a rationalist tradition. The message was progressively stripped of its offensive 'supernatural' elements until it became little different from the best humanistic outlook.

The Student Christian Movement, with its positive enthusiasms and its strong CE roots, had lost its way by trying to draw in leaders and speakers from all sections of the churches on to its platform. It spoke of wanting to stand in the current mainstream of theological tradition. In the prevailing theological scene, that meant that it also moved to a frankly liberal theological position as far as it could be said to have had one.

These movements may have had the best of motives, but they had the most disastrous of theologies. They experienced success for a time. To conservatives it seemed to be a kind of theological kwashiorkor – the deceptive result of a poor diet, or of deprivation of biblical food. Before long, however, they died of a lack of biblical input, while those who had a good diet gained strength, especially those who loved biblical doctrine and tried to base the Christian life upon it in the way that the New Testament does.

If we had lived then, we might well have made the same mistakes. It was a difficult time for the churches. They were losing ground, and it was easy to think that the old paths were no good. If we can learn from both the failures and the successes of the past, we may be helped to avoid falling into the same traps and to look for some guidelines for the future. No doubt there are new dangers also, but we need not repeat history. . . .

1995

What, then, of the present and the future? The portion of history I have sketched suggests strongly that evangelicalism will not advance by cultural and intellectual compromise, as advocated in the LE [Liberal Evangelicals] tradition. Nor will it advance by reliance on extrabiblical 'guidance', as in the Oxford Group/MRA. In the 1990s, we are faced with some of the same temptations as they were in the 1930s. It is again a very difficult time for the churches, and it is attractive to try to find some new theological emphases that resonate with the current culture. The danger is that, as many evangelicals did then, we should either compromise the truth or dilute it to a point where there is little biblical substance left. In a human-centred and experience-oriented generation that is earnestly seeking feel-good factors, it is not so easy to declare a word from God that is more than just the best and most attractive idea to our generation. When our hearers are human-centred, it is easy to follow them and to cease to be God-centred. As David Wells has put it: 'In these last three decades . . . Christian truth went from being an end in itself to being merely the means to personal healing.'[1] The soothing Thought for the Day on radio and the bland 'spirituality' of an outlook influenced by New Age sound more attractive. There is a danger of trying so hard to communicate with that culture in its own terms that we absorb too much of its influences, as the LEs did in the 1930s and 1940s.

If we, quite rightly, recognize some good in the culture and thinking of non-Christians and of other Christian traditions, then we need to be even better informed doctrinally if we are to discern the good from the evil and not to swallow them both together. The old clear-cut positions were in the short run easier to maintain in a simple way, but things are not all black and white and in the long run that position resulted in the loss of many of the more thinking young evangelicals. It is almost certain to do so again if there is not a good foundation in biblical teaching of considerable depth.

There is also a growing tendency to follow the policy that was so disastrous in the SCM of seeking to have 'important' people as platform speakers and, just because of their status, applauding their largely irrelevant pronouncements as if they were clear biblical thinkers. We are easily flattered by the attentions of those with big names, and the desire to be recognized

---

1   David F. Wells, *No Place for Truth, or Whatever Happened to Evangelical Theology?* (IVP, 1993), p. 210.

or accepted contains a hidden trap that leads to pride. We must keep fighting for the truth, even if it gives offence.

At the same time, we are undoubtedly in danger in some circles of a renewed anti-intellectualism and anti-doctrinal superficiality that can feed on implausible uses of Bible verses out of context, especially when coupled with dogmatic statements about what is God's will. Our age is experience-centred, and as a result unstable in almost all relationships. We therefore do well to be aware of the instability, and of the inadequacy from a biblical point of view, of an experience-oriented religion such as was fostered by the Oxford Group/MRA. If experience is stressed at the expense of doctrine (that is, truth) we are in trouble. Jesus was twice described in John 1 at 'full of grace *and* truth' (verse 14, *cf.* verse 17), and Peter urges us to 'grow in the grace *and* knowledge of our Lord and Saviour Jesus Christ' (2 Pet. 3:18). We dare not think that either a little grace or a little truth is sufficient. Therefore we must not run away from the theological and intellectual challenges of our time. We must develop a consistent evangelical theological training. Based upon a good foundation in biblical doctrine, evangelicals should be able to press ahead confidently into every area of thought and practice, and increasingly recapture ground that has been lost to serious Christian influence by liberalism and other distortions and dilutions of apostolic Christianity.

The greatest threat to evangelical strength, therefore, comes if we slip into superficiality of biblical input and fail to address the relative biblical illiteracy of our generation. If we do fail, we shall leave our hearers vulnerable to the latest errors, both at the top academic level and at the 'pop culture' or New Age level. We could again see something like the renewal of a vigorous LE movement on the one hand and a superficial and unstable experience-based pietism on the other. If the form of the disciplined early morning 'quiet time' has to change for many, some better way has to be found.

A good biblical diet may not seem as immediately exciting as a more experience-based approach. As with physical food, however, the attraction of unhealthy foods not only fails to make strong bodies but can produce a dependence on elements that put no iron into the blood or calcium into the bones. We need reserves for the tough days, and the Bible sometimes finds the solution to practical problems in the most surprising and apparently rather obscure corners of revealed truth. We see an example when Paul addresses the questions of going to law with fellow Christians and of immorality with his counter-question '*Do you not know* . . . ?' (1 Cor. 6:3, 9, 19).

Ministers and youth leaders easily forget that the input that they provide – often only one service on Sunday – is far from being enough for those with little background of biblical knowledge. D.A. Carson puts it trenchantly: 'The ignorance of basic Scripture is so disturbing in our day that Christian preaching that does not seek to remedy the lack is simply irresponsible.'[2] Compared with the 1930s and even the 1940s and 1950s, evangelicals are now weak in the biblical content put into work with children and young people. Merely orthodox doctrine is no substitute for the Bible, which has unique spiritual power. That is not to suggest that merely having our heads stuffed with knowledge of the text of the Bible will in itself provide spiritual power. It is, however, a uniquely effective foundation for spiritual growth,

---

2   D.A. Carson, *The Gagging of God: Christianity Confronts Pluralism* (Apollos, 1996), p. 194.

and the Holy Spirit evidently inspired the Scriptures so that they should be his most reliable guide to spiritual life and maturity.

There are two main streams emerging in the evangelical community, and this division may prove more fundamental in its long-term effects than any other. It runs right across denominational distinctions, charismatic and non-charismatic divisions and any special-interest and party groupings. It is between those who make the Bible effectively, and not only theoretically, the mainstay of their ministry, and those who do not. Those who seek to clarify, teach and apply the Bible's message as their controlling principle and as the daily sustenance of the individual will, if this period of history is any indication, produce strong Christians who are able to grapple with all kinds of issues in life, and to face the really tough experiences when they come. Those who fail to use the Bible in this way are almost certain to produce vulnerable Christians or painfully dependent people, who dare not move out from the particular congregation where they have been supported unless they can go somewhere else where they will be equally propped up. Exposure to a new cultural and intellectual atmosphere or a personal crisis will find them weak. . . .

4.2 'THE CHARISMATIC MOVEMENT IN THE CHURCH OF ENGLAND'

From 'What is the charismatic movement' and 'Evaluation', in *The Charismatic Movement in the Church of England*, General Synod of the Church of England, London, CIO Publishing, 1981, pp. 1–3, 44–6.

WHAT IS THE CHARISMATIC MOVEMENT?

Many, if not most, of the main denominations of the world church have over the last quarter of a century experienced a new spiritual movement, sometimes called the 'Charismatic Movement', sometimes the 'Charismatic Renewal', sometimes simply 'The Renewal'. Because it is a 'movement' it does not admit of clear boundaries or definition. It is easier to recognize than to define, easier to describe by its phenomena than to isolate under a magnifying-glass, easier to experience than to report scientifically. If the word 'charismatic' is included in the title, then it appears to make *charismata*[1] too central to the movement; but if 'charismatic' is omitted, then the whole movement starts to lose its identity in discussion. Of these two horns of the dilemma, it is slightly more useful to be impaled on the former, and keep the word 'charismatic' in the title. There will still be difficulty in identifying what makes the charismatic movement the charismatic movement, but at least it will not be muddled with anything else.

Consider the following book titles (each one drawn from a biblical text): *You He made alive; Greater things than these; New Heavens, New Earth; As at the beginning; One in the Spirit; Remove the heart of stone; Not mad, most noble Festus; A people for his praise; When the Spirit comes; Locusts and wild honey.* Here, in a random series of titles mostly from within the movement, we begin to sense a flowing tide of Christian believers characterized by spiritual life, active and visible amongst them, by a strong sense of the power of God at work on earth (often in miraculous ways) amongst them, by an upward-looking faith, by a claim both of continuity with the early days of the apostolic church and also an openness to the future, and by a preoccupation with God himself, even at the risk of seeming to lose touch with the 'reality' of the more earthbound believers and unbelievers. If these titles reflect a movement, then the meeting of man and God – in particular the Spirit of God – is absolutely central to its concerns. The varied *charismata* may be an expression of that meeting in such a way that 'charismatic' becomes a loose shorthand way of identifying the movement. But it remains inexact as a descriptive title – the central feature of the movement is an overwhelming sense of the presence and power of a God not previously known in such a combination of otherness and immediacy. Nevertheless, we join the findings of the BCC's consultation on the value of charismatic renewal (held in December 1978):

---

1. The Greek word means 'free gifts'. It is used chiefly of the Holy Spirit's endowments. (See especially 1 Corinthians 12.)

'(In the early sessions) it had become apparent that there was no immediately acceptable definition for "charismatic renewal", either to those who felt themselves part of it or to those observing it.'[2]

It is our hope that sufficient description and evaluation will clearly identify the areas of the Church of England where there has been 'charismatic renewal' in the recent years. We recognize the difficulty of defining, but both refuse to be distracted by it, and also hope that as the report progresses we shall enable *recognition* to supplant *definition*.

There is an alternative technical term on offer. Sometimes the word 'Pentecostal' is employed, instead of 'charismatic'. This adjective, pointing as it does to the coming of the Spirit in power upon the infant church, has a more general connotation than 'charismatic'. However, its actual denominational and other usage has given it a fairly specific denotation, though modern 'charismatics' are often distinguished from more traditional Pentecostals by the prefix 'neo-', as 'Neo-pentecostals', which usually denotes charismatics in the mainstream Christian Churches, charismatics who have not become members of 'Pentecostal' churches.

The years from 1960 to 1980 have seen no less than 104 official or semi-official denominational reports (some national, some regional, some international) on 'the charismatic renewal', to judge solely from those published in the three volumes entitled *Presence, Power, Praise* edited by Kilian McDonnall.[3] This confirms our confidence that there *is* a distinctive movement, and that a report *is* a way of encapsulating it. We also note that Anglicanism barely figures in the list of 104 documents. So the Church of England is hardly precipitate in stopping to look at the spiritual upsurge which has been occurring within its corporate life in these two recent decades. And our investigations strongly confirm that it not only has been happening, but also, despite some recurrent schismatic tendencies, it has been happening to and among Christians who assert that this experience of the Spirit is the proper outcome of their Anglicanism, that the charismatic movement belongs within the Church of England and its members are not to be driven out. They feel that the whole Church of England stands to gain by a determined holding on in love to what the movement has to offer, and to the hot-headed zealots it may throw up. We concur with this, and look for much growth in true spirituality to flow from this channel of God's power at the heart of our corporate Christian life.

EVALUATION

To establish some secondary causes, even though they be causes through which God may himself have been at work in some special way, does not *of itself* establish the movement as a special outpouring of God's power. Yet the character of those 'causes' does suggest that the charismatic movement has found itself filling a gap in traditional Anglican Christianity. . . .

---

2. *Report of the Consultation on the value of charismatic renewal* held at London Colney in December 1978 (BCC, London) pp. 3–4.
3. Liturgical Press, Collegeville, Minnesota, U.S.A., 1980.

However, if we place the charismatic movement on the world-scene, and note how it has affected Churches from Rome right through to the House Church Movement, then a question starts to emerge: was Newbigin right, in *The Household of God*, to make Pentecostalism a 'third strand' in the character of the world-wide church, seen in its ideal state? And if he was right, then is the outpouring we have seen, in the very years since he wrote, a kind of fulfillment and confirmation of what he wrote? Thus the three strands would be – the 'form' of the church (Catholicism), the primacy of the word (Protestantism), and the experience of the Spirit (Pentecostalism). But the oddity which Newbigin did not foretell (though his whole argument points ideally towards it) is that the Pentecostal experience has been found *within* the catholic and protestant traditions, and not just complementing them from the outside.

If we accept Newbigin's argument, then we have a framework of thought with which to return to the Church of England's own charismatic movement. Is it not likely that a church which has for so long claimed to be unashamedly both catholic and protestant will also need to find a place for this 'third strand'? Its internal ecumenicity calls for this, but not only calls for it, it has got it! The Church of England claims to be catholic in the sense of being primitive and comprehensive, and disclaims being a denomination, if 'denomination' entails only a partial view of the truth of the Gospel or the nature of the Church. It must surely then recognize and welcome this Pentecostal strand which has arisen so astonishingly within its own ordered and institutional life.

Though such an argument may sound fine in a Synod report, it could infuriate some charismatics! Those who are seized of a strong conviction of truth (whether Anglo-catholic or evangelical, radical or charismatic) do not take kindly to being 'patronised' with phrases like 'a valuable contribution', as though above and beyond the differing traditions within the Church of England there were some super-managers, seeing themselves as above the traditions and engaged in blending them into 'the best mix'. The heirs of the Evangelical Revival and of the Oxford Movement both already know the sterilizing effect of such an attitude, for to them it implies that a particular strand of tradition is but a good 'one-eyed' view, needing to be complemented by others in order to become 'two-eyed', thus denying their claim that their tradition *is* already 'two-eyed'. By the same token a charismatic may be unhappy to the point of desperation if he is only to be tolerated and included in a comprehensive Anglican bundle, and denied all chance of making a distinctive challenge that *this* (his experience) is *that* (the apostolic experience) and that he who would practise full-orbed Christianity ought to possess it.

This situation presents to many Christians a major dilemma: they recognize in charismatics a new quality of joy and release yet, *with integrity*, they cannot accept much that the charismatic believes and does (much less the uncompromising demand expressed by a few, that they themselves act likewise). It is this dilemma that underlies much tension and unhappiness in parishes where non-charismatics may experience rejection or the charismatics feel they are not accepted.

Is there a way out of this? An acceptance of the Pentecostal strand that is neither patronizing nor capitulation? Surely there is but it will involve long, hard and frank dialogue . . .

We cannot say how far such serious dialogue would take us. But we do see that there are certain questions which it would inevitably provoke. We set out some of them for consideration:

(a)   Has something of New Testament Christianity been missing from the Church of England's life, something to which the charismatic movement bears witness?

(b)   Does the breath of new life in a parish which charismatic renewal represents have to produce divisive results? If so, is the cost of renewal too high?

(c)   Does the charismatic movement, with its particular preoccupations, involve a withdrawal from the social witness of the Church? It is not sufficient for charismatics to point to one or two notable African or Latin-American exceptions. We think that a more *local* answer is needed in England. We are glad to see some contra-indications in the parish reports already cited.

(d)   Is it possible that the *distinctive* character of the charismatic movement is already past its peak? If so, it may be because the 'behavioural gap' has narrowed *from the non-charismatic side*. In other words, there are now not only many parishes in a 'second generation' stage, where the instinct to the most distinctive features (whether 'tongues' or 'prophecy' or whatever) has been modified by later experience and reflection, but there are also many non-charismatic parishes feeling their way to a greater openness, a deeper experience of the Spirit, an 'every member ministry', and other features characteristic of the movement. Thus the gap has narrowed at the level of 'phenomena'. But this is without prejudice to the outbreak of charismatic renewal in further 'first generation' parishes. This still continues, and in such parishes it all seems very distinctive.

(e)   Is not any evaluation we make made from within the changing times, and therefore very provisional? (And this question calls for the answer 'yes'.)

4.3 'CHRISTIANITY FOR A NEW AGE'

Dave Tomlinson

From *The Post Evangelical*, Tomlinson, D., London, SPCK, 1995, pp. 139–45.

A friend of mine recently asked a well known evangelical leader if he had heard of the term 'post-evangelical'. 'Post-evangelical?' the man replied, 'Post-evangelical? Whatever is a post-evangelical? Surely, my boy, one either is an evangelical, or one is not an evangelical. Which is it?' The plain fact of the matter is, though, that an increasing number of people see themselves as post-evangelical and many others identify with what being post-evangelical means, without actually using the term. Something is happening which is infinitely more significant than whether or not a bunch of evangelical 'drop outs' can find a constructive way forward. My thesis has been that this bigger something is linked to a fundamental cultural shift which is taking place in the Western world: a shift from the modern to the postmodern.

The challenge to churches of all traditions is how to adjust to the changes which are taking place, and how to express eternal truth in and through this emerging culture. It seems to me that there is a basic separation from those who see the only solution to be that of returning (in some cases with a vengeance) to the older certainties; in effect these people are saying that the only response to a sea of uncertainty is to re-establish the presence of absolute certainty. This approach is understandable, and it is clear that there is a considerable 'market' for it. After all, it offers a sense of security and familiarity in the midst of a lot of confusion. But for lots of us, it just will not do. We identify with those who are willing to engage more positively with the new situation and who believe that it has much to offer to Christians, just as they have much to offer to it.

To some extent the separate approaches depend on how much people actually live in the world of the postmodern (or, as I would put it, the real world) rather than bumping into it and trying to avoid it. One of my friends said to me recently, 'I can see that a lot of positive changes are taking place in evangelicalism and I wish the people well. But the fact is, most of it has hardly anything at all to do with me or the world I live in.' . . .

Let me summarize what I think are some of the key characteristics of this new postmodern world in which we live. It is a world in which people now reject truth claims which are expressed in the form of dogma or absolutes. It is a world in which dignity is granted to emotions and intuition, and where people are accustomed to communicating through words linked to images and symbols rather than through plain words or simple statements. It is a world in which people have come to feel a close affinity with the environment, and where there is a strong sense of global unity. It is a world in which people are deeply suspicious of institutions, bureaucracies and hierarchies. And perhaps most importantly of all, it is a world in which the spiritual dimension is once again talked about with great ease. Post-evangelical people, I think, are people who belong to, or are influenced by, this world, and whose Christian faith is increasingly being expressed in and through this frame of reference.

The fact that there is an upsurge of hunger for spirituality can be seen all around, and the selfish prosperity cult of the Thatcher and Reagan years has only added fuel to it....

Our own daughter Jeni speaks of the palpable change of attitudes she detects among her peers: in the early 1980s they were very skeptical of anything to do with the spiritual realm, and talking about God was very difficult, whereas today people readily talk about spiritual things. Yet in most cases, people are not turning to the church to satisfy this hunger; instead, many are turning to some expression of the New Age. Christians often see this as a straightforward rejection of God in favour of satanic deceptions, but is it? John Drane does not see it this way; he states that the vast majority of New Agers are engaged in a serious search for God. 'If anything', he says, 'they are likely to be more open to a radical life-changing encounter with Christ than are many Christians.'[1]

So why is this? Why is it that in an age of almost unparalleled interest in spirituality, the church is still so incredibly unpopular. Even where churches are turning a corner and growing, the majority of this growth is still coming from church transfers. Let me just pinpoint three important points to be pondered.

The first is that the evangelical gospel tends to be much too 'refined'. In other words it is a systematized 'A–Z of Everything You Need to Know about Life, Death and Eternity' – it is a 'big story' approach to the Christian narrative. It is generally assumed that this 'package' represents New Testament Christianity, and yet nowhere was it presented in this way, either by Jesus or the apostles. The pre-packed gospel is really a systematized stringing together of lots of little pieces which in their original context were presented as they stood, without being fitted into a coherent scheme. . . .

We need to take seriously Brueggemann's idea of 'funding the postmodern imagination'. He says that when we offer a full alternative world to people, we are acting in the imperialistic style which postmodern people are actually rejecting. Rather than offering truth in the form of a dogmatic grand scheme, we must offer 'a lot of little pieces out of which people can put life together in fresh configurations.'[2]

In a similar vein, the usual approach to presenting the gospel assumes that 'We've got it – you need it!' But such dogmatic claims are unlikely to cut any ice in today's world. It is much more helpful to use the language of journey. It is quite wrong to think of the world as 'Christians over here on the right and non-Christians over there on the left', with evangelism understood as the task of shifting people from left to right. It is much more helpful to see that people are already on a spiritual journey, in which we can expect that God has been evidently present and at work, even if he is unrecognized by that name. And evangelism should no longer function as a kind of religious sales operation, which often depersonalizes the individual being evangelized, but instead be understood as an opportunity to 'fund' people's spiritual journey, drawing on the highly relevant resources of 'little pieces' of truth contained in the Christian narrative.

1. Drane, *New Age*, p. 213.
2. Brueggemann, *The Bible*, p. 20.

4.4 'CAN EVANGELICALISM SURVIVE ITS SUCCESS?'

N.O. Hatch and M.S. Hamilton

From *Christianity Today*, 5 October 1992.

While visiting my parents in Columbia, South Carolina, recently, I started to reflect on what had changed since the early 1950s when I was growing up there. Like much of America back then and unlike now, Columbia had had no fast-food restaurant or suburban shopping mall. But it also lacked something that we now take for granted: that medley of religious influences we associate with modern evangelicalism.

Columbia was a religious place, to be sure, with Baptist, Methodist, and Presbyterian spires punctuating almost every corner. But religious life had a one-dimensional quality, being confined largely to church programs and activities. The broader culture was mildly supportive of Christian belief, but churches had a virtual monopoly on winning the lost and sustaining the faithful.

When I was a boy, Columbia had no Christian radio and nothing on the airways comparable to Amy Grant, Sandi Patti, or Larnelle Harris. When Elvis Presley became the rage in 1955, all of us in the fourth grade crooned, "You Ain't Nothing but a Hound Dog." By contrast, the church's stodgy hymns and limp gospel songs could not compete for our hearts and minds. While one could tune in Sunday church services on the radio, there was no James Dobson, Charles Swindoll, or John MacArthur offering insight for daily living – and nothing like the string of over 1,000 Christian radio stations that currently blanket the country. Television in the age of "I Love Lucy" and "The Wonderful World of Disney" was just gaining a foothold and did not seem menacing to serious Christians. But one could not look to television for daily Christian instruction as cable television now permits.

While midweek prayer meetings were a staple of church life, small-group fellowships or care groups were unknown, as were Bible Study Fellowship and Walk-Thru-the-Bible. Churches spoke of revival but had few means to bring the laity into the process like the Four Spiritual Laws or Evangelism Explosion. Churches had not yet developed specialized ministries to singles, single parents, or the divorced. Church-growth seminars had not yet interrupted the weekly routine of pastors.

At local high schools there was no Young Life or Youth for Christ, and at the University of South Carolina no InterVarsity, Campus Crusade, Navigators, or Fellowship of Christian Athletes. College students had nothing at their disposal like the popular apologetics of C.S. Lewis, Francis Schaeffer, or Josh McDowell. The 75-member Christian College Coalition had not yet articulated its educational alternative to denominational colleges. Young people interested in the ministry thought in terms of regional denominational seminaries rather than the national evangelical schools of today, such as Fuller, Gordon-Conwell, or Trinity. There was a Southern Baptist bookstore in Columbia with Bibles and Sunday-school materials, but

Christian publishers like Zondervan, Word, and Multnomah had not yet flooded the market with an array of books for Christian living – from child rearing to Christian fiction, from financial planning to biographies of Christian celebrities. And fundamentalists could boast no phenomenal best sellers like Hal Lindsey's *The Late Great Planet Earth* (1970) or Frank Peretti's *This Present Darkness* (1986).

There were few Christian grammar schools or high schools, no Christian counseling centers, no *Christianity Today, Leadership*, or *Decision*. There were no appeals to relieve Third World hunger from World Vision, Samaritan's Purse, or Food for the Hungry. One could not join hands in service with other Christians through Habitat for Humanity or Prison Fellowship. None of my high-school friends had the opportunity to serve overseas in summer missions projects. No mainline churches in Columbia had been touched by charismatic renewal, and Pentecostal churches remained small and restricted largely to the mill section of town.

These stark contrasts between the texture of evangelical life today and that which existed at the end of World War II highlight the success the movement has had over the last 50 years. But they also raise other questions: What will evangelical life look like in the years ahead? Will evangelicalism be able not only to survive but to continue its success? While these questions cannot be answered yet, pursuing them is still profitable. By assessing what has happened to evangelicals in the last 50 years, we will be better equipped to take stock of the current trajectory of the movement.

FROM EMBATTLED MINORITY TO ENTREPRENEURS

Fifty years ago most learned interpreters of American religion expected revivalists, fundamentalists, and Pentecostals simply to wither and die. It was thought that these remnants of a bygone era, these expressions of old-fashioned orthodoxy and overt supernaturalism, could not hope to keep pace with the modern world. They would continue to recede to the margins of American life. In the theological battles of the 1920s and 1930s, most mainline Protestant denominations had purged themselves of these reactionary forces. Mainline Protestants looked forward to growing religious influence in American life as they sought to reconcile faith and modern culture and to narrow the differences among themselves.

What neither scholars nor denominational leaders counted on was the persistence of revivalistic Bible Christianity among ordinary American church goers and the furious organizational counteroffensive launched by those who spoke for them. Taking up positions in a variety of marginal denominations (holiness, Pentecostal, Southern, ethnic-immigrant, Adventist, fundamentalist) and in the transdenominational parachurch agencies, theological conservatives labored to organize Americans around alternative visions of Christian faith that stressed personal conversion, holy living, and direct experience of the divine in daily life.

Their unexpected achievements have surprised, and often flustered, outside observers. Church membership as a percentage of population is up 10 percent in the past 50 years, despite the fact that mainline membership has dropped off. Half the increase is due to Roman Catholic growth, which has tapered off dramatically in the last decade. The other half is the direct result of ongoing evangelical expansion. Evangelicals also present the mainline with a renewed challenge from within. Most mainline denominations now host large, grassroots evangelical caucuses, which function as a kind of loyal opposition, and increasing numbers of mainline pastors have been trained in evangelical seminaries.

Denominational competition is not, however, the most important story of the past 50 years. The organizational structures that house the throbbing heart of evangelicalism are not denominations at all, but the special-purpose parachurch agencies that sometimes seem as numberless as the stars in the sky. These evangelistic agencies, missionary agencies, Bible societies, publishing houses, periodicals, radio and television programs, women's ministries, men's ministries, youth ministries, prison ministries, summer camps, colleges, Bible institutes, day schools, professional societies, avocational societies, charismatic groups, Bible study groups – even the categories seem numberless – all stand outside America's denominational structure. Parachurch groups have picked the denominations' pockets, taking over denominational functions, inventing wholly new categories of religious activity to take into the marketplace, and then transmitting back into the denominations an explicitly nondenominational version of evangelical Christianity.

Evangelical innovations have swept through America's increasingly permeable denominational walls. The church-growth movement, an emphasis on small groups, and the utilization of spiritual gifts have colored a broad range of American churches since 1970. Similarly, charismatic-style worship has spread far beyond churches that speak in tongues. Churches of long sectarian pedigree, like the Seventh-day Adventists and the Churches of Christ, increasingly take on an "evangelical" cast.

Liberated from denominational constraints, evangelicalism has turned loose its women and men of entrepreneurial bent upon American's spiritual problems. The movement's decentralized arrangement has encouraged people with a unique vision to tailor innovative outreach methods to specific groups of people in specific circumstances. Charles Colson's term in prison opened his eyes to prisoners' need for the good news of Jesus Christ, and it also gave him valuable insight into how to go about meeting that need. Evangelicalism's free-market structure gave him the freedom to build a new ministry around his vision, and it gave him mechanisms for selling it in the marketplace. Like George Patton's tank bridges, evangelical parachurch groups can strike wherever and whenever a capable commander sees an opening.

But also like Patton's tank brigades, some ministries are in constant danger of outrunning their supply lines. Their detachment from denominations has loosened their connection to the church and its two thousand years of Christian wisdom and experience. In their freedom to adapt programs to the needs of a particular time and place, they are also at liberty to make the mistakes that Christians have made in the past.

Sophisticated in their use of all forms of mass media and highly attuned to their audience, evangelical entrepreneurs have transformed a popular religious movement into the most dynamic sector of modern religion. One-third of all Americans identify themselves as "born-again" Christians–a phrase given currency by transdenominational evangelicalism. The percentage is even higher for the young adults of the "baby boom" generation, testimony to the evangelicals' unsurpassed ability to gather young people into the Christian fold. Youth ministry continues to be a central and effective thrust of evangelism today–Young Life, for instance, will bring 22,000 high schoolers into summer camps this year.

Nor has evangelical energy been contained by national boundaries. Evangelicals have virtually taken over the field of foreign mission. Fifty years ago evangelical agencies sponsored 40 percent of all American missionaries; today the figure is over 90 percent. Wycliffe Bible Translators alone now has more missionaries in the field than all Protestant American mainline agencies combined.

Its decentralized structure, audience orientation, and what the sociologist has called its "willingness to confront strangers" have helped to make evangelicalism remarkably adaptable to differing social contexts. Abroad, evangelical Christianity in its various forms is the most rapid-growing religion in many parts of the world, redrawing the religious maps of Central and South America, sub-Saharan Africa, and Asia. In the U.S., evangelicalism has been able to translate its message into forms relevant across a wide ethnic and social spectrum, from Hispanic-Americans to African-Americans, from the impoverished underclass to the materialistic middle class.

It has not, however, proven universally adaptable. The truly wealthy are noticeably absent from evangelical circles; and evangelicalism has yet to find a way to communicate in an effective way with the ambitious and well-educated shapers of American culture who guide the mass media, the educational system, the universities, the courts, and the national government.

THE INFLUENCE OF BILLY GRAHAM

It would be difficult to overestimate Billy Graham's importance in the last 50 years of evangelicalism. Raised in Southern fundamentalism and educated in northern fundamentalism, he distilled out of those movements their positive thrusts and brought them onto the national stage.

Graham personally embodied most of the characteristics of resurgent evangelicalism. He stressed personal conversion and the importance of holy living, while de-emphasizing doctrinal and denominational differences that often divided Christians. He was a leader in postwar youth ministry. He worked not through any denomination but through independent, parachurch organizations, taking the gospel into secular arenas–stadiums, television, newspapers.

Graham had strong ties to the National Association of Evangelicals, Fuller Theological Seminary, and *Christianity Today*. He supported the neo-evangelical intellectuals who sought to reform fundamentalism's dispensationalism, moralism, and anti-intellectualism, thereby legitimizing their efforts to a popular constituency that might have otherwise been quite suspicious. He recognized the worth of Pentecostals' and charismatics' forms of Christianity and welcomed them into fellowship. He helped make it easier for evangelicals to return to the public square through his association with major politicians and by taking cautiously progressive positions on a few social issues like civil rights, poverty, and the nuclear arms race. He has been able to adapt his delivery to his audience – for instance, he preaches less about the terrors of hell than in his early years – without compromising his message of salvation through Jesus Christ.

It has often been written that Billy Graham thoroughly reflects the American middle class that attends his crusades. His politics, his language, his concerns, and most important, his religion, are pegged to the values and the aspirations of the middle sectors of American society. But Graham has also transcended the American middle class in his ability to speak to the spiritual aspirations of a broad spectrum of people in other societies. From Latin America to Asia he has been able to draw widespread cooperation and enormous crowds with the same message he preaches in the U.S. However, like evangelicalism generally, Graham has been less successful in winning over the educated classes, who have tended to regard him with skepticism and condescension.

For evangelicalism, Billy Graham has meant the reconstitution of a Christian fellowship transcending confessional lines – a grassroots ecumenism that regards denominational divisions as irrelevant rather than pernicious. Graham was at the storm center when separatist fundamentalists finally split off from the rest of evangelicalism, but he nevertheless led most American fundamentalists out of their enclaves into broader fields of fellowship and activity. In doing so, he gave popular American Christianity an enduring evangelical flavor. Today Graham's is not the most frequently heard voice on the American evangelical scene, but it is still the most respected, still the most winsome.

FROM THE THEOLOGICAL TO THE RELATIONAL

The last five decades of American evangelicalism encompass stories of both continuity and change. Much remains the same – the indispensability of personal conversion, the quest to live lives pleasing to God and in line with his purposes, the firm belief that God acts in individual lives and in human history, the preference to read the Bible literally whenever possible, the centrality of lay leadership and parachurch groups for transmitting the evangelical vision, the ambivalence toward churches belonging to mainline denominations, the democratic bias toward grassroots authority.

There have also been a number of changes that might be understood collectively as a shift away from the theological toward the relational. Fifty years ago evangelicals were fully engaged in battling modernists' attempts to detach Christianity from historic orthodoxy. This kept evangelical concerns centered on the content of Christian belief – on the prepositional truths of Scripture. Today evangelicals seem far more interested in questions of worship. This has led in two different directions: a movement toward the liturgical by the intellectually inclined, and a movement toward the charismatic by the average churchgoer. Both represent a shift in emphasis away from knowledge about God toward the experience of God.

Fifty years ago evangelicals were taught that everyone should witness to non-Christians about Christ at every opportunity. This was understood as plain, direct talk about every human being's sinfulness and need of regeneration through faith in Jesus Christ. The corollary of this teaching was that anyone who could not testify to an evangelical-style conversion experience was presumed not to be a Christian. Today, however, the concept of witnessing has taken on more nuanced forms, such as "lifestyle evangelism." Human spiritual distortion seems more often discussed in terms of psychological maladjustment than as inbred sinfulness. Occasionally, it sounds as though the gospel is directed more toward personal well-being-health, financial security, and stable human relationships – than toward the eternal life of the soul.

Fifty years ago a huge wave of missionaries traveled overseas with the single-minded goal of carrying the gospel to people groups around the globe that had never before heard it. The focus was more on the next world than this – rescuing the souls of all who had never heard the gospel from an eternal death that was as certain as it was terrifying. Today the concern for souls has not diminished, but evangelical missionaries now tend to go abroad with an equal concern for the physical well-being of their hosts. Modern mission agencies are as devoted to the relief of bodies as they are to the relief of souls.

Fifty years ago evangelicals – not without reason – saw secular society as unremittingly hostile toward their faith. One response was to follow moral standards that set evangelicals off from the rest of the world. Movies, dancing, swearing, and alcohol were strictly off limits; tobacco, mixed swimming, jewelry, makeup, and certain hairstyles and types of clothing might also be prohibited. Associating with nonevangelicals for purposes other than evangelism was also usually regarded as worldly.

Today the interest in hard-and-fast moral codes has moved a few notches down the scale of priorities. Fewer evangelical leaders call Christians to self-denial; more provide roadmaps to self-esteem.

Fifty years ago most evangelicals read the Bible through the dispensationalist lenses of the Scofield Reference Bible. This stimulated keen interest in the fulfillment of prophecies preceding Christ's return; along with the tendency of their liberal opponents to emphasize the social obligations of Christians, it gave evangelicals a second rationale for their lack of interest in social concerns. Now, however, dispensationalism does not seem nearly so widespread. Passion for the coming of the Holy Spirit today may have partially displaced passion for Christ's return tomorrow. Evangelicals have shown a new willingness to work in concert with nonevangelicals to effect social change – perhaps a sign that we now read in the prophets a call to work for justice as well as a timetable for the Second Coming.

Fifty years ago evangelicals had virtually abandoned the life of the mind, concentrating instead on communicating their message to a popular audience. All the evangelical scholars in America could have, as one historian put it, "fit into a single boxcar." Today there is a sizable and growing contingent of evangelical scholars making their voices heard in intellectual circles, committed to the proposition that God can redeem even serious intellectual life.

Many doubtless regard these changes as regress rather than progress, but it is clear that they have stemmed to a large degree from evangelicals' reactions to their experiences in spreading the gospel. Fifty years ago evangelical subcultures were highly insular, equipping talented men and women with a clear and unambiguous ideology. But as they went out into the world to proclaim the Christian faith, they contacted human realities for which their ideology had not entirely prepared them.

Evangelists found that direct proclamation of the gospel sometimes hardened people against the gospel, but long-term personal relationships would sometimes soften those same hearts. They discovered many nonevangelicals – even Roman Catholics – who were true servants of Christ in every meaningful sense.

Pastors found that conversion, sanctification, and baptism of the Holy Spirit did not automatically produce harmonious marriages, wise parents, respectful children, and merciful neighbors; and they discovered that strict moral codes could sometimes deflect emphasis from the weightier matters of the gospel.

Evangelicals of a scholarly bent found that the secular intellectual world spoke a virtually different language from that of evangelicals. Evangelicals inclined to activism realized that in abandoning social concern they had left the field to the secular state, which has steadily spread its influence into more and more areas of American life. Missionaries found that their Christian faith was partly shaped by their cultural heritage, and that other cultures possessed liberating insights at times more congruent with the biblical message.

In addition, many of the changes in evangelicalism can be traced to the success of the movement. Fifty years ago the movement had a distinct sense of itself as a small, outsider minority group, bunkered down against the assaults of a hostile society. Today the phenomenal growth in numbers of evangelicals has permitted the growth of subcultural institutions that stretch across the spectrum of human activity. If the subculture is not as deep as it once was – if there is less obvious difference between evangelicals and nonevangelicals – the subculture is broader than it once was, making it easier for evangelicals to isolate themselves from the rest of society than ever before.

4.5 'RECOVERING THE PRIMACY OF EVANGELISM'

Billy Graham

From *Christianity Today*, 8 December 1997, pp. 27–30.

THOSE THINGS THAT DO NOT CHANGE

In the midst of so many changes in the world, it is the unique function of the church to declare by word and deed that there are some things that never change. It is the message that God – the supreme, unchanging, omnipotent Creator of the universe – loves humanity and wants us to know him in a personal way. It is the message that humankind has strayed from God – rebelled against his revealed will, and as a result of sin is alienated from God and from others. It is the message that God has taken the initiative to bridge the gap between God and sinful humanity and he did this by coming down to earth in the person of Jesus Christ. It is the message that there is hope for the future, because Christ rose from the dead and will reign victorious over all the forces of evil and death and hell.

No, God has not changed, nor has the nature of the human heart changed. And that is why the gospel is relevant to every individual in every culture: beneath all the cultural, ethnic, social, economic, and political differences that separate us, the deepest needs and hurts and fears of the human heart are still the same. The gospel is still "the power of God for the salvation of everyone who believes" (Rom. 1:16, NIV).

But there is one other thing that has not changed – and that is the commission of Christ to the church to "Go into all the world and preach the good news to all creation" (Mark 16:15).

That command – thoroughly undergirded by a deep love for Christ and for others – impelled the early Christians to go from one end of the Roman Empire to the other, often paying the price for their commitment with their lives. In obedience to that same command, a host of missionaries and evangelists across the centuries have brought the message of God's love in Christ to the farthest corners of human civilization.

4.6 'THE LEGACY OF JOHN WIMBER'

Todd Hunter

From *Voice of the Vineyard*, Hunter, T., Fall 1998, pp. 12–13.

How do we move forward together in the Vineyard in such a way that is honoring to Christ and that produces lasting fruit for his Kingdom? John designed the Vineyard's values and mission around *What the Holy Spirit is Saying to the Church Today*. That series of conference messages written in the mid-eighties is the mandate for you and I to find out what the Holy Spirit is saying today.

I'm not interested in long debates about our past or about what the "true" Vineyard is. Nor am I going to spend my life being the curator of a John Wimber Memorial Museum: it wouldn't honor John, it wouldn't honor God, and it wouldn't advance the Kingdom of God.

The driving aim of my leadership is to answer the question: "What is God saying to the Vineyard today?"

TAKE THE BEST AND GO!

In November of 1996 John gave his last full-length message called *The Movement I am Trying to Build* to the assembled leaders of the Association of Vineyard Churches USA. In those talks, he explained how new emerging religious movements like the Vineyard follow a pattern.

He taught us that most religious movements usually begin with a sudden visitation by the charismatic presence of God, a "charismatic moment" that propels the group onward and upward like a rocket blast. It's a thrilling, fast paced, intuitively-led, subjectively-experienced ride. But about 25 years after they begin, something happens. What was once spontaneous becomes routine. And as the group tries to hang on to its past, it exerts more control and becomes more rule-oriented.

John knew that if we were going to resist this process of institutionalization, we'd have to prayerfully, thoughtfully and willfully choose a course of action based in humble obedience to God.

How do we combat this insidious process? John told us to continue to re-engineer ourselves by taking the best of our past, our values, what we've learned in our first twenty years, and move forward.

John was right. The best way for me to honor John's legacy and the Vineyard's past is to give full expression to my deep-rooted passion for our future: to discover what God is leading us to do now and discern just what the best is and then go on from there.

I honor our past, but I crave our future more. To *take the best and go*, we've got to prepare ourselves attitudinally and organizationally to receive a new charismatic moment that blasts us off on a new growth curve. It might get scary as we feel the rocket begin to rumble beneath our capsule, but I want to go. I'd rather live in the uncertainty of following God toward the future he sees than celebrate or argue over the past we've seen.

WHERE TO FROM HERE? INTIMACY

I often picture John sitting at the piano early in the morning (as Carol tells me he often did) and composing. I picture tears falling on the keyboards as he sings, *Isn't he beautiful. Beautiful, isn't he?* Or I can see him calling out to Carol, "Babe, come listen to this new melody," and the two of them finish off another love song to Jesus.

I can't see ahead ten years, but I know any positive, Christ-honouring future we have will be directly linked to the Vineyard's staying intimately connected to Jesus. That's why I spend so much time reminding our pastors of the importance of prayer, solitude, meditation on the Scriptures and reflection on their ministries. Or, as John often said, *To go fast you sometimes have to go slow.*

How do we slow down? Focus on being before doing. Take time to know him, to love him and just simply be Christians. If we don't focus on being before doing, how will we be able to hear his voice and thus speak for him as his prophetic people? How else will we be able to communicate the Gospel, in winsome and effective ways like Jesus did through the parables that connected with the people of his day?

I can hear some readers now saying, "Been there. Done that." Yes, but are you doing it now? James 1:22 says, "Do not merely listen to the word and deceive yourselves. Do what it says." Hearing this exhortation, and assuming that because you're a Vineyardite, you're intimate with God, is a deception. Acting on it and building into your life spiritual disciplines is an awakening truth.

OBEDIENCE

Hearing God's voice afresh gives us hope for the future; it shows us our potential (á la the Parable of the Talents). Obedience is the one differentiating issue that makes God's gracious voice and plan effective. Acts 5:32 tells us that "God has given his Holy Spirit to those who obey him."

If God gets his way, we'll be Word workers. We'll do all we can to know him and make him known. Being his ambassadors, doing Kingdom works, planting churches, reaching the lost and making disciples will become our life's passions.

I can't ask John Wimber how to steer the Vineyard. But I think I know what he'd tell me:

- Love the Lord your God . . .
- You are Christ's ambassador . . .
- Go into all the world . . .
- You will receive power . . .

Together, let's take the best of what John gave us, listen afresh to the Holy Spirit, and go!

4.7 'WHICH PART OF THE GREAT COMMISSION DON'T YOU UNDERSTAND?'

Luis Palau

From *Christianity Today*, 16 November, 1998, pp. 74–6.

Much has been made in recent years of the fact that the church in the Third World has taken on the mantle of missions instead of simply being its recipient. I would like to issue a challenge to the North American church to regain the evangelistic fervor so evident among many Third World Christians. As the apostle Paul put it, let us follow them as they follow Christ.

My recent crusades at El Paso-Juárez (Texas/Mexico) and Bristol, England, showed me the sharp contrast that exists in the level of evangelistic energy within the evangelical church. Great hope and a sense of thrill grip the church in Latin America (including the many Hispanics of El Paso-Juárez). Pastors are preaching the pure gospel without apology. Laypeople share their faith with authority.

In North America and Europe, however, I find that while there is much discussion about evangelism, real evangelism is hard to detect. "There simply isn't the same enthusiasm for evangelism there was ten years ago," Anthony Bush, the mission chairman for the crusades in Bristol, told me. Unlike the El Paso experience of revival, Britain greeted us with empty, frigid cathedrals that serve as little more than museums of long-ago revivals. For all but a small percentage of the people in Britain and Western Europe, Christianity is ancient history, not a living relationship.

As an evangelist, I measure the pulse of the church by its evangelistic fervour. Church historian Kenneth Scott Latourette writes that throughout its history, "the primary emphasis of the Church was upon the salvation of the individual for eternal life." Charles H. Spurgeon, the great nineteenth-century British preacher, believed that "the work of conversion is the first and great thing we must drive at; after this we must labor with all our might." And John Wesley reminded preachers, "You have nothing to do but to save souls."

The evangelical Christians of North America cheerfully pay any amount to go to a concert. They fill the civic center for worship sessions and even intercessory spiritual-warfare conventions. But when it comes to face-to-face warfare, which is talking to people kindly but directly about their need for Christ, suddenly the numbers diminish. In too many churches the response to the challenge to proclaim the gospel to their city is, "Why should we be doing this?" and "This is expensive."

I thank God for the continuing health and strength he is giving to Billy Graham. I thank God for the wonderful evangelistic work of Franklin Graham, Greg Laurie, and many other young evangelists, some of whom are partners with us in the Next Generation Alliance. The ministries of Alpha, March for Jesus, Prison Fellowship, Promise Keepers, and Willow Creek Association advance the kingdom of God around the world. Everywhere I go I meet

Christians who gave their lives to Jesus Christ after hearing the gospel on radio or viewing Campus Crusade's *Jesus* film. The growing interest in revival, prayer, and fasting, spurred on in North America by Joe Aldrich. Bill and Vonette Bright, David Bryant, Evelyn Christenson, Ed Silveso, and others is truly a great thing.

But the church must match those efforts with a vision for evangelism that confronts millions upon millions of people with the gospel in every generation. In the West, only small fires of passion for evangelism are lit, not the conflagration that ensures fulfilling the Great Commission. If the church does not take seriously its responsibility to evangelize, to whom does the Lord entrust this priority? The world has experts for everything else of concern to our churches, but the church alone is an expert in evangelism.

GONE "FISHING" OR GOLFING?

A few years ago the missions committee of a large church notified the various mission agencies it had been supporting that they were cutting their giving by as much as 50 percent. Paraphrased, the letter said. "Giving is down. May God provide for your needs." In the same envelope, however, was the church's weekly bulletin. One announcement caught my attention: "The pastor and 20 men in the church will be leaving this week with their wives for a golf tournament in the Bahamas." Was I wrong to conclude that in this church hitting and chasing a little white ball was a greater priority than missionary evangelistic ministry?

In the Spanish-speaking world, the church is showing its evangelistic priority through missions. Argentina, Brazil, and other nations in Latin America have joined Asian nations, such as South Korea, Hong Kong, and Singapore, as missionary-sending nations. The division between missionary-sending and missionary-receiving nations has been obliterated. "From all nations to all nations" is happening.

My colleague James M. Williams, who directs our Latin American ministries, recently returned from El Salvador where a church welcomed home a couple who are planting seeds of the gospel in an Arab country. In fact, many Latin Americans are being sent to the Middle East. As I discovered earlier this year in Cairo, there is a cultural affinity among Latin and Arabic peoples.

CALLED TO CITIES AND CHILDREN

This transnational movement gives me hope for America's cities, which are a ripe mission field. The national majority in America, the Anglo-Saxons, must overcome its fear of the city, where minorities – African Americans, Asian Americans, and Hispanics – are the majority. America's cities are the target of political action, social action, and all sorts of government programs with good intentions, but most of the ruling people, which include those in middle and upper-class churches, have no idea how to relate to minorities spiritually.

The cities need missionaries and the boldness they bring – a sense of purpose and clear-cut commitment. We should have the same missionary purpose in our own culture. We ought to be just as bold and courageous and unashamed in confronting *our* neighborhood and *our* city with the claims of Christ. But it seems to be much harder.

A second ripe – but often overlooked – mission field is children. There are a hundred million abandoned children around the world. Yes, we must feed them and educate them, but we must also win them to Jesus Christ. For 34 years Colleen Redit, a doctor and a single woman from New Zealand, has labored on behalf of abandoned and orphaned children in Madras, India, where more than a third of the population is homeless. Redit herself is mother to 15 or more children at any given time. She supervises educational, nutritional, and vocational programs at the overcrowded Haven of Hope mission, where several hundred young women and teenage girls discover a future. But in the midst of all these vital programs, Redit always makes "the main thing the main thing," helping children to put their trust in Jesus. On every visit to the mission, it is beautiful to see the beauty of the Lord Jesus in their lives.

DREAMING OF JESUS

This evangelistic fervor of which I am speaking is sometimes found in the most unlikely places. I have hope for the Arab world because there is such a stirring among Christians there to reach out in love and respect while clearly inviting others to follow Jesus as the crucified and resurrected Savior and Lord. The Arab world is in a state of deep-seated change. There is a growing hunger to know God. Pastor Menes Abdul Noor of Kasr El-Dobara Evangelical Church in Cairo, where I preached the gospel this past March, told me he talks individually to a hundred searching people every month. Quietly, great numbers of women and young people are coming to Christ.

And where Christians like Noor are moving ahead in faith, God seems to have prepared the hearts of those they are reaching. Every Arabic Christian I have talked to who converted to Christ from a non-Christian background relates a dream or vision in which Jesus, dressed in white as in the Transfiguration, speaks directly to them, telling them he is the Savior of the world. A woman whose father is a top leader in her nation – a nation where there are no church buildings – was converted through a dream in which Jesus revealed himself. The first five years of her Christian life she didn't even have a Bible.

Christians in the Middle East, many of whom are respected professionals with postgraduate degrees, expect God to work in this way. They believe in his supernatural intervention. If God is God, he is going to do supernatural things. No barriers can thwart or frustrate God's redemptive plan. Who could have imagined that Marxism would collapse overnight? But God made it happen. I believe something just as unthinkable will happen to the resistance to the gospel in the Arab world. Already I sense a momentum from God in the Middle East that no one will be able to stop. The gospel still meets strong resistance – in some cases, violent resistance – but I believe that within the next 20 years that is going to change. I am persuaded of this by faith and by Scripture, which says God the Savior wants "all men to be saved and to come to a knowledge of the truth." God will work events, as Isaiah 46 says, so that his purposes will be accomplished. I look forward to the day when I will preach in Riyadh, Saudi Arabia, or Tehran, Iran.

When the door opens, let us be ready to take advantage. After World War II General MacArthur called for ten thousand missionaries to Japan. But after ten years, hundreds – not thousands – had gone. By then the doors began to shut. In Japan today, only 2 percent of the population claims to be Christian.

The relative recent openness of the People's Republic of China is another fact that ought to give us hope. Although there are pockets of religious oppression and need for more freedom, compared to 20 years ago the freedom is enormous. The number of Christians worshiping there is so high that I can foresee in China a similar collapse of the Marxist ideology that we saw in the Soviet Union. The change could be even more pronounced because so many overseas Chinese have been converted to Christ. Along with seminary-trained pastors and biblically knowledgeable lay leaders, thousands of successful businesspeople in the churches of Hong Kong, Singapore, and Taiwan are eager to take the gospel back into China.

CLIMBING THROUGH OPEN WINDOWS

Though Christians in the Third World must address their own weaknesses – many practice intense evangelism but lack a biblically grounded and reasoned understanding of Christian doctrine – they also present a living challenge to those of us who have lost our evangelistic fervor in a secular culture that values toleration and denounces confrontation. The overwhelming sense I have as I travel in that we live in a time of great opportunity. We must go on saturating the nations with pure, simple evangelism and solid Bible exposition while these opportunities last. For they will pass, as history teaches us. In some now-open areas, persecution is rising, and already evangelism is becoming much more difficult.

It was wonderful to see Christians in Western nations pouring into the former Soviet Union and Eastern Europe with Bibles and the gospel when the window (it was hardly a door) opened, even though criticism – some unfair – was launched against this activity. As someone who has lived in a nation under dictatorship and who reads church history, I think this was one of the best moments in world missions. Far better that we are berated for perceived excesses of evangelizing the once-closed countries of Eastern Europe than miss the opportunity altogether.

Our world is in flux. Large populations and ethnic groups are moving from country to country, region to region, city to city. According to missiologist Donald McGavran, such times of transition provide the best moments to lead people to God through Jesus Christ. My prayer is that the church of North America would once again awaken to the Great Commission Christ gave us. Let it begin today with the unsaved around us and then move on to the many lost throughout our world. Now is the moment – perhaps a unique moment in history that may not return for several hundred years. Let us press on.

4.8 'SOME REFLECTIONS ON THE MEANING AND PRACTICE OF WORSHIP FROM INSIDE SOUTH AMERICA'

Felicity B. Houghton

From *Worship: Adoration and Action*, Carson, D.A. (ed.), Grand Rapids and Carlisle, Baker Book House/Paternoster, 1993, pp. 158–68.

INTRODUCTION

One of the privileges I enjoy in travelling within Latin America in order to minister to the student movements affiliated to the International Fellowship of Evangelical Students in this continent, is that of being able to gather with God's people in a variety of places and denominational settings. What I share now is the fruit of what I have seen and experienced in Argentina, Chile, Ecuador, Peru, and Bolivia which is my homeland for the time being. I have tried to be a careful observer of some of the church services in which I have taken part on my travels, as well as here in La Paz, Bolivia, and to note down my observations during the course of the service, putting on one side subjective reactions. . . .

On the one hand we observe that military dictatorships and irresponsible democracy, terrorism and violence, poverty, inflation and economic instability, the strangling foreign debt, corruption, illiteracy, drug traffic and the abuse of natural resources are the milieu in which the churches carry on their work and witness. They are unavoidable realities that entail suffering and could lead to despair. On the other hand, we can see these things as means God may use to instruct his people concerning what he requires of them as the salt and the light of the world. What is clear is that the worship of Jesus Christ cannot be genuine if we shut our eyes and ears to the cry of our neighbour and the groaning of our nation.

THE CULTURAL CONTEXT

I shall refer to a few characteristics that impinge on the practice of worship. First, the attitude to time. At the risk of exaggeration, I would say that the Latin American wears a watch because it is a modern habit to do so, and in order to know the time. But the watch is not consulted as a way of finding out if there is time to do something, or if one ought to be at a certain place, or stop one activity and pass on to another. The clock marks the passing of the hours, but it is one's internal, subjective rhythm that determines the pace of life. Hence, church meetings may or may not begin on time, are generally speaking long and often open-ended, and no one is worried.

Second, it is normal to express one's emotions openly, not only with words that describe them frankly, but also with gestures of the face and hands, tears, embraces and bodily movements. Hence, the raising of arms and hands in church, or clapping, or moving with the music, or a kind of dancing, or greeting with a kiss on the cheek, are all part of normal and expected behaviour in the churches I am describing.

Third, it is an obvious fact, and therefore could easily be overlooked, that the language of all communication is Spanish, a language that is extraordinarily rich in resources to reach the mind and the heart by many paths. Dr Pablo Deiros, an Argentinian pastor and theologian, has pointed out that Latin American culture sets great store by the word, but particularly by the well-spoken word, the elegant turn of phrase, the eloquent flow of sound. The content and the truthfulness of what is said are of secondary importance; what matters is that it should be well said and sound impressive. But we are taught by the apostle Paul that in Christian preaching the values are reversed: that truth is all, and wise and persuasive words are not the secret of efficacy and power (1 Cor. 2:4,5). This inclination towards the word and the sound and their immediate effect may be one of the factors that account for impromptu messages from the pulpit and a widespread lack of serious biblical exposition.

Fourth, modernity has come to Latin America . . .

The danger I see in some churches here is that of a TV show mentality: on the high platform where the lights and the movement engage the attention of the audience, there must be variety, there must be good entertainment, and above all, there must be not only sound but volume, not only volume but noise to shut out thought and shut in feeling. And in the midst of so much 'music', musicality has fled like a shy fairy before the approach of the giants.

In the fifth place, I want to say something about church buildings. Part of the cultural heritage received from Spain is the presence of many Roman Catholic church buildings, of which a large number date back to colonial times. These are often imposing in size, elaborate in style, sombre and dark in their interior, and characterized by the presence of images of Christ, Mary and the saints, and confessionals. Here Mass is celebrated frequently, and from time to time, baptisms, weddings, funerals, and ecclesiastical festivals. Here at any time the individual may slip in alone to pray before a statue or light a candle. Here the weight of tradition and the familiarity of religious custom offer a certain security.

On the other hand, the evangelical understands the church building as a place where he or she meets with God and fellow Christians. Often the buildings themselves are architecturally nondescript, utilitarian, humble in the extreme, and yet 'holy ground'. Sometimes they are cinemas hired for use on Sundays and filled more than once, and sometimes they are elegant buildings raised brick by brick by the sole effort and faith and costly giving of the congregation. In other cases, generous financial help for building is received from overseas. In general, their beauty is in their lightness and simplicity; with no images and no candles, they are truly 'houses of prayer'.

A CATALOGUE OF CONGREGATIONAL WORSHIP EXPERIENCES

In speaking of the church at her best, as also of her need for growth, it has been necessary to generalize. With some relief, therefore, I now turn to the description of some services in which I have taken part, and so move from the general to the particular.

ARGENTINA

Jujuy is a small city in the far northwest of the country, not many hours from the Bolivian border. On two consecutive Sunday evenings I attended a church belonging to the 'Movimiento Cristiano Misionero' (the Christian Missionary Movement). The building is made of stone; on the wall behind the platform, the name JESUS, drawn in bricks which jut out from the wall, is the only adornment. The pastor directed the singing, to the accompaniment of an electronic piano; we sang a few songs several times over. Other elements in the two services were prayer, testimonies from young people in discipleship training, notices,[1] the offering, and the sermon.

Here is the gist of the sermon on the first Sunday that I was present: It is a tremendous thing to draw near to God; he is near and he is holy. We are to deny ourselves the pleasure of giving way to our bad temper. It is time to begin to trust in God. . . .

The preaching began at 8.55 p.m. and went on for about an hour. Though the two Sundays I have referred to were Palm Sunday and Easter Day, there was no reference made to the meaning of Christ's passion and resurrection in the life of God's people, nor to these special days.

When, on another occasion, I asked the pastor of a very large congregation in the industrial city of Córdoba, Argentina, what he considered to be the reasons for God's people to gather together, he replied that it is in order to thank and praise God, to bring our petitions to him, and to preach to those who do not know him.

BOLIVIA

One of the Assemblies of God congregations in the Ciudad El Alto, near the city of La Paz, holds a Sunday morning service in a cinema that faces onto a public square. On the occasion on which I was present, the singing of eleven choruses and one hymn occupied the longest space of time, to the accompaniment of two electric guitars. Other elements were prayer, the reading of Ps.40, words from the pastor addressed to the regular congregation and to possible visitors, an offering, and then the preaching of a young man who referred to Num. 21:4–9 and to his own experience of conversion. When the congregation was asked, 'Who is our God?' all replied, 'Jesus Christ'. Later on there was a round of applause 'for Jesus Christ'. Towards the close there was a prayer for physical healing for the sick, and those who desired to receive Jesus Christ as Saviour were invited to go forward.

In the centre of La Paz a large congregation has recently bought an unused cinema. On the Sunday morning that I went, it was filled to overflowing with people from a variety of social backgrounds. On the platform were two electronic pianos, two drums, two electric guitars, and two singers. Two men between them led the service and the singing; it was long, informal and enthusiastic. Reference was made to three psalms at different moments. One of the leaders gave a long explanation of the financial situation of the congregation in relation to the payment of the building and to God's provision. There was no sermon as such. One of the leaders spoke 'a word of prophecy', followed by a song and a prayer of confession. Many people responded to the invitation to go forward in repentance. They were exhorted to believe

---

1. What Americans would call 'announcements'.

and confess and to read the Bible. 'You haven't changed your religion, but rather have found the Lord of Life.' Later on there was prayer for healing, testimonies, prayer for parents and their young children who went up on the platform, and a round of grateful applause to the Lord. The service concluded at 12.30 p.m., having begun at 8.30 a.m.

A few months later, I talked with a friend who had visited this same congregation. Her comment was that she had been frightened by the lack of respect for the person, and felt that psychological manipulation was used. I asked her how she understood worship; she answered: 'To worship is to pour out our hearts to God. We must worship him, no matter how we feel, for he is worthy of all honour. We practise worship by praise.' I asked then, 'What is praise?' 'Praise is to sing songs which exalt the name of God.' The praise time in her congregation lasts an hour, during which a few songs are sung, each one being repeated a number of times. My friend is aware of the danger of the blank mind during the singing.

'In what other ways do you worship?' I asked. 'Singing in tongues, and praying,' she said. 'Is the Bible read in public in your services?' 'No, we don't have that custom.' I asked her what changes she would like to see in the Sunday Service, and she replied that she would like the leaders to explain what it means to worship God, to create an awareness of this in the congregation, to give more intellectual content to the message, and then to contextualize it for the people now.

CHILE

Surrounded by the Atacama Desert, Calama is at one and the same time an oasis and a small town. A friend and I arrived at the 'Church of God' on a housing estate for 7 p.m. It was the last day of their 'Women's Week'; on the platform were five women dressed in black skirts, white blouses, and a red carnation pinned on the blouse. Behind the pulpit on the wall was a painting, a feature typical of Chilean Pentecostal churches. An open Bible occupied the centre, with rays of light falling on it from above. In the background was a river and waterfall, trees and a snow-covered peak. Pss. 19:1 and 24:1 were written on either side of the scene.

On this special occasion, the whole service was conducted by the five women on the platform, two of whom read the Scripture passage to which the pastor was later to refer in his sermon on Matt. 25:1–13. Two offerings were taken, one near the beginning and the other at the close of the service. There was a prayer of thanksgiving, and a time of joyful singing to the accompaniment of an accordian, an electric guitar, and a group of young girls whirling their tambourines with flowing streamers hanging from them. The music was melodious and simple, typically Chilean, and all the words were known by heart by the congregation.

There was a sense of expectation as the pastor began to preach. It was obvious that he had carefully prepared what he was going to say, and had borne in mind that this was the last day of 'Women's Week' in the church. The Lord is coming for his church, not for any denomination in particular (Matt. 25:1–13). In Luke 8:1–3 we learn of women who served Jesus, and in Luke 7:36–50 we see that love is not something to be talked about, but to be demonstrated. The women who watched Jesus die on the cross, from a distance (Matt. 27:55,56), were grateful women, and we who are now cleansed by his blood should be much more grateful than they.

Here the pastor referred to his own conversion, and to how God had healed and rescued him from misery. In his zeal for us to understand the message, he left the pulpit and the microphone for a few minutes and came down among the congregation, appealing fervently to us. He went on to mention Anna, the prophetess, Rahab the harlot, Ruth the Moabitess. Jesus requires us to love him with all our heart and soul; let us serve him and recognize all the mercies we have received from him. We have been forgiven great sins, and therefore we must assume our responsibility to serve him. Let us serve him with much love for we know what he has done for us.

ECUADOR

Standing opposite the buildings of the radio station HCJB in Quito, the capital of Ecuador, is a church named after the district where it is found, Inaquito. On Sunday mornings they celebrate three services, one after another, in order to give opportunity for all who desire to gather there for worship. The words of the songs were projected onto the wall at the back of the platform where the music group of five members played their instruments. Piano, trumpet and saxophone also made their contribution at different moments. The songs, some of whose words were based on Bible stories, were neither announced nor repeated. Passages of Scripture were read in between the singing of them; often clapping accompanied the rhythm of the music. There was a prayer of intercession before the offering was taken. Then came the sermon, based on 2 Sam. 7, part of which was read. Many of those present had their Bibles with them. Later a member of the pastoral team of this church told me that he had been responsible for introducing changes into the singing habits of the congregation a year ago; the changes involved combining traditional hymns with songs, and eliminating songs that have no theological content.

PERU

In the capital city of Lima I attended a Sunday morning service in a congregation now associated with the Assemblies of God. The structure of the service was straightforward: from 10 a.m. until 10.45 there was congregational singing alternating with prayer led by the man who led the singing. Then came the notices, given by the pastor, after which he preached from 11 to 12 noon. He closed his message with a long evangelistic invitation, which was followed by the taking up of the tithes and offerings. The pastor informed us about the work of construction going on, we sang again and then little by little the 300-strong congregation on that morning slowly left the building, chatting with one another as they did so.

The songs in this case were projected onto the wall and accompanied by an orchestra made up of an electronic piano, an electric guitar, trumpet and drums.

REFLECTION

In a continent nurtured on religious liturgy, it is noteworthy that by and large the structure of evangelical church services is very far removed from that liturgy. Public reading of the Word is absent; prayers of intercession for the nation are rare; baptism of adults receives prominence but the sacrament of the Lord's Supper is not given a central place, except in the Brethren assemblies. The Lord's Prayer and the Apostles' Creed are not used. There is an emphasis on corporate praise, but on the whole I venture to think that this 'praise' is the response to the music and words of a song, rather than to a fresh contemplation of God in Jesus Christ arising from an understanding of the Word. I have already mentioned the dearth of biblical exposition, a situation that opens the door to 'worship' being practised as a 'trip', divorced from daily life and national and cultural situations.

In one city, characterized by violence and poverty, fear and danger, during the course of the church service I attended, the fire brigade with loud sirens twice raced past the church building where we were gathered, but we had been encouraged by the leader, as the service began, to forget the news we had heard and the things which were happening 'outside'. We did not pray for 'the peace of Jerusalem'.

4.9 'VIEW FROM THE OTHER SIDE'

Guido Lombardi

From *Latin America Evangelist*, Maust, J.D. (ed.), January–March 1988, pp. 9–10.

My contact with the evangelical church dates back to my childhood in Tacna, Peru. My school had students from every social and economic background. But only one classmate was an evangelical.

Through some form of tacit agreement, students and professors had singled out this evangelical student for discrimination of various forms. Because I had developed a close friendship with this boy, this mistreatment of him upset me.

And yet, my friend never explained to me about the worship at his church. I was very curious to know what made his worship so different from my own.

Through this experience, I formed the perception that *evangelistas* – as they were called then – were closed unto themselves and self-absorbed. And I got the idea that evangelicals had difficulty communicating with people outside their movement.

This impression of evangelicals may be mistaken. But it traces to the hermetic attitude observed in Carlos and his family.

DEEP CONVICTIONS

My second experience with evangelicals came in 1969, when a small group of us students from the Catholic university did a social work project in Peru's Huallaga Valley.

The area was being settled by poor farmers from the Department of San Martin and Cajamarca, and most were evangelicals.

We students from the Catholic University had formed a link with the local Catholic parish, which was headed by a Canadian priest. This priest told us Catholics lacked the conviction of the evangelicals – people with fewer resources and a spirit of austerity.

I then perceived that evangelicals' lifestyle did not fit with what I might call "the Peruvian idiosyncrasy." That is, they did not have that "little beer" on the weekend. Also, they respected other people's property – traits not common to the rest of the population.

POLITICAL STRENGTH

The 1990 elections gave the evangelical church a new dimension. Alberto Fujimori's presidential election victory was attributed – rightly or wrongly – to evangelicals' word-of-mouth support for his candidacy.

I think evangelicals transmitted the idea that Fujimori was honest. Because evangelicals supported Fujimori and because evangelicals are considered honest people, people thought Fujimori was honest too.

The 1990 elections also helped us see the compactness of the evangelical movement. We perceived that this was a church able to follow a determined political course.

Obviously this scares many people. I remember frequently hearing the comment, "*Caramba*, we didn't know this movement had such power."

When we speak of political participation, we are talking about the need to change society. All of us would like our country to be different and better.

In this respect evangelicals have a tremendous advantage: They've been able to change themselves and so they have greater authority for changing the country.

ISOLATED COMMUNITY

One final anecdote brings me back to the subject of evangelicals isolating themselves. Some friends had a 19-year-old son with serious problems with drug addition.

This youth overcame his problem and radically changed his life. One would expect the family would be grateful for this change, but such was not the case.

When this youth became an evangelical, he began to reduce contact with his family. When his parents asked for my advice about this, I noticed they seemed to prefer their drug-addict son over the evangelical one, because they had lost the latter.

Here is where I see a kind of rupture between evangelicals and their surrounding society, culture and non-religious neighbors. I think the general public perceives evangelicals as being an isolated community, a kind of religious ghetto.

The National Evangelical Council released a small publication, "The Evangelical Church in Numbers," with a series of statistical charts on evangelical pastors – their age, number of children, marital status, etc.

But one finds no data saying whether the pastors like soccer or, for example, if they root for a certain soccer team. In other words, we don't know whether they are people like us.

HELP CHANGE THE NATION

We need to see what we have in common with the evangelicals. We need to see what unites us in our common struggle to build a better and more just country.

The data in this publication reveals that evangelical churches are growing fastest in the poor neighborhoods of the country. And I am convinced the new Peru, the Peru of tomorrow, will arise from these same neighborhoods.

And I think evangelicals, with their characteristic honesty, have the fundamental task of combating corruption in Peru.

These are defining moments for the future of Peru. And I believe evangelical churches have an important task to fulfill when it comes to carving out the new face of Peru.

4.10 'DAWA AND ITS SIGNIFICANCE FOR THE FUTURE'

M. Manazir Ahsan

From *Beyond Frontiers: Islam and Contemporary Needs*, Davies, M.W. and Pasha, K.M. (eds), London, Mansell, 1989.

The word *dawa* has been so used, misused and abused by Muslim and non-Muslim writers and polemicists that in the maze of discussion and counter-discussion, it has lost many of the dimensions of its true meaning. Unless the true nature, scope and significance of *dawa* is understood with all its implications and dimensions, it is not possible to chart any future plan for this noble calling.

Dawa literally means 'call' and in Islamic terminology 'an invitation to Islam', and it is the *raison d'etre* of the existence of the Muslim *ummah*, both at the micro and macro level. It would not be incorrect to say that Islam means *dawa* – for *dawa* is essentially the fulfilment of Islam. One can become a Muslim by declaring the Shahadah: 'I bear witness there is no god but Allah and Muhammad is His Servant and Messenger'. But the true Shahadah, that is witness, cannot mature, flower and bear fruit unless the private confession assumes the form of a public proclamation of the truth. This is what *dawa* means.

Witnessing by word, *Shahadah bil qaul* and reinforcing it by action *Shahadah bil Amal*, are two sides of the same coin – both are complementary and necessary to the other. Muslims cannot offer their lives as testimonies to Islam, and thereby fulfil the demands of *dawa*, unless both aspects of the testimony, words and actions, are properly synchronized and present in their lives. To acquire only one aspect is not only discouraged by the whole body of teaching and ethos of Islam but runs the risk of becoming hypocritical.

It is wrong to assume that *dawa* is aimed only at non-Muslims and that Muslims, by virtue of their birth in a Muslim family or [by] declaring the *Kalimah as Shahadah*, the declaration of faith, at the time of entering the fold of Islam, have been absolved of this responsibility for life. Islam is not a once-in-a-lifetime decision, but a process, a lifelong pursuit. Islam is not a status conferred by the declaration of faith, it is a dynamic state of becoming affirmed by constant activity throughout the course of life – the mechanism of affirmation is *dawa*. So *dawa* must begin with the conscious action of the individual Muslim's lifestyle, to be expressed in the organization of the community to offer an example and invite others to the path of Islam as a complete way of life. To be a Muslim means continually to strive to become Muslim. 'You who believe enter into the fold of Islam completely' (Quran 2:208) and 'Do not embrace death unless you are in a state of Islam' (Quran 3:101).

Dawa is, therefore, a continuous process, a perpetual endeavour aimed at inviting one's own self, every Muslim and all those who are not yet Muslims to embrace Islam willingly and completely. Similarly, *dawa* is not an occupation to be undertaken by any professional group, neither is it a contingent or part-time activity nor one undertaken in reaction to Christian missions or communist onslaughts. *Dawa* is the responsibility of every Muslim, whether a ruler or ruled, a leader or follower, a scholar or student, a Sufi or soldier, a trader or farmer, wealthy or poor, a man of a woman, living in the East or the West, North or the South. No one has a greater or lesser responsibility among *Daiya*, those who undertake *dawa*, and no one can shirk, postpone or evade this responsibility under any circumstances.

Dawa is by no means an easy task; neither is there a mechanical or uniform way of performing it, for no two people perform *dawa* in exactly the same way. Each section of society must accomplish this task in its own way with whatever faculties Allah has endowed them and with whatever wisdom and skill they can muster. The scholars and intellectuals of Islam will have their own methods and techniques of *dawa*, as will soldiers, diplomats, students and people in other walks of life.

Dawa is an essential part of the Sunnah, the way of the Prophet. Indeed, the very nature of the Sunnah, the record of the words and deeds of the Prophet Muhammad, is to be the textbook of *dawa*, a summation of its dimensions. *Dawa* must be undertaken in recognition of the mission of *Shahadah* and *gist*, or witnessing to the truth and justice. Moreover, *dawa* cannot be done correctly and fruitfully unless it is put in its proper place in the total framework of Islam. Similarly, the concepts, approaches and methods of *dawa* cannot be derived from sources other than the Quran and Sunnah of the Prophet Muhammad and the lives of other messengers. Ideally, *dawa* should be done at the macro, intermediate and micro levels of society. If, for various reasons, it is not possible to achieve this in modern times at least it must be done at some intermediate and micro levels.

Since *dawa* is essentially a call for change from sickness to health and the *daiyah* is not merely a transmitter of a message, it is essential that a rapport be established between the proponent and the listener. *Dawa* cannot be a unilateral, one-way process. It must involve a meaningful dialogue to be pursued with care, wisdom and patience. Unless the audience is psychologically attuned to be receptive, the message will not find its way to the heart. This is why all methods of compulsion, exploitation, inciting combative reaction or provoking prejudiced retaliation are strictly forbidden is Islam. *Dawa* has to be achieved with understanding, compassion, *sabr*, and above all, with great wisdom. This is also why the quality of the Prophet's benevolent disposition has been commended as the reason for his successful mission (Quran 3:159).

Dawa should be a gradual process with fixed priorities. Fundamentals must take precedence over details and obligatory duties should come before non-obligatory ones. Faith, *iman*, should be the cornerstone of all *dawa*, through the attainment of which the road to an Islamic life can be followed. Everything cannot be achieved at once. Was not the Quran revealed piecemeal over a period of twenty-three years so that people and society could adopt Islam step-by-step and become firmly rooted in it through a gradual process? Moreover, *dawa* entails the evolution of a system of moral training and spiritual purification, *tarbiyyah* and *tazkiyyah*, so that the mechanism for absorption and consolidation operates along with the machinery for contact and expansion.

The numerical strength of Islam has never been as great as it is today. Yet Muslims as a whole have little, if any, impact on the global scene, neither in economy nor politics nor in intellectual and scientific pursuits. The image of Islam portrayed both in the East and West is mostly negative, truncated, a partial view. There may be some external contributory factors, such as a long spell of colonialism in Muslim lands, but no one except Muslims can be blamed for their dismal failure to make an impact on the world scene. Any perceptive analyst will discern that the Muslim *ummah*, the international community of believers, despite being designated as 'the best' and 'middle most community' in the Quran, have on the whole failed in their duty to carry the message of Islam to mankind at large.

. . .

The theoretical framework of *dawa* being such, the contemporary situation of the Muslim *ummah* does not inspire much hope for we are performing almost no *dawa*. Very little, if any, portion of national resources are spent on this vital duty. Moreover, Muslims living within non-Muslim countries by-and-large are indifferent to this immensely important task. With rare exceptions, *dawa* among non-Muslims commands little of their attention, time and resources, and for the most part the comprehensive nature of *dawa*, its scope and dimensions are not fully comprehended, let alone appreciated. Whether because of unawareness, indifference or neglect, the state of the Muslim mind and attitude, both individual and collective, towards *dawa* is pathetic. The contemporary Muslim *Shahadah*, witness to Islam, in both words and actions does not correspond with the reality of Islam. The gap between ideal and practice is overwhelming and contradictions between Islam as it ought to be and Islam as reflected in Muslim life are pronounced.

The entire Muslim world, with rare exceptions, is in the grip of Western domination, so overpowering and all pervading that there is hardly any layer where the influence of Western culture has not penetrated. Although at village level some Islamic institutions still survive, in the metropolis and urban areas almost all the social, economic, administrative and political institutions of traditional Muslim societies have been replaced by Western-style institutions. These are run mostly by people who have been educated or trained in the West or in Western-style universities in their own countries. This minority administrative cadre, sometimes hand-in-hand with army elites to whom Western values are dearer than Islamic and whose life patterns show all the trappings of Western values, directly or indirectly dominate the entire Muslim *ummah*.

Any analysis of the contemporary Muslim situation has to take into consideration the limitations and obstacles imposed upon the work of *dawa* by internal and external factors. The legacy of hostility between the West and Islam, branching out into misconception and misrepresentation, mistrust and prejudice is not the only obstacle. The limitations of *dawa* at the level of the *ummah*, in Muslim societies and states, as well as at the level of very large groups, institutions and structures such as mosques and schools, which Khuram Murrad calls the 'macro' and the 'intermediate' levels are no less problematic. They are mostly beyond the reach and competence of ordinary Muslims to do anything effective.

This does not mean that efforts are not afoot to Islamize Muslim societies and establish a collective system of Islam to bring about the metamorphosis desired by Islam at macro and intermediate levels. There have always been such efforts in Muslim history and they should certainly be intensified with the aim of eliminating all vestiges of *jahili* culture and domination in the private and public life of the Muslim *ummah*, so that a true living Islamic model is presented to the world. The movement to Islamization whether it be of state institutions or in the intellectual endeavours of Muslim thinkers can all be encompassed within the framework of *dawa* and are the meaning and content of *dawa*. *Dawa* at the micro level is mostly being performed by individuals and small organizations and groups. Even at that level the situation leaves much to be desired: the work of *dawa* is often carried out with limited knowledge and an incomplete vision of Islam and, consequently, is not very effective.

As the whole Muslim world is under the spell of Western secular and materialistic culture, represented by the superpowers and their client states, the furtherance of the practice of *dawa* has to be tackled with great care and propriety.

. . .

The issues which confront the world today are legion. Some are central, others peripheral. The Muslim *ummah* as a whole has to diagnose these at appropriate levels and present their Islamic solutions not only through sermons and literature but also and most especially through practice and example. It would not be an exaggeration to say that Western civilization is now passing through its most critical and perhaps its last phase of crisis and disintegration, and that the stage is set for the emergence of some new order based on values basically different from those of modern Western civilization. For various reasons, such as over-secularization, over-materialism and despiritualization of life resulting in a plethora of problems, the old order is beset by problems and difficulties [which] point to its disintegration and collapse. How much time and how many more convulsions it will need before the new dawn no one knows. But there is little doubt that mankind is heading towards a major change. However, it would be naïve and an oversimplification to claim that the stage is now set for the West's march towards Islam. Ideological and cultural movements take their own time and the historical course they assume to articulate themselves is neither linear, simple nor sudden. What can, however, be claimed with reasonable certainty is that there is an ideological vacuum in the West and, indeed, in many parts of the East under Western influence, and it is a law of nature that a vacuum must be filled. What ideology is going to fill it and over what period of time will depend on a variety of factors, most important of which is the nature of the *dawa* with which Muslims respond to the situation. Like other claimants, Islam also has a chance to fill this gap and the opportunity has to be seized appropriately and immediately. Any delay may prove fatal. A wide spectrum of groups and movements representing different participants in the search for spiritual meaning in life can be seen on the intellectual, literary and cultural scene. A variety of cults, hippy and yippy groups, as well as converts to Zen, Vedanta, Krishna and other more obscure religious manifestations, represent some aspects of this quest. Though these manifestations might be superficial, confused or even counterfeit, they do mirror the phenomena of simmering uneasiness of the soul and a quest for a genuine spiritual and ideological path. This presents Muslims with an exciting opportunity and a challenge of great magnitude.

4.11 'DOES ANYBODY CARE?: THE UMMA AT A CHARITY DINNER'

Seán McLoughlin

'In the name of the Umma', in *Political Participation and Identities of Muslims in Non-Muslim States*, Shadid, W.A.R. and Van Koningsveld, P.S. (eds), Kampan, Kok Pharos, 1996, pp. 214–19, 222–4.

In early March 1994 Bradford Eid Committee organized a charity dinner held in conference rooms hired from the University of Bradford. Tickets were £10 each and the proceeds went to the twin causes of Bosnia and Kashmir.

. . .

This evening of fund-raising was advertised in community centres and Pakistani restaurants with a poster that heralded the question, "does anybody care?" in English and Urdu. The posters maintained that "everyone was welcome" to the dinner and so theoretically addressed all sections of society in Bradford. Indeed the clientele of many Pakistani restaurants is often white and non-Muslim. However on arrival at the dinner it was clear that this was to be an event bounding people on the basis of being Muslim, rather than on the basis of an interest in the multicultural affairs of the city. The white, non-Muslim Lord Mayor had not been asked to preside, as he sometimes was at community events. Instead the organizers had invited speakers, at least two representing notable Islamist organizations in Britain, to address the gathering before the dinner itself. Indeed the evening's speeches would produce an alternative account of agendas for "the Muslim community" to those proposed by the "race" relations industry in Bradford.

By the time proceedings were about to begin probably a few hundred people had gathered. Seating was supposedly gender-segregated with provision made for women at the back of the hall, although as people began to find their seats after prayers in the foyer, some women marched to the front and commandeered those seats for themselves. As the audience waited expectantly for the speeches to begin, the evening's programme opened with a recital of the *qur'an* from chapter *an-nisa* (the Women). First in Arabic and then in English translation, a section of the chapter making reference to the defence of Islam was read aloud from the stage by an *imam* (prayer leader). This recitation set the tone for the evening's speeches.

Adeeb, a businessman from Leeds, was the chairperson for the evening.

. . .

He told us that the organizers had come together after Christmas out of sheer frustration with the fact that after two and a half years of war in the former Yugoslavia, nothing was being done in Bosnia to alleviate the desperate situation of Muslims there. There was a feeling of isolation about his question: "brothers and sisters are suffering…does anybody care?" Adeeb explained that atrocities against Muslims were going on in Kashmir too, under Indian occupation. He acknowledged that the Kashmiri link to the evening's proceedings was special because so many Mirpuri-Kashmiris lived in Bradford. Adeeb continued by thanking the many people that had been of assistance in organizing the dinner. Indeed he maintained that at a time when, "we hear so much of Muslim disunity these days – others play on it – this coming together is a good example of co-operation and unity". He was re-enforcing then, the fact that his question, "does anybody care?", was directed at Muslims themselves. They would have to help themselves given the perceived double-standards of the Western powers who had intervened in Kuwait but left Muslims to die in Bosnia. His point was that they could not help themselves unless they were unified. All the speeches echoed these sentiments but ultimately set up a debate about the best method for transforming Muslims' situation in the world.

KHADIJA: Wearing *hijab* (the veil which covers women's hair and body) and darkened spectacles, Khadija struggled forward to take her place on the stage. We were told that she was recovering from a spate of hospital operations to treat injuries sustained in Bosnia. No mention was made of her membership of any particular organization; her's was a testimony based on personal experience. The daughter of a Bosnian-Herzogovian mother and Polish father, she delivered her speech in an ordinary English accent which suggested that she had grown up in Britain. Her speech began as an evocative recollection of Bosnia; its beauty, the night's sky, the mountains and the way in which all these memories had been wiped out by the carnage: "A girl watching the sky is obliterated and her husband and friends are made *shahids* (martyrs) by the murdering Serbs. Their bodies are gone but their souls are with *allah*, they are well now . . ."

The speech soon moved to the horrific rape of 100,000 Muslim sisters in Bosnia. "The United Nations say that it is not a human rights issue! How does it feel to see your wife or mother or daughter gang-raped before your very eyes? I am sorry if I have offended brothers' or sisters' sensitivities. They must face up to it. The victims of rape want to die; they cry and cry until there is nothing left. Some Europeans and Turks (!) offer abortions . . . What would you do? I know what it is to hate and I hope that those present do not experience what that is like."

Then the emphasis of her speech shifted from offence at the treatment of Muslims to their need to come together in self-defence. Her delivery was slow, steady and deliberate. Every sentence was solemnly calculated to firmly bond those present with the subjects of the recollection. "We may speak different languages but that does not matter. What matters is that we are all Muslims." Khadija demanded protection from the brothers present for their Muslim sisters. She demanded it for all sisters. "It is your duty." She asked whether any of the brothers present would be in Kashmir fighting for its liberation when she next visited? The Quran speaks of iron and *allah* gives us the right to defend ourselves. We must be armed. The only language is that of the gun barrel. Be proud to be a fundamentalist. Perhaps some feel uncomfortable with the title. But it only means being a basic Muslim. Forget small quibbles between you . . ."

She concluded with an emotional vote of thanks to the chairperson: "I want to thank you for the 900 lives of Muslims that you have saved by your efforts so far. So and so from Bosnia thanks for his life to the conference convenor."

This was greeted, as were the other speeches periodically throughout the evening, with one of a number of rallying calls: "*takbir*" repeatedly called out for the praise and glorification of God, to which many in the audience enthusiastically replied, "*allahu akbar*" (God is great).

MAJID: Next to speak was the Human Rights Officer of the Muslim Parliament of Great Britain.

. . .

Majid, dressed in a suit but with no tie after the Iranian fashion, focused his concern, like Khadija, on Bosnia. Claiming that 80% of human rights abuses in the world were directed against Muslims, his argument was that sending charity, money and food *ad hoc* to suffering Muslims there was not enough: "we are simply fattening our brothers and sisters for their death. There are nearly three million Muslims (sic) in Britain and thirty million (sic) in Europe as a whole . . . And all of these donating just £1.00 a week, every week, regardless of status would begin a commitment to arming Bosnia and making a strong Islamic state in the heart of Europe."

From here Majid went on to develop two key points: that giving charity should be regular and planned (along the lines of the Muslim Parliament's welfare system of Islam in Britain, the *bait al-mal al-islami*) and that Bosnian-Muslims should be armed and assisted in their bid to defend themselves in *jihad* (to this second end the "Arms for Bosnia Fund", later renamed 'Bosnia Jihad Fund' after the British government deemed that the former was illegal, was established in 1993). Majid then called, like Khadija, for an individual responsibility for activism given the complicity of many Muslim rulers in the West's project of global domination: "The *Umma* is like a body; if one part of the body if pricked then all the rest of the body reacts (quoting al-Bukhari). It is our individual responsibility to act...At *qiyamat* (the day of resurrection and judgement), it is not the King Fahds who will answer for our inaction; it is ourselves. We cannot always blame an *amir* (prince or commander)."

He concluded by informing those present that Muslims in Britain would be next to suffer the West's opposition to Islam. Thus supporting a *jihad* to defend Bosnians and investing in a strong Islamic state in Bosnia, was necessary to defend all Muslims in their future trials in Europe.

IKRAM: The next speaker, Ikram, was a prominent local member of two national organizations that eventually merged in April 1994: (i) Young Muslims UK, which was launched from Bradford in 1984, and (ii) the recently established Islamic Society of Britain. Both organizations are firmly within the Pakistani Islamist tradition of Sayyid Mawdudi and *Jama'at-i Islami* through the parentage of the latter's offspring in Britain, UK Islamic Mission. However in recent years YMUK have . . . created a distinct organizational and ideological space for themselves in Bradford, reflecting their concern with the experience of Muslims born in Britain.

A young doctor, educated in Britain, Ikram was dressed in an impeccably smart suit and sporting what one neighbour uncharitably called "trendy-Muslim designer-stubble". For

Ikram the transformation of Muslims' depressed situation could only come about with a bottom-up process of missionary activity, *da'wa*. This should be their main activity when: "the greatest injury that is being done to the *Umma* is the loss of a generation in Britain. Our children are falling away from Islam. The Muslims are asleep . . ."

While the materialism and secularism of Western lifestyles was seen as a threat to the faith of young Muslims born in Britain, Ikram also outlined the opportunity that a Muslim presence in Britain presents: offering the invitation of Islam to non-Muslim Britons. He argued that everyone has the right to hear the universalist message of Islam, which itself has a positive contribution to make to the moral and political development of British society. However Ikram counselled that if this message is to be accepted it has to be well presented given the current false images of Islam that dominate the ideas of British people.

. . .

Ikram concluded his plea for *da'wa* amongst Muslims and non-Muslims alike by encouraging the audience to ensure Islam's continued success as the world's fastest growing religion and the second largest religion in Britain through their commitment to a truly Islamic way of life.

SHAKIL: The final speaker of the evening, Shakil, was a white revert (convert) Muslim who was introduced as an "eminent Scottish historian" with a background in the academic study of Islam in universities. Conspiracy against the Muslims was the theme of his talk. He offered an alternative reading of historical and contemporary international relations but after the heavy rhetoric of the previous speeches, here was one shot through with humour that the audience clearly enjoyed. He wove an intricate web which pulled powerful personalities from around the globe into fantastic relationships grounded in their common interest in scuppering the advance of the global Islamic movement. In addition to routine critiques of the West's self-interested intervention in the Gulf during 1990–91, King Hassan of Morocco, had been, he claimed, tutored by the United States' CIA since his childhood. This was why he was their "lapdog". The Queen of England, it was noted, played her own part in the conspiracy as god-mother to a number of prominent Serbians. The double-standards of the ruling political establishment in Britain were exposed. Next Shakil wondered why Muslims were surprised at British support for military intervention in the Gulf War but not in Bosnia?" Don't you read the papers?" he asked. He reminded the gathering that the unchaste sexual manners of government ministers is well reported as going hand in hand with their supposed commitment to "the Family". His conclusion called for Muslims to unite in defence of Islam for only then could they succeed in carrying its message to the world. Thus the evening's speeches came to an end and after *du'a* (supplicatory prayer) we all began to queue in the adjacent hall for dinner.

. . .

All the speeches privileged the idea of a global Islamic trans-nationality that bounds Muslims over and against their other subject positions. Recall how: Khadija enunciated that Muslims in Bradford had a duty to defend their brothers and sisters in Bosnia and Kashmir;

Majid proposed funding an Islamic State in Bosnia to defend all Muslims in an Islamaphobic Europe; Ikram imagined the missionary possibilities of Islam as a universal religion that was now being adopted by twentieth century Britons as it was by thirteenth century Mongols; Shakil outlined conspiracy theories that established a Muslim moral utopia against the moral dystopia of the West. The emphasis was on reaching out from Bradford to realize duties to, and mutual investments in, an *Umma* that transcended attachments to identification positions of nationality and locality, gender and class.

The central message of the evening's speeches, that Muslims in Bradford must defend interests they hold in common with brothers and sisters elsewhere, met with broad approval from the audience. It is also important to note that the dinner was held just after *ramazan* and *'id ulfitr* when giving charity to other Muslims is incumbent upon all. Muslims in Bradford are constantly reminded of their membership of the *Umma* by sermons at the mosque, the work of Muslim charities and the television coverage that has brought the plight of Muslims in Bosnia into their front-rooms – front-rooms which notably often mark membership of the *Umma* with pictures of white-robed figures doing *hajj* (the pilgrimage) or rugs detailing the *ka'ba* (the black cube in Makka which Muslims pray towards) and other holy places. However ordinary Muslims in Bradford do not argue for an Islamic state in Bosnia or for the necessity of doing *da'wa* in Britain as the speakers did. Rather their connection with other Muslims is routinely produced in terms of sharing pain and showing solidarity. Hence the net result of the evening was to raise a few thousand pounds for charity and not to mobilize the sort of activism the speakers called for.

Living at the centre of Western consumer capitalism but marginalized as a minority both in Britain and in the "new world order" of the West, there is a sense in which Muslims in Britain are doubly alert to the politicization of difference in the contemporary world. It is empowering for Muslims at the margins in Britain to take responsibility for other Muslims be they in Bosnia, Kashmir, Palestine or Chechnya, because despite their marginalization in Britain there is a recognition that theirs is a position of relative privilege. Nevertheless in discussions about the *Umma* with Muslims in Bradford a dread of repatriation is discernible. The idea that because they are Muslim they may indeed be, as Majid suggested, "next" to be forcibly expelled from their European homes, haunts even those holding British passports and born in Britain. This, it was suggested to me . . . is one reason, among others, why some minorities still maintain investments in places like Mirpur. I do not claim that this observation explodes the "myth of return" but rather that it signals the importance of suffering as a point of connection between Muslims in Bradford and their co-religionists.

The ideas of the *Umma* was sufficient to aggregate Muslims inside the specificity of the dinner context vis-à-vis an often hostile and uncaring world outside. It constructs a good argument with excluders pointing to membership of something somehow bigger and better than cultural-racist representations of the British nation-state. It is something that Muslims in Britain take pride in. This is reflected in the way in which the *Umma* is routinely produced as a metaphor for utopian racial and ethnic harmony in contemporary Muslim discourses. Muslims will explain how it is a diverse and dispersed trans-national constituency numbering at least 900,000,000, ranging from Morocco in the West to Indonesia in the East, and how it unites Muslims of all colours and cultures, most manifestly at events like *hajj*. Speaking in the name of the *Umma* can also epitomize a desire beyond a Muslim constituency to say something about the world today from a position that is not centred on the West. Among the reasons why Western claims to be universal have been shown to be local eurocentrisms grounded in a copyrighting of the values of modernity, is the power of the *Umma* to name an alternative source of cultural authority in the contemporary world, Islam.

4.12 'NAM-MYOHO-RENGE-KYO: SOKA GAKKAI INTRODUCTION CARD'

Produced by the SGI. The copy shows both sides of the card in their entirety.

Soka Gakkai International – United Kingdom (SGI-UK)
The Buddhist Society for the Creation of Value

Nam-Myoho-Renge-Kyo

The Buddhism of Nichiren Daishonin reveals the existence of a universal Law of Life, which is the essence of life itself and which is Nam-Myoho-Renge-Kyo.

NAM is the act of summoning this law from within us and putting it into action in our lives and environment by chanting Nam-Myoho-Tenge-Kyo.

MYOHO is the power of revitalisation, the emergence of the highest state of life – the Buddha state – from within us.

RENGE is the cause and effect of the emergence of our Buddha nature in terms of benefit, happiness and fulfilment.

KYO is the thread or link of life, connecting everything through sound and vibration, and specifically the sound of the Buddha state which is Nam-Myoho-Renge-Kyo.

4.13 'HAPPINESS IN THIS WORLD'

Nichiren

From *The Major Writings of Nichiren Daishonin, Volume One*, Tokyo, Nichiren Shoshu International, 1979, pp. 161–2.

There is no greater happiness for human beings than chanting Nam-myoho-renge-kyo. The sutra says, "The people there [in my land] are happy and at ease."[1] "Happy and at ease" here means the joy derived from the Law. You are obviously included among the "people," and "there" indicates the entire world, which includes Japan. "Happy and at ease" means to know that our lives – both our bodies and minds, ourselves and our surroundings – are the entities of *ichinen sanzen* and the Buddha of absolute freedom. There is no greater happiness than having faith in the Lotus Sutra. It promises us "peace and security in this life and good circumstances in the next."[2] Never let life's hardships disturb you. After all, no one can avoid problems, not even saints or sages.

Just chant Nam-myoho-renge-kyo, and when you drink saké, stay at home with your wife. Suffer what there is to suffer, enjoy what there is to enjoy. Regard both suffering and joy as facts of life and continue chanting Nam-myoho-renge-kyo, no matter what happens. Then you will experience boundless joy from the Law. Strengthen your faith more than ever.

With my deep respects,
Nichiren

The twenty-seventh day of the sixth month in the second year of Kenji (1276)

---

1. Lotus Sutra, chap. 16.
2. Ibid., chap. 5.

4.14 'THE ONE ESSENTIAL PHRASE'

Nichiren

From *The Major Writings of Nichiren Daishonin, Volume One*, Tokyo, Nichiren Shoshu International Centre, 1979, pp. 221–4.

First, for you to ask a question about the Lotus Sutra is a rare source of good fortune. In this age of the Latter Day of the Law, those who ask about the meaning of even one phrase or verse of the Lotus Sutra are much fewer than those who can hurl great Mount Sumeru to another land like a stone, or those who can kick the entire galaxy away like a ball. They are even fewer than those who can embrace and teach countless other sutras, thereby enabling the priests and laymen who listen to them to obtain the six mystic powers.[1] Equally rare is a priest who can explain the meaning of the Lotus Sutra and clearly answer questions concerning it. The *Hōtō* chapter in the fourth volume of the Lotus Sutra sets forth the important principle of six difficult and nine easy acts. Your asking a question about the Lotus Sutra is among the six difficult acts. This is a sure indication that if you embrace the Lotus Sutra, you will certainly attain Buddhahood. Since the Lotus Sutra defines our life as the Buddha's life, our mind as the Buddha's wisdom and our actions as the Buddha's behavior, all who embrace and believe in even a single phrase or verse of this sutra will be endowed with these three properties. Nam-myoho-renge-kyo is only one phrase, but it contains the essence of the entire sutra. You asked whether one can attain Buddhahood only by chanting, Nam-myoho-renge-kyo, and this is the most important question of all. It is the heart of the entire sutra and the substance of its eight volumes.

The spirit within one's body may appear in just his face, and the spirit within his face may appear in just his eyes. Included within the word Japan is all that is within the country's sixty-six provinces; all of the people and animals, the rice paddies and other fields, those of high and low status, the nobles and the commoners, the seven kinds of gems[2] and all other treasures. Similarly, included within the title, Nam-myoho-renge-kyo, is the entire sutra consisting of all eight volumes, twenty-eight chapters and 69,384 characters without exception. Concerning this, Po Chü-i stated that the title is to the sutra as eyes are to the Buddha. In the eighth volume of his *Hokke Monga Ki*, Miao-lo stated that T'ien-t'ai's *Hokke Gengi* explains only the title, but that the entire sutra is thereby included. By this he meant that, although the text was omitted, the entire sutra was contained in the title alone. Everything has its essential point, and the heart of the Lotus Sutra is its title, Nam-myoho-renge-kyo. Truly, if you chant this in the morning and evening you are correctly reading the

---

1. Six mystic powers: They were expounded in the *Kusha Ron*: 1) the power to appear anywhere at will; 2) the power to observe all phenomena in the world, no matter how large or small, near or far; 3) the power to understand all sounds and languages; 4) the power to read minds; 5) the power to know people's past lifetimes; and 6) the power to be free from all innate desires.

2. Seven kinds of gems: They differ slightly according to scriptures. The Hōtō (11th) chapter of the Lotus Sutra defines them as gold, silver, lapis lazuli, coral, agate, pearl and carnelian. From the standpoint of faith, they indicate the seven jewels of the Treasure Tower.

entire Lotus Sutra. Chanting daimoku twice is the same as reading the entire sutra twice, one hundred daimoku equal one hundred readings of the sutra, and a thousand daimoku, a thousand readings of the sutra. Thus, if you ceaselessly chant daimoku, you will be continually reading the Lotus Sutra. The sixty volumes of the T'ien-t'ai doctrine present exactly the same interpretation. A law this easy to embrace and this easy to practice was taught for the sake of all mankind in this evil age of the Latter Day of the Law. A passage from the Lotus Sutra reads, "During the Latter Day of the Law, if one wishes to teach this sutra, he should employ the mild way of propagation." Another reads, "In the Latter Day when the Law is about to perish, a person who embraces, reads and recites this sutra must abandon feelings of envy and deceit." A third states, "In the Latter Day of the Law, one who embraces this sutra will be carrying out all forms of service to the Buddha." A fourth reads, "In the fifth five hundred years after my death, accomplish worldwide kōsen-rufu and never allow its flow to cease." The intent of all these teachings is the admonition to embrace and believe in the Lotus Sutra in this Latter Day of the Law. The heretical priests in Japan, China and India have all failed to comprehend this obvious meaning. The Nembutsu, Shingon, Zen and Ritsu sects follow either the Hinayana or the provisional Mahayana teachings but have discarded the Lotus Sutra. They misunderstand Buddhism, but they do not realize their mistakes. Because they appear to be true priests, the people trust them without the slightest doubt. Therefore, without realizing it, both these priests and the people who follow them have become enemies of the Lotus Sutra and foes of Shakyamuni Buddha. From the viewpoint of the sutra, it is certain that not only will all their wishes remain unfulfilled, but their lives will be short and, after this life, they will be doomed to the hell of incessant suffering.

Even though one neither reads nor studies the sutra, chanting the title alone is the source of tremendous good fortune. The sutra teaches that women, evil men, and those in the realms of Animality and Hell – in fact, all the people of the Ten Worlds – can attain Buddhahood. We can comprehend this when we remember that fire can be produced by a stone taken from the bottom of a river, and a candle can light up a place that has been dark for billions of years. If even the most ordinary things of this world are such wonders, then how much more wondrous is the power of the Mystic Law. The lives of human beings are fettered by evil karma, earthly desires and the inborn sufferings of life and death. But due to the three inherent potentials of Buddha nature – innate Buddhahood, the wisdom to become aware of it, and the action to manifest it – our lives can without doubt come to reveal the Buddha's three properties. The Great Teacher Dengyō declared that the power of the Lotus Sutra enables anyone to manifest Buddhahood. He stated this because even the Dragon King's daughter was able to attain Buddhahood through the power of the Lotus Sutra. Do not doubt this in the least. Let your husband know that I will explain this in detail when I see him.

Nichiren

The third day of the seventh month in the first year of Kōan (1278)

4.15 'SOKA GAKKAI INTERNATIONAL CHARTER'

The Soka Gakki International Charter, 1996, Soka Gakki International, www.sgi.org/about/sgi/charter.html

We, the constituent organizations and members of the Soka Gakkai International (hereinafter called "SGI"), embrace the fundamental aim and mission of contributing to peace, culture and education based on the philosophy and ideals of the Buddhism of Nichiren Daishonin.

We recognize that at no time in history has humankind experienced such an intense juxtaposition of war and peace, discrimination and equality, poverty and abundance as in the twentieth century; that the development of increasingly sophisticated military technology, exemplified by nuclear weapons, has created a situation where the very survival of the human species hangs in the balance; that the reality of violent ethnic and religious discrimination presents an unending cycle of conflict; that humanity's egoism and intemperance have engendered global problems, including degradation of the natural environment and widening economic chasms between developed and developing nations, with serious repercussions for humankind's collective future.

We believe that Nichiren Daishonin's Buddhism, a humanistic philosophy of infinite respect for the sanctity of life and all-encompassing compassion, enables individuals to cultivate and bring forth their inherent wisdom and, nurturing the creativity of the human spirit, to surmount the difficulties and crises facing humankind and realize a society of peaceful and prosperous coexistence.

We, the constituent organizations and members of SGI, therefore, being determined to raise high the banner of world citizenship, the spirit of tolerance, and respect for human rights based on the humanistic spirit of Buddhism, and to challenge the global issues that face humankind through dialogue and practical efforts based on a steadfast commitment to nonviolence, hereby adopt this Charter, affirming the following purposes and principles:

PURPOSES AND PRINCIPLES

1 SGI shall contribute to peace, culture and education for the happiness and welfare of all humanity based on Buddhist respect for the sanctity of life.
2 SGI, based on the ideal of world citizenship, shall safeguard fundamental human rights and not discriminate against any individual on any grounds.
3 SGI shall respect and protect the freedom of religion and religious expression.
4 SGI shall promote an understanding of Nichiren Daishonin's Buddhism through grass-roots exchange, thereby contributing to individual happiness.

5   SGI shall, through its constituent organizations, encourage its members to contribute toward the prosperity of their respective societies as good citizens.

6   SGI shall respect the independence and autonomy of its constituent organizations in accordance with the conditions prevailing in each country.

7   SGI shall, based on the Buddhist spirit of tolerance, respect other religions, engage in dialogue and work together with them toward the resolution of fundamental issues concerning humanity.

8   SGI shall respect cultural diversity and promote cultural exchange, thereby creating an international society of mutual understanding and harmony.

9   SGI shall promote, based on the Buddhist ideal of symbiosis, the protection of nature and the environment.

10 SGI shall contribute to the promotion of education, in pursuit of truth as well as the development of scholarship, to enable all people to cultivate their individual character and enjoy fulfilling and happy lives.

4.16 'PRESIDENT IKEDA'S GUIDANCE'

Daisaku Ikeda

'SGI President Ikeda's New Year's Message: Happy New Year to my beloved SGI members', *SGI UK Bulletin*, 14 January 2000, no. 259, p. 1.

SGI PRESIDENT IKEDA'S NEW YEAR'S MESSAGE

HAPPY NEW YEAR TO MY BELOVED SGI MEMBERS!

With the magnificent success and development of our kosen-rufu movement, we usher in this New Year that marks the 70th anniversary of the Soka Gakkai's founding. I hope you, my 10 million precious comrades in faith throughout the world, will join me in celebrating this brilliant, hope-filled occasion. I deeply appreciate all of your tireless efforts.

The year 2000, to my great delight, marks the 100th anniversary of second Soka Gakkai president Josei Toda's birth. It is also, The Year of Youth, in which we will raise the curtain on the 21st Century. And this year also signals the exuberant start of our momentous journey toward the third millennium.

As the SGI embarks on a new century, I humbly wish to convey that our membership has now spread from 128 countries to 148 countries around the world. Fellow Bodhisattvas of the Earth are working valiantly and energetically for kosen-rufu in all corners of the globe. I am confident that Nichiren Daishonin, the Buddha of the Latter Day of the Law, would be overjoyed at this unparalleled achievement in the history of Buddhism.

You have made this unprecedented achievement possible. Because of this I am absolutely convinced that the good fortune you have accumulated as a result will shine brilliantly in your lives forever. It will become a boundless and immeasurable treasure, indestructible throughout the three existences of past, present and future, just as the Daishonin promises.

Celebrating a golden age of Buddhism surpassing that which flourished under the ancient Indian king Ashoka, let's keep striving cheerfully for kosen-rufu and courageously advance, like the lion king that roams the plains and the eagle that soars in the sky.

Throughout his life, the Soka Gakkai's founding president, Tsunesaburo Makiguchi, tenaciously fought against evil and injustice. He declared with powerful conviction, 'Happiness and kosen-rufu are contingent on our activity causing devilish functions to appear and eradicating them.'

After Mr Makiguchi died in prison for his beliefs, our mentor Josei Toda stood up with an indomitable resolve to carry on his work. He proclaimed that kosen-rufu could not be achieved without great courage and an invincible fighting spirit.

I, too, have fought for kosen-rufu for more than five decades, without deviating in the slightest from this lofty Soka Gakkai spirit, and I have written an immortal history. In all that time, I have not rested a single day nor retreated a single step. Because the Soka Gakkai has forged ahead with solid unity of purpose centring on the three successive presidents, it has achieved the phenomenal development it has today. As a result, it is hailed by leading intellectuals around the world as 'a miracle of the 20th century.'

There is no life more respectworthy than a life dedicated to kosen-rufu.

In giving guidance, Mr Makiguchi often used to say, 'Rest assured that persecution sends those of false faith into retreat, while it fosters genuine lions.'

Armed with the pride and resolve of true victors that 'no strategy is more powerful than the strategy of the Lotus Sutra' I hope you will join me once again this year in advancing with confidence and light hearts along the great path of peace and culture.

Let us work together to create a Century of Life and a Century of Humanity that will go down in history – an age that humankind has been dreaming of and that will pave the way to lasting happiness for all people.

This life, this existence, is precious. Therefore, let us strive together earnestly and win in all challenges, moving forward intrepidly with optimism, courage and a progressive spirit in order to achieve victory in our lives.

All of you are extremely precious to me and I am praying each day with all my heart for your good health and longevity. I am also praying fervently that each of you without a single exception will lead a life of great happiness and fulfilment.

I also look forward to your continued success and progress in your activities for the sake of kosen-rufu in the year ahead in your respective regions and countries.

Praying for the eternal development of the SGI, I conclude my New Year's message.

4.17 'ADAPTING THE PRECEPTS TO THE LOCALITY'

Win Hunter

'Adapting the Precepts to the Locality (Zuiho Bini)', in *UK Express: A Buddhist Magazine*, February 1997, no. 308.

There's an apocryphal story about an American and a Vietnamese farmer. The American gives the Vietnamese a new strain of rice. 'It's marvellous', the American beams, 'it'll give you twice the yield of the old one.' The Vietnamese smiles, 'Now I'll only have to plant half as much.'

Different cultures, different values. When we start to practise the Buddhism of Nichiren Daishonin, we may wonder if we have to adopt a more 'eastern' approach and make changes to our cultural outlook.

Historically, Buddhism spread from India through China and then to Japan so naturally that the teachings were communicated with relevant cultural references. Buddhism is in essence a universal teaching – Nichiren Daishonin taught that *everyone* has Buddhahood and the capacity to reveal it by chanting Nam-myoho-renge-kyo.

When people who are not Japanese begin to practise Buddhism, they can feel confused about what aspects of the practice are Buddhist teachings and what are cultural overlays. Inevitably, there are cultural overlays because Buddhism spread throughout the world thanks to the great faith and efforts of the Japanese members of the Soka Gakkai after the Second World War.

The answer to this confusion is to be found in the writings of Nichiren Daishonin. He explained the Buddhist principle of *zuiho bini*, or adapting the precepts (of Buddhism) to the locality. The precept appears in the Gobun Ritsu, the *vinaya*, or monastic regulations, of the Mahishasaka school: we may act in accordance with local custom, so long as the fundamental spirit of Buddhism is not violated.

In thirteenth century Japan, the indigenous religion, Shinto, emphasized ritual purity. Women were supposed to refrain from religious observance during their menstrual period. In response to a woman who wanted to know if this observance applied to her practice of the Daishonin's Buddhism he wrote:

> When we scrutinize the sutras and treatises with care, we find that there is a doctrine called the *zuiho bini* precept that corresponds to such cases. The gist of this precept is that, so long as no seriously offensive act is involved, then, even though one should depart to some slight degree from the teachings of Buddhism, one should avoid going against the manners and customs of the country. This is a precept expounded by the Buddha…people born in this country would probably do well to be aware of and honour such prohibitions.
>
> However, I do not think that such prohibitions should interfere with a woman's daily religious devotions (*Major Writings*, Vol. 6. pp. 12–13).

Whilst this is not a problem that western women have to face in their daily lives, we can apply the spirit of this guidance to any questions we may have about practising Nichiren Daishonin's Buddhism here in the UK. The Daishonin does not give the woman a rule to follow, rather, he tells her that she has to take on board what the local customs are and apply her practice to them. Wisdom and common sense are the keynote.

We have to be aware of the laws and the customs of our locality. In the UK, we are free to practise and hold discussion meetings but, in some countries, members are affected by the laws of state religion or prohibitions on public and private assembly. In those cases, members have to practise discreetly for their own safety. In the Daishonin's time, there was much persecution of his followers by the state and by members of other sects. He always encouraged his followers to practise strongly but to exercise wisdom in their daily lives for their own protection.

Nichiren Daishonin wrote:

When the skies are clear, the ground is illuminated. Similarly, when one knows the Lotus Sutra, he understands the meaning of all wordly affairs (*Major Writings*, Vol. 1, p. 82).

Referring to this, President Ikeda said:

This passage means in essence that one who embraces the Gohonzon of the Three Great Secret Laws – The Lotus Sutra of the Latter Day of the Law – can grasp the heart of all mundane affairs. In other words, this passage teaches us that faith finds expression in daily life and that Buddhism is manifested in society (*Buddhism in Action*, Vol. 2, p. 170).

Our basic practice is chanting Nam-myoho-renge-kyo, reciting the sutra, studying Buddhist writings and teaching others. We do that as ordinary people with our own particular characteristics in the localities in which we live and work. Our practice does not involve our undertaking austerities and adopting rules and lifestyles inappropriate to our locality. How are we to prove the power of the practice to ourselves and others except by living as great, yet ordinary, human beings?

In order to do so, we need to reassess ourselves constantly, reflecting on our behaviour as individuals and as members of society. The bottom line in that process is to ask ourselves how we can live to the full within our society, openly, according to the spirit of the teachings of Nichiren Daishonin. We can do this by struggling to understand the precept of *zuiho bini*. President Ikeda wrote:

Religion should by no means be separate or isolated from society. Nor should the philosophy it expounds be empty or idealistic, removed from the realities of daily life. The focus of Buddhism is always among the people and within society. It is directed towards people's suffering and towards improving their daily lives (*Daily Guidance*, Vol. 3, p. 339).

4.18 'FLOOD DISASTER IN VENEZUELA'

Elio Montel

'Flood alert', *SGI Quarterly*, July 2000, no. 21, pp. 14–15.

In December, my brother Alejandro and I moved to a new apartment in Caribe. We never imagined that a few days later our lives would be overwhelmed by a real disaster, that we would see everything around us destroyed. We never imagined, when we saw pictures of floods in countries like India, Bangladesh or other Latin American countries, that this would ever happen to us.

It had been raining nonstop for eight days. We were worried because in other places it had caused landslides, many deaths and much material damage. Fifteen days after Alejandro and I had moved to our new apartment, the city began to flood and enormous mud waves destroyed a number of cars and houses.

We were cut off in our apartment building, with no form of communication except for a battery-run cellular phone that my sister had given me just a few days before. This became the telephone center for our neighbors. The entire building was without electricity, water, elevators and services, and the basements were flooded. We were worried about the health of many of our neighbors because the majority were children and old people.

Creating security groups was one of the first priorities. People who had lost their homes and property were looking for places to stay in the middle of the tragedy, and many of them were out of control. Rape and looting were common during those days.

The second night of the tragedy we received a phone call from one of our friends from SGI-Venezuela, and in the background I could hear the familiar voices of other SGI members and friends. We learned that, throughout Venezuela, SGI members were chanting to support us to overcome this problem. My mother was with us throughout that time. She had traveled across the whole disaster area to be with us and support us. People around me couldn't believe she had done that.

During this ordeal we drew encouragement from the writings of Nichiren Daishonin and President Ikeda not to despair and to try to understand what value we could create in these trying circumstances. My brother reminded me that President Ikeda had said that, as Buddhists, we have a responsibility to work in our community; and this was an opportunity for us to be of help to others. Alejandro started to help people with his medical skills, and I helped rig up an electricity supply from a pole in the street. I also busied myself by collecting water from a well, removing garbage to avoid infection, helping conserve food and generally trying to improve conditions for everyone.

Everybody told us to leave the city, but it took us a long time to decide to do so. We were concerned about our possessions, but mainly we felt that by being there we could help people get over the disaster. We realized that people were putting their trust in us, and we decided to do the best we could until the moment we left the building. We continued to receive telephone calls from SGI members offering their support and concern. We were encouraged to chant for the wisdom to make the right decision about whether to leave or not. Alejandro, my mother and I discussed leaving and, after chanting about it, we decided that we would leave. It was a difficult decision to make.

We went to the rescue center, and three hours later we were aboard a helicopter which took us to the International Airport of Maiquetia, where we took a bus to Caracas.

A family of SGI members was waiting for us. They gave us shelter and food, and a very warm welcome. We began to hear about the efforts that the SGI had been making to help each of the members of my district. I was very proud to learn how the SGI-Venezuela organization, supported by the SGI, had quickly mobilized to provide relief for the many disaster-stricken people in the country. Much of this relief came in the form of donations of various kinds.

SGI-Venezuela made a list of aid bodies so the money and materials raised for relief work could be equitably distributed. We donated 700 toys to the government of the Federal District for children sheltering in schools in Caracas, and learning materials and a radio-cassette recorder to the Education, Culture and Sports Bureau for young children sheltered in a military fort. At the request of the Ministry of Education, we held a workshop on April 28 for 60 teachers from poorer areas in the Federal District affected by the tragedy, in which I had the opportunity to participate. The workshop was based on Soka Gakkai founder Tsunesaburo Makiguchi's value-creating pedagogy and other educational activities.

We donated provisions and foodstuffs such as milk, rice, grains, etc., to the government of Miranda State, where part of Caracas is located. Falcon State was also badly affected by the rains. In this state, SGI-Venezuela donated baby supplies and gas kitchenettes to the governor's relief efforts. We also gave UNICEF Venezuela a donation of US $3,000 to be used in relief activities for children injured by the tragedy. A special donation was made to the Environmental Bureau for building permanent houses for people affected by the tragedy.

Venezuelan Central University and Simón Bolívar University had also been badly affected. Here we made a donation for students who lost everything during the tragedy.

The Venezuelan Institution for Child Protection (VICP) is a national institution working with abandoned and disturbed children. This institution asked for equipment to organize new sheltered housing for injured children from La Guaira. Many of the child refugees in VICP participated in a painting workshop held by SGI-Venezuela members, and some of their paintings are in the Venezuela section in the "World Boys and Girls Art Exhibition." We also made donations to the Child Foundation, led by the wife of the Venezuelan president, Mrs. Marisabel de Chavez, and Carabobo University.

I now have a stronger understanding of the heart of this humanistic organization and why I belong to it. My personal experience during this disaster, and being a part of the broader relief efforts of the SGI, has opened my eyes to the great compassionate core that exists within people. Through this I feel a strong determination to help strengthen and renew this spirit within each person I meet.

Many things have changed in my life and in my surroundings, but the support and optimism of my fellow members in SGI-Venezuela has helped me broaden my vision and enabled me to continue with hope and joy.

Part V:

Belief Beyond Boundaries

The readings in this final section take as their focus those fast-growing and increasingly popular forms of spirituality which used to be considered as marginal to the mainstream of British and North American religious expression. These new categories, which traditionally were termed as 'New Age', or New Religious Movements, include 'revived religion', 'nature religion', post-modern religion, and 'esoteric spirituality'. All of them share a concern, implicit or explicit, with the importance of authenticity, the natural world, and of ritual.

Reading 5.1 introduces the history of pagan theologies and 5.2 and 5.3 discuss the relationship between neoPaganism and the 'New Age'. The following set of readings (5.5–5.9) engage with the phenomena of the revival of Celtic spirituality, both Christian and non-Christian. Reading 5.9 also links to the following set of readings (5.9–5.15), which centre around the conflict between increasing AmerEuropean interests in North American Indian religions, and traditionalists' reluctance to admit the authenticity of what have been called the 'plastic medicine men'.

The next section of the Reader engages with the practice and popular representation of paganism and witchcraft today, employing both scholarly and popular sources, and includes texts intended for children as well as for adults (5.16–5.23). The final group of readings discuss the relationship between religion science, and the relationship between the new tendencies in religion today and the ideas of Carl Jung (5.24–5.28).

5.1 'PAGAN THEOLOGIES'

Prudence Jones

From *Paganism Today*, Hardman, C. and Harvey, G. (eds), London, Thorsons, 1995, pp. 32–4.

I am using the plural here deliberately. A polytheistic religion gives many different accounts of the divine beings, and these accounts, or theologies, reflect the divine patronage of their inventors. People sometimes raise their eyebrows when they hear of *Pagan* theology, but in fact the word 'theology' dates from Pagan times and was first used concerning Pagan deities. In the *Republic* (II,375), Plato discussed the limits to be placed on poets in writing their mythologies or theologies. They must only tell the truth about the deities and must not be allowed to mislead their hearers as, Plato claimed, the ancients had done. Herodotus too (2,53) tells us that it was Homer and Hesiod who described and classified the gods. 'Theology' here, then, is a descriptive account of the divinities, often a poem or song, rather than as we now think of it, an analysis or an explication of the divinely ordered universe and of the place of human beings within it.

Here is some theology in Plato's sense from his own time, an ode by the poet Pindar, written to commemorate the Nemean Games of 463 BCE. Commentators used to say that for the Greeks the divine world was utterly separate from the human world, and that human beings had no part in the former. The Mystery schools of late antiquity belie that sentiment entirely, of course. But even as early as Pindar, the intimate kinship of deities and humans is affirmed, a thought which persisted through the Mystery religions of the ancient world and is not unfamiliar to modern Pagans:

> Single is the race of men and of gods, from one mother (Gaia) do we both draw breath; yet a difference in power divides us, for the one is as nothing, yet for the other the brazen vault of the sky endures as a dwelling for ever.
>
> But we partly resemble the immortals, either in greatness of mind or in our nature, although we do not know, either by day or in the night, what course it is written that we should run.

ANCIENT PAGAN THEOLOGIES

Theology soon moved out of poetry into sober prose. The philosophers took theology as part of natural philosophy, an account of the nature of the universe which included its divine inhabitants. Most people seem to have taken it for granted that gods and goddesses existed, since among other things people had seen them, in dreams and in the visions which were called 'epiphanies'. The Epicureans, following Democritus, understood the universe to be made up of atoms (a doctrine resurrected, like much other Pagan philosophy, in the eighteenth century, by Leibniz in his *Monadology* (2,3)). These were thought to be randomly moved by the force of gravity through a universe of empty space. Deities, like human beings, were seen as fortuitous collections of atoms, living unlike the latter in bliss in the *intermundia*, the spaces between the worlds. They took no part in the affairs of mortals, but could be of use to the latter as objects of contemplation, paradigms of the inner bliss that the wise person might attain. The pursuit of wisdom was the wise pursuit of pleasure, and in this the gods served as a model.

The second great school of the ancient world, that of the Stoics, on the other hand, saw the divine power as one and as immanent in the manifest world. Ultimately, the whole universe, both visible and invisible, was itself divine. Apparent matter and apparent spirit were simply opposite poles of a continuum. Various divinities manifested themselves according to the needs of the time, but they were all manifestations of the universal One. The universe, for the Stoics, was fated and ruled by the laws of Nature, the manifestation of divine Mind. These laws, *logoi* for the Greeks, *rationes* for the Romans, expressed the nature of things and were the same as what people ordinarily call fate. The aim of the good person was to live in accord with Nature. The whole universe was seen as good, bad or unfortunate events only seemed to be so by an error of perception. Similarly, any being which followed the laws of its own nature could do no harm, whatever appearances might suggest. In modern times, the Stoic ontology of a deterministic Nature which has no super-natural beings outside itself has appeared again in the materialistic universe of Newtonian science. But modern scientists have no deities, whereas for the Stoics, as later for Spinoza, another seminal thinker of the Enlightenment, Nature *was* divinity. Stoicism became immensely popular among educated Romans in the first two centuries CE, but it faded before the otherworldly appeal of later Platonism.

Such philosophies of the ancient world contained the theologies of Pagan thought. Their influence on embryonic Christian theology was immense, affecting this at least as much as the Jewish method of rabbinical analysis on which it also drew. It was from these Pagan theologies, as much as from the Jewish method of textual analysis, that Christian theology took its form. The word 'dogma' referred originally to a conclusion of Pagan philosophy.

'PAGAN' DEFINED

Let me state what I mean by 'Pagan'. A Pagan religion has three characteristics. It is polytheistic, recognizing a plurality of divine beings, which may or may not be reducible to an underlying One – or Two, or Three, etc. It sees the material world and its laws (again reaffirmed for the modern age by Spinoza as *natura naturata* and *natural naturans*) as a theophany, a manifestation of divinity. Although the Platonic school, like some schools of modern Hinduism, believed in a definite mind-body dualism, there is no indication that they saw the material world as in itself harmful or 'evil' until the Christian influence of late antiquity, around the time of Iamblichus (*d.* 330). Finally, Pagan religions recognize the female face of divinity, called by modern Pagans the Goddess; taken for granted in Her many manifestations by the Pagans of the ancient world. A religion that does not accept that divinity may manifest in female form is not, on this definition, Pagan.

5.2 'NEOPAGANISM'[1]

Wouter J. Hannagraaff

From *New Age Religion and Western Culture*, Hannagraaff, W.J., New York, SUNY, 1998, pp. 79–81.

THE PHENOMENON OF NEOPAGANISM

As a general term, "neopaganism" covers all those modern movements which are firstly, based on the conviction that what Christianity has traditionally denounced as idolatry and superstition actually represents/represented a profound and meaningful religious worldview and, secondly, that a religious practice based on this worldview can and should be revitalized in our modern world. The very use of the term "neopaganism" as a self-designation clearly contains a polemical thrust towards institutionalized Christianity,[2] which is held responsible for the decline of western paganism and the subsequent blackening of its image. The problems of the modern world, particularly the ecological crisis, are regarded as a direct result of the loss of pagan wisdom about man's relationship to the natural world, and a recovery of this wisdom is regarded not only as desirable but as urgently needed. The focus on ecological problems is particularly prominent in contemporary neopaganism, but it should be noted that – given the above definition – the phenomenon of neopaganism as such is not in fact synonymous with its postwar "New Age" manifestation. Commentators of the contemporary neopagan movement(s) usually seem unaware of the fact that the term neopaganism is also used in quite different contexts, particularly in connection with certain religious and philosophical developments in prewar Germany.[3] The general definition of neopaganism given above encompasses both these often politically suspect movements and tendencies, and the contemporary "New Age" phenomenon. Of course it does not follow that the latter is

---

1. General sources and special studies relating to neopaganism in general: Adler, *Drawing down the Moon*; Anon., 'Witchcraft (Wicca), Neopaganism and Magick', Ruppert, *Die Hexen kommen* (also printed as 'Magic und Hexenglaube heute'; Luhrmann, *Persuasions*; nd., 'Persuasive Ritual', 'Witchcraft, Morality and Magic'; Eilberg-Schwartz, 'Witches of the West'; Kelly, 'Neopagans and the New Age'; Burnett, *Dawning of the Pagan Moon*; Hough, *Witchcraft*; York, *Emerging Network*, spec. 99–144; Weissmann, 'Erwachen'; Kelly, 'Update'.
2. Christianity as such is not necessarily rejected. Surprisingly many neopagans, including well-known figures as Caithlin Matthews or Maxine Sanders, consider themselves both pagan and Christian. They believe that the true esoteric core of Christianity is perfectly compatible with the pagan worldview and that it is therefore not Christianity as such which is to be rejected, but only a particular interpretation which happens to have become dominant in church institutions. These Christian pagans find inspiration in Catholic ritual or in the remnants of Celtic Christianity, and generally regard Christian gnosticism in a positive light.
3. Cancik, 'Neuheiden und totaler Staat'; Feber, 'Einleitung'; Spindler, 'Europe's Neo-paganism'. Cf. especially Von Schnurbein, *Religion als Kulturkritik.*

therefore fascistic, although that opinion has sometimes been voiced.[4] It does imply that, in a strict sense, the term "neopaganism" is not sufficient in itself as a designation for the movements studied here. "New Age" neopaganism should be distinguished from other (earlier or contemporary) attempts to revitalize the worldview of pre-christian European cultures. When in the rest of the discussion I refer to "neopaganism". I will be referring to the New Age variety only.

However, speaking of a "New Age variety" of neopaganism – and indeed, discussing neopaganism as part of the New Age movement – is to invite criticism. Aidan A. Kelly, for instance, states that 'The Neopagan movement . . . parallels the New Age movement in some ways, differs sharply from it in others. and overlaps it in some minor ways'.[5] Obviously, such a categorical statement is possible only if both movements are already clearly defined and demarcated. It is a basic assumption of the present study, however, that at least the New Age movement is not. Kelly's comparison between the "New Age" and the "neopagan" perspective indeed turns out to be based on a rather selective view of the former, which occasionally exerts gentle pressure on the evidence.[6] It is difficult to escape the impression that his attempt to separate neopaganism from the New Age as much as possible is inspired by apologetic considerations – Kelly is not only a well-known researcher, but also a neopagan – rather than by empirical ones. Tanya Luhrmann, in her ground-breaking study of magical groups in London, appears not to have encountered anything like Kelly's distinction: 'In whatever form magicians practice magic, they situate it within what is proclaimed the "New Age"'.[7] Luhrmann's characterization of the New Age, it should be added, is basically the same one as I have outlined in my Introduction.[8] My own research confirms Luhrmann's conclusion that neopaganism is part of the New Age in this general sense at least. Having stated this, however, it must also be said that neopaganism definitely has its own distinctive flavour which sets it apart from other New Age trends. Kelly's position is therefore not totally unfounded, but is

---

4. There is some justification for associating contemporary neopaganism with fascism in the case of so-called "Norse paganism", which uses Norse/Germanic mythology as a source of inspiration. Predictably – considering that neopagans are naturally interested in the mythological heritage of their own country – this variety is especially prominent in Germany. but it also exists elsewhere. Adler notes (*Drawing Down the Moon*, 273) that some groups use Norse paganism as a front for right-wing or outright Nazi activities, but blanket generalizations on the basis of such cases should be warned against. Each specific group should be judged on its own merits (or the lack thereof). Cf. Adler, *Drawing Down the Moon*, 273–82, and Weissmann, 'Erwachen'. In any case, Norse paganism is of only marginal significance for the present study.

5. Identical quotation in Kelly, 'Neopagans and the New Age', 311, and 'Update', 136.

6. For instance, it is true that neopagans 'reject the dualism of Eastern traditions' ('Neopagans and the New Age', 314), but so do many New Age believers. In general, Kelly ascribes a far stronger respect for traditional Eastern notions (such as the role of the guru) to the New Age than the evidence permits. Furthermore, when he says that '*Many* New Agers assume . . . that . . .' ('Neopagans and the New Age', 314. My emphasis) he implicitly admits that not all of them do, but he nevertheless contrasts these assumptions to neopaganism, suggesting a far greater consensus among New Agers than in fact exists. A comparably artificial consensus is suggested by the statement that neopagans are 'not particularly interested in a New Age in the future' ('Neopagans and the New Age', 314). Directly disconfirming evidence can easily be found in most of the standard neopagan literature. Finally, Kelly's statement that 'New Age bookstores rarely have sections labeled magic or witchcraft' ('Neopagans and the New Age, 313) is disconfirmed by my own observations in the Netherlands, Germany and England.

7. Luhrmann, *Persuasions*, 30.

8. Luhrmann describes New Age as 'a broad cultural ideology, a development of the counter-cultural sixties, which privileges holistic medicine, 'intuitive sciences' like astrology and tarot, ecological and anti-nuclear political issues, and alternative therapies, medicines and philosophers. The 'New Age' has become a widely accepted catch-phrase for this matrix of concerns . . .' (*Persuasions*, 30).

best regarded as an overstatement resulting from the exaggeration of real differences at the expense of similarities. The complicated relationship between New Age in general and neopaganism has been adequately summarized by Michael York.[9] York expresses no final opinion for or against the inclusion of neopaganism in the New Age, but his discussion illustrates the importance of both the similarities and the differences. The picture presented by York is confirmed by my own research. . . . The neopagan movement should be treated as part of the New Age movement, but it should nonetheless be seen as a special, relatively clearly circumscribed subculture within that movement.

If our subject is a special case of both neopaganism in general and of the New Age movement, then it may be asked what exactly constitutes its uniqueness.

Very briefly (and predictably) it can be said that the special character of contemporary neopaganism in relation to neopaganism in general is precisely its use of New Age concepts, while its special position within the New Age movement derives from the fact that the specifically neopagan perspective – as defined in the first section of this chapter – is not particularly prominent in the rest of the New Age. In other words, it is precisely the overlap between the two movements/perspectives which constitutes the uniqueness of "New Age" neopaganism.

---

9. York, *Emerging Network*, chapter 4, 'New Age and Neo-paganism: Similarities, Contrasts and Relationships'.

5.3 'RITUAL IS MY CHOSEN ART FORM'

Sabine Magliocco

From *Magical Religion and Modern Witchcraft*, Lewis, J.R. (ed.), New York, SUNY, 1996, pp. 100–103.

THE AESTHETICS OF RITUAL

Like all folk art forms, Neo-Pagan ritual has a well-defined set of aesthetics that operates within the community. Different ritual artists also have their own recognizable styles. Because Neo-Pagans are such a diverse group, not all agree on every aspect of ritual aesthetics. Some feel that rituals should be varied and spontaneous: "I like to keep things different," said Toraine, a witch in his twenties; "I don't like to do the same ritual week after week. If I wanted that, I'd be Christian." Others prefer a more ceremonial style: "I think it's wonderful that people can just rattle off the Lord's Prayer without even bothering to think about it," said Steven. "I aspire to a time when Pagans can do things without having to be so conscious about them." While some prefer a more traditional, regimented ritual style, such as that of Gardnerian Wicca, others revel in a lighthearted, humorous, playful style manifest in freeform, tongue-in-cheek rituals in honor of chocolate or the comic strip character Bill the Cat.

"Ritual should be a transformative experience," said Lhianna. Like many others, she emphasized the educational value of rituals: "If we don't know more on an internal level after we've left the circle, as well as on the cerebral level, then something has not happened." Yet rituals are more than just educational tools; ideally, they need to affect participants on an emotional level as well. Almost all my respondents felt that ritual should express sincere emotions, that it should come from the heart and not be a meaningless rote performance. "I want to learn something, I want to be moved, I want to feel renewed, I want to feel like I've had some sort of participation in something bigger than myself," one man explained. As Steven was speaking to me about the sense of timelessness and transcendence that the ritual along the banks of the Mississippi had induced in him, I became so moved the hair on my forearms stood on end, and I called his attention to it. "That's it!" he exclaimed, "That's how you know a ritual's good."

Not all Neo-Pagan rituals are equally successful for all their participants in this respect. Some rituals are highly successful for certain individuals, but leave others cold; others just don't "work." Negative examples cited included rituals that go on too long and lose the participants' attention; scripted presentations with little spontaneity and few participatory elements; rituals with invocations that take place entirely in a foreign language such as Old Welsh or Gaelic, and thus are incomprehensible to the majority of the participants; and rituals where little planning has taken place and nobody is sure what is going on. These examples emphasize important Neo-Pagan values: a strong participatory ethic, resistance to certain forms of hierarchical esoterism, and an emphasis on spontaneity, variation, and creativity. "In Wiccan ritual, free will is a really important thing," explained Toraine. "I think that's the art form: being able to include that spontaneity and sincerity in worship in a piece…that isn't totally chaotic."

Good ritual does not just happen. It takes organization and artistry, as Toraine suggests, to achieve just the right mix of spontaneity and planning that allows for good ritual to happen. In many ways, ritual is a collaborative performance between the director or facilitator and all of the participants. Lhianna, who often facilitates large rituals, explained: "I like to make sure that not a lot is left to chance, although I don't want to inhibit creativity on the part of the participants, either…. Flexibility is essential…. I want the people in the group to find the deep places within themselves and feel the freedom of expression."

THE STRUCTURAL FRAMEWORK

The highly participatory nature of rituals is possible largely because most Neo-Pagans have internalized a similar ritual grammar or structure, and this structure underlies nearly all rituals. Participants feel free to improvise on this common framework and insert new elements at appropriate times.

This structural framework was probably first outlined by Gerald Gardner in *Witchcraft Today* (1954), and numerous Wiccan publications have printed variations of it (Blacksun 1982; Starhawk 1982; Valiente 1973). But contemporary Neo-Pagan ritual structure probably owes as much to the social movements of the 1960s as it does to Gardner. Books such as Alicia Bay Laurel's *Living on the Earth* (1971) and (with Ramon Sender) *Being of the Sun* (1973) combined ritual techniques with concepts from popular psychology to design "happenings" emphasizing ecological goals; feminist groups, dismayed with what they perceived as the patriarchal nature of Western religions, began to experiment with goddess-oriented worship through ritual (Starhawk 1982). The basic structural framework has by now passed into the folklore matrix of the Neo-Pagan subculture, so that few contemporary Pagans have learned it directly from any publication, but have picked it up informally through contact with other Neo-Pagans and by participating in community rituals.

The core structure is none other than Van Gennep's classic tripartite model of ritual (1909; elaborated by Turner 1968) as separation from daily life (liminality) followed by testing and reintegration into society. While the separation and reintegration phases are self-evident, in the Neo-Pagan case the testing takes the form of the main ritual work itself. Ritual is hard work that requires each participant's undivided attention and tests the strength of the circle; many told me that rituals sometimes do not work if one or more members is unwell, out of sorts, or otherwise unable to dedicate full energy to the task.

Skilled ritualists recognize this tripartite structure and often articulate it as "beginning, middle, and end." Selena, for example, divides the ritual into three parts: preparation and orientation, the work or focus of the ritual, and closure and assimilation. Understanding the core tripartite structure of ritual allows for the development of greater variations, sometimes bypassing certain formal elements of the model altogether.

The following basic outline is accepted by many Neo-Pagans. Ritual begins with the drawing of the circle, sometimes physically, as with chalk or a stick, other times by the presence of the participants standing in a circle. The circle becomes sacred, liminal space

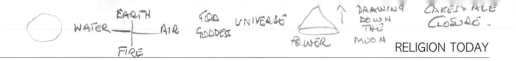

(Turner 1968), marked off from the everyday world. The drawing of the circle serves to separate actions that follow from ordinary time and space.

An invocation of the four elements through the four cardinal directions earth (north), air (east), fire (south), and water (west) – usually follows the opening. Each element/direction corresponds, in Neo-Pagan teleology, to a set of properties or qualities associated with it through the principles of sympathetic magic. Thus earth suggests growing things, material concerns, wordly matters; air, the intellect and thought; fire, passion, the life force, commitment and engagement; and water, emotions, intuition, and the unconscious. These are only basic associations; specifics vary from one individual to another within the ritual context. An invocation of the God and Goddess may follow the salute to the four directions; some ritual artists use additional elements, such as the universe, the planet, spirit or shadow. Through the invocation of elements and sometimes a circular dance or the joining of hands, Neo-Pagans say they "raise the cone of power" – consolidate the combined energies of the participants to focus on the purpose of the ritual. They conceptualize the cone as rising upwards from the participants' bodies.

What follows in the main body of the ritual is the part most likely to vary widely, according to the ritual's purpose, the holy day being observed, the mood of the participants, and countless other variables. Being the least formulaic, this is the part of ritual that necessitates the most planning and is the focus of everyone's attention during ritual planning sessions. Gardnerian-derived practices feature "drawing down the moon," the embodiment of the Goddess in the high priestess, as well as a symbolic Great Rite, the union of the male and female principles in nature symbolized by the priestess plunging the athame, or ritual dagger, into the ritual chalice. Other traditions may include practices such as meditation, focusing and sending group energy towards a particular purpose, or the giving of thanks.

After the main actions of the ritual are accomplished and the energy raised at the beginning has been used or focused on a task, Neo-Pagans say the energy must be "grounded" so the participants can return to the real world. Rituals that end abruptly without closure are thought to be potentially dangerous, since participants have not had a chance to assimilate the ritual experience. Closure is sometimes accomplished through a ceremony known as "Cakes and Ale" in which the group shares food and drink. The ritual may end with one or more formulas which figuratively open the circle and return the group to non-ritual time. One example is:

> The circle is open, but never broken;
> Merry meet, merry part, and merry meet again.

While this tripartite model serves as the basis for most rituals, individuals and covens feel free to modify it according to their needs and wishes. Some cleave tightly to the formal aspects, while others relish in developing new variants.

5.4 'NEW AGE OR PAGAN'

Graham Harvey

From 'Paganism and other religions', in *Listening People, Speaking Earth: Contemporary Paganism*, Harvey, G., London, Hurst, 1997, pp. 219–21.

If Satanism is confused with Paganism because of assertions of their "dark" interests, New Age is distinguishable from Paganism by its obsession with "light". There are similarities between Paganism and New Age – but no more than there are (different ones) between Christianity and New Age.

Margot Adler says:

> There is a funny saying in the Pagan movement: "the difference between Pagan and 'new age' is one decimal point". In other words, a two-day workshop in meditation by a "new age" practitioner might cost $300, while the same course given by a Pagan might cost $30.[1]

Pagans claim that this "one decimal point" is emblematic of the New Age as a predominantly white middle-class phenomenon in which health and wealth are prime indicators of spirituality. New Age celebrates modernity but tries to imbue it with a suitable spirituality.[2] Pagans frequently associate New Age with a "fluffy bunnies" vision of the world: their cosmos is a generous, self-sacrificing and loving place, "all sweetness and light, the lions don't bite and the thorns don't scratch".[3] Being poor or unwell is a result of spiritual wrong or failure to think positively. Humanity is being "allowed" to pollute the world and destroy species as part of a learning process – and the animals and plants are giving up their lives for this great and cosmic good. Cosmic, global and human evolution depend on humanity thinking positively, embracing the "light" and abandoning the darkness, looking to spirit rather than earthiness. While many New Agers celebrate the seasonal festivals which Pagans identify as their own, they combine this with a redemptive and millennial metaphor or agenda that is alien to Paganism. The Earth may be described by New Agers as Mother, but this enshrines the old dualisms of male as active, rational and higher as against the female as passive, receptive and lower. Channelling of alleged wisdom from exalted masters, angels, devas and others is typical of New Age and causes considerable cynicism among Pagans, who feel that if New Agers faced their darkness honestly, they could admit that the "airy-fairy, wishy-washy" messages about being nicer people with more positive thoughts come from their own egos. Spirituality is far more important in New Age than the ultimately illusory material world or existence. Ability to meet the exorbitant and prohibitive cost of New Age events enables its beneficiaries the degree of leisure necessary to indulge in continual self-absorption.

---

1. Adler (1986): 420.
2. Heelas (1996).
3. Quoted by York (1995): 160.

Whether or not these Pagan views of New Age are entirely accurate, they indicate a rejection of the placing of Paganism under the New Age umbrella. The two broad movements appear similar because they celebrate similar festivals, name some similar other-than-human beings (e.g. elves and faeries), use visualization and meditation, eclectically draw on South Asian, Native American and Shamanic ideas and technology (e.g. charkas and sweat lodges) and read widely in astrology, geomancy, anthropology and Celtic mythology. But the exact mix of these elements produces atmospheres and actions which are distinguishable. The devas of Findhorn (a New Age community in Scotland) are much "nicer" and more "cosmic" than the localized, trickster faeries of many Pagans' experience. Paganism rejects the Gnostic denigration of matter and darkness prevalent in New Age, and celebrates the world as real and as given. It does not equate healing with either positive thinking or problem-solving. Certainly its magic asserts that the world can be changed and that what is done affects everything else, but it rejects the "blame the victim' syndrome as well as a rationalized neglect of social-justice issues"[4] that it identifies as endemic in New Age.

As Michael York says:

> Among the further contrasts between the two, we find a theatrical and ritualistic side to Neo-Paganism which is largely absent in New Age. Neopaganism also embraces the idea or practice of ritual/symbolic or sacred sex. Within New Age, we find little if any use of the sexual metaphor.[5]

Sexuality has little place in New Age for at least two reasons: it would, first, require a more Pagan celebration of embodiedness and, secondly, diminish New Age's respectable image. Even though Druidry and Ásatrú court mainstream attention more than the Craft, which makes much of its antithetical status,[6] they share a concern to challenge the status quo of late capitalism in ways completely alien to New Age. Alongside theatricality and sexuality, York might have noted the humour of many Pagan gatherings, in contrast to the seriousness of New Age events.

New Age perhaps constitutes the Gnostic temptation of postmodern spirituality. Its influence on Paganism certainly tends in this direction. Paganism might just constitute

> the this-worldly grounding of New Age – one which counterbalances the tendency otherwise to drift off into the airy-fairy realms of "pure" and transcendent spirit.[7]

To the extent that this is true, it suggests only that two different traditions run parallel for part of their journey. New Age disseminates the perennial wisdom of theosophy in which nature's meaning is to be found in spiritual realities and there is only a passing concern for life's social and political realities.[8] Paganism engages with nature sensually and derives from a critique of modernity answering the needs of post-modernity. All branches of Paganism have

---

4. York (1995): 162. Also see Sjöö (1992).
5. York (1996): 164.
6. See Oakley (1996).
7. York (1996): 164.
8. See Sellon and Weber (1992).

been influenced by feminism while New Age offers women typically patriarchal subordination to male leaders or voices. The centre of attention for Paganism is Nature. While Pagan festivals can be escapist, they encourage deeper engagement with "green" concerns and even with direct action against what assaults the Earth. Paganism's aim – if such a thing can be distilled without doing violence to the multiplicity of Pagan experience and experimentation – is to find more life-affirming ways for human people to live with their other-than-human neighbours. The centre of New Age attention is humanity, some would say Man. Its programme is to facilitate a leap forward in human evolution engineered through self-spirituality.

5.5 'THE STATIONS OF THE SUN'

Ronald Hutton

From *The Stations of the Sun: A History of the Ritual Year in Britain*, Hutton, R., Oxford University Press, 1996, pp. 408–11.

I

. . . The history of the ancient British and Irish year . . . has never been made the subject of a sustained study by any expert in early Irish or Welsh literature, and what has been written upon it has consisted of a paragraph or two provided almost by default, usually in the works of scholars who were not primarily expert in literary sources at all. Nevertheless, this has sufficed to build up a powerful impression of an 'ancient Celtic year', probably uniform from Ireland to Gaul, consisting of the four quarter-days of Samhain, Imbole, Beltane, and Lughnasadh (in various spellings), and commencing on the first of those festivals. The importance of the quarter-days in medieval Irish literature was noticed in the first systematic treatment of those texts, such as the works of Charles Vallancey in the eighteenth century. By the second half of the nineteenth, it had become assumed by English folklorists that they were observed in ancient Britain as well. One of these writers, Charles Hardwick, either borrowed, or made himself, a misreading of the description of the fire rite of Beltane in *Sanas Chormaic* which caused him to believe that it was carried out upon all four feasts.[1] From this error sprang the characterization of them as 'the festivals', which was never taken into academe but has persisted in popular works until the present day.

Most of the academic books upon the Celts produced for a general readership in the 1950s and 1960s made no reference to the subject.[2] Two important publications in 1967 did turn to it, but only briefly and cautiously. One was Anne Ross's splendid pioneering work on pagan Celtic Britain, which only suggested that Beltane and Samhain might have been generally observed in the Celtic world.[3] The other was a joint survey of Celtic civilization by Nora Chadwick and Myles Dillon, which just stated that Celts (in general) observed the four festivals.[4] Then came 1970, with a boom in works for a popular market upon all things Celtic, and two of those authors contributed to it with books which were decidedly less restrained upon the subject. Nora Chadwick declared that the four festivals (and no others) were celebrated by the whole Celtic world, that Samhain was the New Year, and that most were concerned with fertility.[5] Anne Ross said much the same, save that she suggested that each was connected to a particular deity. She did, however, also state that it was only 'probable' that the

1. Charles Hardwick, *Traditions, Superstitions, and Folk-Lore* (Manchester, 1872), 30–40.
2. e.g. T.G.E. Powell, *The Celts* (1958); Nora K. Chadwick, *Celtic Britain* (1963); Stuart Piggott, *The Druids* (1968).
3. *Pagan Celtic Britain* (1967), 57.
4. *The Celtic Realms* (1967), 108.
5. *The Celts* (1970), 180–81.

Celts in general had these feasts, that they might have been distinctively Irish, and that the Irish themselves seemed to have others as well.[6]

During the next twenty-five years, the subject was once again ignored by some of the standard textbooks upon ancient Celtic culture.[7] On the other hand, those by Anne Ross and Nora Chadwick were reprinted, in the latter case twenty years after the author's death. In 1979 Lloyd Laing produced one which repeated the usual information about the four festivals, though he added rather confusingly that while Imbole and Lughnasadh may not have been celebrated in Iron Age Britain 'they certainly had their equivalents'.[8] Another apparent muddle of ideas appeared in 1986, in the first of a series of very successful books by Miranda Green. On one page she told readers that Beltane and Samhain, being suited to a pastoral society, may never have been celebrated in lowland Britain and Gaul. On another, however, the usual four feasts were casually described as 'the great Celtic festivals'.[9] In the same year Graham Webster supplied by far the most detailed consideration of the subject in any textbook of the past forty years, amounting to almost four pages. It was also unusual in that it provided footnotes to support its information. It started from the presupposition that the Celts in general only celebrated the four festivals, with the New Year at Samhain, and went on to suggest what the characteristics of those feasts might have been. None of his references was to original sources, save to well known Irish tales in popular translations; most were to Anne Ross, Maire MacNeill, and Sir James Frazer. Frazer's ghost, in fact, hangs over the whole description.[10] This is hardly surprising. Nora Chadwick never carried out any research into the matter, and Anne Ross, Lloyd Laing, Miranda Green, and Graham Webster could not, for all are not historians but archaeologists (and very distinguished archaeologists at that). They are experts in material remains, not literature, and as their works give only a tiny amount of space to consideration of this question it would be unfair to cite them at all were it not for the fact that they have provided the staple texts upon the matter which colleagues, and everybody else, read. In other words, nobody has carried out any general survey of it since Sir John Rhŷs and Sir James Frazer, about a hundred years ago. John Carey is at present working upon the Irish observation of Samhain, and producing valuable results,[11] but that is a consideration of one festival in one country.

There is, in fact, only one material remain from the pagan Celtic world (as conventionally defined) which bears upon the matter, and that is the famous bronze calendar from Roman Gaul, found at Coligny in what is now south-eastern France. It is totally unlike the Irish system, being a very complex sequence of sixty-four divisions with no equivalent

6. *Everyday Life of the Pagan Celts* (1970), 151–54.

7. E.g. Charles Thomas, *Celtic Britain* (1980); and Lloyd and Jennifer Laing, *Celtic Britain and Ireland, AD 200–800* (Dublin, 1990).

8. *Celtic Britain* (1979), 40–41.

9. *The Gods of the Celts* (1986), 15 and 14.

10. *The British Celts and their Gods under Rome* (1986), 31–35. Perhaps I should also include here the paragraph in Hilda Ellis Davidson, *Myths and Symbols in Pagan Europe* (Manchester, 1988), 38–39, the hesitation being that to ignore it might seem a discourtesy but to discuss it could equally seem an unnecessary finding of fault in another fine book by an eminent scholar expert in, and interested in, other matters. She talks briefly of the usual four festivals in the usual way, her principal citations being not to medieval sources but to the folklorists Máire MacNeill and Kevin Danaher, behind whom stand (again) Rhŷs and Frazer.

11. Outlined in a paper at the Institute of Historical Research, and also in a recent volume of *Eriu* which I was not able to obtain at the time of writing.

names. Nor, as it is now in fragments, does it indicate when the year begins. None of the prehistoric monuments of the British Isles can be said with perfect confidence to be aligned upon movements of the sun at any of the quarter-days. On the other hand, most of the greatest, from the fourth, third, and second millennia BCE, are aligned with remarkable precision upon the midwinter or midsummer solstice. The Coligny calendar suggests that we give up either the traditional notion of a uniform Celtic system of reckoning the year, or the traditional notion of the extent of a Celtic cultural province. The monuments suggest that we either accept that the Iron Age British and Irish celebrated the solstices as well, or else (which is perfectly arguable) that the ritual year in these islands altered fundamentally between the second and the first millennia BCE. What can be suggested is that there is nothing in the material remains to support the fourfold division accepted by the archaeologists. The early Irish literature, on the other hand, certainly does testify abundantly to the importance of the quarter-days, but the Welsh equivalent only mentions one of them (May Eve), and consistently places its favourite feast in midwinter. Even the Irish literary sources, moreover, include references to Christmas, and every time a medieval Irish document marks the opening of a calendar year, it does so either from then or from 1 January or 25 March. The medieval Welsh ebulliently celebrated their New Year at a time identified with the Roman Kalendae, upon 1 January. This apparent practice, of marking the opening of a year at the winter solstice, simply puts these Celtic peoples at one with the rest of ancient northern and western Europe. Even the Irish seem therefore to have operated a dual system, of reckoning time both from midwinter and from the opening of seasons. This is not so different from the medieval English practice, whereby the year was commenced in January or March, and yet rents and other dues were paid quarterly at either the cardinal solar points of Christmas, Lady Day, Midsummer Day, and Michaelmas, or else as the seasons open at Candlemas, May Day, Lammas, and All Saints' Day.

There is, therefore, absolutely no firm evidence in the written record that the year opened on 1 November in either early Ireland or early Wales, and a great deal in the Welsh material to refute the idea.[12] Nor can it confidently be concluded that even the Irish only celebrated the four quarter-days. The whole argument for a 'Celtic New Year' was originally based upon conclusions drawn from relatively recent folklore, and it has been suggested that these were flawed. What the folklorists' collections portray is a general Irish celebration of the quarter-days, midwinter, and midsummer. Midsummer bonfires, with much the same rituals, are recorded all over England, Wales, Ireland, Lowland Scotland, and the Northern Isles, with complete irrelevance to boundaries between Celtic areas and others; but they are apparently not mentioned in the Gaelic speaking parts of Scotland. Since records begin, the New Year (on 1 January) was marked by rituals and merry-making of equal intensity in the Gaelic world of the Hebrides and the Anglicized one of the Lothians. The Irish feast of Imbolc, rededicated to St Brigid, was kept with the same rite all over Ireland, and also in Man and the Hebrides; but not anywhere on the British mainland. There its role was taken by the universal Christian holy day of Candlemas. It embodied a parallel tradition of honouring a divine woman, often through women, and lasted longest in the Celtic land of Wales; but the two traditions may

---

12. Before writing this, I telephoned five colleagues in British universities celebrated for their knowledge of early Irish or Welsh literature, to check this point with them. I would never have dared to assert it so roundly if they had not all endorsed it.

have converged, and medieval Catholic rituals in general survived in Welsh popular culture. The Irish way of celebrating Lughnasadh, by contrast was found in Man but not anywhere in Scotland, including the Hebrides. Elsewhere in Britain it has only one, isolated, parallel, in South Wales. The same feast was, however, celebrated in different ways and under different names all over Celtic, Saxon, or Norse Britain. The ritual of Beltane was found in all the Celtic areas of the British Isles, but also in pastoral regions of Germanic and Scandinavian Europe. A feast with ritual practices at the other end of the herding season was equally well known in both ancient Ireland and ancient Scandinavia, and represented by folk practices in the uplands of Wales and Scotland. There was, however, no common rite as there had been at Beltane. The people of north and central Wales, Man, and the southern and eastern Highlands used fire again, but apparently not those of Ireland and the Hebrides.

Perhaps it may seem unreasonable to expect that prehistoric tribal peoples would employ identical seasonal ceremonies across the whole of the British Isles, let alone the whole of north-west Europe. This is, none the less, the assumption which underpinned traditional scholarly approaches to the subject, from Sir James Frazer to Maire MacNeill and, in the case of the purification by fire or rowan at the opening of the summer pastures, it is actually justified. That does, however, seem to be a unique case. What the folklore record portrays as a rule are strongly marked regional traditions of festivity which bear no strict relationship to nineteenth and twentieth-century notions of Celtic and Germanic cultural provinces. It may therefore be suggested as a proposal worthy of testing, that the notion of a distinctive 'Celtic' ritual year, with four festivals at the quarter-days and an opening at Samhain, is a scholastic construction of the eighteenth and nineteenth centuries which should now be considerably revised or even abandoned altogether.[13]

---

13. I am aware that these suggestions may come to take their place in a diffuse, fitful, and yet still immensely important debate which has been developing since the mid-1980s, over the existence and identity of a Celtic cultural province. At times it has been concentrated briefly and fiercely, such as in a discussion group at the British Museum in November 1992, but these moments have so far been little reflected in print. The only observation which I would make upon the wider issue at this stage is how much the belief in such a province is sustained by linguists rather than by historians or archaeologists. A striking example of this is D.E. Evans, 'Celts and Germans', *Bulletin of the Board of Celtic Studies*, 29 (1982), 230–55, and esp. 239, 253, 255. He asserts that 'there was a fundamental difference; there was antagonism' between Celtic-speaking and Teutonic-speaking peoples in ancient Europe, and that 'Celts and Germans' were in turn expanding, marauding, and conquering peoples, markedly different from each other and for ever, it seems, consciously or unconsciously rejecting each other because of a deep-seated and pernicious incompatibility'. The only evidence offered for these dramatic statements is taken neither from history, nor archaeology, nor literature, but consists of the relative absence of transference from Celtic to Germanic of loan-words for legal, administrative, or political matters! The obvious rejoinder, that cultures frequently use loan-words for objects or concepts unfamiliar or alien to them, not those for which they have domestic parallels, is nowhere confronted. At the same time he notes that 'there may have been a shared Celto-Germanic heritage in material culture, in cult and mythology, in social structure, in language', just to dismiss all this as irrelevant. I would not bother to pick on an essay written some years ago, were it not so characteristic of the genre and by such a distinguished philologist, and were it not still cited as an important prop of the argument that Celts and Germans represented two distinct cultures as opposed to a spectrum or a patchwork; cf. Hilda Ellis Davidson, *The Lost Beliefs of Northern Europe* (1993), 4.

5.6 'THE CELTIC YEAR'

Caitlin Matthews

From 'The year's turning', in *The Elements of The Celtic Tradition*, Matthews, C., Shaftesbury, Element, 1989, pp. 83–5.

The Celtic Year was divided by a mixture of solar and lunar festivals. The equal-armed cross of the solar divisions was offset by the St Andrew's Cross of the lunar fire-festivals, each of which was celebrated on the full-moon.

The solar solstices and equinoxes are the marker points for the sun's path: at its zenith on the Summer Solstice, at its apogee at the Winter Solstice and at the two median points at the Equinoxes. The lunar festivals, frequently called 'Celtic fire-festivals' because of the nature of ritual which attended them, marked important points in the Celtic calendar. Of course, the calendrical dates . . . represent the fixed dates on which these festivals are celebrated today. . . . The lunar festivals are concerned with pastoral and agricultural events, rather than the movements of the sun through the seasons.

Samhain and Beltain were the two major festivals, since they marked the division of the year into two parts: Winter and Summer. This is reflected in the lives of all Celtic peoples. At Samhain, beasts were rounded up and brought into stockades for wintering over: excess livestock was slaughtered, since they could not be kept alive during the hard months of cold and dearth of grain. At Beltain, herds were driven out into summer pasture, for the last of the frosts were safely over and livestock could be fattened up without fear of wolves.

These festivals also regulated the exercise of war and raiding. The Fianna hunted and engaged in warfare from Beltain to Samhain, in the warm months, and from Samhain to Beltain lived off the country, being billeted in different households and tribes.

Both festivals were considered to be the prime time to communicate with the Otherworld. The doors of the *sidhe* were thought to be open on these nights.

The Celtic New Year was celebrated at Samhain, now celebrated world-wide as All Hallows, Hallowe'en or All Saints Day. This festival ushered in the new year, and marked the beginning of winter. The cold time was considered to be under the aegis of the Cailleach and so the rituals of Samhain were concerned with the dead, with divination and storytelling. These customs survive in the modern festival of Hallowe'en as well as more authentically in regional parts as 'Mischief Night' or 'Punky Night'. The Christian feast of All Souls on 2nd November has drawn upon many levels of these customs, but the Celtic festival of Samhain has undoubtedly influenced it most. Many Catholic people in Europe and the Americas go to cemeteries on this day and light candles on the graves of their dead. In Britain, this feature is retained a few days later on Remembrance Sunday or Armistice Day, 11th November, when the fallen of the two World Wars are honoured. The bonfires of Samhain are now more likely to be lit, in Britain, on 5th November where Guy Fawkes Night has taken over the sacrificial aspect of this feast.

The feast of Oimelc marked the loosening of Winter's grip. At this time, the new lambs were born and ewes were in milk. In an age which depends on the artificial production of foodstuffs by modern farming methods, it is hard to imaging what winter would have been like without fresh milk to hand. Yet neither ewes nor cows will lactate unless they have given birth. The protein from new milk, butter, cheese and whey, not to mention the pies made from the docked tails of lambs, would have often made the difference between life and death for the very old and the very young during the hard frosts of February. Little tribal celebration was observed at this dark time of year, but the women met together to celebrate the return of the maiden aspect of the Goddess at the time when the Cailleach's winter was beginning to retreat a little. . . .

Beltain or May Eve marked the real beginning of summer, the time when leaves were beginning to show and when flowers made every meadow colourful. This was the first real opportunity for the tribe to leave its winter quarters and go visiting. An extended clan would be able to gather together to celebrate this feast, discuss the news and make plans for the coming season. It was at this time that major gatherings and fairs were held. Beasts were purified from their long winter confinement in barns and yards by being driven between two fires, so killing off any possible lingering infections. This feast was under the aegis of the Shining One, Belenos, though we lack much reference to the nature of his rites. The release from winter confinement heralded ecstatic celebrations. As the *sidhe* doors were open, this night was also one for the Faery revels. Irish law tracts cite Beltain as the time of divorce. As trial marriages were normally made at Lughnasadh, we can deduce that the couple had had the long duration and confinement of winter to try their relationship and Beltain must have offered the first real opportunity to come before a *brehon* and declare their relationship at an end.

Lughnasadh marked the gathering together of the tribe at high summer. The concerns of the hay harvest would be behind and the prospect of the wheat and barley harvest would be yet to reap. This was a time for showing off the speed of one's horses, of competing in contests of skill and strength: it was a time for arranging marriages also, since young people would be foremost in exhibiting their quality at this festival and would form natural attachments which their parents might, or might not, think suitable. Marriages could be either love-matches or arranged matches, with the interests of the clan at stake depending on the status of the youth or maiden. But it was at Lughnasadh that trial marriages were entered into. Thrusting their hands through a holed stone, the couple would promise to live together for a year and a day, and part after that time if they did not measure up to expectation. Though perhaps none of the maidens would have been quite as demanding as Emer, who in the wooing contest between her and Cuchulainn, says of her fortress: 'None comes to this plain who does not go without sleep from summer's end to the beginning of spring, from the beginning of spring to May-Day, and again from May-Day to the beginning of winter.' In other words, from Lughnasadh to Oimelc, from Oimelc to Beltain, from Beltain to Samhain: in effect, her wooer must not slumber for a whole year!

5.7 'THREE 'P'S'

Ian Bradley

From 'The way goes on', in *The Celtic Way*, Darton, Longman and Todd, 1993, pp. 119–21.

Three 'p's could be taken as the distinguishing hallmarks of Celtic Christianity – presence, poetry and pilgrimage. They have all been rather neglected by the churches of the Western world over the last thousand years. I would like to argue strongly for their recovery.

We are at last beginning to turn our backs on centuries of subscribing to dualist ideas and over-stressing divine transcendence and coming to recognise God's animating presence where we have previously denied or overlooked it – in the world of nature, in the everyday things of life, in the atoms and molecules that are the basic constituents of all matter. We still have a long way to go, however, in recovering the Celts' wonderful and all-embracing sense of every part of the world and every aspect of life being filled with the presence of God. If we do recover it in time, perhaps we will yet save the planet that we have so nearly destroyed. Presence is important in another rather different sense as well. The kind of ministry undertaken by the Celtic Church could perhaps best be described as a ministry of presence. Its monasteries were presences in society which witnessed to the Gospel as much just by being there as by activity and involvement in schemes and projects. There is great stress now in many churches on always doing things, being constantly active, launching new projects and setting new targets. Certainly the church should always be on the move and never standing still, but there is something to be said for encouraging the doodlers and dreamers as well as the doers and planners. We could do with more bards and poets in the modern church and, dare one say, with fewer committees and task forces.

I often reflect on Martin Reith's distinction between the twopence coloured poetry of the Celts and the Anglo-Saxon preference for penny plain prose that has come to predominate in the language and liturgy of our churches. Both theology and worship have become too prosy, over-intellectual and often dull and leaden as a result. We need to learn from the Celts to express our faith in images rather than concepts. In a culture dominated by television and visual imagery this is particularly important. We need to find and develop our own evangelistic aids with the power of the high standing crosses to stop people in their tracks and contemporary icons which will encourage meditation and contemplation as the illuminated manuscripts once did. We need too to recover more widely that rich Christian poetic imagination which still exists in Wales and to stop trying to tie down the ineffable mystery and beauty of God in mere prose.

The third and final 'p' that we would do well to recover from our Celtic Christian ancestors takes us back to those endlessly intertwining ribbons and ever curling spirals of which they were so fond. At the root of the Celts' attachment to the idea of pilgrimage was their understanding that nothing is static. Long before anyone was talking about relativity, quantum mechanics or process thought, they appreciated the essentially open-ended and dynamic character of the universe and realized that creation is a continuous process rather than a once-and-for-all activity in the dim and distant past. They saw, too, that human life is also in a constant state of development, change and growth, charged like the rest of creation with the potentializing energy of Christ, ever becoming rather than just being. To be a pilgrim was to take the outward path which acknowledged the reality of this inner journey of the individual human soul and to embark on a way which involved suffering, sacrifice and pain as well as consolations and companionship along the way and which ended, if indeed it ended at all, at the place of one's resurrection.

We too can both lose and find ourselves as pilgrims within the twists and turns of the Celtic knot. . . . The Celtic knot interweaves the old and the new, the pagan and the Christian, the sacred and the secular, nature and grace, creation and redemption, matter and spirit, masculine and feminine, this world and the next. Along its tangled and twisting threads, with their reminder that all is connected and nothing stands alone, we can make our own journeys of faith and experience, with all their risks and possibilities, circumscribed only by the constant guidance and protection of God who ever enfolds and encircles us.

5.8 'ARE THE MODERN CELTS BOGUS?'

Simon James

From 'Conclusion: are the modern Celts bogus?', in *The Atlantic Celts: Ancient People or Modern Invention?*, London, British Museum Press, 1999, pp. 136–9.

Men run with great avidity to give their evidence in favour of what flatters their passions and their national prejudices.

(David Hume to Edward Gibbon, on the inauthenticity
of the Celtic poems of Ossain, 18 March 1776)

The idea of a race, nation or ethnic group called Celts in Ancient Britain and Ireland is indeed a modern invention. It is an eighteenth- and nineteenth-century 'reification' of a people that never existed, a factoid (a theoretical construct masquerading as fact) assembled from fragments of evidence drawn from a wide range of societies across space and time. This reification served the interests of a range of cultural expectations, aspirations and political agendas – and still does. Yet, as a model for understanding the past, it fails adequately to explain the available evidence, especially the rich archaeological testimony for the insular Iron Age.

'The Celts', then, must be rejected as an ethnic label for the populations of the islands during the Iron Age, the Roman period or indeed medieval times, not least in the direct sense that they did not use this name for themselves. The name is also to be rejected in the more general sense, in that it implies that culturally the Iron Age populations of Ireland and Britain were 'really' all the same kind of people (which is here challenged), and that they were all essentially the same as the continental Celts (who are themselves hard to define and probably also largely a reification). Further, the term 'Celtic' has accumulated so much baggage, so many confusing meanings and associations, that it is too compromised even to be useful as a more general label for the culture of these periods. The peoples in question organized themselves in a diversity of ways, made and used material culture in many different ways, and, it seems, spoke a variety of languages and dialects, which were not all mutually intelligible. The undoubted similarities and relations between them are best explained in terms of parallel development of many societies in intimate contact, rather than of radiation from a recent single common origin. It is inappropriate to give them a single, shared name, whether 'Celts' or any other; if they had clear group identities at all, these were manifold and changing. To the question 'what, then, should we call the peoples of early Britain and Ireland?', the answer must be, exactly that: 'the peoples of Britain and Ireland'. To give them a single name is almost as pointless as asking what is the ethnicity (singular) of the population of Asia.

Yet, as we have seen, the idea of the existence of modern Celts in the British Isles has always been predicated on the assumption that they were the direct descendants of Ancient Celts in these lands. Since the Ancient Celts appear to have spurious historical roots, does it not follow that the modern Celts, too, must be bogus? Paradoxically, the answer is 'No'.

Discrediting the insular Ancient Celts does not make the modern Celts fraudulent. For the more sophisticated understandings of the nature of ethnic identities now available to us, which reveal the Ancient Celts to be a modern construct, equally suggest that the modern Celts constitute a perfectly real and legitimate 'ethnic group'. The resolution of this paradox lies in chronology: the modern Celts are not the present representatives of a people who have existed continuously for millennia, but constitute a true case of 'ethnogenesis' – the birth of an ethnic identity – in *early modern* Europe.

As we have seen, the study of ethnic identities reveals a number of recurrent themes:

- *They arise from a sense of shared difference, and usually perceived threat, from another group with which they are in contact.* In the case of the Welsh, Scots, Irish and others, this common cultural Other was England which, with the drive towards a basically English, uniform 'Britishness' following the Union of 1707, and the incorporation of Ireland in 1801, threatened to swamp other cultural traditions.
- *They express their identity by attaching symbolic value to aspects of their culture deemed characteristic.* In defining themselves, ethnic groups choose particular aspects of their culture which they share in common, but which the Other lacks, and invest them with symbolic significance. The choice of these symbols depends on the cultural make-up of the group, and the particular historical circumstances prevailing at the time. Language is often of fundamental importance, and we have seen that it was possession of a distinctive group of related languages that informed the touchstone for the new Celtic identity. However, the Celts are apparently unique in defining themselves in terms of a group of *mutually unintelligible* languages. This idea only became conceivable as a result of the development of philology and the work of Pezron and Lhuyd. Before this, the notion of such a language family was unthought of and literally unthinkable. Here is a remarkable example of the historical contingency of ethnic self-definition.
- *Such groups also choose an 'ethnonym',* in the present case one derived from the label invented for their newly discovered shared characteristic, their related languages, which semi-arbitrarily were labelled 'Celtic'. This determined that they were now to be called Celts, and retrospectively must always have been Celts (the fact that the term was not used before 1700 is usually glossed over).
- *Ethnic groups create an agreed common history through the selective use and reframing of traditions of pre-existing groups, or the simple invention, from scratch, of 'ancient' roots. . . .* Both the modern Celts, and their English cultural Others, abetted by European scholars with parallel continental interests, shared in creating just such a historical pedigree for the insular Celts. Their linguistic affiliations, and also early interpretations of archaeological remains, apparently gave the insular Celts a remarkably long continuous history, back into pre-Roman continental Europe. That this tradition of historiography is now under attack does not invalidate *modern* Celtic identity, because to some degree *all* modern ethnic and national identities create essentially propagandist histories like this – not least the English, and the British state.

But perhaps the clearest evidence for the reality of the *modern* insular Celts is the simple fact that millions of people feel themselves to be in some sense Celtic.

The concept of British identity, although apparently so different from that of the Celts, has some interesting similarities with it. It, too, was a new creation from pre-existing kingdoms. It, too, was created in response to perceived outside threats. It, too, chose a name redolent with antiquity (its citizens being 'Britons', also harking back to pre-Roman times). It, too, created (and creates) its own history, traditions and rituals to give an impression of antiquity which is often spurious. The exact present meaning, and importance, of 'Britishness' to many nominally British people is also as highly problematic as the 'Celticness' of the nominally Celtic peoples. To many, Britishness seems to mean less than older national or regional identities, as devolution and the resurgence of Scottish and Welsh nationalism demonstrate. Indeed, at the end of the twentieth century, it can be argued that the question mark hanging over the present validity and future prospects of Britishness, and the existence of the largely political entity called 'Britain', is bigger than that hanging over the modern Celts.

. . .

I would suggest the following: the isles have always been home to many peoples, who have fought one another, but also drawn on one another; these peoples have created themselves and also created each other, through their contacts and conflicts, and the islands have always been open to newcomers, who have added to life and modified the course of our shared histories.

The traditional 'story of the island Celts' is exactly that: a story, one of many possible histories which may be written as we struggle to make sense of the fragmentary testimony from the lost past. It is a version which simply does not accord with either the specific evidence for the case, or with general observation of the way the world works. Prior assumption that we know what the past was like buries without consideration the possibility that it may have been different. Imposing Celtic uniformity on the past denies earlier peoples any prospect of revealing to us their true sense of their identity, through the traces they have left of their lives. Prejudged as Celts, they are forced into a mould. This is ironic, since in origin modern Celticness was about asserting identity and difference in the present. Projecting Celtic identity back onto past societies which would neither have recognized nor understood it, obscures the real, complex history of the isles.

5.9 'THREE THINGS THERE ARE, THAT ARE SELDOM HEARD'

J.H.T. Davies

From the pamphlet 'Three things there are that are seldom heard: A comment on modern Shamanism', edited by Jayran, S., House of the Goddess, 1993.

PLAYING AT INDIANS

Consider the Native Americans. They are a perfect example of what happens when the traditions of an ancient culture catch the magpie eye of a certain section of modern society. We are being presented with a bewildering mishmash of courses, by a variety of teachers whose bona fides are seldom vouched for by the elders of the nations whose wisdom they purport to convey. They fall into two groups; native American visitors, and white teachers who claim to have absorbed the wisdom.

The first group may not be all they seem. I heard a rumour[1] that some of them are regarded as renegades by members of their own culture; that far from being the genuine article, they are out to bilk the white man of his money by telling him what he wants to hear. Who can blame them for being a little unscrupulous, considering the white man's record of exploitation and betrayal of their peoples?

As for the whites, how many of them speak any of the native American languages? It's a vital question. Wittgenstein[2] observed, "the limits of my language are the limits of my world". Consciousness is to a great extent a social construct; the grid of selective perceptions through which we filter our awareness of the world is largely a consequence of our upbringing in a particular social milieu. Language plays a vital role. Orwell[3] asked if it is possible to conceive of an idea for which we have no words. If I wanted to enter the culturally-determined mindset of a plains Indian, I would regard learning his language as a vital first step. Yet when a prominent white teacher of "native American shamanism" was asked how many of the languages he spoke, he gave not an answer, but a put-down which was also a rather clumsy sidestep. He said the questioner was being confrontative. I wonder why he didn't answer the question?

I doubt the integrity of much of the "scholarship". I don't just mean the obvious absurdities like Chief Seattle's "Brother Eagle, Sister Sky" speech of 1854, which turned out to have been created by one Ted Perry, a Hollywood scriptwriter, in 1971. (What Chief Seattle actually said is far more down-to-earth and sensible, as you might expect). Native American culture covers a huge geographical area, a considerable timespan, and a myriad of different nations, tribes, and peoples. It would be surprising if the differences

---

1. Dakota Times, Summer '91, Letters.
2. "Tractatus", Wittgenstein.
3. "1984", Orwell.

among such a range were not as important as the similarities. Indeed, the tribes were warring over such differences for centuries before ever the white man arrived.

The question should therefore not be whether we chose to study "native American shamanism"; but rather which form of native American shamanism we chose, and why. I do not get the impression that this point is given any serious treatment.

I think we are getting a sort of pot mess, which consists largely of Sioux and Dacotah, with chunks of Hopi and Kwakluti, with fragments of other tribes thrown in to flavour the stew. A hugely rich and varied range of cultures has been ruthlessly quarried. Pieces have been wrenched loose from their cultural context, and assembled into a composite that will be acceptable to the punters who go on those expensive "workshops" you read about.

Some people seem to be profiting rather well out of this grown-up craze for playing at Indians. It strikes me as an elaborate scam. They may demand that I retract. They may say that the white race is being offered a precious spiritual gift by the red man, and it is merely their vocation to convey it. Fine. Any white teacher of "native American shamanism" who can satisfy me that a substantial proportion of their teaching income goes to the people who gave us this precious spiritual gift: i.e. goes to the reservations, where cash is desperately needed for subsistence and basic medical care, will receive a handsome public written apology. If nobody takes up the offer, you may draw your own conclusions.

THE NOBLE SAVAGE

So if it is such an obvious scam, why do so many otherwise intelligent people seem to have abandoned the faculty of intelligent appraisal? I would suggest we look at Jean-Jacques Rousseau's[4] concept of the noble savage; an idealized picture of life in the state of nature. It has little to do with the reality, which is equally likely to correspond to Hobbes'[5] description; "nasty, brutish, and short." However, it is extremely successful as a picture (left vague in all the difficult places), on to which people can project their discontents about our society, and highlight them by contrast with this carefully assembled construct.

Just like Rousseau, we are making noble savages of the native Americans, for reasons which have little to do with their culture, and much to do with ours. For instance, there is evidence to suggest that the Hopi, far from "walking lightly on the earth", damaged their own ecology quite extensively. No discredit to the Hopi; no society lives up to its self-proclaimed virtues. (For instance, ours claims to be a liberal democracy, in which civil liberties are ensured by the rule of law.) Other native American societies were just as fallible; early European explorers, meeting tribes before they were corrupted by extensive contact with the white man, commented on their penchant for theft, deception, and torture of captives.

Unsurprisingly, native American society seems to have been the usual human mixture of virtues and vices. My point is that if so many people seem determined to concentrate on the virtues, to the exclusion of the vices, they must feel a powerful need to idealize something. Others, who are more ahead of the game, have supplied the need. In the process, some people have done rather well for themselves, and a fascinating group of cultures have been trivialized.

---

4. "Emile" Rousseau.
5. "Leviathan", Hobbes.

But what about the claims made for these courses, that they will change your life, and fill it with a new and beautiful inspiration? Doesn't such a noble purpose justify playing fast and loose with a few cultural niceties? Leaving aside the general question of whether a worthwhile end ever justifies suspect means, there are more specific issues at stake. I have never met anyone whose life was profoundly changed by exposure to a few fragments from another culture. Let's face it, this is all you have time for; even in a week's intensive residential. Human beings are hugely resistant to fundamental change. The most one can hope for is a few small steps in one's personal process. A lot of the time, it's just entertainment and escapism.

Is this such a bad thing? I have often met people who were greatly uplifted by the excitement of meeting aspects of a different culture, well presented, in the company of other enthusiasts. I doubt if any of them fundamentally changed as a result. Sooner or later, the grooves of habit reassert themselves. But while it lasts, it can be enormously enjoyable. This is very important. People seem to have a powerful need for frequent doses of colourful fantasy. So why not indulge? Why not feel able to say that this is precisely what we are doing?

The only caution I would suggest is to try not to be crass. For instance, is it really acceptable to appear in public, wearing a war bonnet? In its own culture, every feather could represent an enemy, whom the wearer had counted coup on, at great personal risk. Imagine how a real native American would feel, seeing one of his people's enemies, wearing such a sacred garment, without having earned it.

As long as you are alive to such issues of basic good manners, why not enjoy? Unfortunately, many of us can't enjoy. As that grim divine John Calvin said, "all pleasure is sin", and his message still contaminates our culture. If more of us could cheerfully say that we do, what we do, for no better reason than that we like it, life would feel far healthier, and a great deal safer. We could enjoy learning about another culture, without feeling the need to disguise our pleasure by dressing it up in portentous terms, as a voyage of personal discovery.

It can be enlightening, to create a "noble savage", as a device to help us air our discontents about our own society. But let us be scrupulously clear about what we are doing. He is a fiction, albeit a useful and enjoyable one.

Best of all, why not dress up in beads and feathers, and drum and shake rattles and chant; be a bunch of grown-up kids playing at Indians? There's nothing wrong with a few magical tricks. People zooming in and out of trances, or catharting all over the place, are guaranteed to lend an atmosphere of exhilaration to any gathering. It's good clean fun. No matter if it has very little to do with saving ourselves, and even less to do with saving the world.

If we could enjoy life more, the spiritual salesmen (who trade on our well-suppressed guilty feelings that we do not deserve any pleasure), wouldn't be making such a prosperous living, and the culture of the native Americans would not be so ruthlessly exploited.

Outrages are almost always committed in the name of religion, spirituality, passionately-held political belief, or some other belief-system which enables its proponents to argue plausibly that its priorities are so important that they override the demands of common human decency. Conversely, it's very difficult to justify atrocities in the name of fun.

I DO NOT WISH

I particularly do not want what has happened to the native Americans, to happen to the heritage of my own people. I do not wish to see us marginalized as the "Dreamtime People" of Europe. We are great dreamers, we Celts: we are good at it. We are also an intensely practical people, with a proud industrial heritage, and a peerless tradition of craft work. To value us only for the haunting quality of our dreams is extremely patronizing.

They are our dreams, not yours. Who are you to define us, still less to get your hands on our dreams? A dream is the ultimate personal experience. I do not want you presuming to define my dreams.

I do not wish to see Ireland marketed for its sad air of the uncanny, when that is because it is full of ghosts; the ghosts of the million who starved to death in the famine of 1846/7, while the English went on exporting corn from Ireland. . . . I do not wish to see the empty landscape of the Hebrides extolled for its beauty, when it is empty because of the brutal clearances.

I do not wish to see you create a homogenized pabulum of Celtic culture, first ignoring the difference between the Goidelic and Brythonic strains, then going on to ignore every other important distinction. "Celtic Culture" sweeps from the Danube to the Atlantic, from about 1000B.C. to the present day. Such rich variety can only be insulted by facile treatment.

I do not wish to see druidism promoted as the latest spiritual fashion. . . .

I do not wish to see the gaps filled in with "inspired" or "channelled" material, which leaves too much scope to the imagination (to put it politely) of the author.

I do not wish to encounter hordes of eager-eyed acolytes who don't know the first thing about the reality of Wales. I do not wish to meet their teacher; some self-appointed Saxon expert on Celtia, whose tongue stumbles over the simplest Welsh place-names.

I do not wish to see the less acceptable aspects of my ancestors glossed over, in order to create yet another sanitized "noble savage", for your consumption. My ancient forebears were warriors, slave-takers and head-hunters. When the hunting was good, they feasted enormously on cauldrons of boiled meat, quarrelled outrageously over the "Hero's Portion", and drank mightily. I honour their memory, warts and all. Let us raise a brimming glass; or better yet, several brimming glasses, to their memory, and lament that we live in such thin-blooded times.

I particularly do not wish to see a horrible, bastardized travesty of my heritage making money for a few English and American teachers who ruthlessly market it.

I most certainly do not wish to see it marketed back to us as the true and real version of our culture, by members of the race that has exploited our economy and killed or imprisoned every leader of our own, from Llewellyn the last, to Dic Penderyn (remember him? We do) by a race which has made sustained attempts to stamp out our language and culture over centuries; which still treats us as . . . fair game for racist stereotypes and odious "jokes" which are only funny to the oppressors who tell them; and who, not content with that, now seem intent on treating the most precious thing left to us; our spiritual heritage; as a sort of a quarry they can exploit, to make magical tricks for their jaded urbanites. This is the very ugliest kind of cultural and spiritual colonialism.

Stop it. Hands off. Enough is enough.

WHAT CAN YOU KNOW?

What can you know of the word the hills speak?

What can you know of the headland above the western ocean, with the islands lying low on the horizon, and the whispering wind in the thin grasses? Short, simple, fierce messages, about belonging and nourishment and protection, are their word.

This is my land; I belong to her, and she belongs to me. She will not speak so to you, because you do not belong to her.

What can you know of hiraeth? There is no adequate English translation, but every person of Welsh ancestry knows it, in all its terrible, lovely, fullness. How can you know what it is like, to be cocooned in my local, pint in hand, listening to the rumble of voices, exchanging jokes, gossip and scandal? My part of Wales is largely English-speaking, but only an insider has a hope of following the conversation. This is as it should be. A private language affords a besieged culture a certain degree of protection. We are on the inside. You are on the outside. I am quite happy for you to remain there, forever.

Do you think I am being excessively rude? I wish I could be ruder, by far. In Wales, the insult has long been respected as an art-form. It is said that, in the old days, a bard of power could create a satire that would raise boils on his enemy's face. I wish I could write a blistering invective which would permanently deter you from attempting to gain entry to our spiritual heritage. Because, you see, you cannot. You are not born to it. But in trying, you have the power to debase it, and cheapen it, and, incidentally, to make fools of yourselves.

SIT QUIETLY

Come to Wales if you will, and be welcome. We value the visitor who proceeds gently. We have seen far too many of the other kind. Enjoy our beaches and hills, craft shops and cream teas. Sit quietly and listen. Don't impose a complex structure of arcane beliefs and magical tricks. Listen, quietly.

The hills may have a word for you, after all. It won't be the word they have for me as a native, but she is unlikely to send you away feeling empty. She is a gentle and a generous lady, this land of Wales. Accept your position as an outsider. The status of guest is an honoured one, but remember that it carries the obligation of mannerly behaviour.

Study our literature, but be aware most of the best interpretative scholarship is surprisingly inaccessible. It tends either to be published by the University of Wales Press, in English, in short print runs, or it is published in Welsh. If you are really interested in Celtic culture, why not learn at least some everyday Welsh?

Finally, don't forget a certain humility. We can never know what life was like in the ancient days of the druidic mysteries. Too much has been lost, and times have changed forever. . . .

I doubt if it is possible to become a "celtic shaman", and it is a mistake to try. Because if you do; if you come to Wales (as I fear you may), wearing beads, and funny hats adorned with feathers and pieces of stick; if you come laden with rattles and spirit callers and suchlike paraphernalia; if you come following an expensive workshop leader who can't even pronounce, let alone speak, any Welsh; whose only qualifications are a set of distinctly cranky ideas, assembled from fragments torn loose from our heritage and a hotchpotch of others; plus, of course, a fast line in chat to convince you that this system offers instant enlightenment at a price; (the fast-food version of spirituality): then you will be obvious for the fool you are. Worst of all, if you lecture us earnestly about our own heritage you will offend us badly. I wonder if that matters to you?

. . .

The instant you're out of earshot, there will be great gales of cynical Celtic mirth. But you needn't worry. You'll never know about the hilarity your antics cause; because to stand in that circle of laughter, you have to belong here.

THE HONOURED GUEST

Well now, if you're still reading, and you're not too put off by a hurt, angry Celt's invective, he will give you a formal invitation.

Come to my land. Come in honour and peace, in our ancient tradition of the deep sanctity of guest right.

Come to Ceridwen's hills, to Morgaine's sea, to Pwyll's hunting ground, and to Blodeuwedd's swift and silent flight. Come and find Mother Non's comfort, and Govannon's mighty craft. But again, it cannot be said too often, be quiet; be respectful of a proud people who are different, and have been much oppressed by invaders.

When you hear Welsh spoken, remember that not long ago in this century, our children in their schools were beaten and humiliatingly ridiculed if they spoke our own language. Remember that until this generation Welsh workers used English names, and arranged English names to get jobs, because of one of the oldest racisms in Europe. Ask why the scholars in universities do not teach the Mabinogion as they do Shakespeare, Homer and Goethe, when its wisdom and art is no less, and Celtia is one of the ancestral roots of Europe?

Is my anger a little more understandable now?

. . .

So finally, go somewhere in my land of your own choosing; sit and listen. Don't TELL the spirit of the land what YOU think about Arthur, about the Mists of Avalon, the Grail, warrior priestesses or the druids. Don't invoke anything according to what you already know. Wait gently for whatever is there to touch you in its own way.

THE CELTIC TEACHING ON SUCH THINGS IS THAT WHAT YOU GET WILL NOT BE WHAT YOU EXPECT

5.10 'APOLOGIES TO NATIVE PEOPLE'

Sara Simon et al

From 'Appendix One: apologies to Native people', in *Bridges in Spirituality: First Nations Christian Women Tell Their Stories*, Simon, S. et al. Toronto, Anglican Book Centre, 1997, pp. 191–3.

In 1986, an apology was presented to Native people by the Moderator of The United Church of Canada at General Council in Sudbury, Ontario.

> Long before my people journeyed to this land, your people were here, and you received from your elders an understanding of creation, and of the mystery that surrounds us all that was deep and rich and to be treasured. We did not hear you when you shared your vision. In our zeal to tell you of the good news of Jesus Christ we were closed to the value of your spirituality. We confused western ways and culture with the depth and breadth and length and height of the gospel of Christ. We imposed our civilization as a condition of accepting the gospel. We tried to make you be like us and in so doing we helped to destroy the vision that made you what you were. As a result you, and we, are poorer and the image of the Creator in us is twisted, blurred and we are not what we are meant by God to be. We ask you to forgive us and to walk together with us in the spirit of Christ so that our peoples may be blessed and God's creation healed.

In 1993, in Minaki, Ontario, the Primate of the Anglican Church of Canada delivered an apology:

A Message from the Primate of the Anglican Church of Canada
Minaki, Ontario,
Friday, August 6, 1993

My Brothers and Sisters:

Together here with you I have listened as you have told your stories of the residential schools.* I have heard the voices that have spoken of pain and hurt experienced in the schools, and of the scars which endure to this day.

I have felt shame and humiliation as I have heard of suffering inflicted by my people and as I think of the part our church played in that suffering.

I am deeply conscious of the sacredness of the stories that you have told, and I hold in the highest honour those who have told them.

I have heard with admiration the stories of people and communities who have worked at healing, and I am aware of how much more healing is needed.

---

* Residential schools forcibly separated Indian children from their families, community, language, culture, and indigenous religion.

I also know that I am in need of healing, and my own people are in need of healing, and our church is in need of healing. Without that healing we will continue the same attitudes that have done such damage in the past.

I know that healing takes a long time, both for people and for communities.

I also know that it is God who heals and that God can begin to heal when we open ourselves, our wounds, our failure, and our shame, to God. I want to take one step along that path here and now.

I accept and I confess, before God and you, our failures in the residential schools. We failed you. We failed ourselves. We failed God.

I am sorry, more than I can say, that we were a part of a system which took you and your children from home and family.

I am sorry, more than I can say, that we tried to remake you in our image, taking from you your language and the signs of your identity.

I am sorry, more than I can say, that in our schools so many were abused physically, sexually, culturally, and emotionally.

On behalf of the Anglican Church of Canada, I present our apology.

I do this at the desire of those in the Church, like the National Executive Council, who know some of your stories and have asked me to apologize.

I do this in the name of many who do not know these stories.

And I do this even though there are those in the church who cannot accept the fact that these things were done in our name.

As soon as I am home, I shall tell all the bishops what I have said, and ask them to co-operate with me and with the National Executive Council in helping this healing at the local level. Some bishops have already begun this work.

I know how often you have heard words which have been empty because they have not been accompanied by actions. I pledge to you my best efforts, and the efforts of our church at the national level, to walk with you along the path of God's healing.

The work of the Residential Schools Working Group, the video, the commitment and the effort of the Special Assistants to the Primate for this work, and the grants available for the healing conferences are some signs of that pledge; and we shall work for others.

This is Friday, the day of Jesus' suffering and death. It is the anniversary of the first atomic bomb at Hiroshima, one of the most terrible injuries ever inflicted by one people on another.

But even atomic bombs and Good Friday are not the last word. God raised Jesus from the dead as a sign that life and wholeness are the everlasting and unquenchable purpose of God.

Thank you for listening to me.

Archbishop and Primate

Vine Deloria Jr.

From *Red Earth, White Lies: Native Americans and the Myth of Scientific Fact*, New York, Scribner, 1995, pp. 13–15.

When Indian bingo games are humming in almost every nook and cranny of our land, stealing the most sacred ritual of the Roman Catholic Church and gathering the white man's coin as quickly as it can reasonably be retrieved, progress is being made. When multitudes of young whites roam the West convinced they are Oglala Sioux Pipe Carriers and on a holy mission to protect "Mother Earth," and when priests and ministers, scientists and drug companies, ecologists and environmentalists are crowding the reservations in search of new rituals, new medicines, or new ideas about the land, it would appear as if American Indians finally have it made. Indeed, some tribal chairmen are now well-heeled Republicans worried about gun control, moral fiber, and prayer in schools. In many respects American Indians are looking increasingly like middle-class Americans.

Beginning in 1960, the federal census allowed people to self-identify their ethnic or racial background, and in the past three decades a startling jump in the Indian population has occurred. Where there were over half a million Indians in the United States in 1960, in the last census the Cherokees alone totaled over 360,000, primarily the result of consciousness-raising efforts of New Age enthusiasts but nevertheless welcome as a politically significant figure. As whites get more familiar with Indian symbols and beliefs we can expect both the national figures and the Cherokee figures to skyrocket beyond belief in the year 2000 and beyond. Indeed, today it is popular to be an Indian. Within a decade it may be a necessity: people are not going to want to take the blame for the sorry state of the nation, and claiming allegiance with the most helpless racial minority may well be the way to escape accusations.

. . .

Indians can always become whites because the requirements are not very rigorous, but can whites really become Indians? A good many people seriously want to know. They are discontented with their society, their government, their religion, and everything around them and nothing is more appealing than to cast aside all inhibitions and stride back into the wilderness, or at least a wilderness theme park, seeking the nobility of the wily savage who once physically fought civilization and now, symbolically at least, is prepared to do it again.

Three areas exist which contain tremendous barriers to any effort of whites to become Indians. These areas, unless they are given careful and serious attention by the next generation of Indians, may prove fatal to Indian efforts to remain faithful to whatever traditions are still being practiced. While it may appear that Indians are adopting the values and practices of American culture, in the field of human knowledge – in science, in religion, and in forms of social interaction, most prominently in government – there is still a tremendous gap between the beliefs and the practices of both whites and Indians.

These three areas of conflict and misunderstanding were present at the beginning of colonial discovery days; they have defined the terms of the conflict between the indigenous peoples and the invaders for more than five hundred years and they remain potent, because they provide the definition of what civilized society should be. Our view of government, our allegiance to high spiritual powers, and our understanding of our world will continue to guide our thoughts and activities in the future and bring us to a complete collapse unless we are able to move beyond present notions into a more mature understanding of our planet, its history, and the rest of the universe. Much of Western science must go, all of Western religion should go, and if we are in any way successful in ridding ourselves of these burdens, we will find that we can fundamentally change government so that it will function more sensibly and enable us to solve our problems.

5.12 'NATURE AND FIRST NATIONS' RELIGIONS'

Catherine L. Albanese

From 'Recapitulating pieties', in *Nature Religion in America, from the Algonkian Indians to the New Age*, Albanese, C.L., Chicago, University of Chicago Press, 1990, pp. 154–8, 162.

Amerindian immersion in nature lives on in a traditionalist version as well as in a New Age incarnation that is decidedly eclectic. Puritan/Calvinist awe at the violent wilderness and respect for its negative forces thrives in the work of some contemporary nature writers. Republican apotheosis of nature in a politicized ideology ranges through the present-day environmental movement, for example, as it manifests itself in the "Greens" and in ecofeminism. Transcendentalists prosper in the general harmonial-metaphysical dialectic of New Age religion and in the special case of Goddess religion. And physical religion persists in vibrational medicines that range from the contemporary laying on of hands to the quest for purity in food. All told, the recapitulating pieties move freely together, mixing and matching, bowing to new partners in a quantum dance of religious syncretism. . . .

If we begin with the oldest Americans – those who form the continuing Amerindian population – the prominence of nature in religious symbol systems is clear. Moreover, Indian peoples have found their tongues and pens. New publications abound. Bookstores carry testimonial tales of religious experience in nature by Indian authors. And militant political activity by Native Americans often grounds itself, literally, in the earth religion of traditionalist medicine persons. Meanwhile, in their own pilgrim traditions of searching, non-Indians go to school among the natives, ritually undergoing sweats, forming medicine wheels for prayer and praise, pursuing shamanic vision journeys to the under and upper worlds.[1]

There is, of course, striking incongruity in linking traditionalists, New Age native teachers, and non-Indian seekers who often know how to turn religion to profit more than

---

1. In this heterogeneous context, the names of Black Elk, Lame Deer, N. Scott Momaday, Leslie Marmon Silko, Russell Means, Sun Bear, Michael Harner, Carlos Castaneda, and Lynn Andrews come readily to mind. For Black Elk, see Raymond J. DeMallie, *The Sixth Grandfather: Black Elk's Teachings Given to John G. Neihardt* (Lincoln: University of Nebraska Press, 1984); and, with caution, John G. Neihardt, *Black Elk Speaks: Being the Life Story of a Holy Man of the Eglala Sioux* (Lincoln: University of Nebraska Press, 1961); for Lame Deer, see John (Fire) Lame Deer and Richard Erdoes, *Lame Deer: Seeker of Visions* (New York: Pocket Books, Washington Square Press, 1972); for a discussion of the work of N. Scott Momaday and Leslie Marmon Silko, see Alan R. Velie, *Four American Indian Literary Masters: N. Scott Momaday, James Welch, Leslie Marmon Silko, and Gerald Vizenor* (Norman: University of Oklahoma Press, 1982), 11–64, 105–21; for Russell Means and religious traditionalism, see the discussion in Vine Deloria, Jr., *God Is Red* (New York: Grosset & Dunlap, 1973), 256–58; for Sun Bear, see any of his works, esp. *Sun Bear: The Path of Power*, as told to Wabun and to Barry Weinstock (Spokane, Wash.: Bear Tribe Publishing, 1983); for Michael Harner, see his *The Way of the Shaman: A Guide to Power and Healing* (New York: Harper & Row, 1980); and for Carlos Castaneda and Lynn Andrews, see, esp., the first published work of each: Carlos Castaneda, *The Teachings of Don Juan: A Yaqui Way of Knowledge* (Berkeley: University of California Press, 1968); and Lynn V. Andrews, *Medicine Woman* (New York: Harper & Row, 1981).

prophecy. Still, examined thematically, there is more striking congruity. Traditionalists and New Age Indians, whether native or adoptive, place nature at the center of religion and life. What unites traditionalists (who politicize the past) and New Agers (who transcendentalize it) is an abiding conviction of the centrality of nature and a continuing enactment of their concern. Nature provides a language to express cosmology and belief; it forms the basis for understanding and practicing a way of life; it supplies materials for ritual symbolization; it draws together a community. In short, like seventeenth-century Indians, contemporary Native Americans and their fellow travelers counter Euro-American Christianity with a religion of their own.

Take, for example, the religious activity of Sun Bear. Born Vincent La Duke in 1929, the son of a Chippewa (Ojibwa) father and a mother of German/Norwegian stock, Sun Bear spent his first twenty years on the White Earth Indian Reservation in northern Minnesota, where he received only an eighth-grade education. An army deserter (for reasons of conscience) in the Korean War, he spent some time in jail. He has also been an activist for Native American people and even a "Hollywood" Indian. But Sun Bear is best known today as founder of the Bear Tribe Medicine Society. Although it has been remarked sardonically that he is the only Indian in it, Sun Bear describes his intentional community as a "group of native and non-native people sharing the same vision, philosophy, and direction toward the Earth and the Creation around us."[2] With an apprenticeship program in Spokane, Washington, and a national following, that direction has become known and shared by thousands of non-Indian Americans. The nature of the vision and its direction is suggested by the Medicine Wheel Gatherings that Sun Bear and the Bear Tribe hold at various locations throughout the nation in an annual calendar of ceremonies and workshops.

Typically, medicine wheels take place over a weekend at a campground location where participants can bring sleeping bags, erect tents, or rent cabins.[3] Balancing ritual with teaching, the gatherings open with the construction of a huge circle of stones (the medicine wheel) to mark a sacred space. Sun Bear begins its consecration by placing at the center the skull of a buffalo or another sacred animal as sign of the creator and of the center of the universe. Then chosen individuals both honor and represent the powers that the stones symbolize as they place them within the wheel. Thirty-six stones, each of them for a part of the universe, become the medicine wheel as the entire community forms a circle around. People have been ceremonially smudged for purification, and they have made tobacco ties of cloth in colors to correspond to the colors of the directions. Most important, they have put into the ties their prayers.

Prayers are offered immediately again in the collective enterprise of a pipe ceremony following the medicine wheel, the two ceremonies consecrating the weekend's activities and providing a prayer and meditation space for participants. Similarly, in the adaptation of a pattern common to many religious cultures, the close of the weekend's work is signaled by the

Symbol & ritual

---

2. "And Life Continues: An Interview with Sun Bear," *Earth Nation Sunrise* 3 (Spring 1983): 14.
3. The description of medicine wheels that is presented here is garnered from my own attendance at the Medicine Wheel Gathering held at Camp Kern, near Lebanon, Ohio, October 3–5, 1986; from the program for the 1986 East Coast Medicine Wheel Gathering at Camp Monroe, New York, the same autumn; and from information gleaned more informally concerning others.

Medicine Wheel Give Away in which participants bring food to give to the poor. Finally, as activities end, with its ritual disassembling the medicine wheel itself is given away.

In between, throughout the weekend, sweat lodge ceremonies offer the chance for individuals to undergo ritual purification in a traditional manner. A crystal healing ceremony provides the focus for group meditation for healing, and a children's blessing honors the contribution of the youngest members of the community. Drumming, chanting, dancing, and prayer form a ceremonial thread that weaves through the medicine wheel's time. Meanwhile, workshop sessions held by Bear Tribe teachers and their associates turn the campground into an outdoor school. United by a common "earth" wisdom, workshop topics may include anything from shamanism to women's "moontimes" (menstrual periods), from Hawaiian huna to star and herbal lore. . . .

In sum, Sun Bear links the visionary to the down-to-earth, even as he links traditional Ojibwa and Plains Indian lore to environmental and survivalist movements and to the popular self-help religion of the New Age. How, then, are we to locate him, and what can we make of his message? Sun Bear is hardly a traditionalist: no traditionalist would tolerate his insistence on sharing sacred teachings and ceremonies with non-Indian people. (Indeed, there have been threats of violence by traditionalists against at least one full-blooded Native American who has offered workshops at Sun Bear's medicine wheels.) Still further, the substance of Sun Bear's teaching echoes the past but also syncretizes and romanticizes it. His teaching is, obviously, not specifically Ojibwa. But beyond his generalizing to a kind of Plains-Indian – and even pan-Indian – orthodoxy and orthopraxy, Sun Bear has entered a world in which the clear, defined boundaries of a Native American heritage have subtly softened. Some parts of the past (such as medicine wheels and crystals) have been lifted to new prominence. Others (such as hunting and burial practices) meanwhile decline.

Moreover, Sun Bear – product not only of a Chippewa past but of a Euro-American one as well – exercises the shaman's ultimate gift. He "makes it up as he goes along." Sun Bear, in other words, creates – out of the past, out of his construction of the past, and out of a California and West Coast present that has left him open to the twin teachings of environmentalism and the New Age. Cleaning up pollution did not figure as a motive in traditional American Indian nature religions. Hugging a tree sounds as likely to be a message from an Esalen encounter weekend as to be a message from an Indian grandfather. Sharing energies in sexual congress has a distinctly contemporary ring. And doing workshops for the uninitiated would hardly occupy the time of a nineteenth-century Ojibwa mother.

5.13 'SPOKESPERSONS FOR INDIAN SPIRITUALITY'

Amanda Porterfield

From 'American Indian spirituality as a countercultural movement', Porterfield, A., in *Religion in Native North America*, Vecsey, C. (ed.), University of Idaho Press, 1990, pp. 153–5.

Non-Indian spokespersons for American Indian spirituality are also influential, especially among non-Indians. They include the poet Gary Snyder, who calls on Americans to restructure their society in terms of the religious devotion to nature characteristic of American Indians and other tribal peoples (1957, 1974); the anthropologist Michael Harner, whose books and workshops instruct Americans in shamanic techniques (1980); and the popular but troublesome Jamake Highwater, alias Gregory Markapoulos, a son of Greek immigrants to America (Adams 1984), who argues that the "primal" consciousness manifest in Indian and African art inspired the pioneers of modern art (1981), and who represents himself in books and television appearances as having Blackfoot and Cherokee ancestry.

All of these spokespersons function independently of one another. The variety of tribal affiliations they represent helps explain the lack of unified institutional organization that permits such an array of independent representatives. These tribal affiliations also explain the persistent idea that some spokespersons are authentic while others are not. Although there is no single institutional supervising entry into and expulsion from the movement, tribal leaders have exercised a kind of de facto supervision over spokespersons for American Indian spirituality who claim tribal authenticity. For example, the activist Indian editor Rupert Costo questioned Hyemeyohsts Storm's ancestry and condemned his book as "blasphemous" (1972). Costo and Cheyenne tribal leaders found Storm's book offensive, not only because his rendering of Cheyenne colors and directions departed from their versions, but also because his published interpretation of Cheyenne religion occurred without tribal sanction.

Distinctions between authentic spokespersons and pretenders is a persistent theme in discussions about American Indian spirituality. Although the nature of these distinctions often seems to be racial, with critics of Storm and Highwater, for example, implying that these men are spiritually inauthentic because their parents were not full-blooded Indians, the real distinction behind this preoccupation with authenticity is a cultural one. Representatives of American Indian spirituality who actually participate in tribal culture speak with the authority of tribal rootedness. Their involvement in tribal culture sanctions their interpretation of American Indian spirituality.

Some direct connection with tribal cultures is essential to the religious movement of American Indian spirituality because its function is one of mediation between tribal and middle-class western cultures. This mediating function accounts for the role difference between religious leaders of tribal cultures and tribally sanctioned spokespersons for American Indian spirituality. For example, Oren Lyons represents the Haudenosaunee to the outside world, but this role is quite different from that of clan chiefs, whose primary responsibility is to represent the Haudenosaunee to themselves. Similarly, Black Elk's role as Oglala holy man was different from his role as representative of American Indian spirituality to non-Indian Americans. The function of American Indian spirituality as a bridge between tribal and middle-class western cultures explains both the importance of tribal representation in the movement and the difference between this representation and tribal leadership.

However divisive questions about authenticity and tribal sanction may be, advocates of American Indian spirituality are remarkably similar in their agreement on certain fundamental points of belief. The belief system of American Indian spirituality is not controversial, although representations of any particular tribe's relationship to that system may be, as in the case of Costo's criticism of Storm. The universally agreed-upon tenets of American Indian spirituality include condemnation of American exploitation of nature and mistreatment of Indians, regard to precolonial America as a sacred place where nature and humanity lived in plentiful harmony, certainty that American Indian attitudes are opposite to those of American culture and morally superior on every count, and an underlying belief that American Indian attitudes toward nature are a means of revitalizing American culture.

The common world view underlying the messages of various spokespersons for American Indian spirituality is both countercultural and religious: countercultural in its reversal of the dominant religious categories of Western culture,[1] and religious in its devotion to the Indian as a symbol of cosmic suffering and redemption as well as in its preoccupation with the immorality of Western culture and the moral superiority of native cultures. The appropriateness of characterizing American Indian spirituality as a countercultural religious movement emerges most clearly through discussion of its historical antecedents and evolution.

The American Indian spirituality movement is the historical successor of the Indian revitalization movements that began in the late eighteenth century with religious visionaries like the Delaware prophet, Neolin. It carries the beliefs and strategies of earlier revitalization movements into the present age by reaffirming the belief characteristic of those movements that American Indian lifeways are sacred and Euroamerican ways are profane and corrupt. Moreover, proponents of American Indian spirituality follow the same strategy as leaders of earlier revitalization movements in appealing to Christian ideas as a means of discrediting American culture and celebrating their own. But as they carry the beliefs and strategies of earlier movements into the present age, spokespersons for American Indian spirituality address a different and larger audience than did the prophets of earlier movements. While participation in those was largely confined to Indians whose tribal structures had been drastically altered by colonization, proponents of American Indian spirituality speak directly to non-Indian audiences disaffected by American government, capitalism, and technology. Moreover, while leaders of earlier movements worked to preserve Indian cultures against destruction and assimilation, proponents of American Indian spirituality work for the transformation of American culture in terms of Indian values. These differences reflect both the assimilation of Indians into American culture and their roles as spiritual authorities within it.

---

1. Sociologist J. Milton Yinger defines a counterculture as an "inversion" of "(historically) created designs for living" (1982, 40).

BIBLIOGRAPHY

Adams, Hank. 1984. The golden Indian. *Akwesasne Notes.* (Late Summer): 10–12.

Costo, Rupert. 1972. *Seven Arrows* desecrates Cheyenne. *The Indian Historian* 5:2 (Summer).

Harner, Michael. 1980. *The way of the shaman: A guide to power and healing.* New York: Harper and Row.

Highwater, Jamake. 1981. *The primal mind: Vision and reality in Indian America.* New York: New American Library.

Lyons, Oren, 1980. An Iroquois perspective. In *American Indian environments: Ecological issues in Native American history,* eds. Christopher Vecsey and Robert W. Venables. Syracuse: Syracuse University Press.

Neihardt, John G. [1932] 1961. *Black Elk speaks: Being the life story of a holy man of the Oglala Sioux.* Lincoln: University of Nebraska Press.

Synder, Gary. 1957. *Earth house hold.* New York: New Directions. 1974, Turtle Island. New York: New Directions.

Storm, Hyemeyohsts. 1972. *Seven arrows.* New York: Ballantine Books.

5.14 'AN EARTH FIRST! ACTIVIST ON THE IMPORTANCE OF RITUAL'

Delores LaChapelle

From 'Thoughts on Autumn Equinox about the importance of ritual', in *The Earth First! Reader: Ten Years of Radical Environmentalism*, Davis, J. (ed), Salt Lake, Peregrine Smith Books, 1991, pp. 232–6.

Most primal or indigenous societies around the world had three common characteristics: they had an intimate, conscious relationship with their place; they were stable "sustainable" cultures, often lasting for thousands of years; and they had a rich ceremonial and ritual life culminating in seasonal festivals. They saw these three as intimately connected. Out of the hundreds of examples, consider the following:

- The Tukano Indians of the northwest Amazon River basin, guided by their shamans, use various myths and rituals that prevent over-hunting or over-fishing. They view their universe as a circuit of energy in which the entire cosmos participates. The circuit consists of "a limited quantity of procreative energy that flows continually between man and animals, between society and nature." Colombian anthropologist Reichel Dolmatoff notes that the Tukano have little interest in exploiting natural resources more effectively but are greatly interested in "accumulating more factual knowledge about biological reality and, above all, about knowing what the physical world requires from men."[1]
- The Kung people of Africa's Kalahari Desert have been living in the same place for 11,000 years! They have very few material belongings but their ritual life is one of the most sophisticated of any group.[2]
- Roy Rappaport has shown that the rituals of the Tsembaga of New Guinea allocate scarce protein for the humans who need it without causing irreversible damage to the land. Ritual dictates the proper ways and times to hunt the pigs which supply their protein.[3]
- The longest inhabited place in the United States is the Hopi village of Oraibi. At certain times of the year the Hopi here may spend up to half their time in ritual activity.
- About ten years ago the old *cacique* of San Juan Pueblo in New Mexico died. The young man elected to take over as the new *cacique* will do nothing for the rest of his life but take care of the ritual life of the Pueblo. All his personal needs will be taken care of by the tribe, but he cannot travel more than 60 miles or one hour from the Pueblo. The distance has grown with the use of cars but the time remains one hour. His presence is that important to the life of the Pueblo.

1. G. Reichel-Dolmatoff, "Cosmology as Ecological Analysis", in *Man: Journal of the Royal Anthropological Institute* (9–78).
2. Richard B. Lee, "What Hunters Do for a Living," in Lee and DeVore, *Man the Hunter*, Aldine Publishing Co, 1968.
3. Rappaport, *Pigs for their Ancestors*, Yale University Press, 1968.

Our Western European industrial culture provides a striking contrast to all these examples.* We have idolized ideals, rationality and a limited kind of "practicality," and have regarded the rituals of these other cultures as at best frivolous curiosities. The results are all too evident. We've only been here a few hundred years and already we have done irreparable damage to vast areas of what we call the United States. As Gregory Bateson notes, "mere purposive rationality is necessarily pathogenic and destructive of life."

We have tried to relate to the world around us through only the left side of our brain, and we are clearly failing. If we are to reestablish a viable relationship, we must rediscover the wisdom of these other cultures who knew that their relationship to the land required the whole of their being. What we call their "ritual and ceremony" was a sophisticated social and spiritual technology for such a relationship.

The Industrial Growth Society (IGS) has caused us to forget so much in the last 200 years that we hardly know where to begin. It helps to begin by remembering. All traditional cultures, even our own Western European ancestors, had seasonal festivals and rituals. The true origins of most of our modern holidays date back to these seasonal festivals.

The purpose of seasonal festivals is to periodically revive the *topocosm*. Gaster coined this word from the Greek *topo* for place and *cosmos* for world order. Topocosm means "the world order of a particular place." The topocosm is the entire complex of any given locality conceived as a living organism – not just the human community but the total community – plants, animals and oils. The topocosm is not only the present community but also that continuous entity of which the present community is but the current manifestation.[4]

Seasonal festivals make use of myths, art, dance and games. Each of these aspects of ritual serve to keep open the essential connections within ourselves. Festivals connect the conscious with the unconscious, the right hemisphere with the left hemisphere of the brain, and the cortex with the older three brains (including the Oriental *tan tien*, four fingers below the navel). They also connect the human with the non-human – earth, sky, animals and plants.

I'm often asked, "What relevance does this kind of ritual have for people who live in the city?" The modern city of Siena in Italy provides a good answer. Siena with a population of 59,000 has the lowest crime rate of any Western city of comparable size. Drug-addiction and violence are virtually unknown. Why? Because it is a tribal, ritualized city organized around the contrada (clans) – with names such as *Chiocciola*, the Snail, *Tartule*, the Turtle, etc. – and the *Palio* (the annual horse race). Each *contrada* has its own territory, church songs, patron saint and rituals. Particular topographical features of each *contrada's* area are ritualized and mythologized. The ritualized customs of the city extend back to the worship of Diana, the Roman goddess of the moon. Her attributes were taken over by the worship of Mary when Christianity came in.

Such famous writers as Henry James, Ezra Pound and Aldous Huxley sensed the energy of the city and tried to write about it, but none of them even faintly grasped the year-long ritualized life behind it. About one week before the day of the Palio race, Siena workmen begin to bring yellow earth (la terra) from the fields outside Siena and spread it over the great central square, the Campo, thus linking the city with its origins in the earth of its place.

---

* Most of these primitive groups' cultures have been virtually destroyed in the last 20 years by the Industrial Growth Society, but they are our only sources of information on what constitutes a sustainable culture.

4. Theodore Gaster, *Thespis: Ritual, Myth and Drama in the Ancient Near East*, Norton and Co., 1977 ed.

Anytime during the year when someone needs to be cheered up, the sad person is told not to worry because soon there will be "la terra in piazza."

The horse race serves two main purposes. In the intense rivalry surrounding the race, each *contrada* "rekindles its own sense of identity." The Palio also provides the Sienese with an outlet for their aggression, and as such is a ritual war. The horse race grew out of games that were actually mimic battles used to mark the ends of religious festivals in the old days.

The Palio is truly a religious event. On this one day of the year the *contrada's* horse is brought into the church of its patron saint. In the act of blessing the horse, the *contrada* itself is blessed. This horse race is the community's greatest rite.[5]

If we want to build a sustainable culture, it is not enough to "go back to the land." That's what our pioneering ancestors did and, as the famous Western artist Charles Russell said, "A pioneer is a man who comes to virgin country, traps off all the fur, kills off the wild meat, plows the roots up . . . and calls it civilization."

If we are to truly re-connect with the land, we need to change our perceptions. As long as we limit ourselves to rationality, we will be disconnected from the deep ecology of our place. As Heidegger explains: "Dwelling is not primarily inhabiting but taking care of and creating that space within which something comes into its own and flourishes." It takes repeated rituals through the years for real dwelling. Likewise, as Roy Rappaport observes, "knowledge will never replace respect in man's dealings with ecological systems, for the ecological systems in which man participates are likely to be so complex that he may never have sufficient comprehension of their content and structure to permit him to predict the outcome of many of his own acts." Ritual is the focused way in which we both experience and express that respect.

Ritual is the pattern that connects. It provides communication at all levels – communication among all the systems within the individual human organism; between people within a group; between groups within a city; and throughout all these levels, between the human and the non-human in the natural environment. Ritual provides us with a tool for learning to think logically, analogically and ecologically. Perhaps most important, during rituals we have the experience, unique in our culture, of neither opposing nature nor trying to be in communication with nature; but of finding ourselves within nature.

---

5. Alan Dundes and Alessandro Falassi, *La Terra in Piazza: An Interpretation of the Palio of Siena*, University of California Press, 1975.

5.15 'DRAWING DOWN THE MOON'

Margot Adler

From 'The Wiccana revival', in *Drawing Down the Moon: Witches, Druids, Goddess-worshippers and Other Pagans in America Today*, Adler, M., Beacon, 1986, pp. 41–5.

What can we learn of this witch figure? . . . She takes energies out of consciousness and pulls them toward the unconscious to forge a link between the two mental systems . . .

We know the roots of our consciousness reach deep into the nonhuman, archaic unconscious. . . . The witch archetype makes visible to us the very depths of what is humanly possible, the great silences at the edge of being. . . .

She stirs up storms that invade whole communities of people. She conducts vast collective energies to our very doorstep. . . . These undirected unhumanized spirit forces are symbolized for us as ghosts, dead ancestors, gods and goddesses come up from the world below. . . .

What do we gain from this vision? A sense of perspective.... The witch-seer makes us see into the proportions of life. . . .

The radical impact of the witch archetype is that she invades the civilized community. She enters it. She changes it. . . . She heralds the timeless process of originating out of the unconscious new forms of human consciousness and society.

Interpreting the word [handwritten annotation]

DR. ANN BELFORD ULANOV

Difficulty in describing the word [handwritten annotation]

The word witch is defined so differently by different people that a common definition seems impossible. "A witch," you may be told, "is someone with supernatural powers," but revivalist Witches do not believe in a supernatural. "A witch," you may be told, "is someone who practices magic," but revivalist Witches will tell you that Witchcraft is a religion, and some will tell you that magic is secondary. "A witch," you may be told, "is a worker of evil," but revivalist Witches will tell you that they promote the good. The historian Elliot Rose observed that the word *witch* is "free to wander, and does wander, among a bewildering variety of mental associations," and the occultist Isaac Bonewits has asked:

> Is a "witch" anyone who does magic or who reads fortunes? Is a "witch" someone who worships the Christian Devil? Is a Witch (capital letters this time) a member of a specific Pagan faith called "Wicca"? Is a "witch" someone who practices Voodoo, or Macumba, or Candomblé? Are the anthropologists correct when they define a "witch" as anyone doing magic (usually evil) outside an approved social structure?

Bonewits does away with some of this confusion, as we shall see, by dividing Witches into many types, including Classical, Gothic, Familial, Immigrant, Ethnic, Feminist, and Neo-Pagan. And in this book we are (mostly) talking about Neo-Pagan Witches – the revival, or re-creation, or new creation (depending on your viewpoint) of a Neo-Pagan nature religion that calls itself Witchcraft, or Wicca, or the Craft, or the Old Religion(s). This religion, with its sources of inspiration in pre-Christian Western Europe, has a specific history – clouded though it may be – and a specific way of being in the world.

We saw that the word *witch* comes from the Old English *wicce, wicca,* and these words derive from a root *wic,* or *weik,* which has to do with religion and magic. We saw that many practitioners of Wicca will tell you that Wicca means *wise,* and that, in any case, the Wicca are seekers of wisdom. Others will tell you that Wicca comes from a root meaning to bend or turn, and that the Witch is the bender and changer of reality.

But etymology does not help one to confront the confusing feeling that lies behind the word *witch.* The very power of the word lies in its imprecision. It is not merely a word, but an archetype, a cluster of powerful images. It resonates in the mind and, in the words of Dr. Ulanov, takes us down to deep places, to forests and fairy tales and myths and friendships with animals. The price we pay for clarity of definition must not be a reduction in the force of this cluster of images.

Among the Wicca, there is a division over this word *witch.* Some regard it as a badge of pride, a word to be reclaimed, much as militant lesbians have reclaimed the word *dyke.* But others dislike the word. "It has a rather bad press," one Witch told me. Another said, "I did not plan to call myself Witch. It found me. It just happened to be a name – perhaps a bad name – that was attached to the things I was seeking." One Neo-Pagan journal stated that the term *Witchcraft* is inappropriate as "it refers to a decayed version of an older faith."

Some Witches will tell you that they prefer the word *Craft* because it places emphasis on a way of practicing magic, an occult technology. And there are Witches – the "classical" ones of Bonewits' definition – who define Witchcraft not as a religion at all, but simply as a craft. Others will say they are of the "Old Religion," because they wish to link themselves with Europe's pre-Christian past, and some prefer to say they are "of the Wicca," in order to emphasize a family or tribe with special ties. Still others speak of their practices as "the revival of the ancient mystery traditions." But when they talk among themselves they use these terms interchangeably, and outsiders are left as confused as ever.

Sadly, it is only poets and artists who can make religious experiences come alive in telling about them. Most descriptions of mystical experiences are monotonous and banal – unlike the experiences themselves. And that is why, after all other chapters lay finished, this one remained unwritten. I had stacks of notes lying in piles on tables: descriptions of Witchcraft by Witches; definitions of Witchcraft by scholars; theories of the Murrayites and anti-Murrayites; theories of modern Neo-Pagan writers like Adrian Kelly and Isaac Bonewits; a hundred stories and anecdotes.

But Ed Fitch, a Craft priest in California, told me, "To be a Witch is to draw on our archetypical roots and to draw strength from them. It means to put yourself into close consonance with *some ways that are older than the human race itself.*" I felt a slight chill at the back of my neck on hearing those words. And then I remembered a quotation from Robert Graves' *The White Goddess* that the true "function of poetry is religious invocation of the Muse," that all true poetry creates an "experience of mixed exaltation and horror that her presence excites." Graves said that one must think both mythically and rationally, and never confuse the two and never be surprised "at the weirdly azoological beasts that walk into the circle."

So perhaps the best way to begin to understand the power behind the simple word *witch* is to enter that circle in the same spirit in which C.G. Jung consulted the I Ching before writing his famous introduction to the Wilhelm-Baynes translation. Do it, perhaps, on a full moon, in a park or in the clearing of a wood. You don't need any of the tools you will read about in books on the Craft. You need no special clothes, or lack of them. Perhaps you might make up a chant, a string of names of gods and goddesses who were loved and familiar to you from childhood myths, a simple string of names for earth and moon and stars, easily repeatable like a mantra.

And perhaps, as you say those familiar names and feel the earth and air, the moon appears a bit closer, and perhaps the wind rustling the leaves suddenly seems in rhythm with your own breathing. Or perhaps the chant seems louder and all the other sounds far away. Or perhaps the woods seem strangely noisy. Or unspeakably still. And perhaps the clear line that separates you from bird and tree and small lizards seems to melt. Whatever else, your relationship to the world of living nature changes. The Witch is the changer of definitions and relationships.

Once on a strange and unfamiliar shore a group of young and ignorant revivalist Witches were about to cast their circle and perform a rite. They were, like most modern Wiccas, city people, misplaced on this New England beach. They had brought candles in jars and incense and charcoal and wine and salt and their ritual knives and all the implements that most books on the modern Craft tell you to use. The wind was blowing strongly and the candles wouldn't stay lit. The charcoal ignited and blew quickly away. The moon vanished behind a cloud and all the implements were misplaced in the darkness. Next, the young people lost their sense of direction and suddenly found themselves confronting the elemental powers of nature, the gods of cold and wind and water and wandering. The land – once the site of far different ancient religious practices – began to exert its own presence and make its own demands upon the psyche. Frightened, they quickly made their way home.

The point of all this is simple. All that follows – the distinctions, the definitions, the history and theory of the modern Craft – means nothing unless the powerful and emotional *content* that hides as a source behind the various contemporary forms is respected. This content lies in the mind. There is something connected with the word *witch* that is atemporal, primordial, prehistoric (in *feeling*, whether or not in *fact*), something perhaps "older than the human race itself." The story of the revival of Wicca is – whatever else it may be – the story of people who are searching among powerful archaic images of nature, of life and death, of creation and destruction. Modern Wiccans are using these images to change their relationship to the world. The search for these images, and the use of them, must be seen as valid, no matter how limited and impoverished the outer forms of the Wiccan revival sometimes appear, and no matter how misreported this revival is in the press.

5.16 'THERE HAVE BEEN WITCHES IN ALL AGES'

Gerald Gardner

From *Witchcraft Today*, Gardner, Gerald B., London, Rider, 1954, pp. 33–8, 50.

There have been witches in all ages and countries. That is, there have been men and women who have had a knowledge of cures, philtres, charms and love potions and at times poisons. Sometimes it was believed they could affect the weather, bringing rain or drought. At times they were hated, at times they were loved; at times they were highly honoured, at times persecuted. They claimed to be, or were credited with being, in communication with the world of spirits, the dead, and sometimes with the lesser gods. It was generally thought that their powers were hereditary, or that the craft was apt to run in families. People went to them whenever they were in trouble for cures, good crops, good fishing or whatever their need was. They were, in fact, the priestesses or representatives of the little gods, who because they were little would bother to listen to the troubles of little people. They are usually thought of as wild dancers, as being 'not too strict'.

In the Stone Ages man's chief wants were good crops, good hunting, good fishing, increase in flocks and herds and many children to make the tribe strong. It became the witches' duty to perform rites to obtain these things. This was probably a matriarchal age, when man was the hunter and woman stayed at home making medicine and magic. Historically, the matriarchal period has been tentatively dated from the middle of the ninth to the middle of the seventh millennium B.C., during which time caves, trees, the moon and stars all seem to have been reverenced as female emblems. So the myth of the Great Mother came into existence and woman was her priestess. Probably at the same time the men had a hunter's god, who presided over the animals. Later, perhaps, came the idea of a future life and thoughts of the next world as being an unhappy place unless you could attain to the abode of the gods, a sort of paradise. This was thought of as a place of rest and refreshment where one would grow young again ready for reincarnation on earth.

Primitive man feared to be born again outside his own tribe, so his ritual prayers to his god were that he might be born again in the same place and at the same time as his loved ones, and that he might remember and love them again. The god who rules this paradise must, I think, have been Death, but somehow he is identified with the hunting god and wears his horns. This god of death and hunting, or his representative, seems at one time to have taken the lead in the cult, and man became the master. But it is emphasised that because of her beauty, sweetness and goodness, man places woman, as the god placed the goddess, in the chief place, so that woman is dominant in the cult practice.

What probably happened was this: there was an organised tribal religion, with a male tribal god, and an order of priestesses and their husbands who looked after the magic. The chief priest of the tribal cult was dominant when he attended their meetings, but in his absence the priestess ruled. My witches speak of him as god of 'Death and what lies beyond': by this they not only mean the life in the next world but resurrection (or reincarnation). He rules a sort of happy hunting ground, where ordinary folk go and forgather with like-minded people; it may be pleasant or unpleasant according to your nature. According to your merits you may be reincarnated in time, and take your chance where and amnong whom this takes place; but the god has a special paradise for his worshippers, who have conditioned their bodies and natures on earth, who enjoy special advantages and are prepared more swiftly for reincarnation which is done by the power of the goddess in such circumstances as to ensure that you will be reborn into your own tribe again. This is taken nowadays to mean into witch circles. It would seem to involve an unending series of reincarnations; but I am told that in time you may become one of the mighty ones, who are also called the mighty dead. I can learn nothing about them, but they seem to be like demigods – or one might call them saints.

At a later time there were, perhaps, other reasons why women may have been dominant in the cult practice, though, as I point out later, there are quite as many men among witches as women. The Bible tells us of the poor persecuted Witch of Endor, working in secret when all other witches had been driven out of the land. It also tells usof Huldah the Sorceress, living in state in Jerusalem, consulted by the King on high points of religion when the High Priest himself could not answer. The unfortunate consequence of the low position of woman in the Middle Ages, when it was against the general tradition of the church to try and improve her status, or raise it to what it was in pre-Christian times, should be remembered. So the Church fulminated against Haracelsus when he wrote a book in praise of women, calling him a 'woman worshipper'. As Mr Hughes says:

> 'This meant that many women resented this subjugation, and a secret religion, where woman was important and which made sexual activity a proud mystery instead of a drudgery, was made. This religion also served as a psychological Cave of Adullam* for emotional women, repressed women, masculine women, and those suffering from personal disappointment, or from nervous maladjustment which had not been resolved by the local resources of the Church.'

The individual motives which persuaded a person to become a witch, other than those to whom witchcraft was an old religion, must have been fairly complicated. As other cults have found, although the practices gave rest, peace, and joy to many, some of their recruits were rather an embarrassment, and as legions of spies may have tried to gain entrance to betray them, from an early date recruits were admitted only from people who were of the blood; that is, from a witch family. The various rituals of worship, secrets of herbal lore, and the Great Secret of what they call magic, have been handed down to what has become more or less a family secret society.

In Palestine and other countries there are two kinds of witches: the ignorant herbalist and charm-seller, and the witch who is a descendant of a line of priests and priestesses of an old and probably Stone Age religion, who have been initiated in a certain way (received into the circle) and become the recipients of certain ancient learning.

---

* A Biblical place of refuge: 1 Samuel 22:1.

At times the Church ignored the witch; but when the Papacy became firmly established the priests treated the cult as a hated rival and tried to persecute it out of existence. The Puritans also took up the work with glee, and between them they practically succeeded.

. . .

As part of this campaign all sorts of false ideas were spread until the popular notion of a witch became that of the common definition: 'a witch is an old woman who flies through the air on a broomstick'. Now no witch ever flew through the air on a broomstick or on anything else, at least not until aeroplanes came in. There is indeed a fertility charm to bring good crops which is performed by riding on a pole, or broom, as a hobby-horse. Doubtless ancient witches practised this rite, leaping high to make the crops grow. In early trials witnesses speak of seeing the accused riding on poles, or brooms, across the fields (not through the air), and this was often accepted as the evidence that they were practising fertility magic, which became a penal offence. In the Castletown Museum there is one of these poles for riding, the head being carved in the shape of a phallus to bring fertility.

WITCH PRACTICES

. . . The people who were attracted to the witch cult were chiefly of the intelligent classes comprising craftsmen, soldiers, merchants, doctors, sailors, farmers and clerks. They were all people who wanted adventure, the 'bright young things' of the period, combined, of course, with those who always flock to anything secret or odd or religious in the hope of relief; that is, people who are to some degree sexually unbalanced. Then, of course, there was the village wise-woman with her cures and curses, and the inmates of the castles and great houses. Not by any means did all these people 'belong', as the witches phrase it – they speak merely of 'belonging', never adding to what – but these were the classes of folk who chiefly attended the sabbats of the men of the heaths; and some of them at least were initiated into the mysteries.

5.17 'THE BURNING TIMES'

Starhawk

From *Dreaming the Dark*, Starhawk, London, Unwin, 1982, pp. 183–5.

She is afraid. Her own fear has a smell more pungent than the needles of pine that her feet crush on the forest path. The earth steams after spring rain. Her own heart is louder than the lowing of cattle on the common. The old woman carries a basket of herbs and roots she has dug; it feels heavy as time on her arm. Her feet on the path are her mother's feet, her grandmother's, her grandmother's grandmothers'; for centuries she has walked under these oaks and pines, culled the herbs and brought them back to dry under the eaves of her cottage on the common. Always, the people of the village have come to her; her hands are healing hands, they can turn a child in the womb; her murmuring voice can charm away pain, can croon the restless to sleep. She believes she has faery blood in her veins, blood of the Old Race who raised standing stones to the open sky and built no churches. The thought of the church makes her shiver; she remembers her dream of the night before – the paper pinned to the church door. She couldn't read it. What had it been? The proclamation of a Witch-hunt? She passes her hands over her eyes. These days, the Sight is a trouble; her dreams are haunted by the faces of women in torment; their sleepless eyes, the lids forced open as they walk up and down, night after night, weak from hunger, their bodies shaved and displayed to the crowd, pricked deep to find the evidence they call devil's marks, then taken for the private amusement of the jailors. And they were mild here in England, where Witches were only hung. She thought of the tales, whispered at Meetings, of Germany and France, of devices to crush bones and tear limbs out of their sockets, of veins ripped apart and blood spilling on the dirt, and of flesh charred as flames rose about the stake. Could she keep silent under that – or would she break, confess to anything, name anyone they wanted as her fellow Witch? She doesn't know; she hopes she will never know.

The old woman makes a banishing sign with her left hand and walks on. Perhaps the paper in the dream was something else entirely. But the bad smell clung to it. Enclosure? Were they going to divide the common land, build fences, tear down the little cottages like her own? She feels a stab under her bodice and sits down, hardly able to breathe. Yes, that was it. What will she do? Who will speak for her or take her in? She has no husband, no children. Once the village would have protected her, but now the priests have done their work well. The sick fear her even when they come to her for help. The villagers fear each other. The bad harvests, the rents, and the always increasing price of food – there are too many rats scratching at the same little pile of grain, and the priests and the preachers are always at them to scratch at each other. Still, there were uprisings in the West and in the North against enclosure. There could be risings here.

She turns and looks deep into the forest. For a moment she is tempted to turn around, to follow the pathway further than she has ever been. Some have said the Old Race still lives in the forest's hidden centre. Would they shelter her? Or would she find the camps of the master-less, the tinkers, the outlaws, those who had been driven, like herself, off the land? Would it be a freer life under the trees? Could they use a healer? And would they someday swarm out from the woods and wastes, an army of the dispossessed, to tear down the fences of the overlords, the manor houses, and the churches, to reclaim their own land for freedom?

She is still. But finally she shoulders her basket and starts off, back toward the village. Young Jonet at the mill is near her time, and the old woman knows it will be a difficult birth. She will need the herbs in this basket.

She is afraid but she walks on. "We have always survived," she tells herself. "We will always survive."

She repeats it, over and over again, like an incantation.

5.18 'SORCERESSES'

Jules Michelet

From 'Introduction', in *Satanism and Witchcraft*,* Michelet, J., New York, Citadel, 1992, pp. viii–x.

Sprenger said, before 1500: "We should speak of the *Heresy of the Sorceresses*, not of the Sorcerers; the latter are of small account." So another writer under Louis XIII: "For one Sorcerer, ten thousand Sorceresses."

"Nature makes them Sorceresses," – the genius peculiar to woman and her temperament. She is born a creature of Enchantment. In Virtue of regularly recurring periods of exaltation, she is a Sibyl; in virtue of love, a Magician. By the fineness of her intuitions, the cunning of her wiles – often fantastic, often beneficent – she is a Witch, and casts spells, at least and lowest lulls pain to sleep and softens the blow of calamity.

All primitive peoples start alike; this we see again and again in the accounts given by travellers. Man hunts and fights. Woman contrives and dreams; she is the mother of fancy, of the gods. She possesses glimpses of the *second sight*, and has wings to soar into the infinitude of longing and imagination. The better to count the seasons, she scans the sky. But earth has her heart as well. Her eyes stoop to the amorous flowers; a flower herself in her young beauty, she learns to know them as playfellows and intimates. A woman, she asks them to heal the men she loves.

Pathetic in their simplicity these first beginnings of Religion and Science! Later on, each province will be separated, we shall see mankind specialize – as medicine-man, astrologer or prophet, necromancer, priest, physician. But in these earliest days woman is all in all, and plays every part.

A strong and bright and vigorous religion, such as was Greek Paganism, begins with the Sibyl, to end with the Sorceress. The first, a virgin fair and beautiful, brilliant in the full blaze of dawn, cradled it, gave it its charm and glamour. In later days, when sick and fallen, in the gloom of the Dark Ages, on heaths and in forests, it was concealed and protected by the Sorceress; her dauntless pity fed its needs and kept it still alive. Thus for religions it is woman is mother, tender protectress and faithful nurse. Gods are like men; they are born and they die on a woman's breast.

But what a price she paid for her fidelity! . . . Magian queens of Persia, enchanting Circé, sublime Sibyl, alas! How are you fallen, how barbarous the transformation you have suffered! . . . She who, from the throne of the Orient, taught mankind the virtues of plants and the motions of the stars, she who, seated on the Delphic tripod and, illumined by the very god of light, gave oracles to a kneeling world, – is the same that, a thousand years later, is hunted like a wild beast, chased from street to street, reviled, buffeted, stoned, scorched with red-hot embers! . . .

The clergy has not stakes enough, the people insults, the child stones, for the unhappy being. The poet, no less a child, throws yet another stone at her, a crueller one still for a woman. Gratuitously insulting, he makes her out always old and ugly. The very word Sorceress or *Witch* calls up the image of the Weird Sisters of *Macbeth*. Yet the cruel witch trials prove exactly the opposite; many perished just because they were young and pretty.

The Sibyl foretold the future; but the Sorceress makes it. Here is the great, the vital distinction. She evokes, conjures, guides Destiny. She is not like Cassandra of old, who foresaw the coming doom so clearly, and deplored it and awaited its approach; she creates the future. Greater than Circé, greater than Medea, she holds in her hand the magic wand of natural miracle, she has Nature to aid and abet her like a sister. Foreshadowings of the modern Prometheus are to be seen in her, – a beginning of industry, above all of the sovereign industry that heals and revivifies men. Unlike the Sibyl, who seemed ever gazing towards the dayspring, she fixes her eyes on the setting sun; but it is just this somber orb of the declining luminary that shows long before the dawn (like the glow on the peaks of the High Alps) a dawn anticipatory of the true day.

The Priest realizes clearly where the danger lies, that an enemy, a menacing rival, is to be feared in this High-priestess of Nature he pretends to despise. Of the old gods she has invented new ones. Beside the old Satan of the past, a new Satan is seen burgeoning in her, a Satan of the future.

5.19 'THE WITCHES OF EASTWICK'

John Updike

From *The Witches of Eastwick*, Updike, John, London, Penguin, 1984, pp. 5, 14–15.

If Alexandra was the large, drifting style of witch, always spreading herself thin to invite impressions and merge with the landscape, and in her heart rather lazy and entropically cool, Jane was hot, short, concentrated like a pencil point, and Sukie Rougemont, busy downtown all day long gathering news and smiling hello, had an oscillating essence. So Alexandra reflected, hanging up. Things fall into threes. And magic occurs all around us as nature seeks and finds the inevitable forms, things crystalline and organic falling together at angles of sixty degrees, the isosceles triangle being the mother of structure.

. . .

She thought she heard the word "hag" or "bag" at her back after she had passed through, but it might have been an acoustic trick, a mistaken syllable of sea-slap.

. . .

Alexandra felt irritated and vengeful. Her insides felt bruised; she resented the overheard insult "hag" and the general vast insult of all this heedless youth prohibiting her from letting her dog, her friend and familiar, run free. She decided to clear the beach for herself and Coal by willing a thunderstorm. One's inner weather always bore a relation to the outer; it was simply a question of reversing the current, which occurred rather easily once power had been assigned to the primary pole, oneself as a woman. So many of Alexandra's remarkable powers had flowed from this mere reappropriation of her assigned self, achieved not until midlife. Not until midlife did she truly believe that she had a right to exist, that the forces of nature had created her not as an afterthought and companion – a bent rib, as the infamous *Malleus Maleficarum* had it – but as the mainstay of the continuing Creation, as the daughter of a daughter and a woman whose daughters in turn would bear daughters.

5.20 'THE WORST WITCH'

Jill Murphy

From *The Worst Witch*, Murphy, Jill, London, Penguin, 1978, pp. 19–21.

First of all everyone sang the school song, which went like this:

> Onward, ever striving onward,
> Proudly on our brooms we fly
> Straight and true above the treetops,
> Shadows on the moonlit sky.
>
> Ne'er a day will pass before us
> When we have not tried our best,
> Kept our cauldrons bubbling nicely,
> Cast our spells and charms with zest.
>
> Full of joy we mix our potions,
> Working by each other's side.
> When our days at school are over
> Let us think of them with pride.

It was the usual type of school song, full of pride, joy and striving. Mildred had never yet mixed a potion with joy, nor flown her broomstick with pride – she was usually too busy trying to keep upright!

5.21 'THE RIDE-BY-NIGHTS'

Walter de la Mare

From *Broomsticks and Beasticles*, Knights Books.

Up on their brooms the Witches stream,
Crooked and black in the crescent's gleam,
One foot high, and one foot low,
Bearded, cloaked and cowled, they go.
'Neath Charlie's Wain they twitter and tweet,
And away they swarm 'neath the Dragon's feet.
With a whoop and a flutter they swing and sway,
And surge pell-mell down the Milky Way.

5.22 'WITCH AT HOME'

Dorothy Edwards

From *Mists and Magic*, Edwards, D. (ed.), Lutterworth Press, 1992, pp. 28–34.

'Several of the inhabitants of these parts are the descendants of witches,' said the woman in grey, waving her hand in a generous sweep that embraced all the valleys and little streams lying at our feet.

She was not at all the sort of person one expected to find upon a mountain summit on a hot afternoon. Clad in a neat suit with a black hat and handbag, and wearing medium-heeled shoes, she had the appearance of a respectable servant of the confidential sort – a lady's maid or companion.

I had set off to climb the steep mountain path that morning. It was a hot day, and I was glad to reach the top. The woman was already there, sitting neatly on a slab of rock. I sat down beside her to get my breath back and enjoy the cool mountain breeze. We fell to discussing the peak on which we were sitting. 'Malkin's Ridge' it was called. The woman told me 'Malkin' was a traditional name for a witch, and that the mountain had been a favourite haunt of witches in olden times.

'Of course, there are drawbacks to having witches in the family,' said the woman. 'Take us, for instance. My Granny was a witch and *her* Granny before her. Indeed, I heard that Great-Great-Great-Granny's Granny was burned by order of the magistrates of her day. My Granny had a pretty bad time with the villagers herself. They pulled down her cottage and threw her into the duckpond which was fortunately not very full at the time.

'But that was in Queen Victoria's time, that was, and what with all the new steam engines and the electric telegraphs, by then the magistrates had given up believing in witches, so half the village was sent to prison and the other half was fined.

'The Squire's lady wife got up a subscription among the local gentry for Granny. They settled her down in a nice new little cottage with lace curtains and everything, and basins of hot soup every day, and free coals and potatoes.

'It was all clean and new to begin with, but Gran soon made herself at home. Once she had encouraged a few spiders and been out on one or two midnight trips round the local graveyards, it looked quite home-like. In fact, in six months you couldn't tell the lace curtains from the cobwebs.

'Mind you, Squire's Lady wasn't pleased. But when Gran made her up a bottle of special medicine that cured her rheumatism, she wouldn't hear a word against her. In fact, she grew quite proud of Granny – said she was "quaint" and used to bring her friends round to watch while Granny made her brews.

'Now, my Gran was very respected in witch-circles. There was always a special place reserved for her at the Sabbat meetings. She had a lot to say in the running of the coven – in fact, you could say she was a sort of chairman of their committee.

'But alas, my Mum was her only child, and she turned out a real disappointment. She just didn't show any interest in the witch profession at all. She hadn't the head for it, I suppose!

'Even a simple little thing like turning herself into a hare went wrong so that she couldn't get back to normal in time for school next day, and my poor Granny had to keep her in a hutch beside the back door telling goodness knows what lies to school inspectors until the spell wore off of its own accord – it hadn't been a strong one, fortunately! The only time Mum ever mounted a broomstick she fell off and went right through the Vicar's conservatory roof! As Granny said, the only use my mother had for a broomstick was for sweeping floors!

'Mad about housework was my Mum. No one knew where she got it from, but there it was. I remember Granny saying that as a baby she'd sit up in her crib and rub away at its wickerwork with the corner of her little blanket for all the world as if she were cleaning it – before she'd grown a tooth to her head!

'Poor Granny did her best, of course. She even engaged a very expensive continental warlock to tutor Mum in the Secret Arts, and she set her up with a fine black cat whose ancestry stretched back to ancient Egypt. But the warlock admitted after only one day's teaching that Mum's was a hopeless case, and was so sorry for Granny that he refused to take a penny of his fee. As for the black cat, after sharpening its claws once or twice on the hearth rug and getting scolded for it by my Mum who couldn't bear the rasping noise, it just got up and walked out of the house, and was never seen again.

'The final blow fell when Mum was eighteen or so. Poor old Granny flew home one night after a particularly successful weekend rally of the Northumberland Malkins to find that her bundles of herbs, her charms, the stuffed alligator and all her bottles of potions had been thrown out onto the rubbish heap.

'In her absence, Mum had given in to temptation and spring-cleaned the house! The windows were shining, the lace curtains had been resurrected, washed and starched and now hung in all their glory with a couple of red geraniums in pots on the window-sill between them, and instead of spiders there was a nice yellow canary bird in the cage singing away happily.

'Granny saw then that she must accept the inevitable. She must just get Mother out of the place. She would have to look around for some nice young man to take her off her hands.

'What my Mum needed was a good husband and a cottage of her own where she could clean and polish and brew and bake to her heart's content.

'Mind you, it was a bitter blow to the family pride and Gran said she sobbed aloud as she carted all her little bits and pieces back indoors. And, as you know, witches are unable to shed tears so it was quite a painful experience for the dear old soul.

'It wasn't easy to find a young man willing to take my mother on – even though she was pretty as a picture and as good as gold – for although the Law mightn't consider our Gran a witch, the villagers weren't taking any chances, and the young men kept away.

'At last Granny had to resort to love-charms. And with Mother grumbling all the time about the smells and the mess on the clean kitchen floor, Granny brewed enough love-potion to start off a hundred weddings. It was so strong that the barest whiff drifting across the village roofs below was enough. In no time at all there wasn't a young man left in the village. They were all clustered around Granny's cottage sighing and moaning and carrying on all night, until Mother couldn't get any sleep for the noise outside, and threw buckets of water out of the window over them – and even then they only went home to change and were back again by cockcrow!

'Naturally the village women were furious, and no one had so much as a nod for my poor mother. If they hadn't been afraid of what my Granny might have done to them, I think they would have done Mum an injury. As it was they sent her to Coventry. She tried to explain that she didn't fancy any of their young men – she said it made her feel silly to have them goggling at her and following her around the village every time she went for a stroll. She asked how they would like it if, every time they went out to shake a mat, they stood the chance of tripping over an exhausted suitor on the doorstep. But it was no use. No one was any the more pleased with her for saying that she didn't fancy one of their lads! Such is the contrariness of human nature. So she was lonely, and like all lonely people she threw herself into her work, and as that meant housework poor Granny had a very uncomfortable time of it.

'I really don't know what Gran might have attempted next, but as it happened, things sorted themselves out very tidily. One day they were having high words about Mother having red-polished the flags of the cottage path, when Squire's Lady, new home from abroad, happened to look in for a chat. The good lady was amazed at the change in the appearance of the cottage, and at the reason for the family discord. She shook her head reprovingly at Granny and said she was to be congratulated upon having such a paragon of a child. "Why," said My Lady, "I haven't a servant in my establishment to compare with her. What a pity you cannot spare her, for I should dearly love to take her into my household."

'This was just the opportunity Granny needed! It took her some time to convince Squire's Lady that she really wouldn't stand in her own girl's light when it came to getting a grand job in a great house, but as soon as My Lady saw that Gran was in earnest, she said she would take Mother into her service at once. "But," she said kindly, "I will send her back to you on one day a week so that she can give the place a tidy-up for you." And Gran was glad to see Mum go – even at the price of having to endure a weekly clean-out.

'When Mother got inside the Big House and saw all those rooms and corridors to clean she was delighted and set to at once to give the place a real going-over.

'After that Mum never looked back. She was in her rightful sphere. She learned to cook and darn and knit, and in due course she rose to be Housekeeper to the Squire. It was then that she married my father who was Head Butler, and they stayed at the Big House until My Lady died. Then, feeling they would like a change, they decided to take on man-and-wife jobs in some of those luxury flats, and did very well indeed out of film people and rich foreigners.

'As for me, well, they got me a job in good service as soon as I left school. And I've stayed there ever since. Of course,' said the woman in grey, 'times aren't what they were.

'Yes it was funny about my Mum,' she went on, after pausing a moment to reflect, 'but Granny always said that she suspected there must have been some respectable blood in the family somewhere. There had been tales of a Second Footman, a sober young fellow, who got caught in a magic ring several generations back. It's funny how misfits happen in families!'

Finding that she had no more to say, and being now completely rested, I said, 'Well, I'll have to be going if I'm to get any tea down below.'

'Me too,' said the woman, jerking out of her reverie. 'My Lady wants me to babysit while she and His Lordship have an evening out.' She looked at her watch. 'Goodness, I must fly,' she said.

With this, she rose to her feet. After brushing herself carefully down she reached round to the other side of the boulder on which we had been sitting, took up a broomstick which I swear I hadn't noticed until that moment and, mounting it nimbly, was soon skimming briskly downwards through the warm air.

5.23 'SCIENCE AND RELIGION'

John Hedley Brooke

From 'Introduction', in *Science and Religion: Some Historical Perspectives*, Brooke, J.H., New York, Cambridge University Press, 1991, pp. 1–5.

One often encounters the view that there is an underlying conflict between scientific and religious mentalities, the one dealing in testable facts, the other deserting reason for faith; the one relishing change as scientific understanding advances, the other finding solace in eternal verities. Where such a view holds sway, it is assumed that historical analysis provides supporting evidence – of territorial squabbles in which cosmologies constructed in the name of religion have been forced into retreat by more sophisticated theories coming from science. The nineteenth-century scholars J.W. Draper and A.D. White constructed catalogs of this kind, in which scientific explanations repeatedly challenged religious sensibilities, in which ecclesiastics invariably protested at the presumption, and in which the scientists would have the last laugh.

Typical was White's account of the reluctance of the clergy to fix lightning rods to their churches. In 1745 the bell tower of St Mark's in Venice had once again been shattered in a storm. Within ten years, Benjamin Franklin had mastered the electrical nature of lightning. His conducting rod could have saved many a church from that divine voice of rebuke, which thunder had often been supposed to be. But White reported that such meddling with providence, such presumption in controlling the artillery of heaven, was opposed so long by clerical authorities that the tower of St. Mark's was smitten again in 1761 and 1762. Not until 1766 was the conductor fixed – after which the monument was spared. White's picture of religious scruples and shattered towers symbolizes the popular notion of an intrinsic and perennial conflict. An ounce of scientific knowledge could be more effective in controlling the forces of nature than any amount of supplication.

A second, quite different view also appeals to history for its vindication. Science and religion are sometimes presented not as contending forces but as essentially complementary – each answering a different set of human needs. On this view, scientific and theological language have to be related to different spheres of practice. Discourse about God, which is inappropriate in the context of laboratory practice, may be appropriate in the context of worship, or of self-examination. Historical analysis is often invoked to support this case for separation because it can always be argued that the conflicts of the past were the result of misunderstanding. If only the clergy had not pontificated about the workings of nature, and if only the scientists had not been so arrogant as to imagine that scientific information could meet the deepest human needs, all would have been sweetness and light.

It has been argued, for example, that much of the heat could have been taken out of the Darwinian debates if only the Christian doctrine of creation had been properly formulated. That doctrine, it is said, refers to the ultimate dependence of everything that exists on a Creator. It need not entail the separate creation of every species. Some twentieth-century theologians, notably Rudolph Bultmann, have gone so far as to say that the doctrine of creation has nothing to do with the physical world. Its correct application is to the creation within men and women of an authentic stance toward their earthly predicament. By such means the spheres of science and religion are insulated one from the other.

A third view, which can also be overstated, expresses a more intimate relationship between scientific and religious concerns. Contrary to the first – the conflict model – it is asserted that certain religious beliefs may be conducive to scientific activity. And contrary to the second – the separationist position – it is argued that interaction between religion and science, far from being detrimental, can work to the advantage of both. This more open position clearly appealed to Whitehead, for he raised the question whether the assumption of seventeenth-century natural philosophers, that there was an order imposed on nature, might not have been an unconscious derivative of medieval theology. And he also argued that interaction between religion and science could purge the former of superfluous and obsolete imagery. Once again, the appeal to history is essential to the enterprise. The thesis of the American sociologist, R.K. Merton, that puritan values assisted the expansion of science in seventeenth-century England, would be a good example of historical scholarship in which the mutual relevance of science and religion is affirmed, rather than constant conflict or complete separation.

There are, of course, many variants of these positions. . . .

Serious scholarship in the history of science has revealed so extraordinarily rich and complex a relationship between science and religion in the past that general theses are difficult to sustain. The real lesson turns out to be the complexity. Members of the Christian churches have not all been obscurantists; many scientists of stature have professed a religious faith, even if their theology was sometimes suspect. Conflicts allegedly between science and religion may turn out to be between rival scientific interests, or conversely between rival theological factions. Issues of political power, social prestige, and intellectual authority have repeatedly been at stake. And the histories written by protagonists have reflected their own preoccupations. In his efforts to boost the profile of a rapidly professionalizing scientific community, at the expense of the cultural and educational leadership of the clergy, Darwin's champion, T.H. Huxley, found a conflict model congenial. Extinguished theologians, he declared, lie about the cradle of every science as the strangled snakes beside that of Hercules.

5.24 'WHOSE SCIENCE? WHOSE RELIGION?'

John Brooke and Geoffery Cantor

From *Reconstructing Nature: The Engagement of Science and Religion*, Brooke, J. and Cantor, G., Edinburgh, T&T Clark, 1998, pp. 62–5.

WHOSE SCIENCE?

Defining science is a notoriously difficult exercise. Some have tried to characterize it in terms of its theories, others by its methods, others still by its social organization. Yet these attempts to define the essence of science are rarely of much assistance when we discuss the past. Moreover, the map of science has changed considerably. For example, Biology (as a discipline) originated early in the nineteenth century, Psychology dates from late in that century, and Physics has been variously dated from the early seventeenth to the late nineteenth centuries. The historian must also be prepared to depart from currently-accepted notions of science and engage those sciences and theories that do not feature in the modern pantheon, such as alchemy, scriptural geology, phlogistic chemistry and phrenology. One of the challenges facing the historian is to study such subjects in a non-anachronistic manner, combining understanding and distance in appropriate measures.

The historical study of science and religion must encompass positions and views that would be entertained by few respectable scientists today – such as scriptural geology and Comte's Religion of Humanity. A further reason why such cases deserve study is because their questionable scientific status has been the subject of long-running controversies that shed light on changing conceptions of science. Thus we would argue that scriptural geology deserves inclusion in the historical study of science and religion since it represents a significant (if ultimately unsuccessful) attempt to construct a synthesis of science and religion (although both selectively defined).

. . .

WHOSE RELIGION?

Many of the issues encountered in defining science recur when we try to define religion. While some writers have emphasized its intellectual content by concentrating on theology, others have sought to interpret it socially and culturally. An example of the latter is Durkheim's claim that a religion is 'a unified system of beliefs and practices relative to sacred things'. However, in contrast to most attempts to characterize science, religion is often conceived as possessing substantial individualistic, spiritual and transcendental dimensions. Thus in his celebrated analysis of personal religious experience an earlier Gifford Lecturer, William James, emphasized 'the feelings, acts and experiences of individual men in their solitude, so far as they apprehend themselves to stand in relation to whatever they may consider the divine'. There is no consensus over the definition of religion. Moreover, as historians of religion have repeatedly stressed, definitions of religion have changed considerably over time. Thus what passes as religion depends on the historical context: for example, under the Roman Empire Christians were denominated 'atheists' since they did not accept the dominant belief system. The situation is further complicated if we move outside the Judeo-Christian tradition and confront non-Western cultures which often lack a word to describe what we understand by religion. That there is no universally-accepted definition of religion is all too apparent.

. . .

CULTURAL RELATIVISM

Our problem of specifying the nature of both science and religion takes on a further level of complexity when viewed through a cultural lens. Some years ago the social anthropologist Robin Horton sought to capture both the similarities and the differences between two ways of understanding the world – first, the Western scientific approach and, second, the world-view accepted by traditional African communities. He argued that we fail to make much headway if we dismiss African belief systems as mystical or non-empirical (in contrast with the assumption that science is manifestly rational and empirical). Instead he stressed that, as with modern science, African cosmologies seek to bring order to the world: 'Like atoms, molecules, and waves…the[ir] gods serve to introduce unity into diversity, simplicity into complexity, order into disorder, regularity into anomaly'. In this respect, at least, Western science and African cosmology are similar.

Despite finding such impressive functional similarities, Horton emphasized one fundamental difference. African belief systems are 'closed', in the sense that their theories are unable to change in response to empirical anomalies. Thus if the remedy prescribed by a diviner fails to work, the patient will conclude that the diviner is incompetent but will not cast doubt on the dominant medical theory. Although some philosophers and sociologists have attributed similar protective strategies to Western science, Horton views science as far more open to revision in the light of disconfirming empirical evidence than its African counterpart.

But Horton also emphasized another crucial issue. If we in the West usually experience no difficulty in drawing a sharp divide between science and religion, this is not so for the African. Our terminology breaks down if we try to decide whether an African diviner diagnosing a patient and offering a medical cure falls on the 'science' or the 'religion' side of the divide. Indeed, for Horton, this difficulty results from viewing their 'closed' system from the perspective of our 'open' one. At the outset we must acknowledge that the diviner's activity is not adequately captured by our conventional terminology. Thus the diviner would surely look at us uncomprehendingly if we were to ask him whether his science is in harmony or in conflict with his religion. From this other-cultural perspective both Western science and Western religion appear strangely parochial. Yet, it may be objected, this line of argument possesses limited applicability in our own culture because of the way we conventionally contrast science with religion. But, if we look closely, and particularly at the past, we shall also find many instances where religion and science cannot be so easily distinguished from one another – scriptural geology being one such case. Indeed, one of the enduring legacies of the conflict thesis is that we have continually to remind ourselves and our students that this is not the natural or necessarily valid way of conceptualizing the relation between science and religion. Moreover, the very term 'the relation between' implicitly demarcates science from religion. Linguistic conventions seem to impose unreasonable restrictions on what we say, write and, perhaps, think.

5.25 'PSYCHOLOGY AND RELIGION'

Carl Jung

From *Psychology and Religion: West and East*, Jung, C.G., second edition, London, Routledge and Kegan Paul, 1969, pp. 6–10.

Inasmuch as religion has a very important psychological aspect, I deal with it from a purely empirical point of view, that is, I restrict myself to the observation of phenomena and I eschew any metaphysical or philosophical considerations. I do not deny the validity of these other considerations, but I cannot claim to be competent to apply them correctly.

I am aware that most people believe they know all there is to be known about psychology, because they think that psychology is nothing but what they know of themselves. But I am afraid psychology is a good deal more than that. While having little to do with philosophy, it has much to do with empirical facts, many of which are not easily accessible to the experience of the average man. It is my intention to give you a few glimpses of the way in which practical psychology comes up against the problem of religion.

. . .

Since I am going to present a rather unusual argument, I cannot assume that my audience will be fully acquainted with the methodological standpoint of the branch of psychology I represent. This standpoint is exclusively phenomenological, that is, it is concerned with occurrences, events, experiences – in a word, with facts. Its truth is a fact and not a judgment. When psychology speaks, for instance, of the motif of the virgin birth, it is only concerned with the fact that there is such an idea, but it is not concerned with the question whether such an idea is true or false in any other sense. The idea is psychologically true inasmuch as it exists. Psychological existence is subjective in so far as an idea occurs in only one individual. But it is objective in so far as that idea is shared by a society – by a *consensus gentium*.

This point of view is the same as that of natural science. Psychology deals with ideas and other mental contents as zoology, for instance, deals with the different species of animals. An elephant is "true" because it exists. The elephant is neither an inference nor a statement nor the subjective judgment of a creator. It is a phenomenon. But we are so used to the idea that psychic events are wilful and arbitrary products, or even the inventions of a human creator, that we can hardly rid ourselves of the prejudiced view that the psyche and its contents are nothing but our own arbitrary invention or the more or less illusory product of supposition and judgment. The fact is that certain ideas exist almost everywhere and at all times and can even spontaneously create themselves quite independently of migration and tradition. They are not made by the individual, they just happen to him – they even force themselves on his consciousness. This is not Platonic philosophy but empirical psychology.

In speaking of religion I must make clear from the start what I mean by that term. Religion, as the Latin word denotes, is a careful and scrupulous observation of what Rudolf Otto aptly termed the *numinosum*, that is, a dynamic agency or effect not caused by an arbitrary act of will. On the contrary, it seizes and controls the human subject, who is always rather its victim than its creator. The *numinosum* – whatever its cause may be – is an experience of the subject independent of his will. At all events, religious teaching as well as the consensus gentium always and everywhere explain this experience as being due to a cause external to the individual. The *numinosum* is either a quality belonging to a visible object or the influence of an invisible presence that causes a peculiar alteration of consciousness. This is, at any rate, the general rule.

There are, however, certain exceptions when it comes to the question of religious practice or ritual. A great many ritualistic performances are carried out for the sole purpose of producing at will the effect of the *numinosum* by means of certain devices of a magical nature, such as invocation, incantation, sacrifice, meditation and other yoga practices, self-inflicted tortures of various descriptions, and so forth. But a religious belief in an external and objective divine cause is always prior to any such performance. The Catholic Church, for instance, administers the sacraments for the purpose of bestowing their spiritual blessings upon the believer; but since this act would amount to enforcing the presence of divine grace by an indubitably magical procedure, it is logically argued that nobody can compel divine grace to be present in the sacramental act, but that it is nevertheless inevitably present since the sacrament is a divine institution which God would not have caused to be if he had not intended to lend it his support.

Religion appears to me to be a peculiar attitude of mind which could be formulated in accordance with the original use of the word *religio*, which means a careful consideration and observation of certain dynamic factors that are conceived as "powers": spirits, daemons, gods, laws, ideas, ideals, or whatever name man has given to such factors in his world as he has found powerful, dangerous, or helpful enough to be taken into careful consideration, or grand, beautiful, and meaningful enough to be devoutly worshipped and loved. In colloquial speech one often says of somebody who is enthusiastically interested in a certain pursuit that he is almost "religiously devoted" to his cause; William James, for instance, remarks that a scientist often has no creed, but his "temper is devout."

I want to make clear that by the term "religion" I do not mean a creed. It is, however, true that every creed is originally based on the one hand upon the experience of the *numinosum* and on the other hand upon πίστις, that is to say, trust or loyalty, faith and confidence in a certain experience of a numinous nature and in the change of consciousness that ensues. The conversion of Paul is a striking example of this. We might say, then, that the term "religion" designates the attitude peculiar to a consciousness which has been changed by experience of the *numinosum*.

Creeds are codified and dogmatized forms of original religious experience. The contents of the experience have become sanctified and are usually congealed in a rigid, often elaborate, structure of ideas. The practice and repetition of the original experience have become a ritual and an unchangeable institution. This does not necessarily mean lifeless petrifaction. On the contrary, it may prove to be a valid form of religious experience for millions of people for thousands of years, without there arising any vital necessity to alter it. Although the Catholic

Church has often been accused of particular rigidity, she nevertheless admits that dogma is a living thing and that its formulation is therefore capable of change and development. Even the number of dogmas is not limited and can be multiplied in the course of time. The same holds true of the ritual. Yet all changes and developments are determined within the framework of the facts as originally experienced, and this sets up a special kind of dogmatic content and emotional value. Even Protestantism, which has abandoned itself apparently to an almost unlimited emancipation from dogmatic tradition and codified ritual and has thus split into more than four hundred denominations – even Protestantism is bound at least to be Christian and to express itself within the framework of the belief that God revealed himself in Christ, who suffered for mankind. This is a definite framework with definite contents which cannot be combined with or supplemented by Buddhist or Islamic ideas and feelings. Yet it is unquestionably true that not only Buddha and Mohammed, Confucius and Zarathustra, represent religious phenomena, but also Mithras, Attis, Cybele, Mani, Hermes, and the deities of many other exotic cults. The psychologist, if he takes up a scientific attitude, has to disregard the claim of every creed to be the unique and eternal truth. He must keep his eye on the human side of the religious problem, since he is concerned with the original religious experience quite apart from what the creeds have made of it.

As I am a doctor and a specialist in nervous and mental diseases, my point of departure is not a creed but the psychology of the *homo religious*, that is, of the man who takes into account and carefully observes certain factors which influence him and his general condition. It is easy to designate and define these factors in accordance with historical tradition or ethnological knowledge, but to do the same thing from the standpoint of psychology is an uncommonly difficult task. What I can contribute to the question of religion is derived entirely from my practical experience, both with my patients and with so-called normal persons.

5.26 'SYNCRONICITY'

Carl Jung

From 'Synchronicity: an acausal connecting principle', in *The Structure and Dynamics of the Psyche*, Hull, R.F.C. (trans), second edition, London, Routledge and Kegan Paul, 1969.

The problem of synchronicity has puzzled me for a long time, ever since the middle twenties, when I was investigating the phenomena of the collective unconscious and kept on coming across connections which I simply could not explain as chance groupings or "runs." What I found were "coincidences" which were connected so meaningfully that their "chance" concurrence would represent a degree of improbability that would have to be expressed by an astronomical figure. By way of example, I shall mention an incident from my own observation. A young woman I was treating had, at a critical moment, a dream in which she was given a golden scarab. While she was telling me this dream I sat with my back to the closed window. Suddenly I heard a noise behind me, like a gentle tapping. I turned round and saw a flying insect knocking against the window-pane from outside. I opened the window and caught the creature in the air as it flew in. It was the nearest analogy to a golden scarab that one finds in our latitudes, a scarabaeid beetle, the common rose-chafer (*Cetonia aurata*), which contrary to its usual habits had evidently felt an urge to get into a dark room at this particular moment. I must admit that nothing like it ever happened to me before or since, and that the dream of the patient has remained unique in my experience.

I should like to mention another case that is typical of a certain category of events. The wife of one of my patients, a man in his fifties, once told me in conversation that, at the deaths of her mother and her grandmother, a number of birds gathered outside the windows of the death-chamber. I had heard similar stories from other people. When her husband's treatment was nearing its end, his neurosis having been cleared up, he developed some apparently quite innocuous symptoms which seemed to me, however, to be those of heart-disease. I sent him along to a specialist, who after examining him told me in writing that he could find no cause for anxiety. On the way back from this consultation (with the medical report in his pocket) my patient collapsed in the street. As he was brought home dying, his wife was already in a great state of anxiety because, soon after her husband had gone to the doctor, a whole flock of birds alighted on their house. She naturally remembered the similar incidents that had happened at the death of her own relatives, and feared the worst.

Although I was personally acquainted with the people concerned and know very well that the facts here reported are true, I do not imagine for a moment that this will induce anybody who is determined to regard such things as pure "chance" to change his mind. My sole object in relating these two incidents is simply to give some indication of how meaningful coincidences usually · present themselves in practical life. The meaningful connection is obvious enough in the first case in view of the approximate identity of the chief objects (the scarab and the beetle); but in the second case the death and the flock of birds seem to be incommensurable with one another. If one considers, however, that in the Babylonian Hades the souls wore a "feather dress," and that in ancient Egypt the *ba*, or soul, was thought of as a bird, it is not too far-fetched to suppose that there may be some archetypal symbolism at work. Had such an incident occurred in a dream, that interpretation would be justified by the comparative psychological material. There also seems to be an archetypal foundation to the first case. It was an extraordinarily difficult case to treat, and up to the time of the dream little or no progress had been made. I should explain that the main reason for this was my patient's animus, which was steeped in Cartesian philosophy and clung so rigidly to its own idea of reality that the efforts of three doctors – I was the third – had not been able to weaken it. Evidently something quite irrational was needed which was beyond my powers to produce. The dream alone was enough to disturb ever so slightly the rationalistic attitude of my patient. But when the "scarab" came flying in through the window in actual fact, her natural being could burst through the armour of her animus possession and the process of transformation could at last begin to move. Any essential change of attitude signifies a psychic renewal which is usually accompanied by symbols of rebirth in the patient's dreams and fantasies. The scarab is a classic example of a rebirth symbol. The ancient Egyptian book of What is in the Netherworld describes how the dead sun-god changes himself at the tenth station into Khepri, the scarab, and then, at the twelfth station, mounts the barge which carries the rejuvenated sun-god into the morning sky.

5.27 'FOREWORD TO THE *I CHING*'

Carl Jung

From *The Structure and Dynamics of the Psyche*, Hull, R.F.C. (trans), second edition, London, Routledge and Kegan Paul, 1969, pp. 591–3.

I do not know Chinese and have never been in China. I can assure my reader that it is not altogether easy to find the right approach to this monument of Chinese thought, which departs so completely from our ways of thinking. In order to understand what such a book is all about, it is imperative to cast off certain of our Western prejudices. It is a curious fact that such a gifted and intelligent people as the Chinese has never developed what we call science. Our science, however, is based upon the principle of causality, and causality is considered to be an axiomatic truth. But a great change in our standpoint is setting in. What Kant's *Critique of Pure Reason* failed to do is being accomplished by modern physics. The axioms of causality are being shaken to their foundations: we know now that what we term natural laws are merely statistical truths and thus must necessarily allow for exceptions. We have not sufficiently taken into account as yet that we need the laboratory with its incisive restrictions in order to demonstrate the invariable validity of natural law. If we leave things to nature, we see a very different picture: every process is partially or totally interfered with by chance, so much so that under natural circumstances a course of events absolutely conforming to specific laws is almost an exception.

The Chinese mind, as I see it at work in the *I Ching*, seems to be exclusively preoccupied with the chance aspect of events. What we call coincidence seems to be the chief concern of this peculiar mind, and what we worship as causality passes almost unnoticed. We must admit that there is something to be said for the immense importance of chance. An incalculable amount of human effort is directed to combating and restricting the nuisance or danger that chance represents. Theoretical considerations of cause and effect often look pale and dusty in comparison with the practical results of chance. It is all very well to say that the crystal of quartz is a hexagonal prism. The statement is quite true in so far as an ideal crystal is envisaged. But in nature one finds no two crystals exactly alike, although all are unmistakably hexagonal. The actual form, however, seems to appeal more to the Chinese sage than the ideal one. The jumble of natural laws constituting empirical reality holds more significance for him than a causal explanation of events that, in addition, must usually be separated from one another in order to be properly dealt with.

The manner in which the *I Ching* tends to look upon reality seems to disfavour our causal procedures. The moment under actual observation appears to the ancient Chinese view more of a chance hit than a clearly defined result of concurrent causal chains. The matter of interest seems to be the configuration formed by chance events at the moment of observation, and not at all the hypothetical reasons that seemingly account for the coincidence. While the Western mind carefully sifts, weighs, selects, classifies, isolates, the Chinese picture of the moment encompasses everything down to the minutest nonsensical detail, because all of the ingredients make up the observed moment.

Thus it happens that when one throws the three coins, or counts through the forty-nine yarrow-stalks, these chance details enter into the picture of the moment of observation and form a part of it – a part that is insignificant to us, yet most meaningful to the Chinese mind. With us it would be a banal and almost meaningless statement (at least on the fact of it) to say that whatever happens in a given moment has inevitably the quality peculiar to that moment. This is not an abstract argument but a very practical one. There are certain connoisseurs who can tell you merely from the appearance, taste, and behaviour of a wine the site of its vineyard and the year of its origin. There are antiquarians who with almost uncanny accuracy will name the time and place of origin and the maker of an *objet d'art* or piece of furniture on merely looking at it. And there are even astrologers who can tell you, without any previous knowledge of your nativity, what the position of sun and moon was and what zodiacal sign rose above the horizon at the moment of your birth. In the face of such facts, it must be admitted that moments can leave long-lasting traces.

In other words, whoever invented the *I Ching* was convinced that the hexagram worked out in a certain moment coincided with the latter in quality no less than in time. To him the hexagram was the exponent of the moment in which it was cast – even more so than the hours of the clock or the divisions of the calendar could be – inasmuch as the hexagram was understood to be an indicator of the essential situation prevailing at the moment of its origin.

This assumption involves a certain curious principle which I have termed synchronicity, a concept that formulates a point of view diametrically opposed to that of causality. Since the latter is a merely statistical truth and not absolute, it is a sort of working hypothesis of how events evolve one out of another, whereas synchronicity takes the coincidence of events in space and time as meaning something more than mere chance, namely, a peculiar interdependence of objective events among themselves as well as with the subjective (psychic) states of the observer or observers.

The ancient Chinese mind contemplates the cosmos in a way comparable to that of the modern physicist, who cannot deny that his model of the world is a decidedly psychophysical structure. The microphysical event includes the observer just as much as the reality underlying the *I Ching* comprises subjective, i.e., psychic conditions in the totality of the momentary situation. Just as causality describes the sequence of events, so synchronicity to the Chinese mind deals with the coincidence of events. The causal point of view tells us a dramatic story about how D came into existence: it took its origin from C, which existed before D, and C in its turn had a father, B, etc. The synchronistic view on the other hand tries to produce an equally meaningful picture of coincidence. How does it happen that A', B', C', D', etc. appear all at the same moment and in the same place? It happens in the first place because the physical events A' and B' are of the same quality as the psychic events C' and D', and further because all are the exponents of one and the same momentary situation. The situation is assumed to represent a legible or understandable picture.

Now the sixty-four hexagrams of the *I Ching* are the instrument by which the meaning of sixty-four different yet typical situations can be determined. These interpretations are equivalent to causal explanations. Causal connection can be determined statistically and can be subjected to experiment. Inasmuch as situations are unique and cannot be repeated, experimenting with synchronicity seems to be impossible under ordinary conditions. In the *I Ching*, the only criterion of the validity of synchronicity is the observer's opinion that the text of the hexagram amounts to a true rendering of his psychic condition. It is assumed that the fall of the coins or the result of the division of the bundle of yarrow-stalks is what it necessarily must be in a given "situation," inasmuch as anything happening at that moment belongs to it as an indispensable part of the picture. If a handful of matches is thrown to the floor, they form the pattern characteristic of that moment. But such an obvious truth as this reveals its meaningful nature only if it is possible to read the pattern and to verify its interpretation, partly by the observer's knowledge of the subjective and objective situation, partly by the character of subsequent events. It is obviously not a procedure that appeals to a critical mind used to experimental verification of facts or to factual evidence. But for someone who likes to look at the world at the angle from which ancient China saw it, the *I Ching* may have some attraction.

5.28 'WHY JUNG WOULD DOUBT THE NEW AGE'*

David Tacey

From *Therapy on the Couch: A Shrinking Future*, Tacey, D., London, Camden Press, 1999, pp. 36–7.

Everywhere the claim is being made that the New Age movement is a product of Jungian interest, and spiritually oriented therapists from a diverse range of fields often refer to Carl Jung as their inspiration. Likewise, Jung and his school of analysis are often automatically dismissed by social critics precisely because of their supposed New Age flakiness.

But just how "Jungian" is the New Age? And how New Age-ey is Jungian psychology? If we try to untangle modern assumptions and links, we find that despite some points of contact, Jung would have been a stern critic of the New Age core.

Jung clearly has several points in common with the New Age approach. They both agree that spiritual meaning is no longer synonymous with the religious institutions of western culture, and can no longer be contained by them. Both are interested in exploring non-Christian, pre-Christian or post-Christian sources of spiritual meaning; both are interested in gnosticism, alchemy, and eastern contemplative traditions.

Unlike the institutional church, which typically looks to the past and a charismatic founder for its standards and moral teachings, Jung and the New Age look forward to the future with a degree of optimism. For Jung the future ideal can be summed up in the word "wholeness", an ideal that he frequently contrasts with the Christian ethic of "perfection". The New Age, too, likes to privilege "wholeness" above "perfection". It sometimes seems that New Age spirituality is simply Jungian psychology writ large, taking his model to the masses in the outer world.

But of course what the New Age seems to be doing, and what it actually does, are very different things. The New Age is not a coherent religious philosophy and often appears to be driven more by commercial interests and market forces than by any particular philosophical position. It is broadly Jungian in its emphasis on the spiritual authority of individual experience, which Jung borrowed from Protestantism, the need for religious and cultural transformation – which he derived from German Romanticism – and on the importance of unorthodox ways of achieving unity with the creator, which he borrowed from gnosticism, hermeticism, and alchemy. However the New Age is non-Jungian or even anti-Jungian in a number of key ways.

The New Age is a popular movement which reverses many of the views found in traditional western religion, especially on the body, nature, and desire. It is a cry to make spirituality relevant to our times and emotionally related to individual human experience. It

---

* 'Why Jung would doubt the New Age' is a brief summary of the book by David Tacey, *Jung and he New Age*, published by Routledge, London, 2001.

does this by extending an archetypal process based on the "feminine principle", compensatory to the patriarchal west. The pagan longings, Gnostic impulses, and unorthodox spiritual strivings that have been repressed for hundreds of years in the west have been released after the collapse of Christendom's authority and now, without any inhibition at all, we find these contents paraded before us. But while it appears to reject mainstream secular culture, in many ways it simply repeats the patterns and preferences of our materialistic and consumerist society.

The New Age is perhaps "Jungian" by default. If it appears Jungian it is not because it has used Jung, but because it draws its life from a particularly strong archetypal current that we might associate with Jung, since he clearly mapped this psychospiritual territory. Jung was especially interested in the archetypal processes that were "compensatory" to the patriarchal west, so this brings him even closer to the interests of the New Age.

However, Jung did not naïvely celebrate these currents in the western psyche. He identified and named them but his response was always detached and ambivalent. Jung continually sought to integrate warring opposites and contradictory elements such as paganism and Christianity into a larger whole, and he almost never championed one set of archetypal claims at the expense of another.

Although Jung prophetically saw that "feminine" and "pagan" contents were on the rise in the western psyche, he never advocated abandoning ourselves to them: on the contrary, he felt that the task of developing the individual sense of self ("individuation") involved resisting such collective forces and developing a critical response to them. "For the development of personality . . . strict differentiation from the collective psyche is absolutely necessary, since partial or blurred differentiation leads to an immediate melting away of the individual in the collective," he wrote in *The relations between the ego and the unconscious* in 1928. "The aim of individuation is nothing less than to divest the self of the false wrappings of the persona on the one hand, and the suggestive power of primordial images on the other."

Any collective movement which identifies with an archetypal process is therefore, virtually by definition, not going to accord with Jungian taste, which is based on the ethics and aesthetics of individuation. Jung's attack on what he called "identification with the collective psyche" is conveniently and deliberately ignored by all those New Age therapists, advocates, and shamans who like to celebrate the newly constellated archetypal contents.

ACKNOWLEDGEMENTS

Every effort has been made to trace all the copyright owners, but if any has been inadvertently overlooked, the publishers will be pleased to make the necessary arrangements at the first opportunity.

Grateful acknowledgement is made to the following sources for permission to reproduce material in this book:

PART I

1.1: Marsh, C. and Moyise, S. (1999) 'Mark's Gospel', *Jesus and the Gospels*. Cassell Publishers Ltd. Reproduced by permission of The Continuum International Publishing Group;

1.2: Borg, M.J. (1994) 'Does the historical Jesus matter?', *Jesus in Contemporary Scholarship*. Trinity Press International. www.trinitypressintl.com;

1.3: Eck, D.L. (1998) 'Seeing the sacred: film images', *Darśan: Seeing the Divine Image in India*. Columbia University Press;

1.4: Roy, R. (1985) 'Idolatory and the defence of Hindu theism', in Richard, G. (ed) *A Source Book of Modern Hinduism*. Curzon Press Ltd;

1.5: Sarasvati, D. (1985) 'Idols', in Richard, G. (ed) *A Source Book of Modern Hinduism*. Curzon Press Ltd;

1.9: 'The principles of the Friends of the Western Buddhist order', *FWBO*. www.fwbo.org/principles;

1.10: 'The FWBO and the Buddhist tradition', *FWBO*. www.fwbo.org/tradition;

1.11: 'Learning about Buddhism', *FWBO*. www.fwbo.org/learning-about-buddhism.

1.13: Gyatso, G.K. (1992) 'Training as a qualified Dharma teacher', *Full Moon*. Summer, 1992. Manjushri Mahayana Buddhist Centre.

1.14: Reprinted from *The Awakening of the West: The Encounter of Buddhism and Western Culture* (1994) by Stephen Batchelor with permission of Parallax Press, Berkeley, California. www.parallax.org;

1.15: Reprinted from *Islam in Contemporary Egypt: Civil Society vs. the State*, by Denis J. Sullivan and Sana Abed-Kotab. Copyright © 1999 by Lynne Rienner Publishers. Used with permission of the publisher.

1.16: From THE PEARLY GATES OF CYBERSPACE: A HISTORY OF SPACE FROM DANTE TO THE INTERNET by Margaret Wertheim. Copyright © 1999 by Five Continents Music, Inc. Used by permission of W.W. Norton & Company, Inc.

PART II

2.1:   Tischner, Jósef, (1992) 'Christianity in the Post-Communist vacuum', *Religion, State and Society*. Vol. 20. Nos. 3 and 4. Taylor & Francis Limited;

2.2:   Beinin, J. and Stork, J. (1997) 'How can a Muslim live in this era?', *Political Islam: Essays from Middle East Report*. I.B. Tauris & Co. Ltd.;

2.3:   Copyright 1948 from 'Human Rights Declaration', *Encyclopaedia of the United Nations*. Edited by Edmund Jan Osmanozyek. Taylor & Francis, Inc. Reproduced by permission of Routledge, Inc., part of The Taylor & Francis Group;

2.4:   United Nations General Assembly (1993) 'The Organization of the Islamic Conference: Cairo declaration on human rights in Islam', *World Conference on Human Rights*. 4th Session, Agenda Item No 5. United Nations Publications. The United Nations is the author of the original material;

2.5/6: Chung, K.H. (1990) 'Who is Mary for today's Asian women?' and 'Asian women writing theology', *Struggle to be the Sun again: Introducing Asian Women's Theology*. Orbis Books;

2.9:   From *Bread Not Stone* by Elisabeth Schüssler Fiorenza. Copyright © 1984, 1995 by Elisabeth Schüssler Fiorenza. Reprinted by permission of Beacon Press, Boston;

2.10: Reprinted from MODELS OF GOD by Sallie McFague, copyright © 1987 Fortress Press. Used by permission of Augsburg Fortress;

2.11: Pauling, C. (1990) 'A Buddhist life is a green life', *Golden Drum*, February–April 1990. Windhorse Publications;

2.12: Batchelor, M. and Brown, K. (eds) (1992) 'A zone of peace', *Buddhism and Ecology*. Cassell Publishers Ltd. Reproduced by permission of The Continuum International Publishing Group Ltd;

2.13 Scott, N. (2001) 'Saving forests so there can be forest monks', *Forest Sangha Newsletter*. http://www.abm.ndirect.co.uk/fsn/35/forests.html. © Nick Scott.

PART III

3.1:   Bellah, R.N. (1974) 'Civil religion in America', in Richey, R.E. and Jones, D.G. (eds), *American Civil Religion*. Mellen Research University Press. © Donald G. Jones and Russell E. Richey;

3.2:   Wilson, C.R. (1980) 'Origin and overview', *Baptized in Blood: The Religion of the Lost Cause, 1865–1920*. The University of Georgia Press. Copyright © 1980 by the University of Georgia Press, Athens, Georgia 30602;

3.3:   Copyright 1999 from 'Completing the theological circle: civil religion in America', *For This Land: Writings on Religion in America*. By Vine Deloria, Jr., edited by James Treat. Reproduced by permission of Routledge, Inc., part of The Taylor & Francis Group;

3.4:   Walter, T. (1990) 'Memorials', *Funerals: and How to Improve Them*. Hodder and Stoughton Limited. Reproduced by permission of Hodder and Stoughton Limited;

3.5:   Pain, T. (1990) 'Say goodbye to Grandad', *Weekend Guardian*, 3rd–4th November, 1990. Guardian Media Group, Plc.;

3.6:   Barker, P. (1999) 'How did Uncle Edmund die', *The Observer Review*, 7th November, 1999. This article was first published in Prospect magazine, www.prospect-magazine.co.uk.

3.7:   Walter, T. 'War grave pilgrimage', in Walter, T. and Reader, I. (eds) (1993), *Pilgrimage in Popular Culture*. Macmillan Press Ltd.;

3.8:   Sutherland, C. (1995) 'Preface', *Hunger of the Heart: Communion at the Wall*. Islewest Publishing. Copyright © 1995 by Larry Powell;

3.9:   Harbutt, C. (1995) 'The things they leave behind', *The New York Times*. 12th November, 1995. The New York Times Company. Copyright © Charles Harbutt;

3.10: Knapp Litt, M. (1998) *Night Rounds – A Visit to the Vietnam Memorial*. www.illyria.com. Copyright © 1998 Marilyn Knapp Litt;

3.11: Scruggs, J.C. and Swerdlow, J.L. (1985) 'Intro' and 'November 1982', *To Heal a Nation: The Vietnam Veterans Memorial*. Harper & Row Publishers, Inc. Copyright © 1985 Jan C. Scruggs and Joel L. Swerdlow;

3.14: Dundes, A. and Falassi, A. (1975) 'The day of the Palio', *La Terra in Piazza: An Interpretation of the Palio of Siena*. University of California Press. Copyright © Alan Dundes;

3.15: Falassi, A. and Catoni, G. (1983) 'Conclusion', in Evans, C.H. and Mann Borgese, E. (trans) *Palio*. Monte dei Paschi di Siena.

PART IV

4.1:   Barclay, O. (1997) 'Looking back, reaching forward', *Evangelism in Britain 1935–1995*. Inter Varsity Press. Copyright © Oliver Barclay;

4.2:   'What is the charismatic movement' and 'Evaluation', *The Charismatic Movement in the Church of England*. CIO Publishing, 1981;

4.3:   Tomlinson, D. (1995) 'Christianity for a new age', *The Post-Evangelical*. Triangle/Society for Promoting Christian Knowledge;

4.4:   Hatch, N.O. and Hamilton, M.S. (1992) 'Can Evangeliscalism survive its success?', *Christianity Today*, October 5th, 1992. Christianity Today, Inc.;

4.6:   Hunter, T. (1998) 'The legacy of John Wimber', *VOV*, Fall 1998. Association of Vineyard Churches, USA;

4.7:   Palau, L. (1998) 'Which part of the great commission don't you understand?', *Christianity Today*, November 16th, 1998. Christianity Today, Inc. Copyright © Luis Palau;

4.8:   Houghton, F.B. (1993) 'Some reflections on the meaning and practice of worship from inside South America', in Carson, D.A. (ed) *Worship: Adoration and Action*. Baker Book House Company. By permission of The Paternoster Press;

4.9:   Lombardi, G. (1998) 'View from the other side', in Maust, J.D. (ed) *Latin America Evangelist*, January–March 1998. Latin America Mission, Inc.;

4.10: Ahsan, M.M. (1989) 'Dawa and its significance for the future', in Davies, M.W. and

Pasha, K.M. (eds) *Beyond Frontiers: Islam and Contemporary Needs.* Mansell Publishing Limited/Cassell Publishers Ltd. Reproduced by permission of The Continuum International Publishing Group Ltd;

4.11: McLoughlin, S. (1996) 'In the name of the Umma', in Shadid, W.A.R. and Van Koningsveld, P.S. (eds) *Political Participation and Identities of Muslims in Non-Muslim States.* KOK Pharos Publishing House/PEETERS;

4.14: The Gosho Translation Committee (1979) 'The one essential phrase', *The Major Writings of Nichiren Daishonin, Volume One.* Nichiren Shoshu International Center. By permission of Soka Gakkai International;

4.15: *The Soka Gakkai International Charter* (1966) Soka Gakkai International. http://www.sgi.org/about/sgi/charter.html;

4.16: Ikeda, D. (2000) 'SGI President Ikeda's New Year's Message: Happy New Year to my beloved SGI members', *SGI UK Bulletin*, 14th January 2000. No.259. Soka Gakkai International;

4.17: Hunter, W. (1997) 'Adapting the precepts to the locality (Zuiho Bini)', *UK Express: A Buddhist Magazine.* February 1997. No.308. Soka Gakkai International;

4.18: Montiel, E. (2000) 'Flood alert', *SGI Quarterly*, July 2000. No.21. Soka Gakkai International.

PART V

5.1: Jones, P. (1995) 'Pagan theologies', in Hardman, C. and Harvey, G. (eds) *Paganism Today.* Thorsons. By permission of HarperCollins Publishers;

5.2: Hannagraaff, W.J. (1998) 'Neopaganism', *New Age Religion and Western Culture.* State University of New York Press. By permission of Brill Academic Publishers, Inc.

5.3: Reprinted by permission from *Magical Religion and Modern Witchcraft* by James R. Lewis, the State University of New York Press © 1996, State University of New York. All rights reserved;

5.4: Harvey, G. (1997) 'Paganism and other religions', *Listening People, Speaking Earth: Contemporary Paganism.* C. Hurst & Co. (Publishers) Ltd;

5.5: © Ronald Hutton 1996. Reprinted from *The Stations of the Sun: A History of the Ritual Year in Britain* by Ronald Hutton (1996) by permission of Oxford University Press;

5.6: Matthews, C. (1989) 'The year's turning', *The Elements of The Celtic Tradition.* Element Books Limited. Copyright © Caitlin Matthews;

5.7: Bradley, I. (1993) 'The way goes on', *The Celtic Way.* Darton, Longman and Todd;

5.8: James, S. (1999) 'Conclusion: are the modern Celts bogus?', *The Atlantic Celts: Ancient People or Modern Invention?,* British Museum Press;

5.9: Davies, J.H.T. (1993) 'Playing at Indians', in Jayran, S. (ed) *Three Things There Are, That Are Seldom Heard: A Comment on Modern Shamanism.* House of the Goddess. © J.H.T. Davies;

5.10: Simon, S. et.al (1997) 'Appendix one: apologies to Native people', *Bridges in Spirituality: First Nations Christian Women Tell Their Stories.* United Church Publishing House;

5.12: Albanese, C.L. (1990) 'Recapitulating pieties', *Nature Religion in America, from the Algonkian Indians to the New Age.* University of Chicago Press. © 1990 by the University of Chicago Press. All Rights Reserved;

5.13: Porterfield, A. (1990) 'American Indian Spirituality as a Countercultural Movement', in Vecsey, C. (ed) *Religion in Native North America.* University of Idaho Press;

5.14: LaChapelle, D. (1991) 'Thoughts on Autumn Equinox about the importance of ritual', in Davis, J. (ed) *The Earth's First! Journal.* Gibbs Smith Publisher;

5.15: 'The Wiccan revival', From *Drawing Down the Moon* by Margot Adler. Copyright © 1979 by Margot Adler. Used by permission of Penguin Putnam;

5.16: Extract from *WITCHCRAFT TODAY* by Gerald Gardner published by Hutchinson. Used by permission of The Random House Group Limited;

5.17: From *Dreaming the Dark* by Starhawk. Copyright © 1982, 1988, 1997 by Miriam Simos. Reprinted by permission of Beacon Press, Boston;

5.18: Michelet, J. (1992) 'Introduction', *Satanism and Witchcraft.* Citadel Press. Copyright © Citadel Press. All Rights Reserved. Reprinted by permission of Citadel Press/Kensington Publishing Corp. www.kensingtonbooks.com.

5.20: Murphy, J. (1978) *The Worst Witch.* Puffin Books. Reproduced by permission of Penguin Books Ltd;

5.21: de la Mare, W. (1984) 'The Ride-by-Nights', *Broomsticks and Beasticles.* Knights Books;

5.22: Edwards, D. (1992) 'Witch at home', *Mists and Magic.* The Lutterworth Press. Reproduced by permission of James Clarke & Co. Ltd.;

5.23: Brooke, J.H. (1991) 'Introduction', *Science and Religion: Some Historical Perspectives.* Cambridge University Press;

5.24: Brooke, J. and Cantor, G. (1998) 'Whose science? whose religion?', *Reconstructing Nature.* T. & T. Clark Ltd. Reproduced by permission of The Continuum International Publishing Group Ltd.;

5.25: Jung, C.G. (1969) 'Psychology and religion', *Psychology and Religion: West and East.* 2nd ed. Routledge and Kegan Paul Ltd. Copyright © 1969 by the Princeton University Press. Reprinted by permission of Princeton University Press;

5.26: Jung, C.G. (1969) 'Synchronicity: an acausal connecting principle', in Hull, R.F.C. (trans) *The Structure and Dynamics of the Psyche.* 2nd ed. Routledge and Kegan Paul Ltd. Copyright © 1969 by the Princeton University Press. Reprinted by permission of Princeton University Press;

5.27: Jung, C.G. (1969) 'Foreword to the "I Ching"', in Hull, R.F.C. (trans) *The Structure and Dynamics of the Psyche.* 2nd ed. Routledge and Kegan Paul Ltd. Copyright © 1969 by the Princeton University Press. Reprinted by permission of Princeton University Press;

5.28: Tacey, D. (1999) 'Why Jung would doubt the New Age', *Therapy on the Couch: A Shrinking Future.* Camden Press. Copyright © David Tacey.

INDEX